Carolyn Fluehr-Lobban is Professor Emerita of Anthropology and Joint Doctoral Program in Education at Rhode Island College and Adjunct Professor of African Studies at Naval War College. Her research topics cover Islamic law and society, women's social and legal status in the Muslim world, human rights and cultural relativism, ethics and anthropology and comparative studies in law and society.

SHARI'A AND ISLAMISM IN SUDAN

Conflict, Law and Social Transformation

Carolyn Fluehr-Lobban

I.B. TAURIS

LONDON · NEW YORK

Published in 2012 by I.B.Tauris & Co Ltd
6 Salem Road, London W2 4BU
175 Fifth Avenue, New York NY 10010
www.ibtauris.com

Distributed in the United States and Canada
Exclusively by Palgrave Macmillan
175 Fifth Avenue, New York NY 10010

International Library of African Studies 30

ISBN 978 1 84885 666 0

A full CIP record for this book is available from the British Library
A full CIP record for this book is available from the Library of Congress

Library of Congress catalog card: available

Typeset by Newgen Publishers, Chennai
Printed and bound by CPI Group (UK) Ltd, Croydon, CR0 4YY

*For peace and reconciliation of the
Sudanese people of the Two Niles*

CONTENTS

ACKNOWLEDGEMENTS

First, I acknowledge the United States Institute of Peace that funded this research and worked creatively with me through the challenges initially of locating a grant administrating institution – rendered problematic due to the severity of the US sanctions against Sudan – and later through the process of obtaining approval from the US Office of Foreign Assets Control (OFAC) for transfer of funds relating to the grant in Sudan. April Hall, Taylor Seybolt, Jon Temin, Andrew Blum, and Doug Smith are specifically mentioned in this regard. Thank you.

Secondly, I am grateful to the Government of Sudan and to its Embassy staff in Washington, DC for facilitating my visas to carry out research during the years 2007–09. I would like to specifically thank Khalid Musa Dafalla who has been both a friend and a colleague in the Sudan Studies Association. This support enabled me not only to benefit from the persons enumerated below, but from thousands of interactions with ordinary Sudanese.

For research in Sudan, first on my list of grateful acknowledgement must be the lady judges at the Sudan Judiciary who have been my friends and research associates in the past and remained loyal up to the present time. These include my oldest and best friend, Moalana Nagua Kemal Mohamed Farid (Associate Justice), Moalana Rabab Abu Gusaysa (Sudan High Court), Moalana Sinia Rashid (Constitutional Court), and Moalana Kawther Awad of the Diem District Court, Khartoum.

At the latter Diem court I also express my gratitude to the Court Ma'azun (Registrar of Marriages and Divorces) Moalana Yusef Kashta who literally opened his books to my research, and to the President of the Khartoum Courts Moalana Sheikh al-Boreii who granted permission for me to visit the courts of Khartoum. I also wish to express gratitude to the Sheikhs at the *Majmi Fiqhi* who graciously hosted me and Justice Rabab Abu Gusaysa and were patient in answering my questions.

In this research I resumed a collaborative relationship with legal sociologist Dr. Hatim Babiker Hillawi of Nilein University who translated the *hudud* Circulars from *Manshurat al-Jan'aiya* (*Criminal Judicial Circulars*) from 1983 to 2006. These circulars formed the basis for the Sudan Criminal Code of 1991 and selections appear in the text. Hatim also brought to my attention a government forum on the controversial, emerging marriage, *zawaj 'urfi*, which we attended together, and I am thankful to him for this unique learning opportunity and for our many interesting conversations over delicious lunches at his home.

At the university of Khartoum I wish to express my sincerest thanks to Dr. Osman Mohamed Osman of the Department of Social Anthropology who extended a warm welcome and lent me his personal laptop computer since I was prohibited by the US sanctions from bringing a laptop into the country. Dr. Osman also invited me to an invaluable conference on 'Shari'a Debates' in February 2007 at the University of Shendi, The conference was sponsored by the University of Beyrouth, Germany and brought together junior and senior scholars from Nigeria, Tanzania, Kenya, and Sudan to discuss the research projects of the younger scholars and their work on various aspects of Shari'a and Islamization in their respective countries. During this time in Shendi town, I was pleased to meet and discuss the Shari'a with Moalana Mohamed al-Dirar and I was introduced to the local Province judge, the town prosecutor, and several practicing lawyers. Among them was Abu Talib Osman, who invited me to spend time in the Shendi combined court which I later visited in 2009, thanks to the generous hospitality of his family, especially his wife Maha.

I am also grateful to University of Khartoum Professor of Political Science, Mohamed Mukhtar whose initial welcome led me to the greatest asset in my research, my research assistant, Salma Mohamed Abdalmunim, then a political science graduate student working on Shari'a, now a doctoral student at the University of Beyrouth, Germany. Salma and I worked very well together, and she provided me with the invaluable perspective of so many of the youth who have grown up under Sudan's Islamism. Her reading knowledge of English and my spoken ability in Arabic were the right combination to get many research tasks accomplished. *Shukran jazeelan*, Salma!

I thank Mohamed Mahmoud for his insights in our interview in Birmingham, England in 2008 and also to Abdel Wahab Aleffendi who welcomed me to his office at Westminster University in London. I thank Noah Salomon who was conducting his own doctoral research for his friendship and occasional notes from the Arabic press in Khartoum.

In Juba, I am indebted to attorney Hoth Chan for arranging a full program of local tourism, as well as matters of law and society. His contacts and insights were invaluable while I was conducting research in 2008 on the impact of the CPA on Shari'a in the South and on the new Judiciary of the Government of South Sudan (GOSS).

I save a warm expression of gratitude to my landlady Mary Portides who always found an apartment for me (and for my husband Richard), and to my roommate and friend, author Wendy Wallace, who shared the apartment in Khartoum's downtown Suq al-Arabi area. Our conversations over the months we shared our living space and beloved balcony were a comfort and a joy and led me to a better understanding of the 'Abandoned' of Khartoum in Maygoma Orphanage.

I acknowledge with the deepest debt of gratitude my friend of the decades Mahgoub al-Tigani Mahmoud, translator of this book and of my previous work on Shari'a published in Arabic in 2004. Mahgoub translated *Islamic Law and Society in the Sudan* (Frank Cass: 1987) purely out of admiration for the work and love of Sudan and Sudanese Sufi Islam. I remain indebted to him for his contribution and loyalty, and I am overjoyed that we can again collaborate in the translation of this work as *al-Shari'a wa al-Islamiya fi al-Sudan: al-Sira wa al-Qanun wa al-Tahawil al-Ijtimaʿiya* that is to be published in 2011 after the English edition.

I thank my publisher and the editors at I.B.Tauris, especially Maria Marsh, who has worked so expeditiously and constructively on every detail of this book.

Finally, I thank my dearest friend and best critic, my partner in Sudan studies over a lifetime, Richard Lobban, Jr. During one phase of this research my elderly mother was living with us in Rhode Island and it fell to Richard to take care of her daily needs, to take her to the Senior Center, to buy her favorite sweets, and to entertain her with his jokes. My mother passed away in 2010 and I will forever keep her in my memory and be grateful to Richard for his support.

C<small>AROLYN</small> F<small>LUEHR</small>-L<small>OBBAN</small>

PREFACE

From 1983 until the present day, Shari'a was, and has been, the main instrument of Sudan's Islamist social and political project. Sudanese religious roots are Sufist, and its history has mainly been one of religious tolerance. Sudan's Islamisation followed that of Iran in 1979 and preceded that of northern Nigeria after 1999, and was born in the desperate effort of military ruler Ja'afar Numeiri who sought to find a new legitimizing paradigm with which to rule, after having failed to successfully utilize communist and socialist ideologies. Its intellectual architect was Muslim Brotherhood (MB) leader Dr. Hasan al-Turabi who drafted the first Islamist laws, known as the 'September Laws' and who was also instrumental in the Islamist 'Civilization Project' institutionalized by the *Inqaz* 'Salvation' regime of al-Bashir meant to project Islamic law and social values upon the whole of Sudanese society, irrespective of their religion. The non-Muslim people of southern Sudan were in insurgency against northern governments in Khartoum since 1955 – at times imposing Arabization as well as Islamization upon them. Sudan is not a homogeneous nation, culturally, linguistically, or religiously. It was, perhaps, one of the worst places to experiment with making Shari'a state law, which it did, in effect, in 1983. This study took place in the wake of the signing of the Comprehensive Peace Agreement (CPA) in 2005 ending decades of civil war, and it continued until the year prior to the historic referendum on separation of the South in 2011. That referendum demonstrated overwhelming support for separation of the South, on 9 July 2011.

This work is not a critique of Shari'a, the noble law of the Islamic faith by which Muslims guide their lives, atone for their offenses against the faith and fellow Muslims, and resolve their differences. However, it does critique the ways in which Shari'a was politicized, misinterpreted, and eventually abused during a quarter-century of a state ideology that used Islam – now unfortunately referred to in the West as 'Islamism' – as an ideology of political repression and manipulation of both non-Muslims and Muslims in multi-confessional, multicultural state of Sudan.

Sudan is one of the major cases of contemporary Islamism in Africa and the Middle East. Islamism is the term now accepted in the West and recognized in the Muslim world as political Islam with a variety of expressions regarded as extremist, or beyond the boundaries of mainstream Islam. Islamism is a regrettable term for its use of Islam in the noun and adjective – extremist Christian activism in the West has not been referred to as 'Christianism,' although it might be. The use of the term Islamism in this book's title and its contents adopts a critical view to what 'Islamiya' in Sudan has wrought over a quarter century, but in no way is this critique one of the faith of Islam or its holy law, the Shari'a, for which I have the greatest respect as I have come to know and admire it in the companionship of Sudanese Muslims. When Muslims oppose Islamism it is not a secular rejection either of faith or of Shari'a, but a rejection of the merging of religion and the state. Separation of the religion and the state is not only a western concept, but many Muslims join others in the world who oppose theocracy.

As Africa's once largest nation, Sudan's immense borders affect eight nations from northern to central Africa. Now with separation and division of the nation after a quarter century of Islamism, the future of Sudan hangs in the balance and with it African stability for the regions of the Nile Valley, Horn of Africa, and central Africa.

Shari'a law has been the main instrument of Sudan's Islamism since 1983 and the resistance to it comes mainly from southern Sudanese. In 2005, the CPA ended Africa's longest civil war through the compromise key to the CPA: withdrawal of the Shari'a from the South and from non-Muslims in the North. The fragile peace was threatened by weak and slow implementation of the CPA, but national elections in 2010 and the CPA mandated referendum on separation in 2011 promise fundamentally changed the national paradigm. The past, present, and future of Shari'a are central to an understanding of events leading up to this crucial two year period of transition and its aftermath.

During the decades of its Islamism, Sudan not only waged civil war in the South but dealt with the domestic and international crises in Darfur and in its eastern and Nuba Mountains regions. But after 1999 it also became a major African exporter of oil to China and eastern emerging markets. Likewise, during this period, where a politicized Islam defined its 'national' identity, massive urbanization and social transformation occurred, especially concentrated in its capital city of Khartoum, which swelled to nearly 8 million. In this major African city the 'new Sudan' is emerging, for better and for worse. With the pariah status that western politics has engendered, few researchers from outside the country have documented the substantial changes that have shaped the emerging 'new' Sudan, and with an informal boycott contacts with Sudanese researchers were difficult to maintain. Thanks to a grant from the United States Institute of Peace (2007–09) and other sources of support, I was able to resume research in order to document the role that Shari'a has played in Sudan's Islamism; to analyze the ways in which it was deployed; and to attempt to comprehend the magnitude of the social change that has taken place since 1983 when Shari'a was made national law, and after 1989, when the al-Bashir *Inqaz* government institutionalized state Islamism. Essentially, this book resumes the story of Shari'a in Sudan that I began with my 1987 book, *Islamic Law and Society in the Sudan*, which detailed colonial and post-independence Shari'a until the eve of its Islamization in 1983.

INTRODUCTION

I began to research in Sudan as a graduate student in 1970 and continued to return regularly until 1988. In 1981 my husband and fellow anthropologist, Richard Lobban, and I organized the Sudan Studies Association (SSA) with five other colleagues and together with other Sudanist colleagues, held annual meetings every year since 1981 and international conferences every three years. The first and last international conference held in Khartoum was in 1988. The SSA has facilitated continuous contact and critical discourse with Sudanese during the years of war and extremist Islamism especially between 1989 and 2004. Fifteen years passed before I resumed research in Sudan in 2004. Along with many western-based Sudanist scholars I had stayed away from the country after the 1989 Islamist coup launched a program of political repression that resulted in the detention, imprisonment, and, in some cases, the torture of colleagues with whom we had worked for decades. Eventually a large number of Sudan's best and brightest chose or were forced into exile. Now, their children have formed a new organization in the Diaspora, Sudanese American Youth Affirmation Project (SAYAP), to create a vehicle to engage with the country they know only through their parents' experience and longing.

In 2004 I returned to a transformed country. Decades of civil war and chronic conflict had internally displaced millions of its marginalized citizens who are now living in and around the capital city. The three towns known as Khartoum – that comprised about a half-million souls when we first conducted research in the early 1970s – had grown to perhaps 7–8 million, making it one of Africa's largest conurbations. No longer a 'northern' city, its streets, informal markets, public transport and parks are filled with multiple ethnic groups from the South and Nuba Mountains, western Sudanese from Darfur and Kordofan, and there is easy movement between the main twin cities of Khartoum and the Blue Nile capital Wad Medani. Politics aside, the 'new Sudan' is actively under construction alongside the dereks and cranes that mark the new skyline of Khartoum, and the capital city now contains over a third of the nation's population.

With the flow of oil after 1999 – presently a half-million barrels a day – the Sudanese economy became one of Africa's strongest and fastest growing. Oil investment dramatically shifted from West to East as Chinese, Indian and Malaysian investment replaced French, British, American, and Canadian oil companies. Western oil interests left or were driven out in the 1990s shamed by an outcry from human rights organizations at the abuses and ethnic cleansing that occurred during the civil war, especially in and around the oil fields in the South. Into this investment vacuum flowed Chinese capital and aid, that – along with a substantial infusion of capital for construction of new buildings from the oil rich Gulf states – turned the capital city center along the Niles into a glistening gem at the confluence of the two Niles. The proprietors of Khartoum's tourist shops began to negotiate in Mandarin with Chinese buying up their stocks of ivory. One of these owners of a well-known dry goods store described to me his surprise in meeting with his Chinese supplier who spoke to him in perfect modern standard Arabic.

In the West the term 'Islamism' has gradually replaced others in use after the Iranian Islamic revolution in 1979, such as 'resurgent Islam,' or 'Islamic fundamentalism.' After 11 September 2001 (9/11) in the US, the 7 July 2005 attacks in the UK and the subsequent wars in Afghanistan and Iraq, the term 'insurgent Islam' gained currency. After the secular democratic revolutions that swept North Africa and the Middle East in early 2011, the long term viability of Islamism is itself in question. Together with the cases of Iran and Afghanistan under the Taliban, Sudan is a major example of state Islamism, and, like Iran, one that has sustained decades of legal change, institution building and social transformation under the banner of a politicized Islam. Sudanese Islamism has exerted influence upon Muslim Africa, especially Nigeria and Somalia, both as a source of inspiration and of caution.

During the extremist period of the Taliban in Afghanistan the following cultural and social practices were enacted: the application of the *hadd* criminal penalties of amputation for theft; the introduction of capital offenses for adultery and homosexuality; the curtailing of female employment and education; bans on the following: female exposure with mandatory wearing of the *burqa*; shaving; secular music on the radio, only Qur'anic reading and *madiyah* chanting; the rearing of pigeons, bird fighting and kite flying; the reproduction of pictures; gambling; British and American hairstyles; *riba*, interest-bearing loans and transactions; public exposure of women, such as washing clothes on river banks, male tailors sewing women's clothes; music and dancing at weddings, playing drums and witchcraft.[1]

In Sudan during its most intense period of extremism, 1983–99, there were similar formal bans and social pressures to conform to Islamist standards including: similar application of *hadd* criminal penalties, head covering with no visible hair became informal practice with similar bans on female public employment. A public morals police enforced the regime's idea of modest Islamic dress and regulated male/female public behavior; the wearing of beards increased; music was restricted to Qur'anic chanting, and comparable bans on reproduction of certain images was introduced, gambling and *riba*, interest-bearing loans and transactions, with a monopoly of Islamic banking and finance institutions imposed; music and dancing at weddings was restrained; restriction were imposed on male tailors sewing women's clothes along with sale of women's shoes in public informal markets. There are numerous examples of the degrees to which extremism was able to affect policy and behavior during these years. One story related to me was of the arrival of an Indian Sikh at the Khartoum airport who was denied a visa to enter the country because he was not a *Kitabi* (a 'person of the Book,' that is a Muslim, Christian, or Jew), thus he could not enter a Muslim state (*dawla*).

During the early years of the National Islamic Front (NIF) backed military regime after 1989, all political parties were banned and internal opposition was crushed thus attracting the attention of international human rights organizations. University of Khartoum professors,

4 SHARI'A AND ISLAMISM IN SUDAN

trade unionists, and real or potential oppositionists, were detained and
some tortured in 'ghost houses' that became emblematic of the era.
Courageous indigenous human rights activists, like Sudan's preeminent northern scholar of the South, Professor Mohamed Omer Beshir,
were subjected to public beatings and had their homes searched for
literature critical of the NIF and their MB predecessors.

The Shari'a criminal, civil, and family law was codified for the first
time in the nation's history, while the *hadd* amputations of previous years
all but ceased. From 1991 to 1996 Osama bin Laden was welcomed in
Sudan by the regime and the Islamist project's acknowledged architect,
al-Turabi. During the Sudan years, bin Laden operated various businesses, laid 'the base' for al-Qaeda and likely planned the first attack on
the World Trade Center in 1993, the Somalia Islamist initiative, and the
attempted assassination of the then Egyptian president Hosni Mubarak.

With the signing of the Comprehensive Peace Agreement (CPA)
under intense pressure from western nations, including the US, Shari'a
law was formally withdrawn from the South and from the considerable
number of non-Muslims residing in the North, thus signaling the formal end of Sudan's Islamism. The beginning of a post-Islamist Sudan
could be observed, albeit neither in smooth, even, nor predictable fashion. Implementation of the CPA was slow and demonstrated a lack of
political will on the part of the Government of Sudan. Mixed messages
promised full legal autonomy free of Shari'a for Southerners living in the
North even as prosecutions, lashing, and imprisonment for alcohol use
by Southerners in the Internally Displaced Persons (IDP) camps around
the capital continued. Although much reduced, *hadd* sentences of lashing
for morals offenses and of amputation and stoning for offenses of theft
and adultery under the Shari'a criminal code continued to be applied
sporadically throughout the North. And in an embarrassing display of
continuing extremism in 2007, a British schoolteacher in Khartoum was
arrested, summarily tried under the criminal code, and sentenced to 15
days in prison for an 'offense against Islam' because her primary school
students named a class teddy bear 'Muhammad.' After the intervention
of two British Muslim parliamentarians President al-Bashir pardoned
the teacher who, after only four months in Sudan, apologized for her
unintentional offense (*The New York Times*, 4 December 2007).

In Iran, comparable formal and informal constraints on public behavior heated and cooled as the country moved to intensify or relax Islamist decrees. As other, more recent cases of Islamism emerge – such as in northern Nigeria, Somalia, and Palestine – elements of the above check list are repeated as features of their Islamist agendas. The challenge for western researchers is to record accurately and assess objectively current and historical events in countries undergoing various stages of Islamism. Campaigns in the West have condemned Islamist regimes that oppose them as part of their own political agendas; scholars have a different agenda. American commentators who condemn the *hudud* (plural of *hadd*) criminal penalties may remain silent on the persistence of the widespread use of the death penalty in their own country, by electric chair or lethal injection, including its application upon women, minorities, minors, and the mentally challenged. This obvious double standard is untenable in an era of increasingly global standards of what constitutes human rights and which nations violate them. The US and the West's *special* relationship with Israel continues virtually unquestioned at the expense of the majority of Muslim and Arab calls for justice and balance.

Western condemnation of Islamist regimes has unfortunately led to a generalized demonizing of Islam and Muslims, leading to further polarization of relations and confrontation rather than dialogue. Western researchers have been avoiding, or are no longer welcome, in areas currently undergoing or emerging from periods of Islamism. This growing mutual avoidance serves to widen the gaps in knowledge and communication that could be improved by engaged and informed dialogue. Dialogue based on mutual interest, and bilateral or multi-lateral translation of ideas; that acknowledges and is respectful of differences; and that presumes equality of the dialoging parties is what is needed in the present moment. Scholars who are engaging in research in these 'hot spots' have a special knowledge, role and responsibility in the current dialogue and debates.

Challenges of Research: From US and Sudanese Sides

From 2007–08, as a recipient of a research grant from the United States Institute of Peace (USIP), I was required to comply with the sanctions levied upon the Sudan by the US government, as the US Congress funds the USIP. Previous research in 2005 was funded by a European Union grant to two Universities, Bordeaux in France and Leiden in Holland, and was not subjected to the same restrictions. Fear of legal complications and potential sanctions violations with the US Office of Foreign Assets Control (OFAC that manages the sanctions) by the attorney for the Rhode Island Department of Higher Education led her to advise my home institution, Rhode Island College, not to administer the USIP grant. For a time I was fearful that the perceived pariah status of Sudan would prevent me from carrying out the proposed research. The US Institute of Peace was patient and advised that any non-profit organization might administer the grant. The Sudan Studies Association (SSA), founded at Rhode Island College 26 years earlier, decided to accept the grant administration responsibility. This unusual problem of locating a grant administrator was just the first challenge.

In order to accept the grant and have it administered by a US non-profit institution, I had to agree to the conditions set out by OFAC, which was actually implementing an 'exemption' as a research scholar from the full measure of sanctions. According to the terms outlined in a formal letter of understanding between me and OFAC, I was not permitted to take with me to Sudan any electronic equipment, including my PC laptop, digital camera, cell phone, or other electronic device. I was likewise prevented from contracting with any Sudanese for any service while in Sudan, and I agreed not to have contact with or interview specified government individuals. In the field, these limitations were challenging, but forced creative response. I coped by borrowing laptops from generous acquaintances who became friends,[2] by using public internet cafes, by bringing mechanical, disposable cameras, and by seeking collaborators willing to assist me without formal contractual compensation.

I was questioned about my travel to Sudan at US and European airports, and was searched once in Boston Logan airport because I was carrying on my person all of the money I needed for my research due to the ban on the use of credit cards as part of an official no-interest Islamic banking and finance system. The majority of my entries and exits through the Khartoum airport searches were trouble free, and only once were two boxes of books searched and the contents questioned, mainly books in English about AIDS internationally and about women and development in Sudan.

Research under the USIP auspices took place from January to May 2007 and from December 2007 to January 2008. During this period it was my great pleasure to renew friendships and contacts at the Sudan Judiciary and at the universities, as well as among the center city shopkeepers and venerable Acropole and Sahara hotels. The women justices who have been my great friends and collaborators in past research were all still at their desks, despite journalistic and human rights reports of their having been summarily dismissed in a purge of female public employees during the early years of the present regime. A multi-building Judicial complex has replaced the single colonial structure of the past, and several lady judges were elevated to the national High Court during the National Islamic Front (NIF) regime, and are now housed in its gleaming, new building, while one of the women justices was made a presidential advisor.

Colleagues in the Departments of Anthropology, Political Science, and the College of Law at the University of Khartoum, at Juba, Ahfad, and Nilein Universities, as well as the Sudanese Studies Center were – as they have always been – open, critical and generous. Some queried what has been gained by the informal boycott by western researchers (with the exception of archaeologists) that isolated scholars in Sudan and did little to isolate the regime. As a returning Arabic speaking foreigner well-acquainted with Sudan, I was interviewed by the electronic and print media generally curious about my long experience in the country, but also eager to engage me in critical political discourse, especially related to the politicization of Shari'a and Islam. My meetings with Sudanese youth from multiple backgrounds were both planned and spontaneous. These were filled with surprise and delight. I found them politically sharp, engaged with global culture, and culturally rebellious, despite decades of war and repression. My research assistant Salma Abdalmunim was very helpful in this respect.

Among entrenched Islamist functionaries with whom I was not previously acquainted, I was held with a mixture of curiosity, suspicion,

Image 1 Research assistant Salma Abdalmunim with members of Sudanese youth organization for democracy and non-violence (author photo)

and mistrust. Whereas in the past access to courts and observation of cases was open without formal permission, during this period of research such access required written permission, or high level verbal approval. In one case, I was admonished by a high level administrator in the Judiciary about the 'agendas' of westerners – whom he presumed to be human rights investigators – coming to Sudan and documenting their version of the 'truth' irrespective of the facts. In some cases barriers and difficulties were erected such that permission to observe court sessions was effectively denied. This occurred despite my habit of carrying and often gifting the Arabic translation of my study of Shari'a[3] that I used as a credentialing device demonstrating my longstanding interest in the law. The book is now on sale in the major bookshops of Khartoum and is being read and assessed for the first time by scholars and jurists. Gauging the reception of this work – a study of Shari'a prior to Islamization in 1983 with Grand Qadi Mohamed al-Gizouli who was out of favor with the NIF jurists led by al-Turabi – was not always possible. Now generally rehabilitated, Sheikh al-Gizouli can be appreciated as closer to the norm of Sudanese legal thinking than the Islamists who followed him. A broad spectrum of readers have received the book favorably, commenting most frequently about its objectivity. I interpret this as having, perhaps, an element of surprise that a non-Muslim expatriate could or would carry out such a study. Beyond the local context, it remains a serious question as to how a western, non-Muslim woman can adequately carry out research on the complexities of Islamic law. I keenly feel this very inadequacy at times. I recall a remark that I overheard when lecturing in Arabic to a generally skeptical class of anthropology students at the University of Khartoum who were reading my book for their course. When I mentioned that I take my American students to visit local mosques for Friday prayers once or twice during a semester, I noticed their surprise and overheard '*ma batal*' – 'not bad' – from one of the students in the front row. It is well to recall that prejudice and misunderstanding is a two-way street.

As a mature western woman long accustomed to modifying my dress and behavior in the majority Muslim North Sudan, I was none-theless surprised to experience the new cultural, or residual Islamist, pressure to dress properly and adopt a modest demeanor. Male friends with whom I used to slap hands and lock eyes in the warm meeting of friends still greeted me genuinely, but with a gentle handshake and eyes modestly cast down. Although tens of thousands of foreign, mainly western, NGO and diplomatic workers live in Sudan and its cities, their presence could mainly be felt in the one and only two-tiered shopping mall, 'Afra,' and in the trendy suburban restaurants and juice bars. In central Khartoum and in Omdurman, I felt conspic-uous as a foreign woman walking around town, but I never felt unsafe or in any personal danger whatsoever, perhaps the result of lingering colonial western, feminine, and white privilege. It is likely that one legacy of the harsh criminal laws applied from 1983 to the present is the general security of life in the great urban conglomeration of 7–8 million that is greater Khartoum today. There is a general sense of personal security, although people do caution about pickpockets in the central market, Suq al-Arabi. I shopped there almost daily and experi-enced no problem; when I asked the doorman (*ghafir*) to my apartment building if there had been much theft in the area, he replied 'Oh, yes, this is a problem.' Inquiring of further details, he responded that a car had been stolen from in front of the building two years ago.

Wearing pants in downtown Khartoum – where I resided in an apartment complex on University Avenue – was distinctly uncomfortable. This was more common in the affluent suburbs, from Khartoum 2 to Riyadh, but virtually absent in Omdurman and North Khartoum (Bahari), except at the long-term Ahfad University bastion of feminism. Careful to wear long sleeved shirts, I resisted the impulse to veil, both as a non-Muslim and in solidarity with the spirit of the recognition of religious difference in the CPA, publicly expressed in the dress of southern women. At times I would veil, in mosques (as I do in the US) and for social visits during religious holidays that might involve visits to mosques or holy places. My choice of dress was met with no objection in Khartoum except for discrete comments from female friends that my long skirts with slits be sewn so as not to reveal too much calf. At home or visiting with close friends a simple *jellabiyas* (long caftans) more than sufficed.

Once I was granted permission to visit the courts, I received a warm welcome by judges in the Family court, and the Labor and Criminal courts in Khartoum, as well as by the Registrar of marriages and divorces, the *ma'zun*, all of whom made this phase of research a pleasure. I was also warmly received in Omdurman Family court. I needed to obtain permission to visit the IDP camps from the government Humanitarian Assistance Committee which was unproblematic[4] and the government official who accompanied us to the camps was helpful and sincerely interested in the welfare of the camp residents. However, this contrasted with a rather unwelcome reception in the Omdurman criminal courts, where I was rebuffed after several attempted visits. In my initial visit to the central Omdurman criminal courts I was asked for my passport, if I was a Muslim, and when I said that I was not, I was still admonished to cover my head. Two days later when I attempted for a second time to visit these courts – after receiving an invitation from one criminal court judge – I did wear a headscarf to the approving nods of the gentlemen at the reception area. After a brief period of observation I was asked to leave to see the president of the Ondurman courts, and was finally told by him, the *Rais al-Jiraz*, that I would have to obtain written permission from the Head of the National Supreme Court in Khartoum in order to continue to visit these courts. Discouraged, I did not return to the criminal courts in Omdurman, but instead began to visit their counterparts in North Khartoum on the advice of Sudanese friends who argued persuasively that sensitive criminal cases were underway in Omdurman, and that I should instead visit less central, less important courts.

Collegial relations at the universities were resumed with great gusto. The long period of isolation between western and Sudanese scholars has left both a vacuum and a longing for mutual exchange. The facility for critical thought and discourse was hardly dampened during the years of political repression and Islamism, and in the present window of opportunity represented by the peace accords and the CPA it has been sharpened. Contacts and exchange at the many venerable and new universities are too numerous to mention here, but my sincere expression of gratitude to them can be found in my Acknowledgements. It suffices to say that in just about all respects the essential character of the Sudanese – generosity, modesty, patience, warmth and hospitality – remains intact. Their democratic spirit was strengthened in the South by their long and successful insurgency against northern abuse and domination, but was weakened in the North by lengthy periods of harsh repression.

There is an increased sensitivity about photography doubtless due to the negative image of Sudan in the western press. Any westerner with a camera might be taken for a journalist with an agenda to show how repressive, or poor, or backward is Sudan at a time when many are proud of the modern look of their larger cities and towns. In 2007, some western visitors at the popular Sufi 'Dervish Dance' (*dhikr Hamad al-Nil*) were asked to stop taking pictures because they would be used for commercial purposes, arguing they were taking their 'cultural property' without benefiting the subjects of the photo.

In spite of, or really because of, the challenges that this research represented, every day in Sudan was full, interesting, and always stimulating. This has left me with a rich set of observations, reflections, and analysis that I share with the readers of this book. Thanks to the USIP grant and to the great talent of translator Mahgoub al-Tigani Mahmoud, the book is published in English and Arabic for critical minds to discuss and debate inside and outside of Sudan in the year of the separation of the colonial Sudan into two countries. May there be many opportunities, inside and outside of Sudan, to reflect upon the role of Shari'a in this outcome with a spirit of mutual, constructive dialogue for the common views we share, and also with respect for our differences of perspective. This work builds upon my previous research on Shari'a prior to its Islamization, and documents and assesses the rise of Sudanese Islamism after 1983 viewed through the lens of the Shari'a, its strengths as well as it weakensses. By treating Islamic law as a living tradition that is as dynamic as it is susceptible to politics, the case of Sudan emerges as a compelling and instructive one for the examination of the ramifications of a concerted policy of Islamism, and indeed, the very nature of Political Islam.

Field research for this book began with the signing of the CPA in 2005 and withdrawal of Shari'a from the South and from non-Muslims living in the North. It asks the question of whether Sudan has entered a post-Islamist transition leading to peace and reconciliation with the South, or whether it is headed back to more conflict. It assesses the effects of a quarter-century of Islamism on the Sudanese people and the dire implications of separation of the South, and the dissolution of the Sudan over its misguided policies of Arabization and Islamization of the non-Muslim South. The leading edge of its Islamist program was the Shari'a, essentially reformed by Muslim Brotherhood (MB) ideology. During this period of state Islamism the society of the North has been transformed fundamentally, and this work documents and analyzes this social transformation. The likely separation of the South and the creation of a new African independent state, largely but not excluisvely stemming from the Islamist program, is anticipated and analyzed. A central point of the book is that the Shar'a, Islamic law of the ages representing justice and mercy for Muslims, was misapplied to non-Muslims and used to repress Muslims who dissented from government policies. This is a wrong that hurts Muslims and damages Islam, and will take a long time for the Sudanese to correct, but surely they will correct this error.

CHAPTER 1

SHARI'A, ISLAM AND ISLAMISM IN SUDANESE HISTORY: ITS CENTRALITY IN WAR AND PEACE

Over twenty years ago when I published *Islamic Law and Society in the Sudan,* I did not even consider using the Arabic term 'Shari'a' in the book title. Then the use of 'Islamic law' was becoming established as more accurate and less Orientalist than the offensive 'Mohammedan law' characteristic of colonial era writings. Since then, the term Shari'a has become an established reference in the English language for Islamic law, as much as is *'intifada'* or *'fatwa.'* However, few of these now well-recognized terms connotes something positive in the English language. Shari'a has come to be the symbol of all that is wrong with Islam and the dangerous harbinger of a fearsome political Islam. Even the briefest mention in a casual remark by Rowan Williams, the Archbishop of Canterbury, resulted in universal condemnation of his suggestion that Shari'a might be a recognized source of law in Great Britain. It will take years for the West to adopt a measure of objectivity toward a religion, society and law they do not understand much less appreciate in the spectrum of global societies in which Islam and Shari'a operate. The Sudanese case is an important one that is both comparable and different from Iran and Afghanistan, and it is one from which Nigeria and Somalia can benefit.

Research for this book covers the period between the signing of the CPA between the Government of Sudan (GoS) and the Sudanese People's Liberation Movement and the mandated 2011 referendum on separation of the South. The longer reach of the book assesses the nearly three decades of Sudan's Islamization of laws and social institutions. It treats critically Sudan's state Islamism (rule using the legitimating effects of the faith of Islam) and its effects, both intended and unintended. The CPA ended Africa's longest running civil war in 2005, and the likely separation of the South in 2011 – whether by legitimate or irregular means – is a direct consequence of Sudan's policies of Islamization and Islamism. Documentation and analysis of this important case for Africa and for the Islamic world is the major purpose of this work.

The single most important issue that symbolized the essence of the events during these years was Islamic law. Shari'a was made state law in 1983 by General-president Ja'far Numeiri and this move precipitated the second period of civil war between the GoS and South Sudan. Shari'a, from 1983 to 2005 was the contrasting symbol of northern intransigence and southern resistance, and its withdrawal was a southern pre-condition for advance in the decades of peace negotiations that preceded the CPA. With the signing of the CPA, brokered by African and European nations and the US, peace was realized through the withdrawal of Shari'a as national law, and the independent development of the South became a real promise for the first time since independence. The CPA has many critics, often justified, but the peace and security that the accords brought to the South is its chief achievement and cannot be underestimated. The outbreak of war in Darfur in 2003 and its international attention after 2005 overshadowed the gains of the CPA and was a distraction from its implementation. The issues of Arabization and Islamization that fueled the conflict in the South are not present in Darfur, but the Darfur conflict demonstrated the depth and breadth of the resistance of the marginalized. The hard won peace for the South – through regional and international negotiation and diplomatic pressure – provide a model for peace in Darfur. In the end, the story of the rise of Shari'a and Islamism in Sudan is essentially the struggle for peace and national unity – or war, chronic conflict and separation.

I was privileged to be in Khartoum at the time of the signing of the CPA and to witness firsthand the joy and genuine optimism of a majority of its ordinary citizens – northern, southern and from all regions in the capital. I remained in Sudan that year, 2005, for several months of initial research on the status of Shari'a after the CPA signing. The signing of the CPA enabled me to return to Sudan in good conscience to a country and people that I love and the study of which I had dearly missed. I returned in 2007 for another three months of research, this time sponsored by the US Institute of Peace to a social and political environment that had changed greatly. Employing the perspective of a legal anthropologist with nearly four decades of observations, friendships, and associations with diverse Sudanese in the country and in the Diaspora, I also bear witness to their half-century struggle to be a nation at peace and with justice for all citizens.

Shari'a Before Islamization

The Early Post-Independence Period

The status of Shari'a was an issue throughout the decades after independence with political maneuvers by various forces seeking a greater implementation of Shari'a and a state more governed by Islamic institutions. It is noteworthy that the nineteenth-century Mahdi, Muhammad Ahmed, is referred to by northern Muslim Sudanese as 'Abu al-Istiqlal,' the father of independence, for uniting through Islam the various ethnic groups of the North and driving out foreign rule. The Mahdist state is acknowledged as anti-imperialist Islamic state unique in its time in Africa. Thus, the twentieth-century movement for restoration of Islam and its institutions as central to the state is viewed by Islamists as grounded in history, and not messianic hope.

The Sudanese MB was founded in 1953 as the country was moving towards independence. Its political lobbying group, the Islamic Front for the Constitution, promoted a clear program for an Islamic state based upon an Islamic constitution with constitution and law based solely upon Qur'an and Sunna (Fluehr-Lobban, 1990: 617). After 1964 it was led by al-Turabi. In 1957 the Umma party (whose leaders descend from the nineteenth-century Mahdi) and the Khatmiya Sufi order (with followers loyal to the noble Mirghani family) both advocated a parliamentary Islamic republic with Shari'a as the sole source of legislation. These hereditary leaders historically vie for power with the MB and their descending organizations, such as the National Islamic Front, but they rarely differed over the increased role for Islam and its institutions in national political life.

From independence in 1956, southern, non-Muslim and regions, now recognized as marginalized, were ignored politically as resistance to northern elites became entrenched and chronic civil war was waged. Political activism toward an Islamic state was interrupted by the first military coup d'etat of General Ibrahim Abboud who began the ultimately failed policy of forced Islamization and spread of the Arabic language in the south.

Shari'a in Colonial and Pre-colonial Sudanese History: British Colonial Policy toward Shari'a

The British colonial policies of its architect, Lord Lugard, were similar in Muslim African countries with the use of indirect rule to govern and control Islamic institutions. Shari'a, under the signature Orientalist designation of 'Mohammedan' law, was relegated to a personal status law only, leaving the important civil and criminal matters to English-derived law. The Sudanese scholars and judges, the 'ulama were carefully observed by the colonial authorities. In Darfur the British extinguished the last sultanate in Sudan in 1916.

Early in the occupation of Sudan Lord Cromer privately commented that he 'did not like the tone' of the Qadi's report. 'He [the Qadi] is evidently opposed to the students learning anything but purely "Mohamedan law." He wants clearly to apprehend that Mohammedan law is founded on equity on all ages and all places and does not require at any time any alternation or amendment, applied to events and circumstances' (Letter to Wingate from Cromer Commenting on Grand Qadi's Report; 11 February 1907, (SA 280/2/82)). He continued:

> These views are held by many in the class to which the Grand
> [Qadi] belongs and they are of course sheer nonsense. Mohamedan
> law requires a great deal of amendment; and what more than

anything else is keeping the Mohamedans back is the impossibility of altering or amending it. Some of the more enlightened among them see this. Mohamed Abdou saw it, or at all events pretended to see it. I hope, therefore, that you will stick to some sort of elementary course of non-Mohamedan law, so that at all events they should they should have some sort of idea of the principles which are in vogue in other countries.

It is perhaps rather rushing at a conclusion, but I am inclined to think that a [Qadi] who holds the views set forth in the report I have just been reading is not altogether the man you want. I quite recognize, however, that it will probably be difficult to get anybody better. They are pretty well all of them alike. Only I would advise keeping a careful watch over him, and not trusting him too far. (Ibid)

After the early period of containing and colonizing Muslim law and its legal personnel, a fear of a Pan-Islamism dating back to the Mahdist period was renewed in the First World War. A recognition of a growing pan-Arabic Islamic movement was of the utmost concern. The English demanded loyalty from the indigenous Muslim leaders while their enemy, the Ottoman Empire, was responsible for the guardianship of the Holy Places at Mecca and Medina. The descendants of the same Mahdists who resisted them on the eve of colonial occupation promised loyalty in a formal letter from Ansar leader El Sherif Yusef Wad El Hindi to the Governor General of the Sudan 11 November 1914/19 El Higga 1332:

In consideration of the brilliant achievements of the British government in the Sudan … and the respect and honour shown to our 'Ulema and religious chiefs … we are enjoying full liberty in the exercise of our religious duties … We pledge our support in your fight against the Turks, against whose oppression we have fought.

There were similar expressions of loyalty by the 'Religious Sheikhs of the Sudan,' including the Mufti, Sheikh of the 'Ulamas of Sudan, Sherif

Yusef al Hindi and 13 others representing the 'Ulamas Committee, dated 8 November 1914 (Sudan Archives, University of Durham).

With British rule, English civil law and a new Penal Code (derived from that developed originally for India) were introduced, displacing Islamic law in all matters except family and personal status affairs of Muslims. An autonomous division of the Judiciary for the Shari'a was established alongside the western-derived Civil and Criminal Division. Nonetheless, a distinctive development of the Shari'a took place during this period. Especially noteworthy were innovations in the law of divorce and changes in the law of inheritance (cf, Fluehr-Lobban, 1987; translation by Mahgoub al-Tigani, 2004).

The attitude of the colonial government left a legacy both of entitlement to full political-religious status and respect for all Islamic institutions, but also some unfinished business of the restoration of Muslim institutions, especially strong among the *'ulama* and the 'second class' Shari'a judges who administered the Shari'a as a separate and inferior system of law and court.

The Mahdiya and Shari'a, 1884–98

The heart and soul of Sudanese Islam lies in the practices associated with the Sufi orders (*turuq*). The spread of Islam in Sahelian Africa was through popular Sufi orders, such as Qadiriyya, or Tijaniyya, while the institutionalization of Shari'a was through the mechanism of the state. Popular Sufi Islam, with its unique brand of spiritual democracy, has a long tradition of resisting oppression. So it was natural that its organization and social consciousness would be mobilized in the struggle against oppressive Turkish rule (Hassan, 1993: 41).

The Mahdist state laid the foundations for the twentieth-century Islamist agenda (Layish and Warburg, 2002: 1–2). Muhammad Ahmed the Mahdi ('expected one' in Sunni Muslim theology) belonged to the Sammaniyya order when he led the most significant and successful nineteenth-century jihad against foreign rule, first Turkish-Egyptian – beginning in 1821 – and later their successors, the British. Through a series of stunning defeats, by 1883 the Mahdi controlled the western provinces of Darfur and Kordofan, and by 1884 most of what had been the Turco-Egyptian Sudan. In late 1884 the Mahdi settled at Omdurman and commenced his siege of the would-be British outpost of Khartoum, which fell to the Mahdists on 25 January 1885. In the context of this research the identity of the 'last Qadi of Khartoum' under Turkish rule – whose picture was taken by the German traveler Richard Buchta in 1880 – has, perhaps, been identified. Muhammad Khojali al-Hitayk, a Mahas from Tuti Island or Burri al-Mahas, was this last judge of Khartoum and he was killed by the Mahdists during the last siege of Khartoum (Fluehr-Lobban, 2009).

During the Mahdist period slave raids, known as *ghazwa*, that began in Turco-Egyptian rule, continued against the southern people. The Mahdist rank and file was drawn heavily from the western ethnic groups of Darfur and Kordofan forming an alliance that can be traced from the Mahdiya to the post-independence Sudan army. These relations forged in Mahdist expansion shaped the relations of the central government with southern and western parts of the country.

Under the Mahdiya, the Shari'a was the sole law in effect, whose decisions were based upon strict interpretation of the Qur'an and Sunna. *Zakat* was instituted as a state tax levied on cattle and grain. A judiciary was established with a Chief Justice (*Qadi al-Quda*) with lesser judges appointed to courts in the towns under Mahdist occupation. The law was rendered more democratic and made accessible to ordinary people, not just the privileged merchant class. Mahdist law sought to purify Sudanese society with a focal point being proper Shari'a dress and enforcement of the seclusion of women. The modern Muslim woman's dress known as the *tobe*, several meters of cloth draped around the body and covering the head, were introduced during Mahdist times. An austerity was imposed in many social and economic affairs, including the limitation of the marital dower (*mahr*) to no more than 10 Maria Theresa dollars to ensure the affordability of the marriage and avoid loose sexual relations and the crime of 'fornication' (*zina*).

The supreme judicial authority was the Mahdi, and later the Khalifa Abdullahi, although this authority was widely delegated and local military officials and provincial governors could act as judges. The *Qadi al-Islam* was the special legal authority representing the Mahdi as Imam, or religious leader of the state. His task was to ensure the 'correct' interpretations of law based upon Qur'an and Sunna alone. There were two *Qadis al-Islam* and both fell out of favor with the state. The four historical schools of Islamic law were set aside indicative of the revivalist state and its isolation from the larger world of Islamic jurisprudence (*fiqh*).

It is noteworthy that the Shari'a was used to prosecute political opponents, defined as 'apostates' during the Mahdiya. A century later a conviction of apostasy and the execution of a dissident Sufi leader, Mahmoud Mohamed Taha precipitated the *intifada* that overthrew Numeiri who gave birth to the modern Islamist movement (Fluehr-Lobban, 1987: 31–34).

The Mahdist movement gave shape to the colonial and post-colonial relations between North and South, between Muslim and non-Muslim, and between center and periphery. While early European scholars saw the Mahdiya as an anti-modernist movement fighting against the forces of progress, post-independence Sudanese and other scholars have viewed it as an anti-imperialist movement and an early 'fundamentalist' Islamic movement as part of an early modern context of Islamic reform and renewal (Lobban, Kramer and Fluehr-Lobban, 2002: 180).

Shari'a in the Funj Kingdom at Sinnar

The first Sudanese Muslim state, the Funj, also brought the first Islamic jurists to its capital city of Sinnar in the sixteenth century. These religious-legal scholars introduced the Maliki school of jurisprudence that became future Muslim practice in the Sudan. Two centuries later during Turkish rule, the Ottoman state introduced its official Hanafi school of law, and the interpretations of law from these two schools continued their influence to the present time.

Intellectuals in the kingdom of Sinnar imported textbooks of Islamic law that Nubian students abroad had laboriously copied as they studied. These 'principles of the Arabs' were foreign to the Funj though many came increasingly to see this as their religious duty (Spaulding, 2007: 81). By the eighteenth century among the Funj kings' high court officials was an Islamic Qadi tellingly to adjudicate the affairs of the *khawajas, jallaba*, and *fuqara* (foreigners, indigenous northern merchants, and Sufis, respectively). The value of the Islamic courts for elites was obvious, making the story of the Mahdist populist revolution all the more compelling. After 1821 and Turkish occupation of the lands of the Funj, a more orthodox interpretation of Shari'a came into force. The transition from indigenous to colonial rule revealed remnants of the prior customary rule of law. According to Spaulding (2007: 127), there was increasing preference for monetary fines over corporal punishment as the Islamic magistrates increasingly served the interests of the propertied and the rich. 'Punishment in kind' for all classes had been used in c.1754–64 CE, according to the last Grand Qadi, but had died out favoring monetary settlement for crimes that previously may have involved physical punishment or mutilation, such as the *hadd* punishment of cutting of the hand of the convicted thief. From the perspective of a commoner this would be viewed as a corruption of the law favoring the wealthy criminal aided by a supportive Muslim judge.

The Funj state, like all states, established itself and ruled through differentiated classes and the unequal access to justice and the law. At the point of its entry to the Sudan, Islamic law was closely allied with the authority and power of the state using Shari'a for its own legitimacy and perpetuation. Shari'a offers strength and the promise of continuity to states in the process of formation, or change of governance – such as in the nineteenth century, from the Funj to the Ottoman states. During British colonialism it was subordinated and marginalized to English law. And under indigenous rule, it served to symbolize the absolute power and unlimited authority of the state in the nineteenth-century Mahdist state and the twentieth-century Islamist states, from the Numeiri to the al-Bashir military regimes.

Shari'a: Mapping the Modern Rise of Islamism

Shari'a is a law whose foundations are the same as those of the faith of Islam – the Qur'an, the revealed word of God, and Sunna, the personal practice of the Prophet to whom the Qur'an was revealed,

Muhammad, and his sayings collected in the books of the *Hadith*. As a religiously-based law the proclamation of Shariʿa is the first visible face of a political program and mobilization in the name of Islam, referred to by scholars and the popular media as *Islamism*. Whether it was popular revolution in Iran, Islamization of the states of northern Nigeria, efforts at state-building in Somalia under the Organization of Islamic Courts, Hamas' takeover of Gaza or the Taliban's taking control of border areas in Pakistan-Afghanistan, Shariʿa is the issue that announces the intention of establishing an Islamic state, or some ideal of the establishment of an Islamic society. Thus it was in Sudan beginning in the late 1970s under the country's second military regime. Steady moves toward Islamization, legalized alms-giving (*zakat*) as a responsibility of citizens, (and not just the private duty of Muslims), illegalization of public acts violating Islamic law, such as alcohol sale and consumption, and prostitution. The political motives were obvious, both to intensify the drive against Sudan's rebellious non-Muslim southern third of its population and to derail secular, reformist northern Muslim rebels. With popular resistance insufficient to stop Islamization, by 8 September 1983, it was simply a matter of proclaiming Shariʿa as state law, however the dramatic addition of Islamic criminal law, the *hudud* (to the limit) penalties drew the attention of the world, the Muslim world and global human rights organizations.

This book analyzes the role of the Shariʿa in the construction and, the deconstruction of the Sudanese state. Its starting point is the withdrawl of Shariʿa as state law according to the terms of the CPA, (*itifaqiyat al-Salam al-Shamil*) in 2005. While Islamic law was withdrawn completely from the South, it was to remain in the North, but not to be applied to non-Muslims. Below the story of Shariʿa in Sudan is told in reverse historical chronology – beginning with the present complex post-CPA Sudan where the issue of Shariʿa has retreated somewhat from the limelight – in no small measure due to the conflict in Darfur – but is still capable of inflaming passions among Muslims and non-Muslims of multiple political persuasions. From the present, the story proceeds through the decades of stalemate in the peace negotiations where the Shariʿa was *the* symbolic issue over which the parties of GoS and SPLM stumbled and failed repeatedly to achieve the needed common ground.

The SPLM demanded withdrawal of the national status of Shariʿa, while the GoS rejected this demand as non-negotiable for a country that is predominatly Muslim. Backward in time, the story reveals the immediate post-independence period after 1956 and the clear efforts of successive governments before the 1983 official date of the rise of Sudan's Islamism to Arabize and Islamize the South, while efforts at nation building stalled repeatedly. From independence to the 56 years of British colonialism and its efforts to marginalize Shariʿa the story turns back to the nineteenth-century dramatic period of the Mahdi who defeated British imperial advance in 1884 and instituted a 'fundamentalist' interpretation of Islamic law that governed the Sudanese Mahdist state until 1898 when the English finally succeeded in colonizing the region and created the boundaries of the modern Sudan. Prior to the Mahdist state were the decades of Turkish rule (1821–84) against which the Mahdist forces rebelled. And before the Turkiya were the kingdoms and states – the Funj based in Sinnar, the first Islamic state – to which I will return – as well as the Sultanate of Darfur, the Shilluk kingdom, the confederation of clans and lineages of the powerful Dinka, and in antiquity the Nubian kingdoms of Kush-Meroë.

Given the protracted crises that have characterized the present moment, let us proceed backward in time from the year 1983 when the issue of Shariʿa moved to the center of Sudanese politics and social life and became the focal point of the nation's future – advance, stagnation or retreat in North-south relations; separation of religion and the state; or unity or dismemberment of the state.

Islamization in Sudan, 1983–2004 and the Shariʿa Issue

Sudanese Islamization intensified under the military rule of Jaʿafar Numeiri in the late 1970s with bans on alcohol production, sale, consumption; suppression of public prostitution, and the institution of *zakat* as a state-sponsored taxation. Various motives are imputed to Numeiri's progression to an Islamized state. One theory is his born-again dedication to the faith after surviving numerous coup attempts, including the 1971 Hashim al-Atta coup against whom he mounted a successful counter-coup. More likely was his opportunistic shift to the religious right after exhausting all of his secular leftist options and allies from the Sudanese Communist party, which helped to bring him to power in 1969, to his experiment with Nasserite socialism in the Sudanese Socialist Union. He had implemented the communist party principle of regional autonomy in the South and had ushered in the only decade of peace in post-independence Sudan, the Addis Ababa Accords that lasted from 1972 to 1983.

However, he began Islamization moves as early as 1977 and in 1983 Numeiri announced the September Laws that proclaimed Shari'a state law. Leaders in the South were already losing faith in the implementation of the Addis Ababa peace accords and openly debated the limitations of national unity. Dr. John Garang was instrumental in the army 'Bor Mutiny' of January 1983 that resulted in the formation of the Sudan People's Liberartion Army (SPLA) before the September Laws were announced, but the failure of the implementation of the Addis Ababa Accords and growing Islamization of institutions pushed the Sudan People's Liberation Movement/Army (SPLM/SPLA) and the region back into civil war against the government in Khartoum. This new face of the Shari'a was dramatically different from the law that I studied and documented in 1979–80 and published in English as 'Islamic Law and Society in the Sudan (1987) and in Arabic as al-Shari'a al-Islamiya wa al-Mujtama'fi al-Sudan (translated by Mahgoub al-Tigani Mahmoud, 2004). This work documented a progressive and tolerant Islamic law, rooted in African Maliki and imported Hanafi law and infused with Sudanese Sufism. Under one of the last Grand Qadis, Sheikh Mohamed al-Gizouli, the first women Shari'a judges in Sudan, indeed in Africa, were appointed.[5] Confined from the legacy of colonialism to a personal status law, many reforms in marriage, divorce, child custody, and inheritance had been instituted under the separate administration of the Islamic Courts over the decades of the application of Shari'a under the British and for the 27 years after independence. These are detailed in this work and provide partial documentation of the Shari'a before it became a comprehensive law and added the harsh criminal penalties (that had not been applied since the Mahdiya) commercial and civil law, including Islamic banking and finance, as well as its traditional role as a family law Muslims. Shari'a thus moved center stage in Sudanese domestic politics, and increasingly it became a topic of international Islamist politics as its chief architect, al-Turabi, projected himself as 'Imam' for Africa's Muslims.

Moreover, the *hadd* punishments were applied in rare circumstances in the history of Islamic societies perhaps reflecting the emphasis on restitution characteristic of Islamic law. Indeed, in many parts of the Islamic world they have not been applied in cultural-historical memory (Bielefelt, 2007: 13).

With the announcement of the September Laws, for the first time in modern Sudanese history the *hudud* punishments of lashing for alcohol use, stoning for adultery, flogging for morals offenses, and amputation for theft were applied. New 'Courts of Prompt Justice' – where appeals were limited or non-existent – were instituted. The Judiciary was allegedly purged of liberals (Gallab, 2008; Ibrahim, 2009). Renewed civil war pitted Muslim northern citizens against southern animist and Christian citizens who viewed the installation of state Islamic law as incendiary. Estimates from dozens to hundreds of amputations were reported in this early, intense period of Islamization and full implementation of Shari'a between 1983 and 1985. Stoning sentences for adultery were 'applied,' but not executed. Reports indicate that the vast majority of Sudanese Muslims opposed the *hudud* especially amputation for theft and this is why referred the laws are referred to as 'September Laws,' so as not to recognize them or conflate then with the Shari'a.

Protesting the September Laws as a misapplication of Islam and Shari'a, the elderly founder of the reformist Republican Brothers (*al-Jamhouriyeen*), Mahmoud Mohamed Taha, was tried, convicted of apostasy, and hung for his 'crime' in 1985. This event precipitated the popular revolution (*intifada*) that overthrew president Numeiri. The war continued for 22 more years until the CPA was signed in Nairobi in 2005.

During the four years from 1985–89, Sudanese democracy flourished with vigorous public debates, forums, and the formation of new parties hoping to challenge the historical dominance of the old parties – the Umma of the Mahdi and its followers (*Ansar*) under the leadership of the Mahdi's descendants, and the Democratic Unionist

Party (DUP) of the Sufi Khatmiya sect with followers loyal to the noble Mirghani family. Sudan's two periods of democracy – 1964–69 and 1985–89 – were bracketed by Numeri's entry into and exit from national leadership. In both cases the central populist concern was an end to the conflict in the South through secular democracy and enfranchisement of all Sudanese regions and ethnicities. After the September Laws, the debate shifted in focus from popular democracy to unresolved issues of nation building and the proper relationship between religion and the state.

The post-Numeiri democracy elected Umma party leader Sadiq al-Mahdi president who promised to reform the September Laws and withdraw the Shari'a from national status. During his four years he was either unable, or unwilling, to do so; some argue he was compromised by his status as leader of an Islamic party, or by his personal relationship with his brother-in-law al-Turabi. Frustrated, because Shari'a had by then become the major obstacle to critical peace negotiations with the SPLM, the Sudanese Parliament moved to withdraw Shari'a in June of 1989. The rival Khatmiyya DUP met separately with the SPLM and made more advance in peace negotiations than the elected sitting government headed by Sadiq al-Mahdi. This peace initiative was hailed by northern Sudanese who showed their support in massive demonstrations in Khartoum giving notice to the NIF which claimed to represent the interests of the 'silent' Muslim majority. Mansour Khalid argues that Sadiq could have earned an honored place in Sudanese history and saved innumerable lives had he captured this initiative and led the way to a peace agreement. But instead he allied with the NIF against the DUP; he undermined the agreement between SPLM and DUP by overplaying the issue of Shari'a and stressing the impossibility of abolishing or freezing the September Laws through Parliament. Utterly frustrated by the stalemate in the civil war, in February 1989 the army sent a clear memorandum to the Prime Minister demanding he take some action to wage war or negotiate peace (Khalid/Garang pp.198–99). Also frustrated, the Parliament was moving to withdraw the September Laws in the spring of 1989, when the NIF made its last move to seize total power.

The corrective move to withdraw the criminal law component of the Shari'a was intercepted by a pre-emptive coup d'etat launched on

30 June 1989, by al-Bashir. This brought the NIF to power under the tutelage of MB founder, Hasan al-Turabi, and ensured that Shari'a would remain the sole law in force, thus further inflaming tensions between the *presumed* solid block representing the Muslim North and the animist and Christian South. The expansion of Shari'a to a comprehensive codified system of law, including Islamic penal law, took effect in 1991 under the NIF. Many Muslims opposed this trend and under the new authoritarian regime they were arrested, tortured in infamous 'ghost houses,' and forced into exile. Meanwhile the issue of a revived slavery in the 'Arab-African' border areas of Bahr al-Ghazal aroused the West, attracting the attention of the American evangelical Christian right who portrayed the civil war as a battleground between Islam and Christianity. Perhaps counter-intuitively, the application of the *hudud* punishments of amputation was actually curtailed under the Islamist regime of al-Bashir, as al-Turabi himself said in a 1993 interview, 'the criminal law [of Shari'a] has only two cases of the application of the harsh punishment [of amputation] in the year and half since the law was promulgated' (interview in the documentary film 'The Islamic State,' 1994).

In the immediate aftermath of the coup all political parties were banned, and the *Inqaz* (Salvation) government expanded the existing Islamist model. The NIF government shortly thereafter welcomed Osama bin Laden to Sudan as a 'base' of al-Qaeda operations from 1990–96. Bin Laden initiated a number of economic enterprises and Islamic investments, including the Tadamon Islamic bank still in operation. Al-Turabi's central role in the new Islamist Sudan enhanced his international recognition as a cosmopolitan 'fundamentalist,' as fluent in French and English as in Arabic, in contrast to other figures such as Ayatollah Khomeini. Al-Turabi's formal power was institutionalized in 1996 when he was elected to the National Assembly and made its Speaker. However, in a 1999 power struggle with President al-Bashir, al-Turabi was dismissed and has since been politically isolated. He has resumed an opportunistic political career in recent years as a backer of the Darfuri anti-government Justice and Equality Movement (JEM) and as an officially denounced defender of the rights of Muslim women to marry non-Muslims and to be Imams leading mixed male and female public prayers. Al-Turabi was himself subjected to the very kinds of *fatwas* condemning unIslamic teachings and ideas, such as those of Mahmoud Muhammad Taha whose writings he had condemned (*Majma' al-Fiqh al-Islami* monograph condemning al-Turabi, *Risala aqul al-fadhal fi al-rad'ali min kharj'an aladhal, 1426/2006*). In 1989 al-Bashir declared a state of emergency that is still in effect, he dissolved the National Assembly, and suspended parts of the constitution. (Hasan, 2003: 378).

The first ever codification of Shari'a in Sudan took place in 1991 instituting a process that consolidated a comprehensive Islamic law through a process of the occasional issuing of Judicial Circulars.[6] Many religious scholars (*'ulama*) argue that Shari'a should not be codified, but should preserve its history of interpretations by the scholars of the religious texts, who base their views upon the Qur'an and books of the Prophet's sayings (the *Hadith*). This process continued through 1983–84 with unification of the Islamic and civil courts. This move legalized and formalized the Maliki School of Islamic law, and thus divested Sudanese Shari'a of its historical ties to Turkish Hanafi law established in the nineteenth century and subsequently adopted by Anglo-Egyptian colonialism. Thus, another vestige of colonialism was removed, yet some of the flexibility of legal interpretation was lost in this move.[7] However, it should be noted that the adoption of Maliki thought is consistent with Sudanese and African Muslim custom and practice.

Although the militarist Ja'afar Numeiri (1969–85) first politicized the issue of Shari'a by making it state law in 1983, it was during the first term as Prime Minister of Umma party leader Sadiq al-Mahdi's (1965–69, great grandson of the nineteenth-century Mahdi) that the political drive for an Islamic constitution began. At the then Constituent Assembly he stated: 'The dominant feature of our nation is an Islamic one, and its overpowering expression is Arabic, and this nation will not have its entity identified . . . except under an Islamic revival' (Yusef Fadl Hasan, 2003: 215). The same position was later argued forcefully by al-Turabi, then head of the Muslim Brother Islamic Charter Front, while the Sudanese Communist Party allied with southern forces in opposition to a central role for Islam in the state. As Sadiq al-Mahdi failed to withdraw Shari'a, John Garang insisted upon the withdrawal of the national status of Islamic law as a precondition to the recommencement of peace talks. As the Constituent Assembly was about to force his hand in June 1989, the Islamist coup blocked the popular will and placed the issue on hold for another 16 years until the negotiated withdrawal of Shari'a with the CPA in 2005.

Sudan's Islamist Rule, 1989 to present

The regime of al-Bashir was committed to a Sudan *unified* under Shari'a law. Sudan's Islamist program immediately acted to ban all political parties except religious ones, and shut down all newspapers and other media, instituting its own publications. One, *al-Inqaz al-Watani* ('The National Salvation'), lent its name to the new regime, which indeed saw itself as the country's only answer to the failure of sectarian-influenced party politics and western-style secular democracy. A large number of politicians and intellectuals representing a broad political spectrum were arrested, and allegations quickly arose of political repression and torture in infamous 'ghost houses,' bringing the regime unwanted attention from the international media and organizations such as Human Right Watch Africa and Amnesty International.

In the face of deteriorating political conditions and harsh repression, unprecedented alliances were formed among the banned political parties, which formed the National Democratic Alliance (NDA) and found common cause in opposing the al-Bashir regime, some from places of exile. All major parties, including the SPLM, were signatories to the National Democratic Charter in Cairo in March 1990. A consensus was reached that the civil war could only be negotiated to an end by the removal of Shari'a as the state law. Also needed was the convening of a constitutional conference, whereby a secular and democratic state, justly representing all of Sudan's diverse regions and minorities, would be constructed.

Offsetting the newfound cooperation of the major political parties was the intransigence of the al-Bashir regime. Initially it pursued a strictly military solution to the civil war, often employing the rhetoric of jihad against the pagan Southerners, while its other domestic and foreign policies were guided by the strict Islamist principles of its chief ideologue, al-Turabi.

Upon first coming to power in 1989, the regime proclaimed itself free of any ideological predilection, and among those it placed in detention were Sadiq al-Mahdi and Muhammad 'Uthman al-Mirghani of the Democratic Unionist Party, and al-Turabi of the NIF. Within four months all three were released, and though the official chief authority in the state was the Revolutionary Command Council, al-Turabi's influence soon became apparent. By 1993, the RCC had been dissolved and al-Bashir was ruling as a 'civilian' president, with the assistance of a 300-member Transitional National Assembly appointed to enact laws. In the parliamentary elections of March 1996 both al-Bashir and al-Turabi won seats, and the NIF emerged as the sole party in government. Al-Turabi's governmental role was further solidified in February 1998, when he was elected secretary-general of the National Congress, the sole legal political organization.

In its attempt to solidify *Inqaz* politics, the al-Bashir regime was adamant that there would be no return to political parties. In 1991 a federal system of government with nine states was announced. Three years later Sudan was re-divided into 26 states with NIF loyalists placed in charge. Popular protests in the towns and at the universities were met with force, and no hesitation to use deadly force. Multiple coup attempts were thwarted, leading to the arrest and execution of scores (and perhaps hundreds) of army officers.

Social conditions in Sudan declined after 1989, especially as a result of the military push to win the war in the South and the consequent flood of refugees into northern cities. Well before the al-Bashir regime came to power, refugee settlements ringing the capital area had grown to township size. After 1990 many of these areas were destroyed in the name of 'slum clearance,' while their inhabitants – mainly non-Muslim Southerners – were either relocated to internally displaced camps (IDPs), desert settlements equally lacking in amenities, or on some occasions killed outright. Behind the government's public health and civil engineering concerns lay a well-documented agenda to coerce or forcibly convert these vulnerable people to Islam. Young men among the displaced were pressed into the popular militias to fight the civil war in the south. These policies made resistance to the symbolic issue of Shari'a even more entrenched among southern non-Muslims.

The early al-Bashir regime withstood domestic opposition and international condemnation and remained steadfast to its Islamist policies, intolerant of dissent. Widespread arrests and torture in so-called 'ghost houses' continued to be reported especially by growing numbers of northern dissidents and human rights activists who fled into exile after their detention. The Sudanese Human Rights Organization (SHRO) was formed in Cairo in 1993 by political exile Mahgoub al-Tigani Mahmoud, and Sudanese Organized Against Torture (SOAT) began to document the regime's human rights abuses after 1993. This repression of all dissent and the failing economy drove many other professionals and educators out of the country. Residents of the capital came under close scrutiny. 'Islamic' Shari'a dress – head covered with hair concealed, long sleeves and long dresses and constraints imposed upon the use of cosmetics, including traditional ones such as henna dying of feet and hands – was imposed on all women including the more vulnerable non-Muslim women. On at least one occasion female students from Ahfad University, the only all women's university in Africa, were flogged for publicly wearing pants. Immorality offenses, especially those punishable by lashing, were executed, although the most severe sentence of stoning for adultery was handed down in a number of well-publicized cases, but never carried out. Several prostitutes were sentenced to death in Khartoum in November 1997.

With the cooling of the earlier, more intense period of application, and gradual withdrawal of Islamist laws and social policies, cultural and social resistance to Sudan's Islamism is noteworthy. The most significant moves away from Islamist policies followed the first commercial flow of oil after 1999 and were paralleled with the relaxation of much of the Islamist program in Sudanese public space. Symbolically, the detention and political isolation of al-Turabi in 1999 was matched by progress in the peace negotiations and gradual retreat on the issue of Shari'a. With oil revenues beginning to flow, the appearance of the capital city dramatically improved, as well as that of the major towns of the North. An estimated one-third of the population of Khartoum was now comprised of the poor, unemployed and underemployed from the South and other marginalized regions. Khartoum grew to a city estimated between 6 and 8 million, with an additional estimated 2 million living in the seven IDP camps around the three towns of Khartoum, Omdurman and Khartoum North. Class differentiation intensified as the Jaʿalin and Shayqiya political elites tied to the regime made their fortunes, while the sub-elites from these relatively privileged ethnic groups migrated to the Gulf and sent home remittances to enrich their families. The issue not only of economic, but political, representation of the whole citizenry of the Sudan has become more acute as the oil wealth of the few is visible in ever more material and non-material ways. The connections between the flow of oil, the advance of the peace negotiations especially after 1999, and retreat from Islamism with its major symbolic issue of Shariʿa are unmistakable and fundamentally inter-connected.

What follows is a summary of the history of attempted Islamization of the non-Muslim South revealing: 1) a pattern of consistent southern resistance to that program; 2) the acknowledgement by the late 1990s that the civil war was not winnable militarily by either the GoS or the SPLM; and 3) and that the strength of SPLM and the presence of the majority of oil reserves in the South won it a major place at the negotiating table, along with the significant presence of international parties with interest in the negotiated end to Africa's longest running civil war.

Shariʿa and the Attempted Islamization of the South

From the first post-independence military regime of General Ibrahim Abboud, a policy of imposed Islamization was pursued by Sudan's North-central elites who inherited a 'right to govern' from their relative privilege as beneficiaries of a half-century of colonial rule in which they were favored by the English. Their newfound identity as 'Arabs' and Muslims was perhaps forged in part by *not* being non-Arab, or *not* being 'black' or *not* being of slave ancestry. The non-Muslim South was viewed as a problem to be solved by what was naively viewed as 'simple' assimilation to the superior 'Arab' and Muslim culture of the dominant North.

Abboud's clumsy program of Islamization included a campaign of forced attendance at Islamic schools, '*khalwas*' established as the sole form of publicly subsidized education, in the Arabic language without accommodation to the diversity of local languages. Christian missionaries who had been granted concessions to operate schools and hospitals throughout the South during colonialism were expelled under Abboud. The lines dividing North and South, drawn during colonial times in the 1933 Closed Districts Ordinance, were reinforced instead of reconstructed, in the first postcolonial opportunity to undo the divide and rule tactics of foreign rule. Small wonder that Southerners began to refer to 'Arab colonialism' as policies emanating from Khartoum were imposed one after the other upon them.

During the decades leading to national political Islamization, the South was politically isolated as resistance to northern Muslim rule became entrenched and civil war became chronic. The western regions of Darfur and Kordofan, eastern and Blue Nile regions were also politically marginalized, but significantly did not move into armed resistance until the maturation and successes of the SPLM.

Over the decades a variety of tactics were used to Arabize and Islamize the animist and Christian south, including forced conversions and the imposition of Muslim names after villages were militarily attacked and 'pacified.' Moreover, the only education provided by the government was in the Arabic language with an imposed religious curriculum in Islamic studies; the opening of mosques in the south was encouraged while permits to build new churches would be denied; outward displays of Christian observance were subject to harassment, along with Christian clergy and leaders; and foreign Christian missionaries and relief agencies were either expelled or had their activities in the country circumscribed.

Peace Agreements: From Addis Ababa
to the CPA, 1972–2005

The viability of the Sudanese state has always revolved around the overriding issue of the North-center and its elites' struggle for power and absolute control of the country, and the insurgent periphery, led by the

South and now enveloping the vast entirety of the nation, Africa's largest until 2011. The Roundtable Conference of 1964 – after Sudan's first popular Revolution – and 9 June 1970 Declaration, during Numeiri's early relatively progressive years, established regional autonomy as a solution to the 'southern problem.' These preceded the first major set of peace accords set down at Addis Ababa in 1972 that lasted until 1983 when the failed policy of Arabization and Isalmization of the South was reinstated.

The Addis Ababa Agreement of 1972 between the Sudanese Government and the predecessors to the SPLM, the Southern Sudan Liberation Movement (SSLM) and Anya-Nya were reached by these parties with Ethiopian Emperor Haile Selassie as official mediator. The main features of this historic agreement included the concept of a unified Sudan with a representative government, allocation of revenue for regional self-rule in the south and economic development with regional security in the hands of Southerners. A caretaker government, to manage the transition, included mechanisms for regional repatriation, resettlement, incorporation of Anya-Nya forces into the Sudan army, police, prison forces and regional civil service. After the peace agreement for regional autonomy was implemented, over one million Sudanese refugees returned home. The Addis Ababa accords recognized the solution to the 'southern problem' as one of a federal system of government. Its greatest objective achievement was the attainment of political autonomy; its greatest weakness the failure to insure economic development and a viable southern economy. And the most serious failure of political consciousness was the characterization of the problem as 'southern,' rather than northern dominion, or equitable nation-building. The renewed outbreak of civil war in 1983 meant not only the political failure of the Addis Ababa accords, but ushered in a new era of a politicized Islam alien to the deep Sufi traditions of Sudanese Muslims, an aggressive and fierce Islamism, and the end to vision of a unified, secular and democratic nation.

After the disappointing failure to implement the Addis Ababa accords, the installment of Shari'a as state law and the harshest period of its application, the execution of the 'apostate' Mahmoud Mohamed Taha, the Numeiri regime was in a protracted state of crisis between

1983 and 1985 leading to its overthrow. At Koka Dam a Declaration on 24 March 1986 included a vision of a post Numeiri nation whereby a reorganized SPLM and the National Alliance for National Salvation met for four days and agreed to create a 'new Sudan' free of racism, tribalism, sectarianism and all causes of discrimination by method of convening National Constitutional Convention. The concept of a 'new Sudan' was the slogan of the SPLM often cited by Dr. John Garang that survived into the post-CPA period as a recollection of Garang's vision, although it can be cynically rendered by activists critical of its failure to be implemented by the Khartoum government. The Addis Ababa accords called for immediate lifting of state of emergency, repeal of the September Laws, adoption of 1956 constitution (as amended in 1964) with the incorporation of the principle of regional government. As a significant part of the peace process of the 1980s, the Koka Dam Declaration was signed by all major parties except the NIF and DUP, but two years later the DUP issued a joint declaration with the SPLM containing all of the points in Koka Dam (SHD3, p.161).

Brought together by Nigerian President Ibrahim Babangida talks between the Government of Sudan and the SPLM met at Nigeria's capital of Abuja in a first set of talks known as Abuja I (26 May 1992) and Abuja II (26 April to 18 May 1993). The GoS argued that as a Muslim majority country they have the right to establish an Islamic system of law and constitution. They nonetheless recognized that religious diversity should be respected by exempting the south from the *hudud,* penalties but not to other Islamic laws relating to business, property and taxes. They continued to argue the fiction that in the long run assimilation would turn the whole of Sudan into an Arab-Islamic nation. As such the GoS refused to accept the idea that *no official state religion* should be a goal of a Sudan at peace in the final communique. Thus, no progress on separation of religion and the state was achieved over the course of Abuja I and II.

Both wings of the SPLM – led by John Garang and the Nasir faction led by Lam Akol – rejected this government position with its counter-assertion of the reality of a 'multiethnic, multiracial, and multi-religious' Sudan. Garang's position held that the key to a lasting and just peace would be by instituting a secular, democratic system with pluralism and equality before the law. By contrast, dissident Lam Akol held that Sudan was actually two separate nations, culturally and ethnically, and they should not attempt to create an artificial unity. The only concession to unity for the Nasir faction was the acceptance of two states in a loose confederation, enabling the North to rule itself according to Islamic law.

Separation of the south, argued GoS delegation head Mohamed al-Amin Khalifa, 'comes from the barrel of a gun' not talks and debates. The SPLM held to the principle that a referendum on separation at the end of any interim period in the South was a fundamental part of right to self determination. The GoS refused to discuss any cease fire or foreign monitors – still trying to win the war militarily – while the SPLM sought an immediate cease fire leading to an interim period in which the South would control its own security. Neutral foreign observers would be engaged to supervise and monitor the process of disengagement and withdrawal by the armed forces.

Despite the impasse over basic principles and security arrangements, the parties devoted considerable time to discussing political and economic arrangements during a possible interim period. Government delegates sought to concentrate authority at the federal level, whereas the SPLM wanted to maximize the powers of the states over social, cultural and economic policies.

When the Sudan government and SPLM reconvened in Abuja in 1993, the government of Nigeria insisted that the first agenda item focus on the issue of religion and state. If that could be resolved, the other issues would fall into place; but if that could not be resolved, no accord was possible on any issue. The delegates immediately deadlocked on that crucial issue, with the government of Sudan insisting that Islamic law had to be maintained, and the SPLM arguing that the government must choose between Islamic law and territorial unity. The talks stumbled, fell, and ultimately failed on the issue of the withdrawal or retention of Shari'a. Given this polarization, there could not be fruitful negotiations on interim arrangements or on security matters. The government continued to deny that the south had the right to self-determination, the issue upon which the SPLM delegation, led by Salva Kiir Mayardit became increasingly insistent. The talks therefore adjourned without any positive result. They illustrated the pitfalls of negotiating in a polarized political context, in which talks served to heighten mistrust rather than to bridge differences (Lesch, SHD, pp.11–12).

The Machakos Protocol: Prelude to the CPA, 2002

One State, Two Systems

The beginning of the resolution of the divisive issue of Shari'a (and, ultimately, the key elements of the CPA) were laid down in the Machakos (Kenya) agreement in 2002. A central compromise was the agreement at Machakos that the South would be secular and the North would be retain its religious character with Shari'a as its source of law. Thus 'two systems' within one state were created. The nature of the state was described as 'democratic,' 'decentralized,' and 'multi-religious' whereby 'races and cultures coalesce and religions co-exist in harmony' (1. Draft Constitution, 16 March 2005). The 'Sources of Legislation' of the states are clearly separated between the northern and southern Sudan as follows:

1) Nationally enacted legislation having effect only in respect of the states outside southern Sudan shall have as its sources of legislation, Shari'a and the consensus of the people (5.1 Draft Constitution);
2) Nationally enacted legislation applicable to southern Sudan and/or states of southern Sudan shall have as its sources of legislation popular consensus, the values and customs of the people of the Sudan, including their traditions and religious beliefs, having regard to the Sudan's diversity (5.2 Draft Constitution).

Separate executive, legislative, and judicial functions of government were established in the South, thus creating the 'two systems' in one 'decentralized' nation. A Government of National Unity was established from constituencies representing in a majority in the North the GoS National Congress Party and a majority in the South of the SPLM.

A Bill of Rights enacted equality before the law (31); including: equal rights of men and women (32); freedom of creed and worship

(38); [equality for] ethnic and cultural communities (47); and 16 other rights not directly related to the issue of religion or Shari'a, with a new Human Rights Commission to monitor application and enforcement.

Under the power sharing sections of the Agreement (2.4.5) a special Commission was to be established by the Presidency to ensure that the rights of non-Muslims were protected and respected in accordance with the 'cultural, religious, and social diversity of all Sudanese' (2.4.3) and according to the 'long-established [Shari'a] principle that non-Muslims are not subject to prescribed penalties' (presumably the *hudud*), and therefore remitted penalties shall apply (156 (d)). Under this provision the rights of non-Muslims in the National Capital would not be adversely affected.

A review of the Draft Constitution by the watchdog group Amnesty International, which it mainly applauded, nonetheless evidenced concern about the language regarding the death penalty that allows capital punishment for 'extremely serious offenses in accordance with the law' (article 36). AI feared that the 1998 Sudan Constitution permits application of the *hudud* penalties for 'serious' crimes of murder and aggravated burglary over a certain amount, and apostasy could be penalized with the *hudud* penalties. They further argued that safeguards in the 1998 Constitution were consistently ignored (Amnesty International Memorandum, ff.8).

The Comprehensive Peace Agreement, 2005

The signing of the historic CPA officially terminated the national status of Shari'a as a comprehensive state system of law. Until the signing of the CPA, Shari'a was a 'non-negotiable' issue in the peace talks, although significant concessions were made at Machakos and Navaisha in Kenya in 2003–04. These ensured that in a post-civil war Sudan the southern states would not apply Shari'a, nor would southern Christians residing in northern cities be subjected to the provisions of Shari'a. However, national and international confidence in the Peace Accords was muted by the long shadow cast by the related conflict and humanitarian crisis in Darfur. The CPA promises to hold the core principles for the resolution of the Darfur crisis.

The CPA was overwhelmingly approved by the National Assembly in February of 2005. After the signing of the CPA trust building by the GoS was seen as essential, not only with Southerners, but also with all marginalized groups who were now seeking to take advantage of the CPA. The SPLM moved into unquestioned leadership among these groups still fighting the government for their place in the nation – not only in Darfur, but in the east and extreme North as well. It would be to the advantage of all marginalized peoples if the SPLM could evolve into a national party of opposition representing their interests as well as those of the South. This has begun to happen as the SPLM organization has grown in all thirteen states of the North where they reported in 2007 that 90 per cent of their membership is northern. In the greater Khartoum area of the capital city conurbation there are seven SPLM offices, which operate as an independent opposition party separate from the partnership with the GoS (visit to SPLM offices in Diem and North Khartoum, 2 May 2007).

Given its historic significance, the Shari'a is ironically rarely specifically mentioned in the language of the CPA. It was perhaps strategically unmentioned in order to create an ambiguous space for negotiation and development according to circumstances and politics. Some activists in Khartoum, both southern and northern, argue that it was largely ignored because it played mainly a symbolic, rhetorical and not substantive role in the politics of the peace negotiations. Widely regarded as a major concession made by John Garang in the final negotiations, ambiguity on Shari'a was balanced by the negotiated potential of separation of the South. Major concessions for wealth and power sharing – a 50–50 North-South sharing of Sudan's considerable oil wealth and effectively two separate governments for the interim period – eased the tensions over the symbolic issue of Shari'a.

With the *de facto* agreement that Shari'a does not apply in the South, or to Southerners in the North, it can be argued that Sudan's experiment with Islamism – 1983–2005 – entered a period of political withdrawal in the post-CPA Sudan. It can also be persuasively argued that the path to peace was paved with real and anticipated oil revenues, now being tallied at c.500,000 barrels a day and capable of doubling to one million barrels by 2006–07.

Further, the following relevant features were agreed to regarding Shariʿa and civil and human rights in the law in the protocols that preceded the signing of the CPA:

1) Respect for all religions, beliefs, and customs shall be guaranteed and enforced in the National capital, and throughout all of Sudan;
2) Law enforcement agencies shall be representative of the population of Sudan and shall be adequately trained and made sensitive to the cultural, religious, and social diversity of all Sudanese;
3) The judicial discretion of courts to impose penalties on non-Muslims shall observe the long established principle that non-Muslims are not subject to prescribed principles, and therefore remitted penalties shall apply;
4) Leniency and granting the accused the benefit of the doubt are universal and especially important in a poor society like Sudan emerging from war, characterized by prevalent poverty and subject to massive displacement;
5) *A special commission shall be appointed by the Presidency to ensure that the rights of non-Muslims are protected in accordance with the guidelines mentioned in this agreement, and not adversely affected by the application of Shariʿa law in the capital.* Additional mechanisms shall be established to make operational these points including: judicial circulars to guide the courts on observing the points; establishment of specialized courts; establishment of specialized Attorney General circuits to conduct investigations and pre-trial proceedings related to offenses involving these principles;
6) Arabic is the widely spoken national language in Sudan and is the national language; English shall be the official working language of National Government business and higher education instruction. Other languages may be adopted, such as the widely spoken languages in the South, Dinka, Nuer, or Bari. (*Comprehensive Peace Agreement,* Between Government of Sudan and the Sudanese People's Liberation Movement, Nairobi, 2005).

Further, the National Judiciary shall be independent of the Legislature and Executive, as guaranteed in the Interim National Constitution. A

National Constitutional Court shall be established in accordance with the Peace Agreement (CPA: 33) that will have independence, original jurisdiction, adjudicate constitutionality of laws and set aside or strike down laws or provisions of laws that do not comply with the National, southern Sudanese, or the relevant state constitutions. The lack of an independent Judiciary was one of the major criticisms of the NIF-National Congress Party government since its period of rule began in 1989.

The CPA and the Role of Religion and the State

The following fundamental principles have been agreed upon in the CPA:

(1) State and Religion: The CPA 'recognizes that Sudan is a multi-cultural, multi-racial, multi-ethnic, multi-religious and multi-lingual country and confirms that religion shall not be used as a divisive factor … all personal and family matters … may be governed by the personal laws (including Shari'a or other religious laws, customs or traditions) of those concerned' (6.4).

(2) According to the CPA Separation of Powers there is a separate Judiciary of the Southern Sudan with a Court of Appeals administering a South Sudan constitution and laws (CPA 3.7.1; 2; 3). Until elections are held in 2008, the government-run National Congress Party holds 70 per cent seats in the northern legislature, while the SPLM holds 70 per cent in the south.

(3) Rights of self-determination locally and to equitable participation in the National Government where a democratic system of governance is established reflecting the cultural, ethnic, racial, religious, and linguistic diversity and gender equality of the people (1.3; 1.4).

The sensitive issue of the withdrawal of the Shari'a in southern Sudan and partial withdrawal in the North, i.e. for non-Muslims in the North, reflects a broader pragmatic withdrawal of the Islamist 'experiment,' and follows the trend of the retreat from extremist Islamism apparent since 2000 when al-Turabi was politically isolated and imprisoned. GoS' chief negotiator, 'Ali 'Uthman Mohamed Taha, spoke to the future relationship between religion and state.

> ... one of the best parts of this agreement is that it would pre-serve the unity of Sudan during the interim period. Moreover, it would guarantee for the first time a satisfactory equation between religion and the state. The agreement does not set the foundation for a secular state. But, it regulates the relationship between religion and the state so that Muslims would resort to their [Shari'a] – Islamic law – and perform their rituals in full, and Christians and non-Muslims in general would have the right to have their religious freedoms, beliefs, and political and social rights in full, side by side with their Muslim brothers. In my opinion, this chapter of the agreement is, perhaps, the best that Sudan could offer to the experiment of reconciling religions and beliefs in a multi-religious and multi-cultural state.
>
> (Quoted in 'Welcome to the new Sudan,'
> *Khartoum Monitor*, 13 January 2005)

By contrast, SPLM head John Garang's words reflect much the same sentiment, but with the added caution that the nation will split into two if this peace agreement fails.

> The solution to the fundamental problem of Sudan is to involve **an all-inclusive Sudanese state which will uphold the new Sudan ... in which all Sudanese are equally stakeholders irrespective of their religion, irrespective of their race, tribe, or gender – and if this does not work, then to look for other solutions, such as splitting the country.** But this all inclusive Sudanese state which we have called the new Sudan must have some basis, for example in history, that makes us one country or one nation. The question is whether there is a basis for the Sudan as a country, and my answer has also been yes, there is. That is, this affirmative answer to this question has guided us and sustained the SPLM for the last 21 years until today.

This is the context and the value and of the peace agreement we have signed today. It provides the Sudan with a real and perhaps the last opportunity to make a real paradigm shift from the old Sudan of exclusivity to the new inclusive Sudan achieved not through force, but through the exercise of the right of self determination.

(John Garang's speech at the Signing ceremony,
Khartoum Monitor, 11 January 2005, p.9)

Demonstrations that I witnessed celebrating the signing of the CPA in Khartoum were overwhelmingly made up of Southerners, many of whom held SPLM/SPLA banners declaring the beginning of the independence of Southern Sudan. It is a broadly held view that a referendum today on separation would overwhelmingly succeed, and that any change in this outcome is entirely dependent upon trust building between North and south, primarily in deeds and not in 'the beautiful words of Northerners which, like birds, fly away' (Scroggins, 2002: 161).

The first serious blow to that trust building was the death, by accident or by conspiracy, of Dr. John Garang just two weeks after his triumphal return to Khartoum to assume the first vice-presidency of the Government of National Unity (GoNU) in July 2005. An estimated one million Sudanese greeted Garang at a public rally just next to the Khartoum airport in a stunning display of his enormous popularity and acceptance as a liberator and political figure with new national status.

As a steadfast advocate of national unity – despite the widespread sentiments for separation among Southerners – Garang was poised to become the strongest candidate for democratic election as president in the CPA negotiated national elections in 2008. His growing popularity and acceptance among unaffiliated Northerners was clearly a new feature in Sudan's history of democratic upsurge. Garang's vice-presidency could easily have eclipsed al-Bashir's presidency. When John Garang's untimely death in a helicopter crash in Uganda was announced, the capital city, with its ring of refugee camps, erupted in a mixture of public mourning, outrage, violence, polarization and fear between 'Northerners' and 'Southerners,' mainly determined by racial and cultural features. The first day of the outpouring of public grief and anger is now known as 'Black Monday' and is referenced both as a reality of the past and a not so veiled threat for future demonstrations. For four days the three towns and the camps that make up greater Khartoum were places of violence and insecurity that might have developed into an urban insurgency had they not been fiercely repressed. Northerners spoke to me of these days in hushed conversation, while Southerners defiantly hailed their display of angry resistance to what was widely held to be a political assassination. The new Khartoum state militia was mobilized to restore security by every forcible measure – breaking up attacks by Southerners against Northerners, arrests and preventive detention, forcible suppression of public demonstrations, and use of the *hadd* penalties for public alcohol consumption and drunkenness that accompanied some of the outbursts. Within a week, the public displays of anger were quelled and a deep, new source of distrust was implanted into the popular southern mind.

The phrase, 'too many agreements dishonored,' coined by former southern vice-president Abel Alier during the years of the Addis Ababa peace, has been invoked periodically to lament the repeated failures at building a just and sustainable peace and unity in Sudan. This phrase has been referenced again in the years after the signing of the CPA, as the pace of implementation has been slow and public review and criticism has suggested a lack of political will to fulfill the spirit, intent, and details of the agreement.

Under the heading 'Sudan's CPA, another born-dead peace,' Kanta Robert wrote:

> With the death of Garang as well as the absence of consistent international pressure, deliberate obstruction of the CPA implementation, particularly the Abyei areas, oil revenue sharing, and the demarcation of the North-south border are putting the hard-fought peace at risk.
>
> (Robert, *Khartoum Monitor*, 1 February 2007, p.6)

Another opinion expressed in 'Make Unity Attractive: the phrase that shall remain to haunt the northern elites' was more harsh in its criticism of the demonstrated commitment of the GoS to trust building and national unity as well as the important role of the media and social relations that have little changed on a mass level after the CPA:

> In Sudan the word 'national' is synonymous with Islam and Arab nationalism. The major media of National TV, radio are still using the words 'Umm al- Arabia,' 'Umma al- Islamia,' and Omdurman TV has only Arabic broadcasting and no programs of interest to Africa; the Azan prayers come on 5 times a day, but we have not heard even on one Sunday a church bell vibrating through these institutions.
>
> The process of reconciliation will never take place because in Islamic states that are ruled by [Shari'a] law it is not possible to publicly criticize their organs or institutions; in the Sudan the war was fought as a holy war; how can a truth commission question those who committed crimes and atrocities in the name of Allah and jihad. For the commission to do so would result in a *fatwa* coming from al-Azhar or from Sheikh al-Mujahidin.
>
> How can our politicians make a unified and peaceful Sudan when there are no proper common grounds for its diverse cultures, religions, ethnic groups to meet; where bonds of marriage are rare, or where antagonism, intimidation, and animosity grow daily.
>
> (Khartoum Monitor, 3 February, p.5 by Chol Mathiai)

Beyond the press warnings about the potential volatility of the slowness of the CPA implementation were critical forums sponsored by universities. I attended one such forum sponsored by the University of Juba's Centre for Peace and Development (at the University of Khartoum's Sharjah Hall, 17 April 2007) that was titled 'On the Critical Evaluation of the CPA and the Protection of Peace in Sudan.' What was interesting was the number of high ranking southern politicians who are members of the GoS, including presidential advisor Dr. Bona Malwal and Minister of Foreign Affairs Dr. Lam Akol, who spoke at the event, supportive of the CPA, yet with remarks tempered by two years of slow progress. The peace is holding so far, and all at the forum hailed the fact that the south is finally at peace after decades of insecurity, death and displacement. The south is developing and the fundamental principle of self-determination has prevailed as the institutions of the new Government of South Sudan (GoSS) have been put into place, including its own Judiciary, Parliament, regional economic and banking system, as well as the start of a much needed infrastructure. Bona Malwal asked rhetorically in his presentation, 'Why do the people of South Sudan want self-determination? Because they have never had it!' The CPA represented the first opportunity for Southerners to legally and officially express their desire to separate or remain part of the Sudan. Lam Akol admitted that implementation is lagging behind agreed to timetables, and that the failure to negotiate the final status of border area Abyei remains an unresolved basic problem. By June of 2007 the GoS declared prematurely that 85 per cent of the CPA has been implemented.

A small but vocal Islamist party, *al-Tahrir*, to the right of the GoS has been an outspoken critic of the CPA as a 'sell-out' to the secular SPLM and a denial of the self-determination of the Muslim majority in Sudan who want Shari'a to remain in full force in Sudan and decry the 'unity that neither side wants.' Their spokespersons are active in public forums and are quoted in the press expressing their criticism of the CPA.

Perhaps more serious criticism of CPA implementation came from a leader of the SPLM and Minister for Presidential Affairs of the GoSS, Luka Biong Deng. While in Washington in 2007 he told a meeting of the House of Representatives Africa Sub-committee that anti-CPA forces within the GoS are now in charge and are deliberately delaying and derailing the implementation of the CPA (AP, Washington, 25 January 2007). Continuing to delay implementation and the possibility of the postponement of the scheduled elections in 2008 is a volatile mix that could lead to renewed violence and resumption of war, or a unilateral declaration of independence and separation of the South.

Commission on the Status of Muslims in the Capital City

The CPA represented an historic turning point in post-independence Sudan and signaled the failure of the policies of Arabization and Islamization directed against the southern region by various governments of Sudan since 1956. Although Shari'a law was officially withdrawn from the South, the sensitive issue of its final status in the capital city of Khartoum was left ambiguous with the issues and their resolution to be determined by a CPA-mandated Commission on the Status of non-Muslims in the Capital. That commission was announced in February 2007 and not fully constituted until May 2007, and in August 2007 the Chief Justice ordered the creation of Courts for Non-Muslims in Khartoum (British Embassy Press Summary, 6 August 2007) over two years after the signing of the CPA. The commission was criticized not only for its delayed formation, but for its composition, having a majority of Muslims thus keeping the 'Christian' vote to a minority. A largely unaddressed issue in the media outside of Sudan is the rights of southern Muslims living in the South. While I was conducting research in the spring of 2007, this issue was resolved with the affirmation of the legal rights of southern Muslims to have their personal status affairs governed by Shari'a. Jurists pointed out that there are many judges and attorneys in the South who studied law while displaced students in Khartoum where study of the Shari'a was mandatory and that their knowledge of Islamic law is adequate to apply the law fairly.

Thus, Islamic law, Shari'a – long the most important symbol of Islamism in Sudan – retreated from the center of political discourse, no longer to hold the pivotal place it held during 22 years of civil war and more than a decade of peace negotiations. However, it's symbolic status is still retained, as its future – in the promised 'new Sudan' or 'two Sudans' – reaches toward its 'final status.' With its withdrawal as the sole state law in force, Sudan entered an early post-Islamist phase. The interim period, transitioning to the 'new Sudan' with Shari'a as a law applicable solely to Muslims – if it is ever to be achieved – is one that requires on site observation, external monitoring, objective study and critical analysis in the years of the national elections mandated by the CPA (which were to have been held in 2008, but postponed until 2010 and the referendum on unity or separation of the south in 2011). If Sudan has, indeed, entered a period of post-Islamism, it becomes one of the important case studies of withdrawal from extremist political Islam. This question will be addressed in chapter three.

CHAPTER 2

ISLAMIZATION, 1983–89: THE POLITICS OF MANUFACTURED IDENTITY, FEAR AND THE MANIPULATION OF SHARI'A

Introduction

The idea of an Islamic Republic is best known in modern times from the example of Iran after 1979 and the Taliban after they expelled the Soviet occupation of Afghanistan in the late 1980s. However, the call for an Islamic Republic has been on the political agenda in Sudan since the time of its national independence in the mid-1950s. The political struggle to Islamize basic institutions of law and government in the Sudan is a central theme in its modern history. It is profoundly tied to the colonial experience, and it is the most deeply divisive issue in post-independence Sudan's quest for national unity for more than a half-century. Islamization, dependent upon making the religious political, is associated with the declining years of the Numeiri regime (1977–85), its alliance with the MB, and the formation of the NIF after the Numeiri military dictatorship was toppled. The MB, with historical roots traceable to the anti-colonial struggles of the 1940s and 1950s, set the modern political agenda for the restructuring of state and society on the basis of Islam. The MB was spread to Sudan from its origin in Egypt. It is important to understand that the exogenous MB in Sudan claims no legitimacy from hereditary rule as do the major northern Umma and Khatmiya/DUP parties. In this respect, like the Communist party, the MB/NIF represents a movement with a political agenda that is broader than Sudan's boundaries and more regional and global than the older lineage-based parties. As English secular colonial rule attempted to undo the Islamist Mahdist state, it tightly regulated all major Muslim institutions. But, although Mahdism and the ideal of an Islamic state retreated, it did not die. Predictably, at the time of independence in 1956 one of the models advanced for the new nation was an Islamic Parliamentary Republic with Shari'a law. This was chiefly backed by the Umma and DUP that expected to govern the independent Sudan. The 1958 military coup led by General Ibrahim Abboud suspended this political dialogue.

War in the South erupted in the year before independence and the government established what would become the basic northern model of resolving the 'southern problem' through Islamization and Arabization of the south. Abboud's rule from 1958–64 proved harsh and insensitive, as it arrogantly and uncritically pursued a neocolonial agenda of northern domination of the South. This period can be understood by the fact that in reaction to the Islamization push the number of Christians baptized in the southern towns of Torit and Isoke trebled between 1960 and 1964, (Johnson, 2003: 31). Ali Abdel Rahman, the Islamic Affairs Department head and Minister for Interior stated in 1958 before Parliament was disbanded and the army took over the country for the first time: 'the Sudan is an integral part of the Arab world and as such must accept the leadership of the two Islamic religious leaders of the Sudan, Sayed Ali El Mirghani and Sayid Abdel Rahman al-Mahdi. Anyone dissenting from this view must quit the country.' (See Second Parliament of the Sudan, first session, sitting No.2. p.3, quoted in *1963 Southern Sudanese Petition to the United Nations.*)

Sudanese have risen up against military rule twice: first in 1964, overthrowing General Abboud and second in 1985, ousting General-president Numeiri. The October 1964 popular revolution arose out of opposition to military rule and the expansion of war in the south. Its first urgent task was the Round Table Conference (RTC) with its call for a peaceful and just resolution of the conflict. Drawing from the first post-independence democratic upsurge, it can be reasonably inferred that popular sentiment in the North has been pro-peace, opposing the model of assimilation to Arab-Islamic culture and the neocolonial designs regarding the South through war. By 1964 civil war had been waged for nearly a decade, and the question of separation or integration of the south was at the center of discussions. All of the northern, by now elitist, parties – including the Umma Party (Mahdi's family), Democratic Unionist Party (Mirghani family), the Communist Party, the NUP, and the Islamic Charter Front – all rejected any moves favoring separation of the south. The southern parties represented by the Southern Front and the Sudanese African National Union (SANU) were divided over the issue. Members of SANU in exile and the rebel group Anya-Nya favored separation. There was no resolution at the conclusion of the conference, however the final proposals of the northern parties included: 1) recognition of the right to self-determination in the south, but not including secession or an agenda leading to a sovereign southern state; 2) advocacy of the principle of regional government with rejection of both models of a highly centralized or federal government as inappropriate; and 3) implementation of an immediate cease-fire.

Ultimately, these resolutions had little practical effect as the elected government in July 1965 continued its military offensive against Anya-Nya, and allied with those Southerners who favored unity. The Round Table Conference supported the remedy of regional self-rule that came to be a hallmark of the Addis Ababa Agreement, which ended the war and promoted talks of unity for the decade 1972–83 during the Numeiri years. However, the failure of the RTC to achieve consensus on the fundamental issues of national unity based in secularism and diversity, economic equity, and political representation continued to haunt the nation, as chronic civil war plagued the country for another forty years.

Instead Islamization of state and society continued to be a part of the political agenda throughout the years of popular rule after 1964. The interim government under the Mahdist heir-apparent, Sadiq al-Mahdi, failed to treat the underlying social ill of the country: the fair treatment of the country's one-third non-Muslim minority. Al-Mahdi revealed himself once in this period, and then again in the second period of democratic rule after 1985, to be incapable of dealing substantively with the issue of the proper relation between religion and the state in a religiously diverse nation in spite of the fact that he had taken a clear position on Shari'a and the state at the time of the September Laws during Numeiri's rule. His hereditary role as successor to Sudan's indigenous ninetheenth-century Islamism proved decisive in the failure to secularize this heterogeneous state and thus secured the retention of Shari'a. The coup d'etat in 1969 led by Ja'afar Mohammed Numeiri, a simple soldier from Dongola, changed the course of Sudanese history in this respect.

Islamic Identity, Islamization, Islamism

The call for an Islamic state is mirrored in the slogan, *Islam, huwa al-hal,* or, *Islam is the solution*: the ultimate solution to the dilemma of the post-colonial state as being the creation of an Islamic Republic. The main architect of the Islamist government in the Sudan, al-Turabi, was Sudan's major proponent of the Islamic state. For al-Turabi, Islamic democracy is ensured by *shura,* or consultation, arguing that all modern Islamic movements are democratic as they operate through a *majlis al-shura,* or consultative council. An Islamic state would be based upon a comprehensive Shari'a, enshrining Islamic values and building a moral community, while the scope of government itself is more limited than the all-embracing Shari'a. Government leaders are also chosen through *shura,* a unique Islamic concept of democracy, not to be confused with western-style one person-one vote democracy. Instead, Muslims in an Islamist democracy work toward a unified community devoid of sectarian divisions, such as occurred with the historical schools of Islamic jurisprudence.

In a practical political sense, the goal of an Islamic state came to mean the Islamization of basic institutions of government and law, a state headed by a Muslim leader guided by Islamic principles, and most importantly, a state governed by Shari'a based solely on the holy sources of the religion, the Qur'an and Sunna. Criticism of the Islamic state in theory as well as practice comes from both Muslims and non-Muslims alike. Fear about any type of religious governance raises basic questions about theocratic rule. Beyond this general fear of the merging of religion with the state are also concerns about the status of non-Muslims and women in an Islamic state. In the West, the most prominent negative examples of Islamic Republics are Iran and Afghanistan under the Taliban, and the case of Sudan is negative, especially on the matter of the treatment of its non-Muslim minority in the southern region.

Before Islam and Shari'a became politicized, to be a Muslim in Sudan was a matter of private practice and quiet observation, and/or participation in a Sufi order, especially for men. During fieldwork in the 1970s, I recall that during the month-long Ramadan fast, secular Muslims would have no fear of public eating or drinking. After 1983 this would be unthinkable, when such behavior became potentially subject to harsh penalty and open public disapproval. Before the days of a politicized Islam, mosques were simple neighborhood places of worship – filled on Fridays for the noonday prayer with observant men, and on other days with the religious few for the dawn prayer, or the elderly and retired with the time to pray during the working hours of the day. Mosques were of simple construction, not the ornate public symbols of the state they have now become, strategically located near to the centers of power. Private observation was more common than public scenes of male prayer.

Today in Islamist Khartoum, not only is there an overflow of men praying outside of central mosques, but also throughout the day on the secular streets surrounding market areas. In the past only religious sheikhs and *'alims* (scholars) would grow their beards, and the sari-like *tobe* of northern Muslim women revealed fashionable coiffures. With politicized Islam, respectable women in public began to cover their hair with additional scarves and headbands so as not to reveal even a wisp of hair. However, like all social movements, there are dialectical forces at work. In the chapter on social transformation, the resistance of younger women in their dress under various phases of Sudan's Islamism is described and analyzed.

For the South, Islamization and Arabization were regarded as necessary and inevitable by every northern government since independence irrespective of political orientation. This fact of Sudanese politics was altered only by persistent southern resistance – first the Anya-Nya and then the Sudan People's Liberation Movement – that consistently challenged these policies both militarily and ideologically. Confusing myth and reality, while consciously manipulating religion and personal faith as identity, successive governments asserted a constructed identity of 'Arab-Islamic' as 'national.'

In the Sudan southern Christian leaders and ordinary believers identified Christianity with the resistance to northern dominance, especially during the extremist military regimes of General Ja'afar Numeiri (1969–85) and al-Bashir (1989–present). As a result, Christian conversion has been on the rise as a reaction to intensified political Islamization (Fluehr-Lobban, 1990). While Sudan's fundamental problems are those of national unity, uneven economic development, and fair representation of the nation's multiple regions and ethnic groups, the battleground rhetoric has been religious – dominant Muslim versus subordinate Christian and animist. Before the Islamists rose to power and relations became more polarized, the presence of Christian missionaries in the south after independence was viewed by emergent Muslim elites as an example of European neocolonialism and interference from the West.

Politicized Shari'a: Bound to Muslim Identity

The main instrument used by Islamists to open, widen, and deepen the divide between Christian and Muslim was the Shari'a. Islamists are politically differentiated – whether in Sudan, Iran, Somalia, Nigeria, or elsewhere – however, the one consistent component of their programs is the centrality of Shari'a in the construction of the Islamic state (Osman, 2004). For Sudanese Islamists, Shari'a was tied to superior Muslim identity, and their politically motivated Islamic identity was bound to the superiority of Arab over African. Given the depth of Sudanese Sufi traditions this was no easy feat, and thus, the Sufis themselves were dragged into the theater of Islamist politics. Their politicization began during the Numeiri years, but their submission became nearly complete under al-Turabi and the NIF. Eventually, all of the complex dimensions of the faith of Islam were were rendered as simple Islamist slogans leading to the supremacy of the Shari'a among the institutions co-opted by the Islamist slogan and answer to every question – *Islam, huwa al-hal* or *Islam is the solution* was Shari'a law.

The Sufi 'heart and soul' of Sudanese Islam was not immune to this onslaught. It had to be controlled and absorbed into the Islamist project. The qualities of the Sufis – personal piety, humility, poverty and devotion to wealth redistribution – were not those practiced by Sudan's military-Islamists. However, their popularity and the devotion of the masses of Sudanese Muslims made them a target of the Islamists' rise to a monopoly of state power. Numeiri began his campaign to incorporate the *turuq* by officially encouraging them and by frequent visits to their leaders in Um Dubban, near to Khartoum, and in Gezira. During Ramadan he would invite sufi leaders to the presidential palace for 'breakfasts.' The seduction continued with financing of leaders' Hajj expenses to Mecca, and then of religious holiday celebrations. With help from Jaafar Bakheit and Omer Haj Musa the presence of the *turuq* became visible within Numeiri's sole party, the Sudanese Socialist Union (SSU) although they were blocked by secular forces from gaining a 'secretariat' within the ruling SSU seats of popular forces (Hassan, 1993: 85). Whether for political or spiritual motives – or a combination of both – Numeiri continued to visit the Sufi sheikhs, and thus gained both their '*baraka*' (blessing) and also the approval of the sympathetic Muslim Sudanese.

My initial research on the Shari'a was during the period between the first impulses toward Islamization in the late 1970s and the decree of the September Laws of 1983. I was, thus, able to witness the end of one era and the early beginnings of another. In 1979 I spent months observing the Shari'a courts in session, and was able to discern what today would be called early Islamist predilections of some judges. Most judges in the late 1970s were not Islamist, as the major purge of non-MB/NIF judges did not occur until after 1983, and especially after 1989. However, I recall the uncharacteristic ease with which one judge whose court I frequented granted divorces to complaining wives.

Normally divorce in an Islamic court was a slow process accompanied by months of investigation that were carried out by delegated relatives of the couple before there was a judicial pronouncement of divorce. This judge, who self-identified as MB, said that his motive for granting divorces in a first hearing, especially to women whose husbands were away from the conjugal home for long periods of time, was to prevent the woman from falling into *zina*, or sinful, adulterous relations with another man. As the women in most cases I observed of the 'absent husband' most often requested support (*nafaqa*) and not divorce, when I asked about this discretionary judgment he replied, 'With her husband away her economic and physical temptation would be too great to resist, so I divorce them on the spot.' This example is just one of the many cases this book will cite of the social consequences of the Islamist political agenda. Divorce, which is permitted in Islam, was, nonetheless, intended by the scholars to be avoided and a careful, deliberative process became the judicial norm.

Arab Identity, Arabization, Arabism, Arabic Language

The term 'Arab' is an elusive ethnic, cultural and linguistic term that has also been used as a racial designation. An 'Arab' is often defined as one who traces descent to one of the Arab tribes (lineages) of the Arabian Peninsula. This would be simple enough were it not for the explosive and dramatic spread of Islam into Asia and Africa by the Arabs from Arabia during the first century after the introduction of Islam in the seventh century CE. The blending of people and cultures in the *Dar al-Islam,* abode of Islam, fostered hybrid concepts, including 'Afro-Arab' that arose in the context of the Sudanese nationalist movement, and was resurrected by Numeiri after the Addis Ababa peace accords in his unity speeches.

Many enslaved persons (*'abd/'abid*) were taken from the Sudan, Ethiopia, and Somalia by people who might be called, or refer to themselves, as Arabs. While some slaves were ultimately incorporated into Arab society, others retained the stigmas attached to a enslaved social underclass, and their enslavers were granted the racial moniker of *Jellaba* connoting 'Arab' but derived from their long white dress, the *jellabiya.* Although often confounding in the Sudan, the terms *'abd* and *jellaba* generally correlate with race and outward physical appearance. Dark-skinned Nubians, other Sudanese, and Africans may experience racial bigotry when they are traveling or working in countries where the legacy of slavery is still apparent, such as in the Arab Gulf countries or the United States. In Arabic the term *zinj/zunuj* is also used to refer to 'blacks,' non-Arab Africans, or African-Americans, and while it carries descriptive and sometimes pejorative meaning, it lacks the specific stigma of slavery.

Slavery in nineteenth-century southern Sudan was a time when 'the world was spoiled,' according to Dinka writer Francis Deng. The capture of humans by soldiers in the Turco-Egyptian army was justified by the fact that they were not Muslims. The British, although involved themselves for centuries in the Atlantic slave trade, encouraged the idea that slavery was favored by Islam. They used this as part of a Christian crusade to rid the Sudan of Islamic rule under the Mahdi in the late-nineteenth century. Indeed, efforts by the Mahdi to bring areas of the south under Islamic control are remembered by Southerners as an encounter like the earlier slave trade, a time filled with bitterness and fear of Arabs and Muslims.

Physically distinct, the Southerners were ready targets for racist referents, most typically and painfully the term *'abd* that can still be heard as a crude remark. Southern Sudanese anthropologist Jok Madut Jok has explored the legacy of racism from this historical relationship (2001). He argues that the British colonizers allied with the northern *jellaba* slave trading merchant elites – who had previously carried out their raids for the Turks – and that neither had a serious interest in ending slavery. The formal end to slavery that the British introduced as part of their 'enlightened' rule, nonetheless preserved intact the relationships born in this trade. This leaves the country with a cruel legacy of slavery, with a strong racist cast to it that must be confronted directly and resolved before if Sudanese unity is ever to be achieved.

The 'true' Arabs of Arabia would not acknowledge Sudanese as their brothers, and the same term *'abd,* used by 'Arab' Sudanese for Southerners might just as well be applied to them in the Arab heartland. This dual consciousness has been probed deeply by some northern intellectuals (Mukhtar, 2003) especially for the role that the legacy of race has played in the civil war. However, the Kingdom of Saudi Arabia with its own brand of Wahhabist Islamism took an active interest and has exerted much influence in the Islamist project in Sudan.

The Arab nationalism of the early Numeiri years and the Sudanese Socialist Union had a distinctly secular cast to its political rhetoric and practice, with religion either irrelevant or separated from politics. During Sudan's Arab nationalist phase the flag was changed from the original tri-colored blue, yellow and white flag of independence to the red, black, and white bands of Arab nationalist flags from Egypt to Syria, Palestine and Iraq. The rhetoric of the 'Arab Nation,' whether in Sudan or elsewhere, was the promise of democracy, that was fundamentally contradicted by the military regimes or single-party governance that proclaimed them as democratic.

The Arabic language is also a symbolic issue, like Shari'a, that has been somewhat eclipsed in the post-CPA Sudan. The SPLM consistently held the view that the Arabic language is not a problem unless it is forced and imposed; eventually the SPLM developed the same view of the Shari'a. John Garang, a fluent Arabic speaker himself, acknowledged the historical development of the Sudan as intimately connected with Arabic, thus he argued that it should be the first national language (Garang/Khalid, 1987: 133) with English as the second national language.

In January 2005, as the CPA was being signed in Nairobi, I stopped by the University of Juba Khartoum branch to investigate advanced Arabic for myself, and my interest was met with a strongly positive response from Southerners who praised my effort for studying 'our national language.' This sparked a spontaneous conversation (in Arabic) of the largely unacknowledged truth that the Arabic language itself was never at issue. 'Language can never be viewed as *the* problem; English remained Sudan's second most widely spoken language after the British left in 1956 – we know that it is an advantage to know English, as it is to our advantage to speak and read Arabic,' they argued.

Today generations of Southerners in their millions have involuntarily or voluntarily become displaced or settled in Khartoum. As a result of Islamist policies of public education in Arabic they are literate and fluent in modern standard Arabic, the language of the educated. This means that they have the potential, at least, to participate in national discourse which I have observed on multiple occasions at the many public forums that were held in the post-CPA transitional period. Often these urban educated Southerners have a linguistic advantage over their 'Arab' northern fellow citizens as they are fluent in both English and Arabic, while most northern youth lack this fluency in English after decades of Arabization and Islamization in their public education. None of this should be interpreted as a new southern ascendancy, although relations between Northerners and Southerners in the capital city have changed dramatically since the CPA was signed and formal peace replaced decades of civil war. As Bona Malwal observed at a public forum in 2007, you can still hear in casual conversation even between a Northerner and Southerner, 'Kan fi sudani wa jenubi fi al-Suq al-'Arabi...' or 'there was a Sudanese guy and a Southerner in the Arab market...' making a distinction between Sudanese nationality and southern difference. The term 'Arab market' (suq al-'Arabi) in central Khartoum was coined during colonial times to distinguish it from the suq al-Franji – the 'Frankish' or European market employing the old Arab/Muslim term for the French crusaders.

Competing Islamist Politics:
Umma Party-MB evolved to the NIF

The MB saw itself as a modernist alternative to the traditional hereditary Khatmiyya and Ansar sects. The MB have been led by al-Turabi since 1964 (he joined in 1954), and under his leadership it ended up outmaneuvering the other sects and isolated the communists (Layish and Warburg, 2004: 14). The rise of this once marginal movement to direct the course of the country after 1983 requires careful analysis to understand not only its past but for what becomes of the Sudanese state. Its evolution from the MB to the NIF made it one of the world's significant cases of Islamism with lasting importance for the CPA and potential division of the country in 2011.

The MB made its debut in Sudanese national politics after the 1964 October Revolution. Its most feared competitor was the Sudanese Communist Party (SCP). Indeed, it was a debate between the MB and SCP at the University of Khartoum that sparked the October Revolution. The heated arguments resulted in clashes that brought police intervention, the death and injury of students, and ultimately mass demonstrations – led by judges and lawyers outraged by the government repression at the university – that toppled the Abboud military regime (El-Affendi, 1991: 72–73).

The MB challenged an SCP led coalition in the 1965 elections under the banner of the Islamic Charter Front, which attempted to form a coalition with the Umma party and the DUP to advance an Islamization program. This marked the appearance of the country's first Islamist organization. It courted its larger rival Islamic movement, the Umma Ansar, but failed then and in subsequent years to consolidate this partnership. Instead the MB allied with marginal Sufis, Ansar al-Sunna, and miscellaneous sheikhs and religious scholars. Al-Turabi was able to convince the Islamic Charter Front to side with his brother-in-law Sadiq al-Mahdi to advocate an Islamic constitution in the 1968 elections, but this coalition failed to convince the electorate.

Both the Umma party of Sadiq al-Mahdi and the MB of al-Turabi are ideological Islamists, although of different hues, who vary in terms of strategies for the creation of a more perfect Islamic society and which of them is *in* or *out* of power, or close to power. Sadiq's view of an Islamic state predominated in Sudanese politics until 1989. This view called for the whole legal corpus of the Shari'a to be reviewed in light of contemporary social conditions on the basis of the core legal sources of Qur'an, Sunna and *Hadith*, and the four legal schools. This could revive Islamic legal credibility and make the Islamic alternative a vital and dynamic one while exposing the incompatibilities and failures of capitalism and communism. Sadiq al-Mahdi rejected military rule absolutely as a route to Islamization because they excel 'only in bloodshed' (Layish and Warburg, 2002: 21), although he sought to overthrow Numeiri in 1975 by military force in retaliation for the brutal assault on the Umma stronghold at Aba Island in 1971.

The MB were a relatively new group, while the Ansar an historical popular movement descending from Mahdist politics. Al-Turabi's political opportunism in the cause of the MB Islamist program is legend. Ideologically he argued for a 'modernist' Islamism, with a democratic Islamic state constructed and supported through *shura* ('consultation,' among the scholars who represent the people). Interviewed by a Tunisian journalist (Hamdi) during the years of his greatest influence in national politics – between 1987–97 – al-Turabi emphasized that his movement and life are devoted to *tawhid,* the one-God truth (22), in every facet of life. If *tawhid* is observed fully, implementation of the entirety of the Shari'a would have to be consolidated in order to build a new culture and civilization. Liberation of women is a key to this revival. Al-Turabi's ideas are largely based upon the Pakistani Jama' al-Islamiyya movement with the ideal model of a state including a Muslim leader and a parliamentary democracy based on Shari'a with all legislation in conformity with Islamic law. Rather than gradual transformation of society, the Islamic state would be developed in a period of five years.

During Numeiri's rule, al-Turabi as Attorney General chaired the committee to bring Sudanese law into conformity with Shari'a. Before seizing total control of the state, the idea in the late 1970s was that of gradual implementation of Islamic law first, with bans on alcohol and imposition of *zakat* as well as the opening of the first Islamic banks. These moves took place five years before the September Laws instituted the *hudud* punishments in the criminal law; with a gradual approach, they were not significantly opposed. By 1983 the Islamist die was cast, the September Laws were decreed, and the formal Islamist project was initiated using Shari'a as its major vehicle.

One of al-Turabi's allies and protégés was Ali Osman Taha who eventually rose to become first vice-president in the al-Bashir regime in 1998. A graduate of the University of Khartoum Law College in 1971, he was posted to the Judiciary where, between 1972 and 1976 he led some of the initial campaigns within the Numeiri regime for the Shari'a laws. His personal success was in the outlawing of legalized prostitution, one of the turning points for the early success of the Shari'a before September 1985.

Competition continued between the Umma party and the MB throughout the last years of Numeiri's militarism with the usual strategic alliances and 'national reconciliations' as each jockeyed for power. Shari'a remained in their political back pockets to pull out as needed, eventually to place center stage as the legal linchpin of the Islamist program was achieved in 1983.

Shari'a Law before Islamization

I conducted research on Islamic Shari'a in 1979–80, just three years before its politicization as national law in 1983. I studied Shari'a law, both in theory and practice, with one of the last Grand Qadis, Sheikh Mohamed al-Gizouli, and from 1979 to 1980 and I observed the application of law in the then sole jurisdiction for Shari'a, the family courts. This was before the Islamic courts were merged with the civil and criminal courts into a single judicial system, thus eliminating the colonial remnant of separate systems for Islamic and Civil courts, each with its own system of appeals. The merger was completed on the eve of the September Laws, but the two events may not have been connected as there had been the plan for some time of a single system of courts under a unified Judiciary, like the Egyptian model.

Prior to the September Laws, the development of Islamic law in the Sudan in the twentieth century included a number of significant reforms that outpaced developments in other countries, including Egypt. The reforms were instituted through the mechanism of the Judicial Circulars issued from the Office of the Grand Qadi, in the following areas of family law that was its only jurisdiction until 1983:

1) Divorce: the right to judicial divorce for the woman was extended due to harm or abuse (*talaq al-darar*) suffered by the woman, this right being derived from Maliki judicial interpretations. Enacted in 1917, it was among the first such legal innovations in the Muslim world. Restrictions limiting the husband's unilateral right to divorce, the triple pronouncement or *talaq talata*, were instituted in 1935. Added to this were judicial grounds for divorce initiated by women that included desertion, mental as well as

physical harm or abuse, and an ability to negotiate an end to her marriage through *fidya,* gaining her release by returning a portion of her dower (*mahr*).

2) Consent in Marriage: In 1960 the right of refusal of marriage was extended to the bride, and legal proofs were established to ensure her consent in marriage. Using Hanafi interpretations, this restricted the absolute role of the marriage guardian (*al-wali*), usually the father, to negotiate a marriage contract for a woman.

3) Inheritance law: Changes in the law of inheritance were instituted whereby the spouse, either husband or wife, is entitled to the entirety of the estate if there are no other legal heirs. This particular reform (1925) placed the spouse on a par with the other Islamic heirs, and is a modification of classical Muslim inheritance law. Other reforms (1939) equalized the shares of full and half brothers and sisters, and the grandfather (who formerly could take a share greater than the full brothers) was placed on a par with these heirs (1943). Each of these moves served to strengthen the nuclear family over the traditional strength of the patrilineal males (*al-'asaba*).

4) Elimination of the practice of *bayt al-ta'a*, whereby wives, who had fled the houses of their husbands due to abuse or domestic violence were forcibly returned by the police to their husbands. This reform, in addition to increases in amounts and better enforcement of support payments to divorced wives (*al-nafaqa*) was part of Numeiri's early progressive attitude toward women and the general improvement of their status.

Many of these reforms antedated comparable developments in other Muslim regions by several decades. The Republican Movement (*Jamhouriyeen*) led by Mahmoud Taha focused on the reform of Shari'a law, especially as it relates to the rights of women and religious minorities in a Muslim state. After two years of sustained protest of the September Laws, Taha was executed for 'apostasy' by Numeiri in 1985.

Thus, Shari'a law was a liberal and progressive law in the Muslim tradition in the decades prior to 1983, its application perhaps reflecting more of the Sudanese sufi spirit. After 1983 this Shari'a was challenged in theory and practice by MB/NIF as the post-1983 development of

Shari'a became reminiscent of the harsh ideological rule of the Islamist movement of the nineteenth century, the Mahdiya.

Secular Numeiri to Islamist Numeiri, 1969–85

Sudan was one of the early manifestations of Islamism. Gallab (2008) argues that Sudan is the first Islamist Republic with legislation on *zakat* and banning of alcohol taking place in 1977, before the 1979 Islamic Revolution in Iran. After the 25 May 1969 coup, for nearly a decade Numeiri and his junta Revolutionary Command Council pursued a secular course of governance in the spirit of the Round Table Conference and the policies of the Sudanese Communist Party (SCP) that supported the coup. The progressive new regime was framed in political terms as the Sudanese Socialist Union (SSU) patterned on the Arab Socialist Union of Nasser's rule in Egypt. Moammar Ghaddahfi in Libya mounted a similarly inspired coup d'etat in September 1969 and Siad Barre in Somalia, (memorialized in Ruth First's *Out of the Barrel of a Gun*). Nimieri claimed that he would turn Sudan into 'the Cuba of the Middle East' (Khalid, 1987: 35). These coups followed the greatest blow to Arab pride, the 1967 Six Day War and the humiliating defeat of Arab armies of Egypt, Jordan and Syria.

Numeiri's first major political crisis was the insurrection in Wad Nubawi and his crushing of the Umma party's 1970 *Ansar* revolt at its Aba Island stronghold, which had challenged the legitimacy of the May revolution. The Imam al-Hadi, the spiritual guide of the Ansar and Uncle of Sadiq al-Mahdi, was executed while fleeing to Ethiopia. This was the beginning of the bloodletting unleashed by Numeiri against political opponents that became routine in subsequent military regimes.

Numeiri's major early achievement was the 9 June Declaration in 1970 that implemented the SCP policy of 'regional autonomy' for the south and led the way to the negotiated end to the civil war in 1972. The Addis Ababa peace accords held for a decade and represent the only sustained period of peace until the CPA. Reforms favorable to women's rights were instituted in the law and rising women's political power was reflected in a number of female cabinet appointments.

A blow to the relatively progressive course of the early Numeiri years came with the coup of 19 July 1971, led by Hashim al-Atta, and the successful counter-coup dramatically led three days later by Numeiri, who escaped their imprisonment. My husband and I lived through these eventful days from 19–21 July 1971 and he observed the beginning of the coup from his motor scooter on Nile street a few blocks from the Presidential Palace that was first to be taken. Within a matter of hours military music was broadcast from Omdurman Radio announcing that a 'Corrective Move' had been carried out by SCP loyalists in the army and that a workers' state would be created to adjust the course of Numeiri's governance that had retreated from its original SCP program. We observed and recorded these events as reporters for the *Nile Mirror* in the employ of the Ministry of Southern Affairs and its Minister, Joseph Garang, one of the few southern members of the SCP. We covered the largely peaceful pro-Hashim demonstrations by thousands of Sudanese communists and supporters along Palace Street in Khartoum, and were working in the offices of the *Nile Mirror* on the afternoon of 21 July when we heard the first gunfire from the nearby Khartoum Army Barracks that signaled the beginning of the counter-coup. After the fact, it was learned that the counter coup was backed and coordinated by Egypt, concerned about a communist outpost by its rebellious neighbor, and with help from pro-Nasserite Colonel Gaddafi who forced down the BOAC airplane in Tripoli that was bringing pro-Hashim supporters back to Khartoum from Britain.

The bold act of retaking of power in Khartoum and seizing the national media infrastructure in Omdurman turned a bloody new page in Sudanese post-independence history. The coup was carried out by the usual force of arms, coupled with a new willingness to eliminate the opposition by mass execution. When Numeiri was ousted by Hashim al-Atta's supporters he was imprisoned, but not executed. However, his return to power was accompanied by great loss of life in street fighting (which we personally witnessed), and in the final hours of the recapture of power, the 'massacre' by remnants of Hashim al-Atta army supporters of Numeiri's officers in the government Rest House on University Avenue near to the Palace. The city remained insecure, and we were not able to return for another two weeks to our flat on a houseboat on the Blue Nile near to the 'People's' Palace.

After this correction of the 'corrective move,' the tenor and character of the regime and of subsequent Sudanese politics in the North changed in fundamental ways. The bloodshed and harsh rule to which Southerners had been subjected since 1955 was applied in selective ways against citizens in the North. Military tribunals of alleged coup planners and SCP leaders, Secretary General Abdel Khaliq Mahgoub, trade union leader Shafie Ahmed al-Sheikh and southern Minister Joseph Garang, ended in their immediate execution by hanging. Numerous officers supporting Hashim were also executed, and 'mopping up' exercises in the three towns continued for some time. Elimination of regime opponents by imprisonment or execution became more common and eventually became an accepted part of militarist politics. The power and symbolism of those heady days in the summer of 1971 was again in the news in 2007 when the wife of Shafie al-Sheikh, Fatma Ahmed Ibrahim – a communist and an historic figure herself as the first woman elected to parliament in 1965 – verbally and physically attacked Numeiri's vice-president Abul Gassim Mohamed Ibrahim in the Popular Assembly whom she accused of 'murdering her husband' thirty-eight years earlier.

Having dealt with leftist opposition, and with myriad problems besetting his regime, by the late 1970s Numeiri increasingly turned to Islam and Islamic forces to solve his political problems. Islamic banking and financial institutions, pioneered by the Faisal Islamic Bank, were opened in the late 1970s. Officially promoted by Numeiri, they grew rapidly and dramatically to about 40 per cent of all capital investments by the early 1980s. Legislation introducing *zakat* and a total ban on alcohol were introduced. When other, more comprehensive Islamist measures failed in the People's Assembly, Numeiri needed MB support. In exchange for this support he introduced the all-encompassing September Laws, thus instituting Islamic law as state law for the Sudan.

Abdullahi Ibrahim (2009) offers a new theory for Numeiri's September Laws and the notorious courts of 'prompt justice.' He argues that Numeiri had run out of political ideologies and seized the opportunity of populist demands for 'law and order.' Shariʿa was accepted as a better, cheaper deliverer of justice to the masses, comparable to the popularity of the Islamic Courts movement in recent years in Somalia. While there is merit to the 'law and order' argument, Sudan's overriding crisis in 1983 was the resumption of war in the South, months before the September Laws were announced. The target of the September Laws was more likely the rebellious Southerners and their potential northern allies. Making Shariʿa law effectively state law flushed them out, sent the message of the pre-eminence of the Islamic state, and restarted the civil war which the generals still believed was militarily winnable. However, Ibrahim acknowledges that Numeiri's Islamization of the state was an instrument to terrorize the population into political submission. By separating the political from the professional, Ibrahim affords the judges their due respect for having survived political events while trying to retain standards of impartiality despite intense pressure from rulers.

Many observers have attempted to explain Numeiri's shift from the leader of the single party Sudanese Socialist Union to a pro-MB Islamism. In his own reflections (from his book *Why the Islamic Way?* 1980) he said that he began to reassess his faith during the three days in July 1971 as he awaited his fate in detention after having been overthrown by some of his closest personal friends and associates (El-Affendi, 1991: 121). It can also be argued from a psycho-social standpoint that two basic influences in Numeiri's life were both based in team efforts where loyalty and winning are primary – soccer and the army (Bechtold, 1976). The seeming opportunism of Numeiri was possibly fueled by his sheer desire to win. Not being an intellectual like the communists, there were lots of jokes about his intelligence and abilities, fueling an inevitable personal insecurity. He understood that the SCP had used him and these intellectuals probably made him feel as an outsider. Also as a Nubian from Dongola he was not part of the Jellaba elite (from whom the communist leaders also descend), and perhaps when they broke their loyalty to him he reacted with vengeance and the executions. This psycho-social explanation cannot suffice to explain the complexity of the transformations that took place in Sudan from the early days to the last years of Numeiri's rule,

but it may help to explain the bloodletting against northern elites
before the country turned to the bloodiest years of its civil war against
Southerners after 1983.

The September Laws of 1983

On 8 September 1983 President Ja'afar Numeiri decreed that Shari'a
would be the sole state law in force in the Sudan. Shortly after, al-
Turabi was appointed Attorney General and the Judiciary fell under
the direct influence of the ideology of the MB. Immediately following the decree all of the University of Khartoum faculty and students
were summoned to the largest lecture hall and were instructed by Dr.
Abdel Awad of the Medical Faculty that all knowledge emanates from
the Qur'an. This began the assault on intellectual secularism.

Along with this decree, Numeiri also called for a restructuring of
the Sudanese legal system which included: 1) giving a stronger hand
to the Attorney General; 2) revising court procedures in order to attain
prompt justice by simplifying the legal process; and 3) establishing
the application of Islamic laws in all fields (in addition to the former
jurisdiction that administered personal status laws only), including
the concept of aggravated theft punishable by *hadd* punishments ('to
the limit,' such as limb amputation; flogging for defamation, alcohol
drinking, possession, manufacture or sale; and the death penalty for
adultery and armed robbery).

Fair trials, irrefutable proof, or admission of guilt, along with the
non-applicability to non-Muslims were to be guaranteed in the implementation of the new laws. However, within a year of their promulga-
tion, it was clear that these guarantees were not being met. Courts of
Prompt Justice replaced the previous courts along with a large portion
of the trained judicial officials who were purged if not supportive of
the changes. Non-Muslims were charged and punished for alcohol-
related offenses, while Muslims and non-Muslims alike had limbs
amputated after the Prompt Justice courts determined their guilt for
property crimes. Several hundred amputee victims, primarily between
1983–85, organized themselves into a social welfare society after
democracy was restored with the overthrow of Numeiri in April 1985

(Mahmoud, 1985). The *hadd* punishments were discontinued during
the period of democracy, 1985–89, and were not resumed with the
same force after the NIF seized power in the June 1989 coup d'état,
led by al-Bashir.

The problem with Numeiri's Islamization of law – 'the legislative
coup d'etat of 1983' – according to an early critic Abdullahi An-Na'im,
is that the Shari'a lends itself so easily to political manipulation (1989:
19). The opportunistic nature of the 1983 Islamization had the appearance of legitimacy with the acceptance by the People's Assembly of the
first Presidential Decrees leading up to the September Laws in August
of 1983. The Assembly perfunctorily approved all of these laws, including the new Penal Codes and Codes of Criminal Procedure, in two
days: 8–9 November 1983. Obviously, to have rejected these would
have meant a confrontation between military and 'popular' rule and
action by the Assembly to reject or modify the new codes would have
been labeled as anti-Islamic, politically impossible for a predominantly
Muslim Parliament owing its very existence to the President who
issued the decrees. The president could have dissolved the Assembly
(Ibid: 20).

The reinstatement of Shari'a criminal law, from the time of its last
application during the Mahdiya, was explained to the judges through
the mechanism of the Judicial Circular. The Circular on cross amputation for aggravated theft reads as follows:

The following directions, however, should be observed when cross
amputation penalty is issued:

1. The right hand and the left foot should be amputated;
2. The right hand should be amputated first followed by the left foot;
3. Though amputation should be immediate and without delay, yet
    the health condition of the accused should be observed. In cases
    when the accused could not bear both organs at the same times
    his hand will be amputated first and after a while the foot. The
    executing authority should refer to medical authorities to deter-
    mine the health condition of the suspect;
4. Prison authorities are responsible for execution in the presence of
    the magistrate and in a public place.

The new flogging (*jald*) *hadd* punishment (Circular No. 87/1983) was enacted as a deterrence by causing physical pain to the offender. The Circular is specific as to the flogging instrument, the degree of severity, and gender differences in application. A leather whip should be used in flogging, its force must be moderate i.e. not be light nor severe. Whipping in all *hadd* crimes must not vary in severity from one *hadd* offense to another. All lashes should be administered at once and the accused (male or female) should have his clothes on while being flogged. Males should be whipped while standing and females should be seated. Flogging should not touch sensitive parts of the body i.e. head, heart, stomach, and should only be on the back and shoulders. The penalty should be administered in a public place and in the presence of a magistrate. Although in practice flogging sentences were administered through the Courts of Prompt Justice and carried out immediately after sentencing, the Circular does specify that 'appeals to the flogging penalty may delay execution until the date of the appeal elapsed when the sentence becomes final. In the meantime the suspect should be kept in custody until the penalty is executed.' (The *Hadd* Judicial Circulars were translated by Hatim Babiker Hillawi, Professor of Sociology at Nilein University.)

Using the legislative and judicial apparatuses of the state, the basic language, structure, and application of Sudanese law was changed with consequences that continue to this day. Ultimately, the independence of the Judiciary was fundamentally compromised, from which it has not recovered. After the September Laws, when the Judiciary resisted implementation of the new legal order, Numeiri declared a State of Emergency on 29 April 1984 and brought into existence the 'Emergency Courts' that evolved five months later into 'Courts of Prompt Justice' to implement the new laws. The Judiciary Act of 1984 further gave the president absolute power to establish any 'special' criminal court with appointments of new judges by the High Judicial Council which the president appointed himself (Ibid: 20). In this way the Sudan Judiciary was turned into a partisan force losing its history of independence for which it was praised in the years before 1983, and the ranks of judges were nearly gutted of its professionalism.

Many left the country to be employed as judges or university professors in the Gulf countries. Numeiri consulted often with the Mufti of Saudi Arabia Bin Baz and he advised him that 'even if the whole world is against you, you must continue with the Shari'a (interview Mahgoub al-Tigani, July 2007).

Within a matter of weeks the first *hadd* penalties of amputation began. The first at Kober prison was supervised by physician Dr. Kamal Zaki who renounced the Hippocratic oath replacing it with an Islamic oath. Al-Turabi was also present and is alleged to have fainted when the blood began to spurt (Mubarak, 2001: 91). The greatest number of amputations – perhaps as many as 200 – took place between 1983–85, mainly in Khartoum, but also in northern towns. According to scholar and human rights activist Mohamed Mahmoud, ethnic minorities and the underclass were the primary victims, mainly displaced young males from the marginalized areas of the south and west, non-Muslims and Muslims. While the exact number of *hadd* victims in this period is not known, some put it as high as 215. Initially the amputations were carried out in public in accordance with the exhortation that the punishments be well-known for the purpose of deterrence. However, when the Numeiri regime realized the unpopularity of these extreme measures, the sentences were carried out secretly in Kober and Omdurman prisons (Mahmoud, 1985: 31).

At this time Mahgoub al-Tigani[8] was Brigadier in the Department of Corrections. According to his account, Numeiri visited the department in November 1984 as he was feeling the growing criticism of the public about the application of the *hudud* and the number of amputations. Numeiri had come to the DoC to obtain *bay'a*, the oath of loyalty to him as the new 'Imam,' and to respond to the many public critics of the application of new Shari'a laws, including from the corrections officers themselves. He came to the Prisons Headquarters in Khartoum near to Nilein University, and the Prisons Commander after thanking him for accepting their invitation they confronted him on the application of the *hudud*. The criticism was delivered on grounds of Corrections professionalism arguing that prison personnel are not trained properly for carrying out *hadd* penalties for which they were now made responsible. 'These punishments represent a great responsibility for us,' the

Commander argued, continuing that the application of *qisas* – retaliation 'eye for eye' – means that corrections officers can be sued, or be subject to revenge. This represented a great liability for officers as the Prisons Department was not only charged with the application of the *hudud,* but they also had to locate the surgeons required to carry out the surgery in the prisons. Even if the amputations were carried out in the hospital, the Prisons Department is in a supervisory role. The professionalism exhibited by the Corrections Department in this respect may have played a restraining role upon the excesses of the overly zealous early use of the *hadd* punishments.

Al-Tigani recalls that some officers asked Numeiri if they might be permitted to continue to uphold international law regarding treatment of inmates since the very founding of the Prisons Dept is rooted in these international norms. The President responded to the Corrections officers:

> Look Gentlemen, I know that people are complaining [about *hudud*] and you are telling me your concerns, but I want to assure you that I will not abandon Shari'a. I know you are humanitarian with prison inmates and uphold professional standards in Kober (main prison) and I always defend these practices that reflect the kindness in the Sudanese nature. But I am here to ask you to be more firm and to be my right hand with the Shari'a.

The officers were silent and were effectively blocked from further protest.

There were also protests from the Doctors Union saying that cooperating with application of *hudud* violates the Hippocratic oath and medical ethics to do no harm. Only a few physicians cooperated with the MB/NIF to work on amputations. Amputations were also carried out in the Army Medical Corps and not in the civilian hospital. In response, Numeiri annexed the Prisons Department because the civilian physicians refused to carry out the amputations enforcing the rule that any officer refusing an order could be court marshaled and even hung. In Pakistan physicians also refused to carry out these penalties.

According to Shari'a, the *hadd* application of amputation for theft is inoperative in times of starvation. The 1982–85 years of 'grave drought' and rampant famine in the Sahel coincided with the installation of the Sudanese *hadd* penalties, and therefore theft for reasons of hunger should not have been prosecuted.

During this same meeting Numeiri asked about the Shari'a penalty of exile (*ib'ad, nafiu*) and whether this meant imprisonment in a far off jail, such as exile in Port Sudan, or simply incarceration itself. Sociologist and criminologist Dr. al-Tigani responded to this question that the intent of exile or imprisonment is removal from society, thus imprisonment in itself is sufficient to fulfill exile in Shari'a.

This account, recalled by a member of the Corrections Department, conveys much about the sentiments of a class of officers who reacted as professionals to the extremist application of a law, with which they had no experience. And they argued against the *hudud*, not on moral or political grounds, but on professional ones as their training did not prepare them for the tasks they were compelled to execute. Numeiri did not respond to their concerns, but referenced only his own ideology. To be clear, no training programs were planned or financed with those experienced with the *hudud* penalties, such as the Saudis with whom Numeiri was in close contact. As an officer in the army, he asked only for the loyalty and support of the prison officers.

The Execution of an 'Apostate' and the issue of Shari'a

According to Mohamed A. Mahmoud, political debate in the period before the 1985 *intifada* was centered on the issue of Shari'a, and the debate was unlike that anywhere else in the Muslim world at the time.[9] Highly respectful debates about Shari'a took place in the late 1980s before the al-Bashir/NIF forces seized power in 1989 and included well-known Sudanese democrats, such as Mahgoub al-Tigani Mahmoud, Ali Osman Mohamed Taha, Mohamed Mahmoud, al-Hibr Youssef Nurreddine, and Peter Gatkouth. While still an active Corrections officer, al-Tigani had seen statistics showing that initially the crime rates dropped after the *hudud* were imposed, however they then quickly returned to normal levels. A small percentage were non-Muslims showing that the application of Shari'a to non-Muslims started early in Sudanese Islamization. Mahmoud recalls a case in the early 1990s, after al-Bashir's *Inqaz* regime, of the amputation of a southern Christian in Port Sudan, and another in the North in Dar al-Islam.

The MB cemented its relationship with the Numeiri government during this earlier period of the application of the *hudud,* 1983–85. When Numeiri failed to break the critically important judges strike, the MB exerted their newfound influence to promote fuller implementation of Shari'a that stood at the heart of their program. However, according to Mahmoud, the regime was divided over the *hudud* from these early days of imposed Islamic law, and it divided again over the execution of Republican Brother (RB) leader, Mahmoud Mohamed Taha.

The targeting of Taha by the MB can be traced to 1968 when the first charge of apostasy was raised against him in Sudan, followed by *fatwas* from prominent sheikhs in Mecca and at al-Azhar University in the 1970s. The campaign was resurrected in December 1984 and January 1985 after the RB had strenuously criticized the September Laws. RB Mahmoud Taha issued a statement referring to the September Laws as 'violations of Islamic Shari'a and of Islam itself . . . Moreover,' he added, 'these laws have distorted Islamic Shari'a law and Islam and made them repugnant . . . and [they] were enacted to terrorize the people and humiliate them into submission.' The laws were also seen to jeopardize the national unity of the country, by discriminating against the one-third non-Muslim population (An-Na'im, 1987: 14). Ironically, Taha was not opposed theologically to the *hudud,* but to their misuse and abuse by Numeiri.

Before the zeal whipped up in the wake of the September Laws, Numeiri had relatively good relations with the RB (*Jamhouriyeen*) who had generally supported him in his early progressive years. The case of 'apostasy' mounted against Taha was substantively more one of alleged sedition. The judicial argument read on 8 January 1985 suggested that Taha may have committed the offense of 'apostasy in mind,' but the judgment concluded the defendants (four others were tried with Taha) were guilty of sedition, undermining the constitution, inciting unlawful opposition to the government, disturbing public tranquility, and membership in an unlawful organization (Ibid: 15). Thus, the crime of ʿapostasy' was never specifically mentioned, underscoring the political and not theological essence of the trial. Apostasy was later ʿconfirmed' by the special court of appeal and the original sentence of death was confirmed. The four charged with Taha were originally given one month, and later just three days by Numeiri, to reconsider their views, to recant and repent. All four did so, and they were freed the day after the execution by hanging of Ustadh Mahmoud Taha on 18 January 1985. As President of the Republic, Numeiri publicly announced his confirmation of the death sentence by reference to the Shariʿa theory of apostasy.

Abdullahi Ibrahim has a more provocative answer to the question ʿWho killed Taha?' He negates the usual response that it was the MB and al-Turabi. Instead, Ibrahim argues that the Qadis of the Judiciary had a better motive. Taha, who was condemned as an apostate in 1967, was actually the victim of a political vendetta from a longstanding conflict between him and the Qadis. He mocked their authority and accused them of false interpretations of Shariʿa in their September Laws of 1983, and by 1985, the second apostasy trial, he mocked them again for failing to execute their own decision of 1967 and for building a Shariʿa based upon their ʿfalse 1983 laws.' ʿBoycotting Shariʿa courts did not endear Taha to his adversaries,' Abdullahi opines (p.310). The Appellate judge in the 1985 trial (later the engineer of al-Bashir's state Islamism) was al-Makashif Taʾa al-Kabbashi, who did not give the final chance for Taha to recant his heretical views, he argues, because of his habitual disrespect for the courts. So, according to Ibrahim, it was vindictiveness of the Qadis that pushed for Taha's execution and marked the turning point that ended traditional Sudanese Islamic institutions and their reputations for tolerance. This view of a tolerant Islam, the author argues, is indicative of the overlooked and understudied aspect of power and orthodoxy when analyzed through the lens of the law and its implementers.

The 1985 *Intifada*

Taha's execution was clearly an object lesson to any opponent. However, in less than three months, Numeiri was overthrown by a combination of popular democratic uprising and new military rule – which many have argued was sparked by the hanging of a peaceful Muslim reformer and respected teacher in his mid-1970s. General Suwar al-Dahab restored military rule on 6 April 1985, allegedly to stabilize the country. But many argued, especially the SPLM/SPLA leadership, that military intervention was wrong after such a massive outpouring of populist anti-military sentiment.

In November 1986, the Supreme Court repudiated the judgment against Taha as violation of the constitution and of the September Islamic laws themselves. Annual commemorations of the anniversary of Taha's execution for years were held by members of the Republican Movement, but in recent years the spirit of Mahmoud Mohamed Taha as a national martyr to the cause of Sudanese democracy has been resurrected from Khartoum – where they were legal and undisturbed – to California. With respect to resistance to imposed Islamization and extreme Shari'a, two national figures are recognized, John Garang and Mahmoud Taha.

During the final 20 months of Numeiri's rule, at least 90 persons convicted of theft had their limbs amputated. After Numeiri's overthrow the military and civilian governments from 1985–89 suspended the September Laws and began work on a new penal code to replace them. This was delayed by the parliament pending constitutional assembly that would include the SPLA and determine what the fundamental sources of law in Sudan are. After 1985, the more extreme *hudud* sentences such as amputation were not handed down; the flogging *jald* offenses were extended to the point of non-execution, and any *hudud* sentences handed down during Sadiq al Mahdi were converted to jail sentences.[10]

Legal Methodology for Erecting the Edifice of Shari'a

The architects of the codification of Shari'a, al-Mukashfi Taha al-Kabbashi and Abdel Munim Uthman Muhamad Taha employed a method of organizing selected domains of Shari'a and then codifying them through statutory legislation (Layish and Warburg, 2002: 94). Chief Justice Dafalla al Hajj Yusuf issued Judicial Circulars, most pertaining to criminal matters as a dramatic break with past legal traditions. However, the method of issuing circulars to change the law or 'evolve' it dates back to colonial times, when the English Legal Secretary periodically published such circulars to innovate legal interpretation or practice, or to change established practice (Fluehr-Lobban and Hillawi, 1983).

Layish and Warburg document the discretion employed by the Shari'a judges in imposing the *hadd* punishments (p.113). Circular #89 affirmed a prohibition of tying an amputated limb around the neck, and specified that this *hadd* punishment must be administered, assisted with medical and scientific consultation. Criminal Circular #2 provided for appeal of *hadd* sentences of amputation and cross amputation as well as other *hadd* punishments for theft, illicit intercourse, robbery, and that flogging of women should be inflicted moderately (Ibid: 100). They argue that much of the penal code is a mixture of broadly extant applications of a revivified Shari'a. The penal laws of the Shari'a were more frequently sentenced than applied, except for lashing that remains in force. Amputations diminished in application, but were reported to still be used for their repressive effect in Darfur throughout the years of its rebellion after 2003.

Debates over the Interpretation and Correct Status of Shari'a, 1985–89

What happened between 18 January 1985 and the April *intifada* was the mobilization of secular elements in Numeiri's regime, such as Khalid el Kid head of the *al-Amn al-Qawmi*, who were anti-MB forces within the regime. Al-Turabi and others were arrested before Numeiri traveled to Washington, DC to meet President Reagan. The situation was dynamic and fluid with pressure mounting about the cruelty of the *hudud* applications. However, the US and President Reagan did not protest the amputations and it has remained silent over the full application of the *hudud* in the Kingdom of Saudi Arabia.

On the strength of the popular uprising, General Suwar al-Dahab engineered a temporary military intervention to stabilize the nation as it prepared for democratic elections in the following year. This promise was kept and, in the immediate post-*intifada* period, Shari'a became *the* vehicle for the power struggle among Sudan's northern Muslim parties. The debate was framed in the following terms: 1) The pro-Shari'a position, led by the MB and future NIF vice-president Ali Osman Taha, argued that the real struggle is between *kufr* (heathenism) and *iman* (faith). This is an eternal struggle, and there is no possibility to argue against it, or the debater faces the charge of being a *kafir* (heathen). The strategy was to frame any political critique as an attack on Shari'a. 2) For the liberals the strategy was to avoid criticizing the Shari'a directly, although the real issues were human rights, freedom of expression, the status of women and non-Muslims in a context of increasing Islamization.

According to activists during this period, the discourse was intellectual and respectable. However, had it been less polarized and more diplomatic, the Republican argument for Shari'a reform might not have been cast as *kufr*.

The *intifada* was one of Sudan's great democratic upsurges, but, ironically it actually strengthened the hand of the MB. Their plan of attack to secure state power, using the Shari'a as the battering ram, was set. Critics, such as Mohamed Mahmoud,[11] were characterized by the Islamists as hopelessly western, and protégés of the Orientalists who frame Islam according to western motives and interests. He argued that the force and eventually the brutality of the MB/NIF assault meant that the formerly wide space in Sudan that was progressive, moral and democratic was shrunk because of the intensifying fear of what the Islamists might do next. In 1988 after Mahmoud spoke out against the Iranian *fatwa* against Salman Rushdie and the publication of *The Satanic Verses,* he was in fear of his life and needed to have a body guard to move around the city.

SPLM, John Garang, and Shari'a

Islamism was consolidated in absolute state power terms in 1989, and the Shari'a was legally codified and institutionalized in 1991. However, it has been the ideological and military success of the SPLM/ SPLA that has liberated the Sudanese masses and Muslims from the grip of the harshest face of Islamist rule. This was symbolically and really achieved through the signing of the CPA in 2005 that withdrew Shari'a as a national law.

In his political speeches between 1983 and 1985 John Garang rarely mentioned Shari'a. But in SPLM negotiations with the GoS and in reaction to successive post-Numeiri governments, Islamic law emerged as the major symbol of northern oppression and insensitivity to Southerners, and emerged as their central point of resistance. Despite an expectation that the SPLM would join the new democratic forces gathered around Suwar al-Dahab after the overthrow of Numeiri, Garang, speaking for the SPLM, refused to recognize the Transitional Military Command (TMC) for its having usurped the popular revolutionary momentum. Moreover, Garang alleged that the TMC isolated the SPLM in its planning to take power in the name of the *all* of the people, and was in fact planning to resume the military offensive against the South (Garang/Khalid, 1987: 89).

After what the movement perceived as belated overtures, the SPLM demanded the following of the Transitional Military Council (TMC):

1) Return of power to the people and dissolve the TMC;
2) Commit to resolve the 'Problems of the Sudan' not the 'Problem of the Southern Sudan';
3) Lift the state of emergency;
4) End the joint military pacts with Egypt and Libya;
5) Cancellation of Numeiri's Shari'a laws, noting that it is pointless to participate in a national dialogue within the context of Shari'a laws.

Furthermore, Garang argued that it was an objective indication of the lack of seriousness to talk about exempting the south, or any other region, from national laws, and it was meaningless to talk about *modifying* Shari'a laws (Response of John Garang to Dr. el-Gizouli, 1 September 1985, Khalid/Garang, p.94).

In response to the Shari'a issue, the TMC Prime Minister El Gizouli Dafalla wrote to Garang that the Shari'a laws would be on the agenda of a proposed National Congress leading to a new permanent constitution that would resolve matters regarding the source and type of law by which justice, economic and social equality would be ensured (Ibid: 94; 99). These points were reiterated in communiques between the SPLM and the TMC during the period leading up to the Koka Dam, Ethiopia talks. In various expressions the same message was communicated regarding the September Laws:

1) 8 February 1986: 'The September 1983 Laws and the State Security Act 1973, be immediately repealed.'
2) 20 March 1986: 'abolition of the so-called Islamic laws imposed by Numeiri in September 1983.'

Since the TMC and the Government of Sudan refused to meet these conditions, the SPLM refused to accept their invitations to come to Khartoum for talks. The SPLM did agree to meet with Sudanese polit- ical forces outside of Sudan in Ethiopia at Koka Dam where the forego- ing issues were boiled down to their political essence: abolition of the September Laws; freezing the military pacts (that had been deployed against the south and SPLA); and lifting the state of emergency.

   Note that Garang and the SPLM only referred to the 'September Laws' and the 'so-called Islamic laws imposed by Numeiri in September 1983' and never to the faith of Islam or its religious law, the Shari'a. Over time, as rhetoric replaced any hope of real, candid dialogue, Shari'a became *the* issue, the word to inflame passions on both sides of the divide between GoS and SPLM, and then more generally between the North and south. For its part the NIF in its negotiations with the SPLM offered a solution of federalism as an compromise to the com- prehensive model of an Islamic state.

Concluding Remarks

By the end of the second period of multi-party rule, as the efforts by the Popular Assembly to do what Sadiq al-Mahdi had failed to do, that is, withdraw the September Laws, it was in this vacuum that the NIF moved to seize total state power. Shari'a had been the best tool in their kit for this seizure of power and, in a sense, the consolidation that followed the NIF takeover in 1989 was anti-climactic. The status of Shariʻa as Sudan's unquestioned national law – its place as the sole source of legislation, governance, and social regulation – was secure. It would not be challenged for another decade until Sudanese oil began to flow and global forces after 9/11 placed intense pressure upon the regime that had been a haven for the architect of al-Qaeda, Osama bin Laden.

CHAPTER 3

SHARI'A AND THE ASCENDANCE AND DECLINE OF THE ISLAMIST 'CIVILIZATION PROJECT,' 1989–PRESENT

After the June 1989 coup d'etat, the Sudan joined the ranks of nations referred to in the West as Islamic 'resurgent,' or Islamist, especially after the Islamic Revolution in Iran in 1979. For Sudan, the emblematic phrase *al-Mashru' al-Hadari,* the 'Civilization Project' came to be equated with Sudanese Islamism. As with the Iranian Revolution, Sudan's 'Civilization Project' imposed comparable restrictions upon popular culture and symbolically upon women as the vessels of social propriety. As has also been the case with life under the Taliban, public appearance bans were instituted on female exposure, shaving for men who sought to be in the government's favor, the reproduction of pictures, western fashion and music, gambling, interest, *riba*, on loans, music and dancing at weddings, playing drums, and tailors sewing women's clothes.[12] Most of these bans were also true of Sudan in its ascendant Islamist period, after 1989. Nearly two decades after these Islamist initiatives as I was conducting research for this book and living in downtown Khartoum, I searched in vain for a female public tailor as a substitute for the male tailors who declined to measure me as they had in the pre-Islamist past. Despite the decline of much of the institutional-structural Islamism with the CPA, much of the cultural change instituted under Sudan's Islamism remains.

While pressure mounted against Prime Minister Sadiq al-Mahdi in advance of the 1989 coup, it was clear that he had failed to repair the country's political and religious problems (Perlez, *The New York Times*, 23 October 1988). The Islamists refused to join Sadiq's proposed new cabinet and vowed to keep the strict Islamic laws and to fight to extend Islam (Reuters, 15 March 1989). Sadiq equivocated to the end and parliamentary moves to act in his stead were pre-empted by the 30 June coup d'état, led by al-Bashir and backed by al-Turabi, the third since independence. Dubbing itself a government of *Inqaz,* became the preferred referent for the regime.

The term 'Islamist' characterizes governments that seek to Islamize political and social institutions and favor a present or future establishment of an Islamic state. Al-Turabi provided the ideological framework to the new military government which moved quickly after seizing power to abolish all parties and all publications except those approved of by the NIF. Although the Sudan did not declare itself an Islamic Republic (like Iran or Afghanistan), it was regarded as such since it Islamized government and social institutions, banks and economic organizations, and refused to negotiate with the SPLM/SPLA over the removal of the Shariʿa as state law. The coerced Islamization of Sudan's non-Muslims was unique and not like Iran or Afghanistan and political and human rights groups representing the peoples of the Nuba Mountains and southern Sudan raised an international outcry.

Internationally, al-Turabi emerged after 1989 as a rising star among Islamists, gaining prominence for his key role in the NIF shaping of the al-Bashir regime. His charm and ease in interviews in Arabic, English and French gained him attention as a cosmopolitan Islamist. His writings, the translations of his works, and his accessibility to the international press made him one of Sudan's most recognized personalities on the global scene and a significant voice of Islamic resurgence until 1989.

In the third year of *Inqaz,* 1992, the year of jihad to win the war in the South was officially announced while al-Bashir was proclaimed as 'Imam al-jihad.' On 27 April 1992 six pro-government religious leaders (*'ulama*) issued a *fatwa* legalizing jihad against the SPLA rebels in the Nuba Mountains, and in South Kordofan to liberate these areas from the 'infidel' (*kufar*) rebels. This *fatwa* called into question whether an Islamic state can order the killing of alleged 'non-believers' when the war is not waged in self-defense.

The Popular Defense Forces (PDF) and Mujahideen were officially established, and a state tax with the title 'financing the jihad' was levied. New Islamist Voluntary organizations were established to advocate for jihad, *Nida al-Jihad* (Call for Jihad), Munazamat al-Shahid (Organization of Martyrs), and *Salam al-Izza* (The Peace of Prosperity) to provide material support to *mujahidin* families and *Zad Al-Mujahid* (food for the holy warrior). By 1993–94 'jihad' against the southern rebels was the government's central theme. Even after the signing of the CPA in 2005, jihadist propaganda using war footage from GoS-SPLA battles continued to be broadcast on Sudan TV. To encourage and reinforce Muslim perceptions of the war against Southerner 'infidels,' the *Inqaz* government developed a special policy toward northern martyrs' families by training their sons to replace the fathers in continuous jihad (Abdel Moneim, 2006).

Al-Turabi's right hand man, Ali Osman Muhammad Taha (b. 1947), was active in the MB while a student at the University of Khartoum. He captured the attention of al-Turabi as a leader during his student years 1966–71 and as Khartoum University Student Union (KUSU) president in 1969 after Numeiri took power. Al-Turabi pioneered the growth of the movement at the university, traditionally a bastion of leftist and progressive politics led by the Sudanese Communist Party. By 1973 Taha was a leading opponent of Numeiri's May Revolution. Posted to the Judiciary in 1972 he led the initial moves to implement Shari'a law, one law at a time through the late 1970s. His personal rise to political success and his prominent role in Shari'a stemmed from his role in outlawing legalized prostitution. From the Judiciary he was appointed by the al-Bashir regime to Minister of Social Planning in 1996, and by 1998 he was made Minister of Foreign Affairs. He survived al-Turabi's political isolation in 1999–2000, and was promoted to first vice-president. Taha was the GoS chief negotiator in the talks leading to the CPA. After its signing John Garang was made first vice-president, and after his death he was succeeded by Salva Kiir. Ali Osman Taha was then made second vice-president; however, he is widely regarded as al-Bashir's right hand man.

Shari'a after the NIF Takeover

After securing power and banning all political parties except the National Islamic Front, the first major political act of the al-Bashir-al-Turabi regime was to move decisively on the Shari'a, making its national status final and comprehensive thus fulfilling one of the central pillars of the Islamist agenda. The al-Bashir government turned its primary attention to codifying Islamic law, instead of discussing its retention or removal. This strategy, unique in Sudanese Islamic history, codified and fixed Shari'a in comprehensive codes of law embracing criminal and all aspects of civil law (mainly in the banking and finance sectors), as well as the traditional personal status law. The Muslim family law that I studied before the September Laws was never codified but was interpreted by the traditional *'ulama* and the judges in the Sudan Judiciary according to the times and cases as they arose (cf. Fluehr-Lobban, 1987; Arabic translation, M. al-Tigani, 2004).

The penal code drafted by al-Turabi in 1988 – which is briefly summarized below – was codified and instituted in 1991. For the first time it included the crime of apostasy (*rida*), although the only time that the death penalty for apostasy was carried out was against Mahmoud Taha in 1985. The code also included specified penalties for adultery, in one of several extensions of the 1983 laws. The first anniversary of the September Laws had been celebrated by an international conference in 1984, while Numeiri was still in power, which also signaled the new era of comprehensive Islamic governance. On 30 December 1992 al-Bashir and al-Turabi celebrated the second anniversary of the implementation of a comprehensive codified Shari'a – although the September Laws of 1983 were as significant – demonstrating that military rule reinvents the state with each new coup and government. By the third anniversary of the installation of Shari'a in its new codified form there was no mention made either of 1983 or 1991 (*al-Inqaz al-Watani*, 3 January 1994, quoted in Mubarak, p.81).

Codification of the Penal law also institutionalized the *hudud* punishments of lashing, amputation, and stoning for criminal offenses, building directly upon the September Laws. Although the major innovations were to the criminal and civil laws, the personal status family laws were also updated and brought closer to Islamist interpretations. This political stage was set in a January 1990 government conference on the 'Role of Women in National Salvation' whose major recommendation was that a new code of personal status law be drafted. A legislative committee drew up the 1991 Act on Personal Law for Muslims which was passed by the ruling military and its Council of Ministers and came into effect on 24 July 1991. The new code consists of five volumes and represented the first codification of Islamic personal status law in the Sudan. The major drafter of the code was High Court Justice, Sheikh Siddiq 'Abd al-Hai. Although codification of law has been an anathema in the history of Islamic law, it is often projected as a modern reform by Islamists. This is strongly rejected by many Muslim jurists who argue that the genius of Shari'a is its flexibility and continuous tradition of interpretation of the holy and exclusive sources of the law, the Qur'an and Sunna of the Prophet Muhammad. Codification fixes the law in a specific time and place contrary to the views of historical and revered religious scholars, the *'ulama*, who offered lengthy commentaries and reflections on various aspects of Islamic law, compiled over fourteen centuries in the four major schools of Islamic jurisprudence, the Hanafi, Maliki, Hanbali, and Shafi'i schools. Codification was practiced by the colonialists as a way to aid foreign and indigenous administrators in applying a limited version of Islamic law, historically limited to family law. Thus, codification of Shari'a not only represents a break with the past, but it is one of the innovations Islamists have undertaken in the present era.

Inqaz, Southern Policy and Shari'a

Immediately following the coup on 2 July 1989 al-Bashir pledged to end the civil war in the South, then in its sixth year, and it offered a referendum on the future of Islamic law, the central issue driving the conflict (Alan Cowell, special to *The New York Times*, 2 July 1989).

However, the consistent position of the SPLM was not to recognize imposed military rule from Khartoum,. About two weeks after the coup on 17 August 1989 the two parties did meet, possibly with mediation assistance from Egypt, but it became clear immediately that the parties were deadlocked.

A National Dialogue Conference in Khartoum, lasting more than a month from 9 September to 21 October 1989 yielded a set of recommendations to which the new government agreed. These included a federal system for Sudan under a national president and Shari'a or *'Urf* (customary law for non-Muslims) proposed as main sources of law developed so as to reflect majority and protect minority rights (Khalifa, 1989: 9). But in meetings in December in Nairobi, in which former President Jimmy Carter acted as mediator, the talks broke down over the SPLM's insistence on the abrogation of military pacts with Egypt and Libya and the government delegation holding firm on non-negotiation of the issue of Shari'a withdrawal. Shari'a from this point on became the symbolic issue by which the GoS held its ground and declared its legitimate right to represent the interests of the majority of Sudanese Muslims. Although opposition amidst intense repression is difficult to gauge, there is little indication that this move – or others toward Islamization of basic institutions – were fundamentally unpopular in the North. With more pressing concerns of the civil war and general economic impoverishment in the pre-oil era, and with potentially troublesome members of the Judiciary dismissed, the changes in the Shari'a were more noted by legal and academic professionals, rather than by the masses of Sudanese Muslims.

As such, opposition to the comprehensive Shari'a codes came mainly from outside Sudan in relation to the use – some would argue the abuse – of Shari'a for alleged human rights violations. The main opposition group outside of the country, the National Democratic Alliance (NDA) comprised of the traditional parties in a tactical alliance with the SPLM, called for a secular government with Shari'a as the source of law for Muslims, while non-Muslim customs and laws would be respected. In 1993, Pope John Paul II – whom al-Turabi once met – warned Sudan against applying Islamic law on Christians in an address made to the Bishops of Benin on 4 December 1993. Throughout the decade of the 1990s international human rights organization from Amnesty International to Human Rights Watch published regular reports about the deteriorating conditions in Sudan, often featuring Shari'a cases where the rights of women and non-Muslims were being violated.

The role of the military as a quasi-independent force in encouraging peace negotiations has received little attention. But just as the pro-peace role of the US military was evident in the years of the worsening war in Iraq, the Sudanese military has a strong civilian component. With a compulsory draft system the popular base during the decades of war has been northern in the majority, but many southern rebel leaders, including John Garang, have cut their military teeth in the national army. During my visits to northern towns between 2004 and 2007, I raised the question about the apparent absence or reductions of young males to which I was consistently offered the twin explanations of labor migration to the Gulf and 'the war in the south.' Some pointed to individual houses in our views, 'one soldier from that home; two brothers from that home.' The public dialogue on this sensitive sub-ject has predictably been suppressed by various military regimes, but casualty numbers absorbed by the Sudan armed forces are unknown at present.

International Criticism, Sanctions and Civil War Stalemated by the Shari'a Issue

During the 1990s – with virtually no western social scientists conduct-ing research in what was becoming a pariah state due to the deten-tion and alleged torture of the regime's dissidents – documentation of conditions on the ground was left to the international human rights monitoring organizations. While the role of the international human rights NGOs in raising international awareness of abuse by the gov-ernment is important, nonetheless objective reports during this period are rare. One such report by the US-based Lawyers Committee for Human Rights analyzed the impact of Islamic law on Sudan's criminal justice system. It found that many abuses in Sudan were not directly related to the government's Islamist ideology, but followed patterns common to many repressive governments irrespective of ideology. The first years of the regime were characterized by alleged gross human rights violations of a kind common to secular regimes worldwide, such as extrajudicial killings, arbitrary detention, torture, unfair trial procedures and repressive security measures. However, these initial brutal measures gave way to more subtle methods of social control, such as restrictions on the right to freedom of expression, opinion, religion, association and movement. However, by criminalizing political and ideological dissent, the government installed a system of rewards and punishments based on adherence to its policies and observance of government approved Islamic practices. Though less conspicuous than mass arrests and summary executions, these control mechanisms proved equally debilitating to the fundamental freedoms of Sudanese citizens. What I observed in the research years 2005–09 was a subdued and careful populace in the public domain, but with a private and increasingly public critical facility still intact.

In essence, the *Inqaz* regime set up a parallel system of justice to deal with threats to its security. The Report noted that the harassment, purging, voluntary retirement of the judicial profession and the replacement of half of the judges since 1989 is the 'primary cause of the deterioration of the quality and competence of the judiciary.' These judges were replaced by those largely sympathetic to the regime and the purge has meant under-representation of women, Christians and Southerners in the Islamic criminal justice system. Sudan, which had been among the pioneers for the appointment of women judges in the Islamic world, including the first woman appointed to a Shari'a judgeship in 1970 (Fluehr-Lobban, 1987), curtailed the appointment of women judges during its Islamist venture and it was reported to me that only three women judges had been appointed since 2003, one of whom is a southern woman. Contrary to international human rights reports, no women judges appointed before the al-Bashir-al-Turabi regime were dismissed and several advanced to the highest judicial posts in the land, including six women sitting on the High Court,[13] Hon. Rabab Abu Gusaysa and Hon. Amal Muhammad Hasan, while Hon. Sinia Rashid was appointed to the Constitutional Court in 2005. Moalana Rabab Abu Gussaysa also sits on the influential Magmi'

Fiqhi that debates and decides matters of Islamic interpretation and issues *fatwas* on matters of contemporary relevance and concern. Hon. Ishan Fakhri (b. 1938), the first woman judge appointed in 1966, to Court of Appeals in 1980, retired in 1991.

According to the report, the Public Order Courts (*al-Nizam al-Am*) that deal with petty infractions of Islamic law (e.g. dress and alcohol), fail to meet the minimum standards for a fair trial,

> These courts are characterized by rapidity of judgment, political dependence, incompetence of judges, irregularity of trial procedures, and absence of safeguards against abuse. Procedures contained in the CCP were replaced by summary procedures and execution of the sentence, particularly sentences of flogging are carried out almost immediately without chance for appeal. A large percentage of Public Order court defendants have been non-Muslim women from IDP camps around Khartoum raising the issue of equality before the law.
>
> (Lawyers Committee for Human Rights,
> Report on Sudan, 1996)

This characterization of Sudanese justice in the 1990s although structurally altered by the CPA, nonetheless remained in effect for several years after the CPA as its implementation was slow, uneven, and lacking in political will, and the IDP camps remained isolated from even limited national standards of justice.

Application upon non-Muslims and discrimination against women by using Islamic devices such as honor, reputation, and morality are used by the Public Order Police (*al-Shurta al-'Ama*) and Popular Committees (neighborhood associations) to protect the 'moral health' of the Sudanese society. The report concluded correctly that the GoS conflated its own interpretation of Shari'a and policies with Islam itself. In response to international criticism the GoS invoked freedom of religion and protested attacks on Islam, although Muslim critics declare that, ironically, both Muslim and non-Muslim citizens were denied freedom of religion in the name of the application of religious law. The government preferred to rule with the aid of emergency laws granting it wide powers of political repression and social control. The Report concluded that the GoS should not seek to evade its civic responsibilities by invoking cultural or religious particularity, and such arguments should be viewed with skepticism as attempts to rationalize her violations, (1997 from Lawyers Committee Report, 17 January 1997 *Lawyers Committee for Human Rights*).

NIF/NCP Split in 1999 – Isolation of al-Turabi

The outside world was stunned when it learned of al-Turabi's ouster from the National Congress Party (NCP, descending from the National Islamic Front) and his arrest and detention in 1999–2000. The isolation of the regime from world press reports and the unreliability of the censored Sudan press at the time made explanations of this dramatic development problematical. What was certain was the effect of al-Turabi's isolation. The regime took a decidedly more pragmatic turn and this political turn of events coincided with the first commercial flow of oil. Since al-Turabi was the chief architect of Sudan's Islamism from his central role in the September Laws through the codification of Shari'a with Bashir, his ouster was viewed as the initiation of a possible post-Islamist transition. Shortly after, al-Turabi's breakthroughs in the peace talks began to take place, thus making it tempting to see the connections between these events.

In 1998, al-Turabi was Speaker of the National Assembly when he led a political move intended to weaken al-Bashir's monopoly of power by recommending a constitutional amendment whereby regional governors (*walis*) would be elected by their regional constituencies instead of being appointed by the president, according to the 1998 constitution. Al-Bashir requested in writing that al-Turabi cease and desist, but he was undeterred, and the move triggered a full division within the Islamist ranks and dissolution of the National Assembly. The al-Turabi move was hailed by marginalized Islamists, especially Darfuris and other western Sudanese who formed a sizeable majority in the assembly. The fight continued in a 10,000 strong meeting of the NCP General Assembly that voted in al-Turabi's favor, but he won this battle and lost the war when he was ousted four months later by the more commanding military power of the President, who issued the Presidential Decree as Party Secretary General. This was a preemptive move to keep al-Turabi from engineering a strategic shift in power through the elected governors of the 26 states, thus decentralizing state control (Kamal al-Din, 2007: 106). Arrested and held at Kober prison, and later detained under house arrest, ironically given his political past, Amnesty International called for his release as a political prisoner. Ever the political survivor, after his ouster al-Turabi formed the Popular Congress Party (PCP) as an opposition movement to the NCP, a party that he had innovated from the discredited NIF after the 1985 *intifada*. So, the removal and political isolation of al-Turabi was a major turning point, both for domestic and international consumption, that paved the way for the pragmatic changes to come that may be described as early post-Islamism, or the end of Sudan's extremist Islamism. After 2000, significant progress in the peace talks occurred leading to the Machakos breakthrough position resolving the long-standing obstacle of Shari'a with the 'one state, two system' approach, Shari'a in the North and secularism in the South. The new order was symbolized in one way by the December 2007 opening of a 'national' beer brewery in Juba, South Sudan, an impossibility in the North, although the illegal underground market in *merissa* and *aragi* has never dried up.

By 2003, although in his 70s, al-Turabi's ability to influence national politics was not erased. The Justice and Equality Movement (JEM) that fomented the Darfur conflict is widely viewed partly as a revenge for his ousting from power in a proxy war for bitter Khartoum politics. The Darfur Sudan Liberation Movement (SLA), nurtured by the SPLM, followed its secular ideology of separation of religion and the state (*din* from *dawla*). Although the security apparatus dismantled much of the PCP's assets and resources and arrested its members, the movement has strengthened and led a dramatic attack on Omdurman in May 2007 that brought the remote Darfur war home to the capital.

In his self-appointed role as Imam and in a reversal of previous statements about the immutability of the Shari'a, al-Turabi issued a number of controversial religious opinions favoring women's ability to become Imams and asserting their equal right to marry men 'of the Book' – Christians and Jews. He also said that women's testimony was equal to that of a man and even more so in areas where her expertise is greater. He went on to advocate dialogue with the West and stressed that jihad should be waged only in self defense, despite being a central part of the regime that waged the fiercest jihad against the South (*Sudan Tribune*, 30 April 2006). Al-Turabi was quickly branded a heretic by government religious scholars and threatened with trial for apostasy like Taha in 1985. A special pamphlet directed against al-Turabi and declaring him an apostate was published by the official *Majmaʿ al-Fiqh al-Islami* in 2006 under the title *Risala al-Qul al-Fasl fi al-Rid al min al-Kharjʾan alaʾsl*, wherein al-Turabi's statements which are contradicted by the Qurʾan are repudiated.

In 2007, al-Turabi continued his attack on the government, in which he was once central, with interviews in the local press, where he was quoted: 'It [the *Inqaz* government] has provided a bad example of Islamic corruption that is now being practiced in broad daylight.' Belatedly, he warned of 'growing government influence on the Judiciary. The GoS has done unspeakable things to us and had halted the practice of religious rites.' He further demanded a 'system of *shura*, consultation, and full disclosure about how and where the oil revenues are being spent.' As a master of political rhetoric, he warned about Darfur secession denying any role in the rebel movement JEM. Finally, the old Muslim Brother declared in this interview that leftist ideologues have collapsed globally in the face of the Islamic tide (*Khartoum Montitor*, 16 January 2008, p.2).

In private conversations, I often asked about why al-Turabi is not still in jail or why he was not in exile or assassinated, as has been the case with many powerful government opponents. The most consistent response to my query was '*lisa khayafeen*,' 'they are still afraid of him.'

Post-al-Turabism showed its face openly in 1998 when ten members of the NIF (prominent among them Abdel Rahman Ali) signed a memorandum, *muskrat*, against al-Turabi in which the first ten years of the Islamist experience were critically assessed and reforms, including stripping al-Turabi of his powers, were recommended. Thus, al-Bashir asserted full political control and 'the end' (Gallab 2008: 129), or the beginning of the end of the Islamist Republic was accomplished.

Populist Approval of the Islamist Agenda?

When regimes are repressive, it is not surprising that public protest is kept at a minimum. Throughout the decades of Sudan's Islamism – 1983 to present – the only major populist uprising was the one which overthrew the Numeiri regime in 1985, repeating what the masses had done in 1964. The Numeiri regime had become repressive – indeed the September Laws are a *prima facie* case of this, but the execution of the elderly Mahmoud Taha deeply offended the Sudanese people, irrespective of political affiliation. When the September Laws were introduced, there were protests from Taha and the Republican Brotherhood and from some intellectual-politicians, such as Sadiq al-Mahdi and the Sudanese Bar Association, but mass sentiment was not to oppose the imposition of Shari'a as state law, but to object to its misapplication, especially the ferocity with which the *hudud* penalties regarding theft were executed. In a pure Islamic society, such as that during the time of the Prophet Muhammad, such penalties were implemented out of pure faith and were accepted by pious Muslims as righteous. When the *hadd* punishments are used for politics, pious Muslims recognize the sham that has been made of them.

Likewise, the general acceptance by Muslims of Islamic banking is notable from Numeiri's time in the late-1970s through its displacement of all competitors (including major international banks such as Citibank and Barclays) and complete domination of the banking sector after 1989. The introduction of foreign capital through the influence of Saudi Arabia and Iran, might not have been noticed as the two successive Islamist governments used the Islamic banks to control currency and the economy. Osama bin Laden's Tadamon bank may have been viewed as a curiosity.

Shari'a forbids currency speculation and hoarding (both are *haram*) and one of the first crackdowns of the al-Bashir regime was the death penalty for individuals accused of possessing dollars in the early-1990s. After this crackdown black marketeering disappeared and remained absent in Khartoum during the years of my recent research. But as Simone (1994) reported that the *Jabha* (NIF) grew rich on these very practices 'hoarding' currency and commodities for themselves in the early, austere days of the al-Bashir-al-Turabi government when the slogans went 'We grow what we eat and we use what we produce' (p.33).

The Islamic banking and investment movements ran their course, and although they still dominate the economic sectors (and some banks remain open in the South) they have become more flexible and realistic about global economics using the principles of *darura* (necessity) and *maslaha* (for the greater good) as rationales for their 'contamination' with western, interest-based banks. Islamic investments often yield high returns on investment, and in the recent economic recession Islamic financial institutions, as non interest-based, faired very well and were generally insulated from the western crisis.

The Decline of the Islamist 'Civilization Project': Post-Islamism? Post-Extremism?

Early in the *Inqaz* regime cracks in the Islamist façade were exposed by astute commentators and first hand observers (Simone, 1994). As moves toward Islamization steadily intensified after 1983, generally Muslims were supportive as part of their religious obligation to defend the faith and its religious law, however implementation of parts of Shariʿa, especially the *hudud* penalties, were unpopular. Early in the *Inqaz*, drug smuggling and alcohol brewing took on increased economic importance in the 'second economy' as prohibition was imposed. Many urbanites, not just non-Muslims, were driven to these practices to survive.

The mileposts throughout the years of the *Inqaz* leading to the reduction and partial withdrawal of the Islamist program are the following:

1) The expulsion of Osama bin Laden, associated with the Somalia attacks on the US and the attempted assassination of Egyptian president Hosni Mubarak, planned in Khartoum and attracting the attention of the US and its key ally in the region, Saudi Arabia;

2) The bombings of the American Embassies in Nairobi and Dar as Salaam and the retaliatory bombing of al-Shifa factory in Khartoum North by President Clinton;

3) After the boycott and withdrawal of western oil companies, Sudan's opening to Chinese, Indian and Malaysian oil companies permits commercial flow of oil; peace with South becomes an economic necessity;

4) The isolation of al-Turabi deterring his likely role in obstructing the GoS peace process with calls for solidarity among Muslims with the symbolic retention of Shari'a;

5) Multiple internal factors analyzed by Sudanese social scientists, including the aspiration of the growing middle class.

Historically the Islamic movement in Sudan grew in opposition to the Sudanese Communist Party, which briefly held the reins of power during the early years of Numeiri (1969–71). The mantra that one should be close to your friends but closer to your enemies played out in Sudanese politics with al-Turabi's and the NIF's obsession with the SCP, as it progressively destroyed in its career even as it modeled its Leninist tactics (Gallab 2008: 53). As the centerpiece of its agenda, Shari'a became the Islamist's tool in all matters, especially critical in the announcing that the Islamist agenda was here to stay with the brief period of the intense application of the *hadd* penalties. Because of their symbolic status the *hadd* penalties only needed to be used for a few years of popular intimidation, and then they would remain codified on the law books for fear, deterrence and selective social control in the year to follow.

Simone (1994) observed the nascent contradictions inherent in the application of Shari'a from early on in the regime. The application of *hadd* penalties for theft require absolute social justice, obviously not existing in Sudan, but the regime relied on the prediction that every Muslim would defend Shari'a, or at least not oppose it. Simone argued further that no African city can survive economically while adhering to the full strictures of Shari'a. And the hope that social justice will flow from Shari'a, a view held by many Islamists, is not supported as yet by experience and history of modern Islamist movements.

The Sudanese Islamists took upon themselves the establishment of a twentieth-century Islamic State while Islamists from around the world gathered in Khartoum, especially those persecuted on their homelands while al-Turabi launched the International Islamist Movement (Sunni Majority) as a forum for all Muslim revolutionaries fighting against imperialism. Initially the regime was on the offensive, exporting the 'Revolution' and not in a defensive, retreating position. A review of foreign policy between 1989 and 1995 reflects how al-Turabi and his disciples tried to isolate Egypt and Eritrea, that Sudan supported Saddam's invasion of Kuwait, and organized visits of Islamic Congresses in Baghdad.

The question as to why the al-Bashir regime began to move away from Shari'a involves a mixture of the commercial flow of oil in 1999 and the events of 9/11. Pragmatic politics required the isolation of al-Turabi prior to the dismantling of the project. Sudan's de-Islamization also involved the fact that peace talks with the SPLM had stalled over Shari'a, but eased when the SPLM was promised that non-Muslims would not be harassed using Shari'a in Khartoum.

Mohamed Mahmud (2007) argued that the Islamist's regime bid to implement Shari'a failed for three reasons:

> First, Shari'a began to lose its legitimacy after Numeiri's harsh and cruel implementation of the hudud penalties; second, the determined resistance of Southerners, particularly the political and armed resistance of the Sudan People's Liberation Movement, forced the regime into recognizing the South as a non-Shari'a zone, a measure which has weakened the case for Shari'a as a national law. Third, was the consistent and vociferous criticism of Sudanese secularists and human rights advocates inside and outside the country of the aspects of Shari'a that are incompat-ible with human rights standards has made adherence to Shari'a particularly costly (p.284).

Haydar Ibrahim (2004) argued that the Islamists retreat began after the first Gulf War and the failed assassination attempt of Hosni Mubarak in 1997, widely held to have been plotted in Khartoum. After these the regime began to talk of national reconciliation, a new constitution, and peace orchestrated from within. Venezuelan Ilych Ramirez Sanchez, Carlos the Jackal, one of Europe's most notorious terrorists, long offered safe haven in Sudan, was captured in connivance with the GoS (as he was undergoing anesthesia for a tooth extraction) and was sacrificed for a deal between Sudan and France. The regime thus sent a message to Osama bin Laden who abandoned Sudan but left behind a great deal of money among unknown brothers, among his assets the Tadaman Bank that still operates in downtown Khartoum. It was this direct strategy that necessitated the 'downfall' (*Suqut*, in Ibrahim's terms) of the 'Civilization Project.' Some NIF leaders saw a solution in winning external media and financial support so long as they could coerce and terrorize the local population. The Muslim Brothers, he argued, became more royalist than a king. This may explain why a colleague from the University of Khartoum complained to me bitterly about a senior scholar and university chancellor, who bowed deeply before his former student, Ali Osman Taha, al-Bashir's right-hand man. The project remains in words only, such as President al-Bashir's words after the signing of the CPA that, 'There will be no bars in Khartoum.' What remains is only the struggle to hold and maintain power. The biggest achievement is their 'humiliation of the Sudanese people and the taking away of their dignity for the sake of safeguarding political power. Resorting to torture, repression and the dismissal from work, the flogging of women, unlawfully pursuing the students and the young, imposing dress restrictions, were all tools used to safeguard the regime but humiliated the citizenry' (Ibrahim, 2004: 20). Regrettably all of this was linked to religion. Whether Sudan is 'post-extremist,' as sociologist Hatim Babiker suggested, or post-Islamist, the harm done to Sudanese people and their traditional egalitarian and tolerant values may never be undone.

The *Inqaz* Regime and Relation with the US, Europe and China

The *Inqaz* Regime failed to develop good relations with USA or Europe during its first decade. Despite lobbying efforts within the Clinton administration by those who favored continued engagement with the Islamist trend in Sudan prior to 9/11, the human rights record of the regime was the major stumbling block. For their part the Islamists were keen to support a pro-Sudan lobby in US but failed on this propaganda front despite a $1 million pro-government advertisement published in *Newsweek* (21 December 1992). Nor did this did not prevent the attack on the Shifa plant in August 1998 following the Embassy bombing in Nairobi and Dar al-Salaam. There was a similar propaganda campaign with its publication of a major multi-page advertisement in *USA Today* after the CPA signing in Nairobi but this also failed to break Sudan's isolation from the US. By the time of the CPA various European actors – notably the UK, Norway, the Netherlands and Italy – had taken active interest in the peace negotiations and were witnesses to the historic CPA signing.

China moved decisively into the void left by a decade of US and western-imposed sanctions and boycotts, IMF restrictions, and withdrawal of oil concessions, thus sealing the Chinese-Sudanese relationship. As China supported Sudan through its veto power on the UN Security Council, the influence of sanctions and political isolation of Sudan in the West were effectively neutralized. Chinese investment in oil production, with Indian and Malaysian petroleum interests as well, has driven the relationship which has now transformed Sudan's orientation as 'toward the east' and not the West, remarkable given its colonial history. Besides the highly lucrative joint venture between the China National Petroleum Company and the Sudan Ministry of Energy and Mining, such that Sudan now supplies China with about 8 per cent of its total imports, China has built Sudan's major refinery for export through Port Sudan, and a major dam at Merowe opened in 2009, and three new bridges spanning the Nile in Khartoum. As such Sudan played a significant role in a new Chinese-African economic alliance, that is part of a broader Afro-Asian partnership that connects the past success of the Asian tigers to the new African economic lions, Sudan among the main roaring lions.

A key feature of Chinese relations in Africa has been its non-judgmental approach to indigenous politics and human rights. This has been persuasive in many a relationship even though there are complaints about the import of Chinese labor to carry out the various projects while local labor still migrates to the Gulf in their droves for economic opportunity. This contradiction has yet to sharpen largely due to the *Inqaz* (and before them the Numeiri regime) suppression of the once strong trade union movement.

Needless to say, the issue of the national status of Shari'a, human or minority rights, or the war in the South did not factor into the economic and political ties forged between China and Sudan. Members of the western press that continued to visit Sudan reported a deteriorating Islamist social project. 'Islamic law is disintegrating barely a decade after its initiation by the "Pope of Terror", Hasan al-Turabi,' reported Phillip Smucker of the UK *The Telegraph*. He was among the first to report the growing promiscuity in Khartoum, 'where poor women are prostituting themselves for university fees.' Setting the tone for many western reporters, he continued, 'While Osama bin Laden was in the country during the early period of the Islamist project, discos and western films were banned – now he [al-Turabi] is in the same prison where he presided over many amputations' (Smucker, 3 March 2001).

The CPA and Civic Discourse on Future of Shari'a in Sudan

The CPA opened a democratic space for civil discourse on multiple issues regarding the future of Sudan, including the future of Shari'a. Delays in the implementation of the CPA led many commentators to conclude that political will is lacking and the CPA mandate to 'make unity attractive' was not a priority of the *Inqaz*.

However, initially the CPA unleashed a sense of optimism and freedom of expression in the capital city, as ordinary citizens began to discuss the politics of the 'new Sudan' or to debate whether, in fact a 'new' Sudan can emerge, while the actors and political parties that waged war are the same ones charged with building the peace. I attended several open public forums on democracy and civil society in the immediate interim period after the signing of the CPA where individuals from across the political spectrum spoke and responded to questions and comments from the audience.[14] Effectively speaking from the sidelines of the political process leading to the CPA, representatives of Sudan's old parties, the Umma party leader Sadiq al-Mahdi said that 'the greatest benefit of the CPA is that the era of religious wars (*hurub al-din*) is finished in Sudan,' while Sayed Osman Ali Hasan Mirghani of the DUP, asked if the CPA is a lavish wedding party between North and south, or the beginning of divorce proceedings?'

Dr. Riek Gai, a southern MP and member of the GoS Congress Party argued that 'the idea of one country/two systems is not new as it resembles Numeiri's policy of "regional autonomy" [in 1969–70]. So Shari'a in the North and not in the south is not a problem for us. He added that Sudan needs secularism for all [*almaniya*]; we are not an Islamic state, we are Sudanese, and we all [Northerners and Southerners] have experienced racism in Saudi Arabia (ansur al-'Arab).'

DUP commentator Ali Mahmoud Osman Hassanain argued that the essential question during the Machakos negotiations was religion and state; now, after Nairobi, it is the question of democracy and the state. Murtada Ghali, an editorial writer with the independent daily, *Al-Ayam*, emphasized the importance of the power and independence of the Constitutional Committee (*Lajnat al-Dustur*), pointing to the lack of a final status on Shari'a as a problem remaining for them to resolve. As with other speakers, he questioned the CPA being an agreement between only two parties (the ruling Congress Party and the SPLM), asking how it can claim to be representative of the Sudanese people or the political spectrum?

Johnson Chol (southern MA student from the University of Khartoum, speaking in perfect Arabic), said: 'The fundamental problem is that you have religion in the North and secularism in the south. This division will be a source of continuous friction. Should the Shari'a stay? We must recognize that it has brought enormous problems and carries this legacy of bitterness.' These public forums, attended primarily by intellectuals and journalists, continued on a regular basis. If they continue without government restraint until the elections schedule for 2010, they could play a vital role in the resurrection of civic discourse and democracy that prevailed in the years after the 1985 popular revolution against Numeiri and before the al-Bashir-al-Turabi coup of 1989.

Status of Non-Muslims in the Capital City – Commission on the Shari'a and Non-Muslims in the Capital

The Commission on the Shari'a and Non-Muslims in the Capital, mandated in the CPA, was formed two years after the CPA on 15 February 2007 (Sudan TV, Nightly News). Prominent southern political and legal figures and women jurists and academics were included in its membership, such as Joshua Dao (Chair), Moalana Rabab Abu Gusaysa, Dr. Akolda Tier, and Dr. Mahasin Safi. But, within one day of the Commission's formation there was bitter criticism from the nation's preeminent southern journalist, Alfred Taban (*Khartoum Monitor*, 17 February 2007) outraged by its composition, with 15 Muslims and 13 non-Muslims. He challenged the mission (section 1(b)) in how to protect the rights of non-Muslims within the framework 'of the imposition of Shari'a law,' a phrase that repeated throughout the decree. Moreover, the presidential decree did not give the Commission the right to take legal action against those violating the rights of non-Muslims. He argued that the decree demonstrates to the non-Muslim community in the capital that they are welcome in theory, but not in practice: 'This is not what the non-Muslims want, all they want is to live according to their culture, tradition and religious beliefs and not to be victimized.'

From my own observations in courts and in public interactions, there is prejudice against Southerners evident in the streets, in public transport, in housing and residential areas, in government institutions, and in the domestic realm where most house servants are southern. The marginalized people of Sudan are physically and socially isolated in most major institutions functioning in daily life in the northern cities. Southerners are concentrated in low status, low income jobs with lengthy, unregulated days of work in the informal sectors of public construction or private domestic work. While the prosecution of alcohol related offenses and appropriate dress for non-Muslim women has relaxed in the public spaces of the northern cities after the CPA, the more fundamental economic and political grievances remain. Among Northerners there is a persistent fear of southern rebellion especially after the nearly week long urban uprising they witnessed beginning on

'Black Monday,' the day after the death of John Garang was announced. The reign of the police in the IDP camps is real, but people in the camps are no longer afraid of them and subject their official overseers to private and even public ridicule. Shariʿa for these urban disaffected citizens of the Sudan has ceased to be an issue now that it is no longer directly being used to oppress them in daily life.

The 'final status' of Shariʿa and other questions or ambiguities were theoretically resolved in the new permanent Constitution. There is agreement that Shariʿa as a comprehensive civil, criminal, and personal status Islamic law will not apply to Christian, non-Muslim citizens, but it is still unclear whether animists residing in the North are likewise excluded. As might be expected, Christianity expanded among Southerners during the years of intense Islamism, however current, accurate numbers of Christians in the North are not available. This issue has been addressed by critics of the peace agreement and by human rights activists favoring clearer evidence of non-discrimination for non-Muslims living in northern cities where comprehensive Shariʿa still applies.

The most important outstanding issue that remains is how Shariʿa law will continue to be applied in metropolitan Khartoum. It is clear that there will be no comprehensive withdrawal of Shariʿa from Khartoum, while its non-applicability to non-Muslims is now secure in the Draft Constitution. Quiet withdrawal of the application of Shariʿa upon Southerners in the courts has occurred. The large number of Southerners in northern cities is unlikely to be reversed by the fragile era of peace that followed the CPA and with the positive vote for separation the status of Southerners remaining in the North is uncertain. Most who are not scheduled for return (like those in the IDP camps ringing the city) are adopting a wait and see attitude about returning to their homes in the South after war and hunger forced their migration and in anticipation of the 2011 referendum. Although this demographic shift is one of the positive factors favoring a united Sudan – as northern-southern familiarity has increased and Arabic language competence among Southerners has been voluntary rather than imposed by the government – the case for meaningful northern-southern social integration is still weak. Still old patterns of prejudice and discrimination persist and few socialize together on an equitable basis or intermarry.

Southern politicians and elites adamantly state that neither Shari'a nor the Arabic language are central issues any longer. Southern Member of Parliament, Helen Lalyec Oller, (National Assembly, Omduman) expressed a common sentiment among Southerners regarding the issue of the status of Shari'a:

> Most of the Northerners are reluctant to withdraw or compro-mise on it [the Shari'a], because most Sudanese Muslims believe the Shari'a is the best way to lead a good life and to raise their families. Only a few [northern Muslims] are willing to speak publicly against any modification of the present status of Shari'a, and they are divided among themselves [about what to do]. All that we Southerners want is that Shari'a is not applied on the non-Muslims.
>
> (Interview 7 February 2005)

Others expressed the view that Shari'a is just a symbolic issue that will fade away. One observer opined that Shari'a was used by the NIF to build their movement and now they are finished with it. Reflecting the present ambiguity, he also argued that the GoS will neither fur-ther press the issue of Shari'a, nor will they issue a formal withdrawal of Shari'a as state law, as that would be too politically controversial.

Human Rights and Islamist Shari'a

International and Sudanese human rights groups have criticized not only the imposition of Shari'a as national law in a country with a one-third non-Muslim population, but have also been sharply critical of its application of the *hadd* penalties on Muslims as well as non-Muslims. They have likewise criticized the 'Courts of Prompt Justice,' instituted during the successive waves of Islamism, for their lack of an appeal process. On balance, it is evident that during the early period of Sudan's Islamism members of the Sudan Judiciary exercised restraint in reviewing *hadd* penalties on appeal (*The Sudanese Judgments and Precedent Encyclopedia*, 1956–99, the Sudan Judiciary; Court of Appeal citation; Layish and Warburg, 2002). Statistics are extremely difficult to obtain, but the human rights cases, if correct, reflect application of the *hadd* penalties upon Sudan's most vulnerable populations, Southerners and Westerners. However, the *hadd* penalties were executed in the greatest numbers in the period 1983–85. I raised the sensitive issue of the *hadd* punishments with a broad spectrum of persons – from human rights attorneys to lawyers in private practice, to former judges, sociologists and journalists – and they all agreed that the *hadd* punishments of amputation for theft and flogging for morals charges had not been implemented in the capital city for a decade or longer, but that harassment of southern women beer brewers only began to ease after the CPA came into effect. Human rights reports point to the application of *hadd* punishments of flogging and amputation in Darfur, underscoring the possible use of these extreme punishments for political motives of suppression of an insurgent population (SHRO, Cairo Annual Report, 2003).

No sentence of the *hadd* punishment of stoning for adultery has been carried out in Sudan. Criticism from human rights groups and international pressure has helped to monitor *hadd* punishments incorrectly handed down against non-Muslims, such as in the 2002 sentence of death by stoning of a pregnant 18 year old Christian woman in Darfur, Abok Alfa Abok. She appealed the sentence; New York-based Human Rights Watch condemned the original sentence as 'cruel and inhuman,' and it was commuted to 75 lashes. Sudanese Chief Justice Ali Mohamed Osman Yassin defended the punishments of stoning and flogging, but acknowledged that in this case the implementation was incorrect. He described the punishment as 'excessive and cruel' and said that the ruling was not appropriate. 'Flogging is a humiliating punishment because it is painful and degrading' (SOAT Annual Report, 2004).

The 2004 annual report of the human rights group, Sudanese Organized Against Torture (SOAT) summarized its concerns about the application of Shari'a with the following: the lack of independence of the Sudanese Judiciary from the executive power; political appointments to the judiciary, often of unqualified judges, is still a common practice; general exclusion of women from the judicial bench, beginning in July 1989, especially the appointment of new women judges.[15] The 'Special Courts' established by Section 10 of Criminal Procedures Code 1991 continue. 'Special Courts' have no fixed rules or procedures, and it may be that unqualified politically appointed judges have incorrectly handed down *hadd* sentences.[16] After lengthy discussions with the Ministry of Justice, SOAT believes there is a political will to reform the Judiciary. Abdullahi Ibrahim's study of the Sudan Judiciary (2009) documents its history of professionalism and hints at the possibility for its eventual reform after many years of manipulation by the Islamists' agenda.

According to the CPA all human rights agreements should be a part of the new constitution. Significantly, certain citizens – women, Southerners, and marginalized persons – were excluded from the constitutional process. Implementation of Shari'a *hadd* sentences on non-Muslims continued to be reported by human rights organizations, including the well-publicized case in 2005 of a pregnant Christian woman sentenced to flogging while the implicated man was acquitted of any wrongdoing. Despite spirited debates in conferences hosted by international NGOs, no consensus was reached on the interpretation of the application of Shari'a and its prescribed *hudud* penalties, indicative of the lasting symbolic importance of the issue outside Khartoum. Although some non-Muslims converted under pressure to obtain or keep a job – for promotions, job advancement, or social services or benefits, there is no evidence of forced conversions after the CPA. However, reports continue of rewarding persons for converting to Islam in the South to promote North-south unity ahead of 2011 referendum. Street children are presumed to be Muslim regardless of their origin; teachers and the media still characterize non-Muslims as non-believers; and in the South non-Muslim women whose husbands were killed in the war have no rights to widows' benefits, while Muslim women do receive the benefits, thus, some women are reported to have converted to receive these benefits.

The US State Department issues Human Rights Reports annually. For years they have confirmed continued police abuse of their authority in the IDP camps. In 2007, they reported that victims who complained were punished, including harassment of southern women in Omdurman, one of whom was seven months pregnant, who were beaten by police after they resisted police attempts to steal money from their home. The women were taken to the Thowra police station, and were taken to court the next day, where one of the women complained about the abuse to the judge. Three police officers accused her of lying and defaming the police. The judge ruled in favor of the police, and sentenced her to 30 lashes and a $23 (SDD 5,000) fine for defamation (2007: 10). Impunity remained a serious problem, although on a few occasions during the year courts prosecuted police and other officials for abuses they had committed. Continued problems with arrest and detention, denial of fair, public trials, non-discrimination on the basis of ethnicity and gender were also mentioned in the report. Consistent with my own findings, the 2007 report indicated that no amputation had occurred in that year.

An Unsteady Road to Post-Extremist, withdrawal of Shari'a

The official language of the GoS before and after the signing of the CPA was one of mixed messages regarding withdrawal of Shari'a. President al-Bashir received a standing ovation in Nairobi in January 2005 when he ended his speech immediately following the signing of the CPA with 'La Allah – Hallejuiah,' cleverly employing both familiar Muslim (the beginning of the testament of faith in Islam) and Christian joyful invocations. However, in stark contrast, he angered many Southerners by announcing 'Khartoum as a Capital of Arab Culture' in the month before the CPA signing as part of a promised cooperation with Arab development funds.

In the months immediately following the CPA, while I was actively researching this question, the mixed messages regarding Shari'a continued, causing some uneasiness but affirming the continued symbolic importance of the issue of Shari'a. Within a month of the historic CPA, President al-Bashir was quoted in a speech in the central Sudanese town of al-Suqi that 'Islam will remain *the* main source for legislation even after the peace deal with the south.'[17] An editorial in the southern-controlled *Khartoum Monitor* opined, 'No to Islamic legislation' must be our response, cautioning that the people of the South must carefully monitor these public statements and actions (11 February 2005, p.3).

A few days later, at a rally in the northern border town of Kosti the president remarked that 'Islamic Shari'a will always exist, and it is stabilized in the peace agreement and will be included in the transitional and permanent constitutions.' However, the president also affirmed in the same speech that the 'door of participation in power is open to all political forces, but added that the capital will not be secular and no bars will be opened in Khartoum' (translation of al-Bashir speech, from Arabic daily, *Al-Sahafa*, 15 February 2005).

In one commentary, pessimism was expressed: [when] 'Islam is used as a source for legislation and Arabic language as a medium for instruction in schools throughout Sudan, Sudan's unity is surely being killed. Sudanese unity should serve as a blessing but with the North insisting on Islam as the sole source of legislation, Southerners are left with only one option … Brothers, let us go forward for separation' (M. Koma, *Khartoum Monitor*, 16 February 2005, p.12).

In 2002 Chief Justice (*Rais al-Quda*) Ali Osman Yassin was quoted: 'People try to avoid it [referring to use of the *hadd* penalties] and therefore crimes that result in flogging are curtailed. Despite the particularity of the emergency courts, I stand for a court being compatible with the imperative of justice, such as proper procedures, proofs, and rules of law.' Reflecting only partial compromise on Shari'a, Yassin added that 'criminal penalties shall be applied to Christians and Muslims alike wherever they are in place. Exemption from Islamic laws is subject to geographical basis, but a Christian living in a state where Islamic laws are observed is subject to their enforcement.' He added, 'If a displaced person wishes to come to one region of the country then he has to be ready to observe the laws in force in that region.'

Shari'a raised other issues of Sudanese identity. Leading up to the CPA, John Garang was criticized for proposing that the SPLM obtain observer status at the Arab League. Opposing views argued that the SPLM would be well-served by dialogue with member states of the Arab League who might be interested in economic as well as political relations with the Government of South Sudan and its substantial

Image 2   Sudan Judiciary exterior and Chief Justice Ali Osman Yassin, 2007, (author photo)

potential in oil and water resources. The plan to change the currency from the Sudanese *dinar* (changed during the height of the al-Bashir-al-Turabi rule) was 'associated with Arab nationalism and racism,' according to one commentator reported to be in place (Ori-Ayo, KM, 30 December 2004, p.5). The restoration the old Sudanese Pound took place in 2007.

It is significant to note that the independent pro-southern news-paper the *Khartoum Monitor* – in which many of the critical editorials cited here appeared – has been closed repeatedly by the government for its coverage of anti-governemnt demonstrations by Southerners.[18]

Withdrawal from Islamism in Regional and Global Perspective

Sudan's period of withdrawal from Islamism, makes it one of the important examples of withdrawal from extremist political Islam. 'Post-Islamism' has been analyzed from several well-known cases: 1) post-Islamists who evolve to more modest agendas for electoral pur-poses, such as Hamas in Palestine and the Refah party in Turkey; 2) post-Islamists who create a secular space by re-routing religious activism away from the state, such as mobilizing activism by Sufi orders, northern Nigeria; and 3) post-Islamists who employ reformist theology, such as Iran (Lauzière 2005: 241). It would seem that the Sudanese case is a hybrid of both the first and third examples as the NCP prepared for elections in 2010 and the official ideology of the regime, as reflected in its own pronouncement and the pragmatic *fatwas* handed down by the state-backed *'ulama* in the Magmi Fiqhi, such as those on the new marriage forms of *zawaj*, *'urfi*, and *misyar*, and the relaxation of strict adherence to Islamic banking standards.

Assessing the stage of post-Islamism, or post extremism is a vital part of the analysis of the future of Sudan – no longer as a unified state, but as two states generally at peace, or as conflict-ridden after the division into two nations. The present situation is one of heterodoxy in Islamist political thought and practice in Sudan. All current Islamist activist groups share the same objective – the creation of an Islamic state – but they evolved different strategies. There are reformist groups – the 'Islamic Movement' and 'Ansar al-Mahdi' who advocate a return to the original Muslim society and consider Shari'a as universal, subject to contemporary interpretation through *ijtihad* – and conservative groups – the 'Ansar al-Sunna,' who reject all but the strictest interpretations of the Shari'a – and there are moderate groups – the Sufis and the Republican Brothers who condemn violence and consider and advocate a gradual socialization toward an Islamic state (Osman, 2004). At the moment none critically address the role of Shari'a in the resumption of civil war in 1983, nor do they articulate a future substantive role for Shari'a in the peace and trust-building essential to the construction of the 'new Sudan.' One model is for the return to the status the Shari'a held in the pre-1983 period where it constituted *a* source of law, not *the* source for state law in the North. Shari'a in the south now operates within a secular context, utterly depoliticized and able to offer southern Muslims the family law they require without having to travel to the North for legal services.

In the light of the fragile and failing peace with the mixed progress implementing the CPA, continued inter-communal conflict in Darfur, the 2010 elections and 2011 referendum – each of which threaten national unity and the stability of the state, the following questions remain:

1) Will Sudan's Islamism survive the 2011 referendum on separation?
2) Will the separation of the South in 2011 be viewed historically as traceable to the Islamist program and its main instrument the Shari'a?
3) Will the Sudanese Judiciary, with its history of independence before 1983 remain subordinate to the state, or return to its tradtion of independence?

CHAPTER 4

THE NEW 1991 CODIFIED SHARI'A: CRIMINAL AND FAMILY LAW COURTS AND JUDGES

Introduction

Few have written in detail about the key institution of the Sudan Judiciary, its corps of professional judges and its management of the courts whose role has been the implementation of the laws of Sudan, whether colonial, post-independence, or Islamist.

The most critical works, appropriately in my view, have been written by Sudanese, for example, Abdullahi an-Na'im, Francis Deng – both trained in the law who have added human rights and diplomacy to their legal writings – Mohamed Mahmoud, Mahgoub al-Tigani Mahmoud and Abdullahi Gallab, each of whom who lived through the tumultuous years of legal change and have, as scholars in the Diaspora, reflected and commented upon the political and social transformation that has occurred in and around the legal institutional change. Added to this distinguished group is Abdullahi Ibrahim who's *Manichaean Delirium: Decolonizing the Judiciary and Islamic Renewal in Sudan, 1898–1985* offers details of the inner workings of the Judiciary and a unique critical perspective on the years of post-independence Sudan and its march toward Islamization under Numeiri and state Islamism under al-Turabi and al-Bashir. Works by various non-Sudanese have sought to create objective historical chronicles of the law, such as Layish and Warburg's work *The Reinstatement of Islamic Law in Sudan under Numeiri* (2002) that refers to the Islamist legal project – from 1983 through the al-Bashir-al-Turabi *Inqaz* regime – as a 'legal experiment.' My early work, *Islamic Law and Society in the Sudan*, combined the study of Shari'a as it was on the eve of the September Laws, with an ethnographic account of the law in practice. In this book, I reviewed briefly the history of the Sudan Judiciary. Since then two other works have added significantly to our knowledge of the Judiciary – Abdullahi Ali Ibrahim's *Manichean Delirium: Decolonizing the Judiciary and Islamic Renewal in Sudan, 1898–1985* (2008) and an insider historical appreciation by Judiciary Librarian Muhammad Ibrahim Muhammad in Arabic, *Tarikh al-Qadaiya al-Sudaniya bayn 'Ahdayn 1899–2005* (*History of the Sudan Judiciary between two eras 1899–2005* in 2005.[19]

In this brief introduction I highlight select features of these recently published works. Quoting from late scholar Abdulla al-Tayeb describing the colonial era, Mohamed sets the colonial historical background:

> It [colonialism] has succeeded in turning the Islamic Shari'a into a stranger in its own home. Shari'a was buried in 1898. The colonialists persisted in their opposition to Islam under the pretext of fighting the tyranny of the Mahdiyya to the extent that no speech from any of the successive Governors-General was free of this bias.
>
> (Mohamed, manuscript, forthcoming English translation)

Mohamed continues that Sudan's colonial administration was military and divided the country and its legal administration into fourteen provinces, with all functionaries under the English Governor-General. All districts, including the South, had a Shari'a court [strictly for the handling of family law matters only], but the administrative center was in Khartoum. This office also had oversight for the administration of mosques, their Imams, religious students, as well as Ma'azuns (recorders of marriage and divorce). 'Despite the unsuitability of this method and its inhumanity the judgments were executed. I do not rule out that the colonists wanted to offend Islam' (Mohamed, 121). The war against the Shari'a during the colonial era caused the judges to be popularly ridiculed as 'the judges of women' and 'an insult to what God glorified' – they were masters of the undermining of Islam in the guise of suppressing Mahdism. The development of the Judiciary was delayed by the priority given to the suppression of all resistance from 1906 through the White Flag anti-colonial Revolution in 1924–28. Kitchener (who conquered and pacified Sudan from 1898) militarized the criminal courts by establishing military tribunals, thus judicial power rested in the hands of Provincial Governors and District Commissioners. Adding to the colonial structure and administration of Shari'a was the fact that all Grand Kadis were Egyptian until 1947, and first Sudanese was Sheikh Ahmed al-Tahir. The six British Legal Secretaries were all knighted.[20]

Of the controversial Chief Justice Dafalla al-Haj Youseff, the President of the Judges (*Rais al-Qada*), during Numeiri's Islamization moves, Mohamed writes appreciatively, 'He issued several criminal law circulars of outstanding jurisprudence' (p.222). Abdullahi Ibrahim's work analyzes the decolonization of the Judiciary after 1956 and sees the installation of Shari'a as a corrective move to that legacy. His analysis of the Judiciary and of the Qadis' courts as 'Manichaean' pays a deep bow to Frantz Fanon, whereby a bifurcated world exists and the colonial is 'civilized' and the colonized (persons and their institutions) are 'savage.' Their dichotomous opposition and ranking is rooted in the colonial experience that sought to undermine Islamic institutions, but was fearful of eradicating them with the experience of Mahdism fresh in their minds. The Shari'a was not given a full measure of respect during colonialism and this legacy continued well into post-independence times where the Shari'a court judges were paid less, worked in inferior buildings, and were marginalized in the Judiciary. I observed this distinct legacy in my original research in 1979–80, three years before Islamization. Thus, the 'pride of turbans' that Ibrahim recounts so well was a reality, whereby the religious legal tradition was carried forward more by symbols than by real government affirmation until 1983. The Shari'a remained separate from the Civil and Criminal divisions until 1983 when the three divisions were combined into a single

comprehensive system. The nineteenth and final Grand Qadi of the
Shari'a Courts was not Sheikh Mohamed al-Gizouli, as I had reported
in my 1987 work, but Sidahmed El Awad (1980–83), last of the separate Shari'a Court system.[21] After 1983 the posts of Grand Qadi and
Mufti entered history. The reluctance of both qadis and judges to accept
the merger reveals the 'Manichaean delirium' stalking the post-colonial
state and stalling the process of decolonization. Merger was inevitable
after independence but it took decades to accomplish due to the lega-
cies of colonialism. The new Islamic alliance (identified by Ibrahim as
al-Turabi, al-Mahdi, Numeiri and al-Bashir) discovered a new source of
political legitimacy by decolonizing the law and Islamizing the state.
The Committee on Revision of Laws to Conform to Shari'a, headed by
al-Turabi in 1979 took the first steps toward the merger.

Having decolonized Shari'a, it is virtually impossible that it will
be withdrawn. But this history helps to explain why anti-imperialist
rhetoric by Islamist politicians remains so vehement and effective.
Abdullahi offers a new theory for Numeiri's September Laws and
courts of 'prompt justice.' He argues that Numeiri had run out of
political ideologies and, seized the opportunity of populist demands
for 'law and order.' I would differ having conducted research in the
Khartoum courts in the years prior to the 1983 laws; I detected neither
mass sentiment for or against the moves to Islamize the law. The first
Islamization moves in 1977 were mostly unopposed. However, the
Shari'a qadis in the Judiciary were very pleased, and viewed the trend
toward Islamization as a major opportunity ('*fursa kabira*,' as I heard
time and again). Ibrahim's treatment of the development of Sudanese
law and the Shari'a legal professionals is respectful, yet also critical of
the Islamist project that has done so much harm to the independence
of the Sudan Judiciary. After the 1989 coup, the 1991–92 Codification
of Shari'a Act (*Iftaa Shari'a*) was chaired by Sheikh Siddiq Abdel Hai.
A New Constitutional Court was established on 24 November 1998,
making the Judiciary no longer competent to interpret the constitution and law. Since the 1992 '*Inqaz* Revolution' the number of courts
expanded including the following numbers to date, 2004: 61 General
Courts; 154 Family Courts; 170 Civil Courts; 192 Criminal Courts;
122 Special and Municipal Courts; and 898 Town and Rural Courts.

After 2001 the judicial organization in every region consisted of:
1) Court of Appeal; 2) Provincial Judges court; and 3) District court.
The following represents the national structure of the judicial system:
1) The Supreme Court; 2) District Civil/Criminal /Family Law/Labor
Courts; 3) The Constitutional Court; 4) Military/Security Courts; 5)
Customary Courts; and 6) Magmi' Fiqi (the newest addition in 2000,
outlined and discussed in this chapter).

The 1991 New Codified Shari'a

Criminal, Civil and Family Law, Selected
Summaries and Commentaries

The new comprehensive Shari'a Code of Law, with 458 sections, may
be seen as totally innovative, although it retains much of colonial law,
the Indian Penal Code adapted to Sudan in colonial times, and the
evolved family law until 1990. Justice Ahmed Dirar, whom I met in
Shendi, spoke of Sudanese law after 1991 as 'Anglo-Islamic law.' The
function of the Commission drafting the 1991 law was to consolidate
the totality of Sudanese law into a single code. However, the process
also served to institutionalize, through codification, Islamic concepts,
legal principles, and remedies and punishments that were previously
scattered in Judicial Circulars, presidential decrees, and miscellaneous
legislation. Some new subjects, such as criminalizing terrorism, were
specified, and some customary practices were elevated to codified law,
such as *diya* (compensation) payments. Codification profoundly signaled that Shari'a is *the* law of the land, not to be meddled with again,
and the centerpiece of the Islamist agenda of *Inqaz*.

In order to avoid a dry legal discussion of the codified law, I will
discuss the applications of these laws using either case material that
I personally collected, or data that is derived from current Sudanese
social scientific studies, or from the Bureau of Statistics and the Sudan
Judiciary cases and discussions of current legal practice. Given the
political isolation Sudan experienced after 1989, this is the first summary for an English language audience that combines details of the
recent law with current research and observations.

The Criminal Act, 1991[22]

The criminal law contains 188 sections that depend upon Shari'a exclusively as the main source of law. Entirely new are laws criminalizing *irhab* (terrorism) and, for the first time, attacks on personal freedom were introduced. Otherwise the criminal law retains definitions and categories of crimes already contained in the Penal codes of 1923 (under British rule) and 1983, the September Laws. The existing wording on *attempt* (to commit a criminal act), *abetment,* and *the right of personal defense* were retained because they were consistent with Islamic jurisprudence (el-Bushra, 1998: 18). However, specific Shari'a punishments of *hudud* (to the limit), *qisas* (equal retribution), and *ta'azir* (imprisonment, fine, whipping and detention) were instituted in Sudanese law for the first time after they were introduced in the September Laws. The southern states were exempted from laws regarding alcohol consumption, apostasy, highway robbery, *qadhf* (false accusation of fornication), *zina* (adultery) and *qisas,* retribution (Badri, 2003). While the southern states were exempted from these penalties, Southerners residing in the North were not until the CPA in 2005.

The most serious crimes for which these Islamic punishments were established in the new law were as follows:

1) Theft – equivalent to or more than 4.25g of gold – is punishable by cutting of the right hand (Section 171), or cutting off a hand and a foot alternately (Section 168);

2) Highway robbery *(hiraba)* is punishable by death, death by crucifixion, or cutting off a hand and a foot, or with imprisonment and expatriation (Section 168);

3) Adultery is punishable with death by stoning, if the offender is married. If unmarried, the punishment is 100 lashes (Section 146);

4) Drinking alcohol, if a Muslim, is punishable by 40 lashes (Section 78);

5) Offenses against the human body, murder and assault causing physical injury are punishable with qisas or by its alternatives, *diya* and forgiveness. It is the personal choice of the victim to forgive or to accept the *diya,* in whole or part; otherwise the qisas punishment is to be applied; and

6) Offenses for which *hudud* or *qisas* are not prescribed are punishable by *ta'azir* – imprisonment, fine, whipping and detention in reformatories – and are subject to great discretionary power by judges.

Islamic law embodies the same recognition of the rights of the accused as in other major legal systems in the world including the presumption of innocence, the right to freedom from arbitrary arrest, detention or torture, the right to a public trial, the right to counsel, and not to be compelled to testify against oneself, as well as the right of appeal (El-Bushra, 1998: 21). As with all legal systems, their justice and efficacy rests with the application of the laws, not with legal theory or laws on the books.

The severity of the Shari'a punishments attracts the greatest attention in the West, and rightly so when they are used for repression, abuse, or discrimination against individuals or groups. Whether they are violations of emerging standards of global human rights is a significant dialogue for jurists, human rights professionals and citizens to have. However, what is overlooked by western critics of Shari'a is the strong measure of fair compensation for loss, forgiveness, and the explicit and powerful rights of the victims to have the final say in the punishment or resolution of a case where they or their family suffered disability, death, or loss of property. The use of *diya* and *qisas*, emphasizing equal debt, punishment equal to the offense, or compensation for the loss suffered is a salutary part of Islamic criminal law that has no real parallel in any western legal system. Only in recent decades have the rights of victims been asserted in the US, primarily through advocacy by victims' groups themselves, and very little of this movement's proposals have found their way into legislation.

The age of criminal responsibility is set at the time of puberty. A mature person of free will is criminally responsible, but a child who has not attained puberty is not. In 2007 the Constitutional Court determined the conditions for the onset of puberty agreeing that this is not fixed by age, but by the appearance of the secondary sexual characteristics of the youth.[23] A Judicial Circular following the September Laws made the initial Islamic legal definition of the age of criminal responsibility to be established by natural features or onset of menstruation in females; and if there is a question regarding these, then the age of the person is next considered according to both the Maliki and Hanafi schools that Sudan has followed. The age of 18 years is the age of majority if natural features have not appeared (Circular Number 106, 1984).[24] The correctional measures for juveniles (between 7–18 years of age) include reprimand, whipping, handing over to parental or guardian, or detention in a reformatory.

There is no responsibility unless a criminal act is done with intent, or by negligence (8.2). Mental infirmity, insanity or involuntary intoxication all remove criminal responsibility (10), as does a criminal act in the performance of duty (11). *Darura*, necessity, absolves a person of criminal responsibility if a person is compelled to commit an offense to protect his person, honor, or property, provided that necessity does not justify the death (15). A major difference with western criminal law is the protection of personal honor mitigating criminal responsibility. Juvenile offenders are defined as between 7 and 18 years of age. The juvenile accused of a criminal act may be punished by reprimand in court in the presence of the youth's guardian, by whipping (not to exceed 20 lashes, 'by way of discipline'), by handing the juvenile over to the father or another trustworthy person, or placing the juvenile under social supervision for not less than one year and not more than 2 years, or, finally, sending the youth to be detained for reformation in social welfare institution for a term not less than 2 years and not more than 5 years (47). It is noteworthy that elderly offenders are similarly treated. Without prejudice to the implementation of the *hudud* penalties and the provisions of *qisas*, the court may order the following for an offender over the age of 70 years: handing the elderly offender over to a relative or trustworthy person, expatriation for a term not exceeding the prescribed period of imprisonment, consigning him to a reformatory or social welfare institution for a period not exceeding 2 years (48).

Retribution (qisas)

Qisas is literally the 'eye for an eye' retributive concept traceable to the Hammurabi code. This is the ancient *lex talionis*, punishment by the same offensive act committed. The right to retribution is given first to the victim and then to the relatives; if the offense is murder, *qisas* is death by hanging, if the court sees fit in the same manner in which the death was caused; in case of wounds, according to the code's Schedule, 'Parts and Wounds subject to Retribution.'

Retribution for wounds is subject to the conditions of similarity of the affected body part or organ. The penalty of *qisas* is carried out without causing the death of the offender, or exceeding the injury caused (29). The relatives of the victim(s) are entitled to retribution, and these follow those specified as the Qur'anic heirs. They have the right to claim *diya* from the offender which in turn may reduce the penalty.

Reconciliation or Pardon (diya)

The custom of the payment of *diya* (sometimes translated as 'reconciliation or pardon,' or 'blood money' in older Orientalist jargon), for disability, loss of limb, as well as for loss of life, was utilized frequently by the British in cases of unpremeditated and accidental homicide (cf. Fluehr-Lobban, 1972; 1976). It is currently widely used by the US government in Iraq and Afghanistan to pay compensation for losses suffered by civilians in these wartime situations. In the rural areas where customary law supersedes any national law, *diya* prevails as the key to resolving conflicts from property to personal offenses, and it is central to the prevention of more serious long-term feuds or simmering, unresolved conflicts.

Diya is based on the use of compensation/restitution through payment and it works exceptionally well in quelling conflict and reducing the chance of further conflict. *Diya* can be paid not only for death, but also for disability to the face, the senses, the limbs, the sexual organs of a man (The Criminal Act 1991, 'Parts and Wounds subject to Retribution'). Defined as 100 camels in the Qur'anic passage or its equivalent in money as determined by the chief justice, *diya* multiplies by the number of victims not the number of offenders. It is paid by each offender according to his participation in the offense, and no other compensation for homicide besides *diya* shall be executed. In the case of homicide and wounds caused by negligence, the amount of the *diya* should be decreased proportionately to the offender's participation in the harm (42.1-5).

Diya is due originally to the victim and then passes to his heirs according to their shares in inheritance; where the victim has no heirs, the *diya* is awarded to the state (44). *Diya* is to be collected from the offender, and then from his clan/lineage (*aqila*) in offenses of negligent homicide [as in the past with British]; the *aqila* include the paternal relatives, his insurer or persons jointly liable, or his employer of the offense is committed during the course of employment. *Diya* for murder or intentional wounds is due immediately, and may be postponed or paid in installments with the consent of the victims or the relatives, but the responsible person must produce the necessary guarantee the payment if requested (45.1-5). *Diya* may be ordered by the court as restitution from the property of the accused to be paid to the victim or his relatives, according to the provisions of the Civil Transactions and Procedures Act (46).

Death Penalty

The death penalty is by hanging or stoning, *ta'azir* (specified penalty by judge); it may be accompanied by crucifixion for armed robbery, and may not be executed on anyone younger than 18 years or over 70 years of age (27.1.2.3).

The death penalty may be withdrawn if the family of the victim pardons the murderer and revised to a sentence of not more than 10 years. This occurred in the case of the slain American USAID worker John Granville who was murdered with his Sudanese driver in the early morning of New Year's Day 2008. Four men were convicted and sentenced to death for the two murders, however the family of the murdered Sudanese pardoned the guilty men and all of the death sentences were commuted (AP news report, 18 August 2009).

According to an Amnesty International Report (BBC News, 27 April 2007), globally 90 per cent of all death penalty sentences are carried out in six countries: Iran, Iraq, Pakistan, China, Sudan and the US. Often jurists with whom I have spoken in Sudan bring up this fact and justify application of the death penalty using similar religious and social arguments for its retention owing to its deterrent value and religious sanctioning.

Hadd/Hudud *Penalties*

These are often applied to the most vulnerable. The *hadd* penalties are flogging, amputation, cross-amputation, death by crucifixion, hanging, or stoning as specified in the Criminal code of 1991 for immorality, theft, highway robbery, adultery, and prostitution. Documenting these penalties is a sensitive topic of discussion with many in the judicial system, but one that human rights activists are keen to discuss. The *hadd* penalties are quickly defended by the judges with whom I have spoken, with the proviso that they are to be properly applied, which is to say, with restraint. Warburg and Layish (2002) indicate that there was, indeed, a measure of judicial restraint the 'legal experiment' of the reinstatement of Islamic law in 1983. They note the analysis of one of the early European scholars of Shari'a, Joseph Schact, who concluded: 'There is a strong tendency to restrict the applicability of *hadd* punishments as much as possible ... narrow definitions of the crimes, short statutes of limitation, and extremely high evidentiary requirements ensured that those punishments would be executed only in exceptional cases' (Bielefelt, 1995: 13).While there are a few cases that were heard before the High Court[25] and are on the public record (2003, *The Sudanese Judgements and Precedents Encyclopedia,* Khartoum), obtaining reliable statistics for the execution of *hadd* penalties in Sudan proved to be difficult.

According to one human rights activist and writer on the subject Mohamed Mahmoud, the greatest number of amputations – perhaps 200 or more occurred in 1984–85 while the Numeiri regime was a US ally and little protest was heard from the West.

Nearly all with whom I have discussed the issue of *hudud* – jurists, lawyers, professors, human rights activists and ordinary citizens – say that the *hadd* penalties are no longer applied in Khartoum, and have not been since the 'days of Numeiri.' Nonetheless, there were occasional reports in the Sudanese media that a case of *hadd* sentencing was

Image 3   Association of Amputees, 1985 (photo courtesy of Mohamed Mahmoud)

withdrawn as a result of the formulaic triple denial by the defendant that he did not commit offense which the judge accepted, in one case while in the hospital awaiting the surgical amputation of a hand for theft.

Human rights organizations documented the application of the *hudud* in December 2001 of at least six men in northern and southern Darfur who were sentenced to 'limb amputations for robbery and possession of weapons' (2002). Human Rights Watch expressed concern about Sudan's continued use of 'emergency courts' where the amputation sentences are issued, as such courts restrict legal representation and appeals and consist of one civil judge and two military ones. Legal representation of defendants is not allowed and only one week is permitted for appeal to the District Chief Justice. These courts were reported to have begun in May 2001. On 27 December 2001, Adam Ibrahim Osman and Abd Allaha Ismail Ibrahim from Um Kadada were sentenced to cross amputation convicting them of banditry (*hiraba*) and possession of unlicensed weapons. This report suggests that the *hudud* were resumed or intensified in Darfur as a tool of government repression, in this case of men in possession of arms in the lead up to the outbreak of conflict in Darfur in the following year, 2003. It is the view of HRW veteran activist, Jemera Rone, that the effects of limb amputation are amplified as it mutilates the convicted person and disables them for future gainful employment. Human Rights Watch described the *hadd* punishments as 'barbaric,' as did the United States Manual on Counterinsurgency (2006) which also condemned the 'emergency courts.' The Sudan Human Rights Organization-Cairo (UA 7/02) and Amnesty International consider the *hadd* punishments of amputation and stoning to be cruel, inhuman and degrading and violations of the Convention Against Torture (CAT) that Sudan has signed.[26] The Sudan Human Rights Organization-Cairo criticized the Sudan Penal Law of 1991 as endorsing and not revising the provisions in the September Laws of 1983 concerning harsh physical punishment. Moreover both the penal code and the criminal procedure enjoined as Sudan Criminal Law, taken together, constitute 'gross violations to international human rights norms.' The law, equally important, contradicted significant aspects of modern Islamic jurisprudence on principles of justice that could have been adequately consulted to establish a common understanding with international human rights norms. Physical punishments such as crucifixion, stoning, and cutting of limbs have been frequently used for crimes for which alternative non-physical treatment could have been legally and appropriately applied in accordance with the modern jurisprudence' (SHRO-Cairo Memorandum to the Human Rights Commission, 2001).

Women and the Hudud Penalties

With emphasis on public morality, the long shadow of the *hadd* penalties was cast not only on the poor and vulnerable, but on all women as the repositories of a chaste and proper Islamic society. Propriety in public, averted eyes in the presence of men, proper length of skirts and long sleeved blouses, covering of not just the head (as with the traditional *tobe*), but the hair and ears as well, and avoiding any cosmetic or perfume that might attract the attention of men who are not relations all have been used in determining whether or not a woman is violating 'public morality.' Women unwilling or rebelling against the new conservative conventions, dubbed *Shari'* (lawful in Islam) would be harassed at a minimum, or could be subjected to arrest and prosecution for violating the new criminal law, (sections 145–160, 'Offenses of Honor, Reputation and Public Morality').

Adultery (*zina*) is defined as a man and woman who have sexual intercourse with one another without a lawful bond between them, through penetration (145.1.2.3). Whoever commits adultery shall be punished with execution by stoning if the offender is married (*muhsan*) or with 100 lashes if the offender is not married (*ghayr-muhsan*) (146, a.b.). True to the near universal double standard regarding criminalization of sexual offenses, the male non-married offender is punished with whipping, and also with expatriation (exile) for one year (146.2). Being *muhsan* means having a valid, persisting marriage that has been consummated (146.3). Under this law adultery in the southern States was punished by one year imprisonment and/or fine, and where the offender is *muhsan*, with prison not to exceed 3 years and with a fine, or both (146.4). The southern-married male adulterer was not subject to criminal penalty. Significantly, remittance of the penalty of adultery may be permitted, and indeed no sentence of stoning or execution for adultery of a convicted woman was ever carried out in Sudan, although a number of sentences were handed down. The well-known case of Abok Alfa Akok, who in 2002 was accused of adultery and sentenced to stoning, took place the in Criminal Court of Nyala, southern Darfur, although she is Dinka and Christian. Like every other sentence of stoning in Sudan, it was never executed. Less well known internationally were the cases of Amural Abdalla (23 years old) and Sa'adia Fadul (22 years old) who were both sentenced to death by stoning for adultery in Al-Azazi Criminal court, Manajil Province, al-Jazirah state. Both were from the Tama people of Darfur and were held in Wad Madani prison, one with a 2 year old daughter. There were no further reports that the sentences were carried out.

Prosecution of women for not wearing proper *hijab* was common throughout the decade of the 1990s, but eased after 1999–2000 coincidently, or not, with the beginning of the flow of oil and the political isolation of Hasan al-Turabi. One example of the extreme and generally non-Sudanese nature of the origin of these laws (many argue their inspiration was linked to Saudi Wahhabist influence in Sudan at the highest levels) was the prosecution of what was described as 'excessive' henna dying. Anyone familiar with Sudanese feminine culture is aware of the cosmetic and status-bearing importance of henna. It is first applied in association with a girl's circumcision, is strongly associated with wedding rituals and childbirth, and signifies the status of being a married woman when displayed on the hands and feet of a woman wearing a *tobe*, it is the very symbol of respectability. Through simplistic and culturally irrelevant arguments – in this case that henna poisons the body through the skin – the Islamist program instilled fear but eventually lost credibility on this point among a majority of Muslims, except for hard core NIF activists.

The *hadd al-zina*, stoning for adultery, was privately opposed by many citizens and several women judges on the High Court who noted that the problem for women is that her very pregnancy, under whatever circumstances, is proof of the crime, therefore the law in inherently discriminatory.

Flogging (*jald*) is still practiced and is the most persistently used *hadd* punishment. Today when it is carried out in a semi-public environment, it is in the Shari'a courtyards, thus limiting its general past justification as a deterrent. However, *jald* may be less applied as an outcome of a court case and more dispensed as paralegal 'justice,' carried out by the police in local stations where the poor are concentrated, in the IDP camps primarily for alcohol offense, and, perhaps most alarming, in hospitals where flogging of women who have born children out of wedlock is mandated if/when such births come to the attention of the authorities. Any childbirth in a hospital where there is no father's name to put on the birth certificate must be reported to the police who will enforce the sanction of 100 lashes for an unmarried woman. A married woman can still be sentenced to death by stoning, although, as mentioned, no sentence has been carried out in Sudan. British journalist Wendy Wallace reported to me that a woman who came to Maygoma orphanage (where she was doing a report in 2006) who wanted to reclaim her baby three weeks after the birth had to be lashed 100 times before she was able to take the child. The World Organization against Torture, OMCT, unreservedly condemns corporal punishment which violates international human rights standards, and it reminded Sudan that it is a signatory to the Convention on the

Elimination of All Forms of Discrimination Against Women, which cites 'cruel, inhuman and degrading punishment'[27].

Women tea sellers and *merissa* (local beer) brewers are the most harassed for their occupation of public space and for their connection to public drunkenness of men. It is well-documented that the Shari'a criminal law regarding alcohol brewing, sale, and consumption is prosecuted on a daily basis in the camps. I have personal testimony from long-time residents of the IDP camps around Khartoum that this persecution is carried out mainly by the camp police, Northerners who use the law allegedly as a means of intimidation and control of the potentially insurgent, angry residents. Camp residents complain bitterly about their being subject to Islamic laws when they are not only non-Muslims, but have been deprived of any other means of earning a living while forced by conditions of war and displacement to live in the North, albeit in segregated and sub-standard living conditions.

Women in the Sudanese prison system are mainly there for beer brewing. Before my research and the relaxation of the enforcement of public morality early in the new millennium, a law was drafted that compelled the lady tea sellers to wear socks so that their bare legs not be seen as they prepare their beverages in the informal markets of the city streets, and that they needed to have a box in front of their legs so that nothing forbidden (*haram*) could be seen. By the time of my research – 2004–08 – this was not in effect. On 6 August 2007, about 1,000 southern women and children detained for brewing alcohol were released (British Embassy, Khartoum Press Summary, *al-Sahafa*, 6 August 2007).

A flogging sentence cannot be passed upon a person over 60 years, or a sick person, or on one whose life would be endangered or a sickness exacerbated by the punishment (35.1). In such cases an alternative punishment may be directed if whipping penalty is remitted for any reason (35.2);

The Sudanese Organization against Torture (SOAT) reported that between 12–20 November 2002, 17 women near to Nyala, Darfur were convicted of adultery and sentenced to 100 lashes each. Proof was based solely on facts that all of the women were unmarried but had children between the ages of 6–12 months. Women were tried in Courts of

Prompt Justice, *al-Mahkama al-Ijaziya*, in summary trials under article 146 of the Sudan Penal Code as punishment for being unmarried fornicators. None of the women had legal representation and the punishments were carried out on the same day. According to the law no men were punished in conjunction with these acts; the 17 women were between the ages of 18 to 22, only five of whom were aged 18, the minimum age of criminal prosecution. There appears to be a pattern of the selective application of the criminal *hudud* in Darfur, especially as it entered its insurgency against the government, one of the important political functions of the law. As a result of international protest a special investigation was order by the GoS, including High Court judge Mohamad Ali al-Khalifa and a woman judge Sirhan Sameer.

Women and the Criminal Law

Abortion is criminalized for the 'quick unborn child' (from the time of quickening or the time when a woman 'feels' the baby in the womb) unless the abortion is carried out to save the woman's life. Abortion is permissible when the pregnancy results from rape not more than 3 months previously, and the woman desires the abortion, or where it is proved that the 'quick unborn child' has died in the mother's womb. If convicted of impermissible abortion, the penalty is no more than 3 years, a fine, or both with right to *diya*. For abortion after 90 days, the penalty is five years imprisonment, a fine, or both. Acts leading to abortion, or causing the death of a 'quickened' ['living' fetus, the time when a mother feels life in the womb] unborn child is criminalized with prison sentence of two years and/or a fine (136; 137).

The offense of rape is deemed to take place whenever sexual intercourse by way of adultery or homosexuality is committed without consent (not including the rape of the virgin). Consent shall not be recognized where the offender has custody or authority over the victim. The punishment for rape is 100 lashes, and imprisonment not to exceed 10 years, unless the rape constitutes the offense of adultery or homosexuality, then it is punishable by death (149.1.2.3.).

False accusation of un-chastity (157), *qadhf*, is committed when the false accusation of un-chastity, whether expressed or by implication, or in writing or clear signal, imputes adultery or homosexuality, or negation of lineage (illegitimacy) to a chaste person, even if the person is dead (157.1). A person is deemed to be chaste if she/he has not been convicted of adultery or homosexuality, rape or incest, or practicing prostitution. Whoever makes a false accusation of un-chastity shall be punished by 80 lashes (157.2.3.). Recent statistics reported by an Ahfad University study of the impact of the 1991 law upon women shows the relatively large number of convictions of persons convicted of 'false accusation' (*qadhf*) of *zina*, adultery with 14 persons in Kober prison for this offense in 2003 (in *Mashru' Muqtarah li Ta'dil ba'd Mu'ad Qanun al-Ahwal al-Shakhsiya*, 'Contesting Project Proposals after a period of the Personal Status Law,' edited by Balghis Badri, Ahfad University Center for Gender and Development, 2004). The penalty for false accusation is remitted when there is a pardon by the defamed person before the execution, or when there is equal exchange of defamatory statements, by *li'an* between the spouses. When remitted, the offender shall be punished by the penalty for the lesser offence of defamation (158.1.2.).

In an analysis of the impact on women of the 1991 Criminal Law, Balghis Badri argues that the legal and social orders are not one and the same, and that Sudanese society is mixed with African values thus calling for a more nuanced view of the law. From her studies of women and the law, the abuse most experienced by women include sexual harassment while homicide, robbery, assault as the most common offences against them (2004: 27).

Hudud *in other Muslim Countries*

While the *hadd* punishments are strongly associated with extremist, Islamist regimes, they are not exclusively applied in these contexts. The Kingdom of Saudi Arabia (KSA) is a major case in point. The Geneva-based UN Committee Against Torture has criticized KSA over the amputations and floggings it carries out under Shari'a law. KSA rejected the criticism saying that the Shari'a forbids torture, and that the practice of *hudud* dates back 1400 years. Likewise non-Muslims are not exempt, and expatriates have been convicted and sentenced to lashing for alcohol-related offenses.

Lashing for morals offenses is practiced in United Arab Emirates where it has been applied against prostitutes and brothel owners. Comparable punishment is meted out in Pakistan and in Saudi Arabia for the same offense where the courts are also summary, 'prompt' courts. Iran regularly sentences men and women to flogging, as well as fines, for consumption of alcohol, especially at mixed gatherings. The youths are charged with 'illegitimate relations, promoting corruption and drinking alcohol.' The Dubai Shari'a court in 2002 sentenced an Indian man and an Indonesian woman to two months in prison, and to be lashed 60 times, but the sentence was dropped when they agreed to marry. However, the Federal National Council of Dubai has proposed amending 33 articles in the criminal code, moderating current punishments. Article 85 modifies flogging and sentences of more than two months for morals offenses to ones that can be suspended or revoked at the recommendation of the prosecutor. Sentences of lashing may not exceed 200. They lifted the death penalty except in cases of premeditated homicide.

A 19 year old woman in Lagos who brought her fiancé before a Shari'a court over an unwanted pregnancy, and was sentenced to 100 lashes with the sentence to be carried out four months after the delivery of the child. This latter case drew attention from international human rights groups for its perceived sexual discrimination and the innocence of the young woman who was seeking relief from the court for a pregnancy that was perhaps not consensual. Likewise the case of Amina Lawal attracted world attention for the sentence of stoning handed down upon her in a case of alleged *zina*. This case is discussed in depth in chapter 7.

In Sudan, repeated homosexuality is punishable by life imprisonment, or death. Prior to 2010, I know of no case where homosexuality was prosecuted; however, in August 2010 a transvestite party, mainly composed of men dressed as women dancing together, was raided in Khartoum and all present were arrested. Presumably prosecution for the criminal offense of homosexuality would be pursued. Until this time, unlike its neighbor Egypt, there had been no special crackdown on homosexuality in the capital city, or elsewhere. Homosexuality is legally defined as a man penetrating the anus of a woman or a man, or permitting another man to penetrate his anus or glans (148.1.). *Whoever commits the offense of homosexuality shall be punished with 100 lashes and he may be punished with imprisonment for term not exceeding 5 years; the second offense carries the same punishment. The third offense carries a penalty of death or life imprisonment* (148.2.a.b.c.). Prosecution of homosexuality is not mentioned in the criminal statistics I gathered for 2005 for the country, nor is it mentioned in the social science studies of the applied criminal law that I consulted (see statistics below).

By 1991, the intense period of the application of the severest of the *hudud* penalties in the capital city had ended and the subsequent decades shows their selective use for persecution or harassment of minority and vulnerable populations, southern women and men and Darfuris. Judicial Circular No. 2/1991 allowed for the retroactive withdrawal of the enforcement of *hadd* penalties. The Circular clarified Section 4 of the Criminal Code that delay in the execution of *hadd* penalty implies doubt on the verdict which may be considered as a withdrawal from the penalty. The Circular thus directed all courts not to execute any *hadd* penalty on cases tried before the issuing of this law even if these sentences are final. Courts should revise all *hadd* cases and *ta'azir* penalty should be enforced instead. What remains of the *hudud* are the lesser sentences that have targeted the poor and vulnerable women. The targeted women were the public tea sellers, but this has been withdrawn in the last few years, and now they must pay a monthly license fee.

Offenses Causing Public Nuisance: Alcohol and Gambling

According to the 1991 Criminal Code, public sale and consumption of alcohol is specified. 'Public nuisance' may provide a justification that some Muslims use who continue to drink despite the repeated crackdowns. It is an open secret in Khartoum that the local brews of *'aragi* (fermented from dates) and *merissa* (millet beer) continued to flow from the initial ban on alcohol in the late 1970s, through the September Laws, and after the 1991 Criminal Code. Prosecution, however, is another matter and the brunt of the laws was felt by southern women as brewers and southern men who were open consumers (justifying their right to consume alcohol as non-Muslims), but prosecution of northern Muslim men was never more than symbolic. The law reads:

> A Muslim who drinks, possesses, or manufactures alcohol shall be punished with whipping of 40 lashes (78.1); whoever drinks alcohol and provokes the feelings of others or causes annoyance or nuisance, or drinks in a public place or comes to that place in a state of drunkenness shall be punished with imprisonment not exceeding one month and whipping not exceeding 40 lashes, or a fine (78.2). [southern provision] Whoever deals in alcohol by storing, sale, purchase, or transport … shall be punished with imprisonment not more than one year, or a fine. In all cases the alcohol in question shall be destroyed (79).

Likewise gambling was not eliminated despite its criminalization (80.1.2) with sanctions of prison for running a gambling house that include fines and lashing (limited to 25). Gambling includes the drawing of lottery and any other game of luck. A highly popular form of online gambling known as 'BusiNas,' 'Gold Quest' and later 'Quest Net,' originating in Malaysia, were questioned and critiqued by the Islamic Jurisprudence Council. *Whoever gambles, or runs a game or a house for gambling will be punished with imprisonmnt of no more than one year, or fine, or whipping not exceeding 25 lashes.* The question before the religious scholars was whether these hugely popular pyramid-like games were in effect a 'gambling house' and whether it is *halal* (lawful), *makruh* (questionable), or *haram* (forbidden). Estimates of 10,000 or more members in Khartoum – university students, professionals such as engineers, physicians and members of the military – register by paying the equivalent of $600, and begin to get returns on their 'investment' after members convince two other persons to join, and they recruit two more members, and so on. This religious debate ended with a *fatwa* issued by the Magmi Fiqhi against these forms of online speculation as, indeed, forms of gambling. According to my research assistant and university student, Salma Mohamed Abdalmunim, the most interesting thing about these schemes is that their participants do not really care whether their behavior is *halal* or *haram* so long as they are profiting from their participation.

Offenses Relating to Religions

In Section 125, an insult to religion can be punished by one year imprisonment, and/or fine, and/or whipping of up to 40 lashes. In my 1976 study of over 400 cases of homicide in Sudan, among Muslim men an insult to religion as part of a physical altercation was often the precipitating event to a homicide (Fluehr-Lobban, 1976).

Apostasy (*ridda*) is a crime by which a Muslim who renounces Islam, or publicly declares this renunciation by an express statement or conclusive act. Whoever commits apostasy shall be given a chance to repent during a period determined by the court, where if he continues to assert the apostasy, and is not a recent convert to Islam, he shall be punished with death. The penalty for apostasy shall be remitted whenever the apostate recants before execution (126.1.2.3). (It is noteworthy that executed Republican Brother leader, Mahmoud Taha made no public pronouncement of apostasy, but was declared an apostate by the Shari'a court.)

Offenses Against the State are detailed in sections 50–57 and what is notable for the post-CPA period is Section 50, 'Undermining the Constitutional System,' in which anyone undermining the constitution or endangering the unity and independence of the country will be subject to the death penalty, life imprisonment, or confiscation of property.

Offenses relating to Public Tranquility criminalizes much of what is known as freedom of assembly. The offense of 'rioting' is committed by any assembly of five persons or more using force, terrorism or violence, or one of the following: resisting the execution of a law or legal process; criminal trespass; exercise of an alleged right likely to lead to disturbance of public peace (67.a.b.c.). The penalty for rioting is imprisonment not exceeding six months or a fine, or whipping not to exceed 20 lashes (68). This punishment was meted out to southern protesters who 'rioted' after John Garang's death was announced in July 2005 and urban uprisings lasting nearly a week took place all over the greater Khartoum area and in the IDP camps. Beginning on 'Black Monday,' the uprising fundamentally challenged the existing order by which Southerners live in the North. Demonstrators in Sudan during 2011 when the region was undergoing revolutionary change were likely prosecuted with the same law. The penalty for disturbing the peace is three months, or a fine, or 20 lashes and is also meted out often for alcohol related offenses (69).

The penalties for theft (al-saraqa) were mainly applied during Numeiri's time, a fact reiterated to me by many lawyers, judges, and human rights activists with whom I spoke. Hiraba (highway robbery for which the hadd penalty is death) is still present in Darfur, where it is likely used for political repression as much as criminal justice.

Offenses Against Property

Armed Robbery (hiraba) [muharrib, trafficker]: whoever intimidates the public or hinders users of the highways with the intention of committing an offense against the body, honor, or property. Hiraba is punished with death, or death and then crucifixion, if the act of robbery results in murder or rape. Amputation of the right hand and left foot is applied if his act results in grievous hurt or robbery of property equal to the minimum (nisab, the right proportion) for capital theft. In all other instances, the punishment is imprisonment not exceeding seven years.

Whoever commits armed robbery in the southern States shall be punished with death, if his act results in causing death, or life imprisonment, if his act results in the commission of rape, or imprisonment for a term not exceeding 10 years if the robbery results in grievous harm imprisonment for term not exceeding seven years. Penalties for armed robbery can be remitted if the offender declared his repentance before his arrest, however remittance does not affect diya (which is also customary in the South), or compensation and return of property if remitted. The penalty for capital theft (public property, property associated with waqf (Islamic bequests for public benefit), or guarded property in its hirz, fortified place), is amputation of the right hand from the joint.

Mitigation of the hadd penalty of amputation is permitted if the offender is a close relative of the victims and if the crime of theft is deemed not to be a result of necessity (whether personal need, or that of his dependants), or if the alleged thief makes resitituion before trial or declares his repentance, or where amputation endangers the life of the offender (172).

Theft: whoever dishonestly takes any moveable property from a person without his consent will be subject to imprisonment not more than seven years or whipping not exceeding 100 lashes (174.1.2). Extortion, Criminal breach of trust, cheating, falsifying checks, criminal misappropriation, receiving stolen property, criminal mischief, criminal trespass, lurking with criminal intent, manufacturing an instrument for a criminal purpose are all subject to fines and imprisonment, but not lashing. Where the penalty for capital theft has been remitted the offender may be punished with imprisonment not exceeding 7 years, or a fine, or both, or whipping not exceeding 100 lashes (173).

The following table enumerates the official statistics for all crimes in the Sudan, for all states. The total gross number of crimes reported in 2003–05 of 641,134 can be used to compute a very rough rate of criminal activity assuming a population base, conservatively at 35 million for this time period. Thus, a crude figure of one crime per 62 citizens can be calculated, with the understanding that multiple variables of enforcement, recording, rural-urban differences and a myriad others, affect the value of any such estimate.

Clearly across the country crimes against property exceed crimes against the body, although the disparity is less in the peripheral states of Sudan's vast margins, such as in the eastern states, and certain western states, as well as in the South. The urbanized states, such as Khartoum, have almost double the number of property crimes to those against the person likely reflecting the growth in wealth disparity and class differentiation that generally are association with theft.

Criminal cases involving drugs and illegal substances, referred to as 'brain affecting materials' were also reported for the country as a whole at totals for 2005 of 2,589; for 2004, 2,720; and for 2003, 2,602. Predictable, almost half of these totals were in Khartoum (respectively 826 for 2005; 828 for 2004; and 1000 for 2003). In El Gezira the totals were: 279 for 2005; 214 for 2004; and 201 for 2003, (CBS, pp.322–23).

The statistics for crimes in Central Omdurman and Bahari (Khartoum North) are among the first to analyze the effects of the

Table 4.1   Total Crimes Reported and Registered for all States
2003–05

State	2005	2004	2003
Khartoum	174,658	174,750	277,593
Northern	13,612	12,068	13,702
Nahr elNil	15,201	14,763	23,731
El Gezira	52,076	57,800	40,950
Blue Nile	14,590	12,749	11,291
White Nile	29,201	25,351	35,567
Red Sea	26,507	23,191	26,326
Kassala	20,182	17,889	20,182
El Gedarif	18,022	21,078	24,152
Sinnar	20,200	21,875	24,152
North Kordofan	23,886	23,368	22,717
South Kordofan	9,762	9,728	11,973
West Kordofan	13,809	14,995	14,846
North Darfur	12,643	12,576	14,638
South Darfur	24,083	26,351	24,195
West Darfur	6,793	5,772	8,478
Equatoria Sector	4,079	3,591	4,690
Upper Nile	3,223	3,185	5,793
West Bahr el-Ghazal	3,932	2,879	3,370
Public Facilities Police Force	3,838	4,632	3,130
TOTAL	490,297	488,591	641,134

new codified Shari'a criminal code. Of note are the newly codified Shari'a crimes including 'false accusation of un-chastity' (*al-qadhf*), as well as *zina*, and 'improper sexual contact not amounting to *zina*.' These are new morals offenses. Likewise, terrorism (*al-irhab*) is a new crime, and it is interesting that there were ten cases of terrorism in Khartoum North in 1996.

The Criminal Law and States of Emergency

States of emergency were declared during Numeiri's rule, were re-imposed by Sadiq al-Mahdi in 1987, and have been continuous since al-Bashir seized power in 1989. Under normal conditions the criminal court system has extensive guarantees of due process prescribed for the

Table 4.2　Comparison of Crimes against the Body and against Property for 2005

State	Crime against Body	Crime against Property
Khartoum	39,126	74,333
Northern	2,135	3,681
Nahr elNil	3,322	6,626
North Kordofan	6,222	8,428
South Kordofan	4,057	3,015
West Kordofan	5,296	3,967
North Darfur	2,896	6,158
South Darfur	7,779	9,444
West Darfur	2,301	3,016
El Gezira	11,216	16,139
Blue Nile	4,569	5,931
White Nile	7,759	9,238
Sinnar	4,971	7,468
Red Sea	6,120	7,011
Kassala	4,752	6,193
El Gedarif	5,056	6,304
Equatoria	1,430	1,818
Upper Nile	932	1,072
West Bahr El Ghazal	1,486	1,060
Public Facilities Police force	280	1,226
TOTAL	121,705	182,128

accused. Trials should be held in public except when an accused person requests a closed trial. The accused should be brought before the court within 48 hours of arrest and legal aid services should be available for the poor. Defendants have the right to speak in court and present evidence on their behalf, and to appeal judgments from magistrate level to High Court of Appeal.

However, under states of emergency the government has wide powers to arrest and use preventive detention for an indefinite period of time in areas declared to be emergency zones. Military personnel cannot be arrested by civilian authorities, nor is there any provision for judicial review of the military whose acts remain legally uncontested. Sadiq al-Mahdi declared emergency zones in southern and western

Table 4.3   Criminal cases Central Omdurman/Bahari (needs work with proper translation)

Crime	Central Omdurman	Khartoum North
al-irhab/terrorism	1	10
al-ta'adi/bodily harm	1	2
al-adha al-jassem/stabbing assault	114	1
al-itlaf/destruction of property	1	2
zina/fornication	1	1
a'fal fadhiha/improper sexual contact not amounting to zina	1	3
al-khatf/kidnapping	1	3
al-shuru' fi al-qatl/attempted murder	1	1
al-isā'ah wa asbāb/insulting	35	7
isha'nat al-sum'ah/libel	11	11
al-qadhf/false accusation unchastity	14	5
al-ightisab/robbery	3	1
al-adhi/assault	1	79
al-jarh al-'amd/injury	90	1
al-shuru' fi al-intihar/attempted suicide	9	1
Isti'mal al-quwa al janaiya/abuse of power	1	3

conflict areas of Sudan and used detention powers to arrest persons suspected of being in sympathy with rebels. About 60 judges who protested these emergency detentions were themselves detained, and remained so right up to the al-Bashir coup.

After the 1989 coup the criminal courts continued to handle offenses under the old criminal code. After experimenting with various models, the GoS established special security courts that had both military and civilian judges. These courts tried security and drug cases. Attorneys in these cases were permitted to sit with defendants but not to address the court. Sentences handed down were to be carried out immediately and they gained a reputation for harsh sentences.[28] Since 1989 the power of the state to use its discretion in applying the criminal law has remained unfettered by the judges or the Judiciary.

The IDP camps are the most obvious expression of the effect of the chronic state of emergency where criminal law is applied in the context of a military encampment. There was a certain sensitivity toward my observing criminal courts, and on one occasion I was asked to leave a major criminal court in Omdurman, although I was welcomed into a comparable criminal court in North Khartoum.

Family Law Changes

With a few exceptions, the major change in Sudan's Law of Personal Affairs (*Qanun al-Ahwal al-Shakhsiya*) was its codification and the adoption of Maliki interpretations over the historic Hanafi law that the Ottoman Turks introduced in the early nineteenth century which was then substantially revised through Judicial Circulars issued by the British and Sudanese throughout the twentieth century. Since Shari'a law was exclusively a law of personal status during colonialism and remained so after independence until Islamiszation and state Islamism, its theory and practice in Sudan were documented in my 1987 study of Shari'a in Sudan. Rather than repeat the details of this established law of marriage, divorce, maintenance and support of wives, child custody and support, and the law of inheritance which are detailed in my earlier work. Rather, I will focus in this section on the relatively minor changes is the codified family law. I will also comment upon the myriad social changes evident in the transformed society detailed in chapters 5 and 6. Added to this are commentaries by judges and lawyers and recent research by social scientists.

The 1991 Family Law reinforced through codification the following provisions:

1) The requirement of the consent of the marriage guardian (*al-wali*) with the agreement of the woman;
2) The *wali* retains the right to refuse the marriage or to order its dissolution if equality of standard (*kafa'a*) is not met in the contract of marriage, that is a woman effectively marrying a man 'beneath her religious or economic status;'
3) Polygamy is lawful according to classical Muslim interpretation;

4) Obedience (*ta'a*) is defined as lawful cohabitation of the wife with the husband and disobedience on the part of the wife (*nashiza*) exists from her departure from the conjugal home;

5) Maintenance (*nafaqa*) is the responsibility of the husband and can be claimed for up to three years post-divorce;

6) Divorce (*talaq*) by triple pronouncement is legal provided that the wife is informed of her divorce during her three month '*idda* period (three monthly periods to determine that she is not pregnant from the husband);

7) Judicial divorce by the woman is legal for the following grounds: incurable physical or mental illness in the husband making life between the spouses impossible; impotence in the husband; the husband's cruelty and discord in their relationship; the husband's absence for more than one year, or his imprisonment for two or more years. Divorce by 'ransom' (*fidya*) is legalized whereby the *nashiza,* 'disobedient,' wife requests divorce and the husband refuses. Two arbiters are then appointed by the court and if they recommend separation of the couple, the court may divorce the couple at the wife's request;

8) The 'divorce present' (*mut'a*) is provided as support to the divorced wife for six months;

9) Child custody (*hadana*) is legal for the divorced mother up to seven years for a boy and nine years for a girl. Extensions of custody for the mother can be ordered by the court when the best interests of the child are favored. The court has discretion to allow a re-married mother to retain custody of her children from the previous marriage if the 'best interests of the child' are favored. The custody of a child whose mother is different from the father ends at the age of five years, or earlier if the court fears the child will take a faith other than Islam. The father is obliged to support his children until the girl is married and the boy is able to support himself; and

10) A judge can affirm a marriage for a minor of ten years amending the prior legal marriage age of eighteen years for a man and woman.

Social Change and Family Law

While the family law became more conservative in line with other measures of the *Inqaz* government, Sudanese society became more liberal with respect to marriage and social mobility. The new 'public order' of the 1990s, along with rapid urbanization and economic restructuring, yielded an increase of the loose liaisons characteristic by *zawaj 'urfi* and *misyar* marriage. Polygamy increased, as the wealth of ruling class and those allied with it was enhanced, and President al-Bashir admonished men by citing the Qur'anic verse legitimating polygamy to 'marry the widows' from Sudan's chronic wars. Polygamy is difficult to measure in absolute or relative numbers, as second marriages may be more informal, but its increase is consistent with the official promotion of marriage as an absolute good for the promotion of social morality over *zina*.

In line with the promotion of marriage has been the lessening of the tradition barriers to marriage, such as the reduction in the amounts of the marriage dower, *mahr*. This has positive effects of enabling men to marry earlier than in the past and may be a class leveling device, but it also results in less economic security for the woman to begin her marriage with a smaller dower. All that is required now for a marriage to be validated is the signing of a valid marriage contract, (*qasima*), the presence of two witnesses, and registration of the marriage with the Registrar, the *Ma'azun*.

Lawyer Sonia Abdel Malik reports that the courts have been lenient in family law matters that come before them involving rape and adultery, *zina*. She reports that the new judges in the last few years are better educated and as a result are more enlightened.

Tradition of High Interest by Women in Family Law Reform and Revision

My 1987 book highlighted the strong role played by the Sudanese women's movement in the reform of family law after independence. The reforms of the 1960s and 1970s strengthed women's consent in marriage and broadened her rights in divorce. These were much discussed, debated, and were subject to public education about the legal rights of women. The growth of Islamism did not stem this interest, but it became more ideologically differentiated than in the past with the influence of an Islamist feminist movement with ties to the government. However, these Islamist activists respected the gains made by the democratic and even communist-inspired feminism of the past.

Research on women and a tradition of rich commentary based at Ahfad University for Women in Omdurman, Africa's only university for women, provides a steady supply of feminist scholars who observe, research, and comment upon Sudanese law as it relates to women. The latest example is a commentary and study of the impact of the new codified family law upon urban women in the three towns comprising greater Khartoum (Badri, 2004).

Badri (2004) argues that this first codification of family law did not break new ground in legal innovation, but summarized points of law already having precedent in High Court cases. The codified law explicitly prefers the local and more African Maliki interpretations over Hanafi law, associated with Ottoman Turkish rule. For example, it recognizes the increased authority of women in marriage and rejects the six conditions required for a valid marriage in Hanafi law: religion, freedom, job, financial situation, place of residence, and reasonable pedigree. These conditions when formerly applied in the Sudan raised many cases involving ethnic, racial and class differences as well as objections raised by marriage guardians to grooms with alleged slavery in their backgrounds. The new law requires only mutual respect between the families. The new law widens the concept of *nafaqa* or support to include education and medical treatment of the wife that were previously excluded under Hanafi law. The major accomplishment of the codified family law is the consolidation of nearly a century of applied law in the Sudan and the ending of the conflicts between the Hanafi and Maliki interpretations.

Some Sudanese women activists have strongly criticized the new law. Lawyer Mona Awad[29] stated that the law is largely influenced by a male-dominated ideology that is, in fact, contradictory to true Islamic teachings. In principle, Islam emphasizes egalitarian relations between males and females and urges men to treat women as their sisters.

Further, the codified law ignored some major achievements of Sudanese women prior to June 1989, including their participation in government affairs and high-level decision making. This legislation treats women as legal minors, who are incapable of deciding upon their own marriages, with the reaffirmation of the primacy of the male marriage guardian. Women's testimony in courts is still not equal to that of men, and maternal status is eroded as children (especially male) may be easily separated from their mothers at a young age. Some feminists insist that the Sudanese Personal Status Law must reflect the UN international Convention on the Elimination of All Forms of Discrimination Against Women (CEDAW), to which Sudan is a signatory.

Feminist scholar Balghis Badri recommends the following be taken into consideration in the application of the family law:[30] 1) The Codified personal law needs change according to the contemporary needs of women, and should not be based on ideology. 2) *'Unf* (violence or harm) against women of all types is growing among the marginalized populations. The judges need to understand this and bring the Sudanese law into conformity with development of domestic violence law internationally. 3) Further they need to cooperate with civil authorities so that laws meet international standards of human rights along the following specific lines: a) women should be above 18 years of age for all matters; b) there should be equality in law for marriage and divorce between men and women; c) consent in marriage, *wilaya fi zawaj*, should be the woman's solely; d) in the marriage contract the woman must learn to negotiate her rights into the contract for divorce; e) women should be informed of her of her rights in court; f) evolution of the *al-nizam al am* courts with greater training for judges – i.e. judges should be open minded to the contemporary social problems; and g) court procedures should be simple and prompt.

These three towns are of mid-size: Bahari is Khartoum North and is part of greater Khartoum; Hillet Kuku is a poor area in Khartoum; and al-Fasher is the capital of North Darfur. What is noticeable about these statistics is the predominance of divorce and support cases, underscoring the brittleness of marriage under current economic pressures, migration and internal displacement, particularly in the greater Khartoum communities of Bahari and Hillet Kuku. The small number of *nasab* (genealogy

Table 4. 4   Numbers of Completed Cases in Family Law (*al-Ahwal al-Sha-khsiya*) Courts in Selected States, 2003–05, pp. 310–311 CBS Yearbook 2005

State	2005	2003	2004
Khartoum	30,288	35,941	35,003
El Gezira	8,249	9,520	11,013
White Nile	4,446	4,621	4,827
El-Gedarif	3,025	3,118	3,081
Red Sea	2,156	2,046	2,379
South Darfur	6,861	6,997	8,384
North Kordofan	4,366	4,773	4,699
Southern states	536	544	507

(Source: The General Secretariat of the Higher Judicial Council, Department of Judicial Statistics and Research)

Table 4.5   Family Court (*Mahkamat al-Ahwal al-Shakhsiya*) Court, 2002

Type of case	Khartoum No.	Hillet Kuku	Al-Fasher
Talaq/divorce	171	334	52
Nafaqa/marital support	164	180	106
Khūla/negotiated divorce	0	0	0
Farqah/separation	4	34	0
Hadāna/child custody	18	32	23
Nasab/determination of paternity	3	9	6
Talaq ala Fidya/divorce by ransom	4	0	0

(Source: Statistics from Badri (ed) book, pp. 12–13, from cities of Bahari, Hillet Kuku, al-Fasher in *Mashru Maqtara Li Ta'dil ba'd Mu'ad Qanūn al-Ahwāl al-Shaksīa* (*Contesting Project Proposals after a period of the Personal Status Law*), edited by Balghis Badri, Ahfad University Center for Gender and Development, 2004).

through the patriline) cases involving the legitimacy and paternity of children belies their importance as only a fraction come before the courts. Once they would have been too shameful to bring to court and may have ended with the mother burying the child to hide her shame (Fluehr-Lobban, 1976). Fewer cases of *nasab* in Darfur likely reflect its relatively homogeneous population where marriages are arranged and stable, as they once were in Khartoum before its demographic and economic transformation.

Ethnographic Observation of the Courts

Ethnographic description of the actual functioning of the Sudanese courts, in English or Arabic, is rare, while more attention has been paid to the legal texts. In comparison with my court observations in the 1970s, the most obvious change is the size of the Judiciary complex in Khartoum that has more than doubled in size and numbers of offices since the late 1970s.

The old colonial structure has been upgraded in appearance and facilities. The offices of the highest officials are wood-paneled and richly appointed. The judges' offices are modern, air conditioned and spacious. The Library is a state of the art facility with extensive online services and research assistance. There is an extension to the old Judiciary across the way on the intersecting street between Shari'a Jama'a and Shari'a al-Nil that is a multi-story office complex. And the newest addition is a gleaming new High Court building directly across the street from the historic colonial building.

In order to visit the courts of Khartoum and Omdurman, I needed to obtain permission from the President of the Courts' Organization (*Rais al-Jiraz*).[31] In Omdurman before entering the Courts building, I was asked about my national identity, my religion, and why I wanted to visit the courts; there was some concern that I was a journalist. Possibly confirming that case of mistaken identity, when I entered the building a man immediately came up to me and spoke in English, 'I am from Darfur.'

At such times, I imagine a Sudanese researcher entering any American court and trying to explain to the police or court officers that she/he was there just to observe and conduct research. What we do as anthropologists is certainly out of the ordinary, and social science research has been limited, especially by Americans, since 1989. Needless to say, I was not the proverbial 'fly on the wall' in the greater Khartoum courts.

Overall Observations of the Courts' Physical setting and Proceedings

These observations contrast with my earlier research in 1979–80 when the Shari'a courts were separate from the Civil and Criminal courts, and when Khartoum was a city of about a million, not the eight million of the twenty-first century.

The courts are busy places, as always, but my first impression was that overall more lawyers are present, and that was confirmed by the hours I spent in diverse courts. There were almost an equal number of men and women lawyers, unlike the past when male lawyers predominated, but the courts of the past were filled with more women, while today the law has been unified and family law is only one part of the courts operation. The court rooms are relatively small and intimate and can accommodate about ten people seated in the back. Three chairs are placed in front of the judge's seat and a table for lawyers and claimants waiting to be heard by the judge with a nod of her head. The judge's chair and desk are elevated slightly above these, maybe by a foot or less. The courtroom is air conditioned; the judge still writes everything by hand so that what is said is recorded. Computers may be planned, but there may be a certain reluctance – not because the GoS and Judiciary do not have the money – but because the personal hand of the judge would be lost. Nonetheless, judges in the past complained about this, and they still do today.

Except for the judge's desk, the court is simply furnished, and other than a file storage cabinet, the court room is devoid of any decoration or pictures, including those associated with Islam, which surprised me. In fact, the court had the look and feel of a secular court. In the past pictures of President Numeiri were in every court whereas in no court did I see a picture of al-Bashir.

Court Proceedings

Unlike the courts of the past crowded with the poor, the courts I visited in Diem, North Khartoum, and Omdurman seemed to be comprised mainly of middle class litigants. Moalana Kawther Awad, whose family law court I visited frequently, described the area of Diem in South Khartoum as 'lower middle class.' My impression and the judge's description of class reflect Khartoum's changing class structure, but judging from the standard of Arabic that I heard being used by litigants there was very little colloquial 'darjiyi' Arabic being used and the standard was one of an educated 'lower middle class.'

For the majority of cases I witnessed lawyers were employed to represent the claimants, unlike the past when lawyers were only engaged for serious cases, or large estates in inheritance cases. There were no visible security court police with sticks, as in the past. Order was kept in the court by the judge by knuckling or gaveling the desk, telling people to turn off their mobiles or go outside, followed by a stern admonition about quiet and order in the court that was uniformly observed.

Unlike the past when there were no female judges sitting publicly in Shari'a courts (they generally worked in the Judiciary to hear cases on appeal and only a few women Civil Courts judges presided in public courts), there are many women judges in public courts. For the lady judges whose courts I observed,[32] I witnessed only respect comparable to the more numerous male judges. My good friend Justice Nagua Kemal Muhmmad Farid who paved the way for these court visits remarked that she did not sit in court because her mentor Sheikh el-Gizouli (and mine in 1979–80) did not approve. She went on to say that eventually she *needed* to sit in court for the experience to improve her work in the court of appeal. 'A judge has to practice in order to have the proper feel for the law,' she said.

The women judges and lawyers wear the professional white *tobe*, while the male lawyers appeared in western dress with ties or the professional Sudanese short sleeve suit, appropriate to the hot climate. This differed from the old colonial legacy I observed 25 years earlier where male lawyers often donned black robes when appearing in court. Male judges either wore western dress or *jellabiyas*; judicial robes are gone, and *jellabiyas* have increased. The cases are heard in quick succession, mainly because most cases cannot be completed in a single session and future court dates are appointed according to the judge's calendar. Justice Kawther estimated that she heard 20 or more or cases in one day between the hours of approximately 9:00am and 2:00pm. In the past perhaps four or five cases were heard in a day, and were completed in the same day.

Litigants are sworn in with a Qur'an (a presumption that all are Muslim) that sits atop the judge's desk, as in the past. The formula for the swearing in is no longer the simple 'I swear by God to tell the truth and the whole truth' (*Wilahi lazim, aqul al haqq wa kul al haqq*), and the judge has to read the words – continuing, *ow fi yamin ow ghayr al-haqq* – 'and if the truth or not the truth,' which the witness repeats.

It is still relatively inexpensive to litigate a case and carry it forward, 10SD = $5.00 to initiate a case and 10SD (dinars) for appeal in 2007. Since then the *dinar* has been replaced with the old Sudanese pound.

Continuity and Change

As will be described in chapter 6 on social transformation, the courts mirror directly changes in society. Whereas in the past there were few estate and inheritance cases brought to court, they now are a majority, perhaps a reflection of increasing wealth in families. Mainly the estate problems arise over houses and land that is difficult or undesirable to divide among the multiple mandated Qur'anic heirs. In one case the house of the dead father could not accommodate the sons wishing to use the physical space to house a newly married couple. The problem of too many heirs and not enough space must be reconciled by the judge fairly and reasonably given Khartoum's immense growth. Likewise, family land that was once agriculture land is now expensive real estate in the capital city, and some heirs want to sell and divide the profit, while others seek to retain the family homestead, or wait for land values to increase even more. Khartoum land and building costs for new dwellings are now among the highest in the region.

Divorce has increased, and while the old grounds of harm or abuse (*talaq al-darar*), desertion or lack of support (*ghayaba*), impotence (*'ayb*), ransom (*fidya*), and negotiated divorce (*khula'*) are still present in significant numbers, there are new grounds for divorce after 1991. Added after 1991, was *hajjura* (flight) from the marriage, which is an extension of harm or *darar*, but is a new phenomenon where the husband abandons the wife, and presumably his family. Why the husband abandons his legal responsibilities can only be speculated upon, one being that he became impoverished, or that he found opportunities that excluded marriage. In either case abandonment is another measure of social breakdown consistent with urbanization and intensified class differentiation.

Talaq al-mal, which is a version of *khula*, where the couple contract divorce as they had marriage, has expanded to accommodate the class that always preferred it. The terms of the divorce, usually involving a monetary settlement (*al-mal*) are mutually agreed to and confirmed in front of the Registrar (*ma'azun*), whose office is now attached to the court. A new interpretation of the divorce law permits a woman's testimony that her husband is abusing her, although there are no witnesses to confirm the beating. If she continues to complain for three months, the judge can divorce her based on her testimony alone, contrary to the usual standard of proof by witnesses. This strengthens the divorce law on the side of the abused woman, and is a step in the direction that Badri called for in 2004.

Bayt al ta'a (literally 'house obedience') in which the police were able to return a 'disobedient' wife to her husband and the conjugal home was abolished during the early days of the Numeiri regime. However, as with Egypt – where it was also abrogated – the husband still has the ability to obtain an obedience order (*hokum al-ta'a*) from the family court if the wife has fled or left the home, but it cannot (or should not) be executed with police force and is used so that the wife may not claim the support (*nafaqa*) to which she is normally entitled, due to her being in a state of legal disobedience (*nashiz*). *Zawaj 'urfi* and *misyar*, both seeming forms of temporary marriage, are not mentioned in the 1991 code but have come into legal practice through their widespread appearance in society and the resulting *fatwas* from the *Majma' al-Fiqh al-Islami* that they have prompted.

The IDPs surrounding Khartoum: The Chiefs (*Salatin*) and Public Order (*al-Nizam al-Am*) Courts

The demography and social conditions within the IDP camps surrounding Khartoum are described in chapter 5. Social research is possible in the IDP camps. My research assistant Salma Mohamed Abdalmunim conducted her Master's research in Political Science at the University of Khartoum on Christian-Muslim relations in the camps after the CPA. She was of great assistance in helping me to obtain research permission for the camps from the oversight body, the

Muslim Humanitarian Assistance Commission (MHAC), in Erkoweit. There copies of my passport, visa, research proposal and questionnaire were evaluated before permission was granted. Permission was granted within a week of my formal request, and only one visit to Erkoweit was necessary. The questions I submitted relating to the Shari'a after the CPA were as follows:

1) How long have you been in this camp?
2) What is your ethnic/tribal background?
3) What do you know about Shari'a in the camps?
4) Do you know of any case of arrests or detention for 'Shari'a offenses'?
  5) If yes, are these old cases, or recent ones?
  6) Are these people both men and women?
  7) For what offenses have people, in your knowledge, been arrested or detained?
  8) In your opinion, what differences have occurred regarding Shari'a before and after the CPA?
  9) According to your knowledge, what has happened to the people arrested or detained for Shari'a offenses?
10) Are the Salatin Courts a good way to solve disputes?

With each visit to the camps a representative of the MHAC accompanied us. Khalid Abdel Rahman Ahmed was a compassionate man who has been working for this agency in the camps since 1991, so his sympathies for the camp residents was high. He was keen to point out both the services that are provided, as well as those still urgently needed. For example, as we entered Mayo camp, he pointed to a children's clinic, and the IMO/OMI (International Migration Organization), a large high-walled compound with lorries outside that were loading people and goods to be transported and repatriated to the South after the CPA. We asked to visit inside but were denied permission by the SPLM, or other responsible southern officials. The language of our interactions and interviews was Sudanese colloquial Arabic, except for a few of the Dinka chiefs (Salatin) who knew little Arabic despite years of living in the camps next to Khartoum, and for whom we used an Arabic-Dinka translator.

Customary Law and State administration of Justice in the IDP Camps

The camps are divided by ethnicity or region of origin, Dinka, Nuer, Nuba Mountains, Darfur. Any case involving a Southerner must go before a customary court. Most of the work of the 'Chief's Courts' (*Mahakim Salatin*) has to do with marriage and divorce, or serious quarrels or physical fights among camp mates. The courts administer customary law according to the ethnic group of the South or Nuba Mountains. The courts are usually held weekly, or if needed several times a week. They are held in a *rakuba,* an open place with chairs shaded by a makeshift awning, with the 'Sultan' presiding over the customary court. However, some chiefs reported that their courts were closed after the CPA and have not received government funding, ever since on the ground that they are soon to be repatriated to the South.

The work of the Salatin has devolved to simple maters, such as the negotiation of marriage contracts, often with written IOUs for cattle promised once normal life is resumed and the couple returns to the South.

> If there is a small problem between husband and wife they go the sultan. If she is Muslim they go to the Shari'a, court. If they are Christian, they go to the local sheikh, 'omda or sultan. If there are major problems they go to the police. Men can marry five or six wives, *zawaj mut'a* (with just with a simple present) and their children become the woman's responsibility, so the new camp family is the woman and her children by themselves in shelter. Most of the women have two jobs, the work in the house and then a small enterprise such as selling tea or sunflower seeds in the suq in Omdurman or Khartoum; the men have no work. The men just sit *sakit* (doing nothing) in the camps all day.[33]

The most serious problem for law and justice in the camps is the dynamic of the brewing and sale of *khamra* and *merissa* (alcohol and beer). Women make the brew, while their husbands or male relatives sell it to other camp residents or to consumers in greater Khartoum at known distribution points. The government police may seize and prosecute the brewers and sellers and then consume or re-sell the seized illegal brew. The police have immunity from prosecution and use their legitimate force to harass and intimidate the camp producers of alcohol, all the while keeping the illicit trade throughout the city flowing.

Omdurman prison remained a problem because many women from Mandela Camp were held there, despite an amnesty after CPA. They were fined $75, which most could not pay, or were given three months sentences that have been extended indefinitely. 'After the CPA the police became rougher with us and they do not need the same proof as before,' offered Sultan John. The word of the police against the accused is sufficient to convict a person of *merissa* or *khamra*, and this opens the door wide to corruption of the police – the fine is 400,000 SD ($400) per day.

The police in the camps are a mixture of Northerners and camp locals who are from different ethnic groups. The latter are known as 'popular police' – *shorta sha'biya* – and are young men who don't know the law, according to Umm Asha. The *hadd* flogging punishments are meted out in *al-Nizam al-Am* courts adjacent to, but outside of the bounds of the camps. The punishment is whipping (*jald*) for khamra, 80 lashes for a Muslim and 40 for a Christian. We were not permitted to visit and observe these courts.

We spent one day with the Dinka Chiefs originally from Aweil in Wad al-Bashir camp. They also reported that after the CPA the government closed the Chiefs Courts, whereas before they heard many cases every Friday, now they have none at all. As outsiders they first wanted to tell us that they are hungry because they don't get the small government subsidy as before when they were treated as government employees. One reported, 'Now it's only the police and they run everything – closed the court – the police hear about a murder and go looking for the *khamra* instead. The police work in *merissa* only. Only a few days ago a man was killed with a knife, but when the police came they only asked "where is the *merissa*?".'

Although there are 12 sultans, one *'umda*, and a court president (*Rais al-Mahkama*), it is the police who run the camp and administer 'justice.' The Salatin report that before the CPA they were strong and people were afraid from them. They could apply fines and adjudicate small crimes for up to three years imprisonment. But now they have lost the respect of people because they have no power. 'Actually it was better before the CPA when we had some power. Now the only cases that go to court are the big ones and they go to the *Mahkama Niaba* outside of the camps. We are "*salatin bidun sulta*" (chiefs without power)' – they agreed laughing sardonically. That morning there were many cynical, sarcastic comments made that reflected a high degree of consciousness of the absurdity and hopelessness of their situation.

Already mentioned is the fact that the *hadd* punishments are still meted out in the camps, primarily for alcohol related offenses for men and morals offenses for women (*akhlaq*, morals or *sharaf*, honor). These were reported even after the CPA when Shari'a law was not supposed to be applied to non-Muslims. The camps exist in a political no man's land where IDPs have neither the status and protection of refugees nor the rights of full citizens. The CPA treats Southerners as persons whose 'home' is in the South, making the IDPs akin to foreigners in their own country. As such their legal administration is neither in the hands of their own leaders nor subject to the state's formal legal apparatus. The camps are left to raw social control by the police, more like prison guards than guardians of justice.

Morality offenses, such as prostitution, are tolerated for much the same reasons that alcohol brewing and sale are accepted. Women in the camps can be harassed for their 'immoral' dress, but my research assistant reported that several cases she knew of occurred on days when there were demonstrations in the camps over conditions, and the police retaliated by accusing female demonstrators of not being 'properly dressed.' The new constitution has equal protection by gender and ethnicity language, and southern women in Khartoum have given up wearing head scarves and long sleeves, although some still report being harassed by police when out alone in public. In 2009, southern women wearing trousers were arrested for 'immorality,' but in this case several have filed suit for this violation of their constitutional right not to be harassed as non-Muslims for their dress.

Law enforcement agencies have been ordered not to harass non-Muslims and not to detain drinkers unless they are disturbing the peace. According to an Associated Press report in October 2005, ten months after the signing of the CPA and three months after the new constitution formally stopping Shari'a from being applied to non-Muslims, a Southerner was sentence to 45 lashes for being drunk in Joborona IDP camp. After sentencing he was publicly whipped in the courtyard of the *al-Nizam al-Am* court, and then had to pay a fine of $20.[34]

There is little joy in the camps about the immediate effects on them of the CPA. 'They stopped the war but it did not end our troubles. Conditions were supposed to improve but they did not, in fact some of the police harassment increased because some of the police were against the CPA, as they saw it as a loss of their power.' One sultan said, 'we are not speaking freely as we do not know if you will go and tell the government what we have said.'

Nearly everyone with whom we spoke in the camps, including the salatin, agree that there are no problems between Christians and Muslims. In fact, Wad al-Bashir has the largest ethnic and Christian/Muslim mix, with 70 per cent Christian and 30 per cent Muslim. They complain that the Muslims have the better houses, not the *beut showlat* (rakuba with cloth).The problems between people are all about food and money (*akil wa grush*) and are never about religion.

The police often focus on the youth whom they allege steal in the Khartoum main market, the *suq al-'Arabi,* to buy a 600 ml bottle of *merissa*. In 2007, a stolen mobile was equal to three 600 ml bottles. If they are caught, they pay a fine of 200,000 Sudanese dinars (about $2,000) or go to prison for four months. Camp residents report being sent to prison for possession of the ingredients to make *merissa*, dates and sugar.

On our last day in Wad al-Bashir camp final words were offered to us that bear repeating. 'We need your help to tell the truth about these things. We still do not feel free to speak without fear.' They talked further about racial discrimination and 'the color of our skin.' 'Here we have together an American lady, a northern Sudanese man and a northern Sudanese woman, how do we come together to make peace in this land and in the world?'

Law and Justice in the South before the CPA

In the South, normal judicial procedures could not be carried out during the years of the civil war. The administration of law and justice was carried out by the SPLM who developed their own military-civil code of law.[35] In rebel areas, where the GoS armed forces were in charge, the accused were summarily tried and punished, especially for offenses against public order. However, in SPLA-held areas justice could either be through the SPLM code or through traditional means, and was administered by the village elders.

In 1983 the SPLM/SPLA initiated the Punitive Law to regulate the conduct of the armed forces. A year later a committee headed by the late Major Gai and Joseph Oduho drafted the Penal and Discipline law of the SPLA, signed by the Chairman John Garang. In 2003 these laws were repealed and replaced by the SPLA Act with a Penal Code, Civil and Criminal Procedures. Customary law is currently being codified under several auspices, including a UNDP Rule of Law project for South Sudan (Chan, 2008). Unifying the customary laws of the fifty or more ethnic groups and the ten states of the Government of South Sudan (GoSS) has proved a challenging task for a new nation and for building and re-building civil society. There is resistance to writing down a system of law that has flourished as an oral system based on talking things out and negotiating compromise. There is a fear that a written law would destroy the strength of the oral customary law.

The 22 years of civil war from 1983–2005, destabilized all institutions and upturned the Chiefs' Courts system that dated back to the days of English colonialism. During the years of war civil law was subordinated to martial law as an imperative of a wartime situation. With peace, even an unstable one, the construction of a South Sudan government is a key part of normalizing government and society. The codification of customary law is a priority for the development of inter-ethnic relations which then will proceed in logical, progressive stages of development. The Chiefs' Courts must be incorporated and their wisdom and experience valued. Judges must be trained in the unified legal system; ultimately the laws of South Sudan will have to reconcile with Shari'a law, international humanitarian law, and for a time, military law (Chan, 2008: 20).

As the former GoSS Chief Justice Ambrose Riny Thiik has opined: 'Customary law is a manifestation of our customs, social norms, beliefs and practices. It embodies much of what we have fought for these past twenty years. It is self-evident that customary law will underpin our society, its legal institutions and laws in the future.'[36]

Transitional to Parallel Judicial Systems and Eventual Separate Southern Judiciary

Given the decades of war and disruption of every institution in southern Sudan, it is not surprising that the transition to a functioning independent or autonomous region is presently in a state of flux from an old order to a new one. After visiting Juba in 2008 to observe first hand this transition, I can report that optimism in most affairs – neither unbounded nor incautious – is the operative word. This includes those who are working on the legal transition, like Hoth Chan whose work on codifying customary law is described above. In addition to this challenge, there is the overarching structural problem of the two existing legal systems, as holdovers from the former era of war and resistance – the laws of the Government of Sudan and the laws of the SPLA.

Two parallel legal codes operating in the south can cause serious confusion for the Judiciary. Both the 1991 Unified Code and the 2003 SPLM Laws operate in southern Sudan according to the interim constitution. According to the President of Southern Sudan's Court of Appeal, Justice Kuc John Akot, there are as yet few clear guidelines. He said that in general the 1991 laws are associated with the Islamist program and relate more to criminal cases, while the SPLM 2003 laws focus more on civil society. Justice Akot used the example of a man in Aweil who refused to accept the judgment of his criminal case under the 1991 Khartoum criminal laws. He has appealed to the High Court in Greater Bahr al-Ghazal which reached the Supreme court in Juba as a constitutional case. 'There is no clear margin as to how best to apply the laws which creates many problems' said Justice Kuc (*The Juba Post*, 6–13 April 2007, Swangin Isaac, p.9).

Summary of Courts of South Sudan

The following is a summary of the present state – pre 2011 – of the courts of southern Sudan:

1) Customary courts: these form the greater part of the 2003 laws than the 1991 Khartoum laws because they side with the person whose interests are damaged as a result of the crime. 'If we find a case that relates to culture we are most likely to refer it back to the customary courts,' said Justice Akot.

2) County courts: these deal with cases that do not relate to cultures which are dealt with by the customary courts. It is possible to appeal a ruling of a County court to the High court in each state.

3) State High courts: in addition to hearing from the County courts, the High courts in each state are responsible for judging more important cases. These include those involving foreigners, intellectual property rights, as well as rape and murder cases. If a ruling by a State High court is questioned, it is then revieded by the Court of Appeal.

4) Court of Appeal: there are three Courts of Appeal in South Sudan – Greater Equatoria, Greater Bahr al-Ghazal, and Greater Upper Nile. As well as dealing with appeals from the State High courts, these courts are responsible for administrative disputes within the government, for example a civil servant whose contract is terminated without clear evidence as to why.

5) The Supreme Court: in south Sudan the Supreme Court is based in Juba and is the center of the Judiciary. It deals with cases referred on appeal from the three Courts of Appeal while also making judgments on high profile administrative cases. The Supreme Court is also responsible for confirming death sentences in murder cases. The SC deals with all constitutional cases such as cases where there is a conflict between GoS laws and SPLM laws. In contrast to the Supreme Court in Khartoum that has 70 members, the Juba SC has only 7 judges.

(Extracted from 'Understanding the courts in South Sudan,'
The Juba Post, 6–13 April 2007)

There is also an assessment of legal institutions in all of the ten states initiated by the Judiciary of South Sudan working with UNDP. 'New buildings are needed for states that do not currently have County Courts and High Courts because it is important that cases be tried close to where alleged crimes took place,' added Justice Akot.[37]

Periodic reports in the southern press available in Khartoum reveal yet more challenges for the effective functioning of law in the South. In Bentiu it was reported in 2007 that 75 per cent of the inmates in prison had not had their criminal cases adjudicated and remained in prison although never convicted (*The Juba Post*, 20–27 April 2007). This 75 per cent are those accused of murder cases, reported the Unity State Director of Prisons Brigadier Kon Kudum Thot. 'Killing has been a common practice in the state. In the past they used guns, now that civilians are disarmed they use spears, arrows and dangerous tools.' He said the quarrels leading to death are over 'girls, cattle and clan conflicts.'

Heavily armed fighters have killed more than 200 people in raids on villages in South Sudan, where bloody tribal disputes over cattle are jeopardizing peace efforts in the oil-rich region, officials said on Sunday. The commissioner of Pibor County Akot M. Adikiu told Reuters he had seen more than 200 bodies, but had heard reports that hundreds more may have been killed in a string of attacks over the past two weeks.

The surrounding Jonglei State, where Malaysia's Petronas is searching for oil and France's Total owns a huge concession, has long been plagued by interethnic violence, often sparked by disputes over livestock. But ethnic fighting has escalated, fueled by the huge supply of weapons left over from the two-decade North-south war. Adikiu said that about 6,000 people had also been displaced by the recent attacks and thousands of cattle were taken. Cattle are highly prized by southern pastoralists and represent wealth, status as well as stability in fraught times. Efforts by south Sudan's semi-autonomous government to disarm communities have been patchy and in some cases have descended into bloody battles when civilians fight back ('Hundreds Killed in South Sudan Cattle Attacks,' Reuters, 15 March 2009).

Status of Muslims and Shari'a in the Government of South Sudan

The GoSS maintains an Islamic Affairs department within its Ministry of Gender, Social Welfare and Religious Affairs. The town of Malakal in Upper Nile State has the largest southern Muslim population and the total number of southern Muslims – born to Islam, or recruited through voluntary conversion or coercion through war and displacement in predominantly Muslim areas of North – can only be crudely estimated. Nonetheless southern Islam is a reality, as is a large number of southern Muslims living in the North. This fact can be a painful reminder of the bitter past, but what I have observed and heard from Southerners is that the war was never about religion and there is little interest in discrimination against the victims, or persecuting the victimizers who may have used religion as a tool of oppression and control.

As such mosques openly operate in the South; however I must confess that I did not once hear the call to prayer during my stay in Juba. The Islamic banks may be perceived as more of a symbol of the Islamist program and they were gradually shut down in the major southern towns since the CPA.

However, an announcement came in April 2007 that the Islamic Corporation would be responsible for the affairs of the South's Muslims (*Khartoum Monitor*, 24 April 2007). Mango Ajak, the Secretary General of South Sudan's Islamic Corporation, accepted this post at the invitation of the GoSS. The two parties agreed on six items, the most important of which is that all personal status matters of Muslims will be referred to Shari'a judges who will be appointed to arbitrate Muslim affairs, such as marriage, divorce and inheritance. Religious education would be supplemented with Islamic subjects but the standard southern syllabus would be primary. There will be no establishment of private Islamic schools.

Owing to the seriousness of the subject of Islamic affairs in the South other religious matters concerning *Hajj*, *'umra*, *zakat*, and *waqf* were negotiated with the president of GoSS and the Speaker of South Sudan Parliament.

CHAPTER 5

DEMOGRAPHIC TRANSFORMATION: THE 'NEW SUDAN,' UNDER CONSTRUCTION IN THE CAPITAL CITY

The 'New Sudan' under Construction in the Capital City

The new Sudan, for better and for worse, is actively under construction in greater Khartoum, including the northern cities and peripheries with the most rapid and transformational growth in the three towns of Khartoum, Omdurman, and Khartoum North. This vast, new African conurbation, with a combined population of about 8 million, now comprises perhaps a quarter or more of Sudan's entire population.

When I first conducted research in 1970–72, the population of Khartoum was estimated at 500,000; in the census of 1993, it was perhaps 3–4 million. In the decade after the NIF came to power, the three towns nearly doubled in size, placing Khartoum in a class with Africa's other great urban centers of Cairo, Lagos, and Nairobi. Sudan's chronic civil wars and conflict created huge internal displacement of its peoples – from the South, the Nuba Mountains, the East, and the western regions of Darfur and Kordofan. Environmental crises – drought and resulting famine – have likewise played a significant role in this internal resettlement of diverse peoples. While many fled across

Image 4   New Khartoum skyline

borders into Uganda, Egypt, Chad, Ethiopia, and Kenya, huge numbers left home to find haven in their capital city where urban clusters
of regional settlements of the marginalized have grown over the past
two decades. Significant among these are the IDP camps, five of which
ring the capital city's three towns, where over 2 million people reside
in the limbo that characterizes life in the camps, but are now increasingly part of the conurbation. These factors, plus the continuous draw
of the primate-capital city, make Khartoum the place of destiny for all
of Sudan's future whether as a unified or broken state. This complex
and fundamental transformation of Khartoum has made it an indis-
putably African city, despite al-Bashir's declaration of Khartoum as an
Arab capital in 2005, the same year as the CPA was signed.

The creation of a 'new Sudan' was the dream of John Garang, the
visionary founder of the *all* Sudanese People's Liberation Movement.
A unionist in the midst of an insurgent southern majority who in
their majority desired and have achieved separation from their northern oppressors, Garang saw a 'new' Sudan born of liberation from
militarism and Islamism. He envisioned a new pluralist and secular state governed by and for Sudanese – neither Arabized Africans,
nor Africanized Arabs, but Sudanese. This would emerge from the

re-structuring of power relations in the nation's capital of Khartoum. 'The new Sudan as a socio-political mutation will be qualitatively different from its present form,' he wrote (Khalid/Garang, pp.202–03).

If there was one defining moment for the 'new Sudan' in Khartoum, it was the triumphal and much anticipated arrival of John Garang in the capital city in July 2005, six months after the signing of the CPA. I was carrying out research in Khartoum in the months following the signing of the CPA and anticipation of the arrival of Garang was running high. He held virtual rallies addressing large numbers of followers by telephone from Juba or Rumbek in which he maintained the vision of the 'new Sudan' so long as unity could be made 'attractive' by the North. When Garang announced he was coming to Khartoum to be sworn in as national vice-president in July, expectations had mounted to unprecedented levels for a political figure in Sudan. Estimates of a million or more Sudanese crowded the area near to the Khartoum airport where the newly sworn in vice president of Sudan addressed the multitudes. The visual of this event is striking and according to SPLM officials and members whom I interviewed, there were many northerners in the crowd, along with the majority of Southerners who flocked to greet their leader. Many northern friends describe Garang's triumphant return came to Khartoum as *'yom saeed jeedan'* – 'a very happy day' – and the days of the aftermath of his death as *'ayyam soda'* – 'dark days.' For better and for worse, the new Sudan is being forged by tragic events, such as this, and by more hopeful encounters between stranger-citizens in the capital city.

Two weeks after his swearing-in, Garang would be dead as the result of a helicopter crash on his way from Juba to Uganda – ruled an accident by an independent aviation mishap commission, but widely believed to have been an assassination plot. When the announcement of Garang's death in Uganda spread throughout Khartoum, spontaneous bursts of outrage and anger developed into mass demonstrations of protest over the 'killing' of Garang just as he had assumed the nation's second highest office with hopes running high of his being elected president. The outpouring of grief and anger, of dashed hopes and fear, were expressed on a mass scale in all of the three towns in a series of clashes known as 'black Monday,' rioting that continued for days. Instead of celebration, the three towns were locked down as

Southerners roamed the streets smashing shop windows and burning automobiles. The 'Monday uprising' lasted for almost a week before the urban riots were put down by the security police and the army. The three towns were in lockdown with the closure all of the seven bridges spanning the Niles – Blue, White, and the Nile proper after the confluence – and citizens were forced to walk to their homes as all public transport ceased. Southern rage exploded in random violence against Northerners and the looting of stores and burning of cars in public areas. Americans who recall the race riots of the late 1960s, especially after the assassination of Martin Luther King, would recognize and understand this urban upheaval. Two years later, when I spoke about these days with Southerners, their anger was still apparent, and in conversations with Northerners, their fear was still evident.

The old social paradigm of domination of the North over the south has been exhausted, due to the military and political victories of the SPLM/SPLA and the triumph of peace over successive governments in Khartoum that varied little in respect to southern policy. SPLM ideology envisioned that the historical elite minority would ultimately be overwhelmed by the vastly greater peripheral majority, and the new 'Sudanese' person would emerge with a complex identity embracing the whole of the nation-state – if it survives.

Perhaps two-thirds of greater Khartoum today is comprised of non-Arab, non-central-northern Sudan peoples – which is to say, the majority of the capital city are people from the peripheral regions of the country. Khartoum may be as much as one-third southern, with several hundred thousand Westerners from Darfur and Kordofan also residing in the capital added to this number. Men from these areas dominate the new informal economy that lines the sidewalks of the commercial districts of downtown streets in the capital. They sell men's clothing, shoes, watches, billfolds, items of personal care, CDs, and a smattering of southern handicrafts. The few women who have access to these prime locations are restricted to selling tea, peanuts, peanut butter, and a variety of edible nuts and seeds. For many, if not a majority, their hero is John Garang.

Education in the IDP camps is minimal and emphasizes Islamic studies and Arabic. This helps to explain why for so many Southerners their Arabic is fluent in reading and writing and why some may choose to stay in Khartoum, despite the estimated 17–20,000 who were repatriated in 2007.

An Increasingly Cosmopolitan City and Country

Khartoum has not only been transformed by internal demographics, but it is also more international, cosmopolitan, and more 'African.' Historic populations of Ethiopians and Eritreans have swelled to the hundreds of thousands in greater Khartoum where their presence is visible in new ethnic neighborhoods with stores and restaurants in Amharic or Tigre, their music mainstreamed into mass culture, and a high demand for Ethiopian musicians and dancers at middle class weddings.

Long sought after as nannies and domestics in Khartoum, the expanded middle class has reinvigorated this demand. These long established communities have become permanent residents, have their own popular Ethiopian market on Sunday, and significantly they represent another segment of the Christian community in the North

Image 5   Sunday Ethiopian market in Khartoum Two (author photo)

added to the large southern Christians community, neither homogeneous by denomination or ethnicity. Greek and Syrian Orthodox Eastern
Christian churches and populations have dwindled in the decades of
the *Inqaz*, and the old Syrian Club is now a hall that can be rented for
social events and Muslim weddings. The Christian Ethiopian community has been exempted from religious discrimination because of their
outsider status, but the possibility that an alliance could be formed
between the permanent resident southern and Ethiopian Christian
communities would add another dimension to the 'new Sudan.'

Eritrean immigrants resident in Sudan are more heavily Muslim
than Christian and blend in religiously, but intermarriage with
Sudanese Muslims is still relatively rare suggesting continuing importance of language and cultural differences.

In Juba, Ugandans, Kenyans, Ethiopians and Eritreans, predominate in the work force, and they are a strong presence in the growing
small and large entrepreneurial sectors that also includes some Indians.
This is a significant issue to address for southern economic development and reflects the obvious legacy of displacement and impoverishment resulting from decades of civil war. Unlike Khartoum, these
immigrants are unlikely to become permanent residents.

Changes in Public Space

For those who knew the more homogeneous old Sudan and old
Khartoum, the changes in the physical environment of the capital city
are stunning and dramatic. In place of the three bridges that connected
the three towns, now there are seven, the new ones built with Chinese
materials and labor. The sidewalks and streets of center city are still
recognizable, except that they are now dwarfed by gleaming new high
rise buildings, and the still recognizable colonial era government ministry building have mostly been upgraded or replaced by high rise,
high security buildings, such as the Ministries of Foreign Affairs and
of Interior. Some of the last vestiges of old central old Khartoum, the
Suq al-ʿArabi (Arab market) and *Mahata Wusta* (transportation central),
have been removed, for many gutting the heart of the old downtown,
and, for most, making life less convenient. The one and only Cinema
on Sharia Jamhouriya is still functioning, and it is still the domain of

young men. The streets are cleaned at night, and after dark the city is quiet and safe with little in the way of night life.

The decision in 2007 by the Governor of the Khartoum State to empty areas in downtown Khartoum and turn them into green squares is consistent with the beautification efforts the capital has gone through over the last years. An editorial in *Sudan Vision* (17 July 2007) supporting the clearing of downtown areas as the city center reflects the face of a national capital and the cultural identity of the nation. The editorial opined that Sudanese cultural identity has been distorted by some street boys, pickpockets and litter that is left lying in front of shopping centers and cafeterias. 'Even those suffering from infectious diseases and others practicing magic are seen sitting on pedestrian walkways. The Governor's decision will therefore put an end to these scenes that do not match our image as a nation.' The editorial further argued that the Public Order police should tighten control on the appearance of these squares lest they be abused.

Traffic jams that were unknown a decade ago now clog the streets that were created during the colonial era when only the elites owned automobiles. A trip from *Suq al-'Arabi* to Khartoum North across the Blue Nile Bridge that used to take 15 minutes might require an hour during the periods of high congestion. The trip to Omdurman from Khartoum can take an hour or more. Rush hour, that used to begin as offices closed for the day around 2.00pm, now extends from mid-morning to late afternoon, as the work day has also been extended. People complain about stresses of time, the commute via private car or public transport, and the inability to remain faithful to the old patterns of frequent visits to family and friends, except on the only non-working day, Friday. The highly affordable and ubiquitous mobile phone has moved in to fill this void.

The gap between rich and poor has widened in every respect, but is most apparent in the burgeoning suburbs, new malls, and high end shopping areas that line Airport road, resembling the elite suburbs of Cairo or the glittering cities in the Gulf. Elite cafes, such as 'Ozone' and a growing variety of 'ethnic' restaurants – Indian, Korean, Chinese, and Turkish as well as the universals of global fast food – are all in evidence. The culture of male-public/female-private dining has been transformed. Whereas in the past only men dined together in public, now not only are families dining together, but couples are as well, with no questions asked. While modest female dress is more in evidence in the city, more relaxed, western-style clothing is apparent in the suburbs. Although the wearing of pants by women is still relatively rare, this is rapidly changing along with other manifestations of a growing global monoculture, especially among the youth.

In short, Khartoum is no longer the dusty, sleepy capital once imagined by outsiders. Despite its political isolation, with its booming oil economy it has entered the world driven by the realities of globalization, and it has become one of Africa's largest and eventually its most important cities. With its immense population of the displaced and dispossessed – of new migrants and traditional elites – of burgeoning universities and bureaucracies, it is a city full of complexities and contradictions, of competition and opportunities, of ethnic encounters and conflicts. In other words, it is a world class city, for better and for worse.

Demographic Transformation

The demographics of new Khartoum – *Khartoum Jadid* – have been born of chronic war and displacement, as well as by the economic opportunities fueled by the oil economy and attraction of the primate city. While the following statistics measure some indices of demographic and social transformation, they are in desperate need of being evaluated and assessed by demographers and social scientists. The data reported illustrates the breadth and depth of the changes in urban life and society. They have been derived from Sudan's official *Statistical Yearbook for the year 2005*, (Central Bureau of Statistics, Khartoum, 2006).[38] The commentaries are mine.

Basic Demography

Sudan as a whole is 63 per cent rural and 36 per cent urban (p.46).

Table 5.1   Ages of the general population (p.52):

Age Group	Percentages (%)
0–14	41.7
15–59	54.2
60+	4.0

Table 5.2   Life Expectancy (p.54)

	Northern Sudan	Southern Sudan
Males	52.5 years	45.9 years
Females	55.5 years	48.7 years

Table 5.3   Number of Households (excluding 'collective' ones, i.e. extended families) by religion of head and population by religion and sex: Khartoum, 1993, (cited in 2006 Statistical Yearbook, p.55, indicating that new urban household data has not been collected since the early 1990s):

Households	Both sexes (joint)	Male heads	Female heads
Muslims	510,830	3,157,405	1,467,536
Christian	57,025	350,536	161,313
Other religion	506	2,663	1,276

Table 5.4   The number of Mobile phone customers doubled between 2003–04, and doubled again in 2005 (p.25)

Year	Number of Mobiles
2003	546,262
2004	1,048,558
2005	1,808,239

The large number of female heads of households in the city from 1993 is worth noting. It is likely much higher today. The global rise in the number of female heads of households and matrifocal families is apparent in Sudan despite its strong patriarchal cultural and familial traditions (Billson and Fluehr-Lobban, 2005). In Sudan the formal number of female-headed households has been estimated at 13 per cent (Badri, 2004) which appears to be a gross underestimate as the above official 1993 figures suggest that female-headed households comprise 28 per cent of the total number of Muslim households, and an equal number of Christian households are female-headed. Any regular visitor to the neighborhoods of Omdurman, Khartoum, and Bahari or a commuter on public transport would notice this new social phenomenon of the increase in women workers in the formal economy and of their increased prominence in family affairs at home. The last available data for 1993 would surely have increased due to steady northern male labor out-migration, and an as yet undetermined number of male casualties of soldiers in Sudan's chronic wars and conflict.

Mobitel and Sudatel are the major companies that met the increased demand for mobile phones while Areeba and Kanartel are also active in the Sudanese market. LGF, a Saudi company, invested $2 billion on Sudan mobile communications, and started operations in southern Sudan (*al-Hayat al-Siyasiya*, 5 September 2007, p.3).

This figure speaks for itself, as the number of mobile phones in use has nearly doubled each year since 2003. Mobile phones are affordable, and phone cards are cheap and ubiquitous making this means of communication the new standard, displacing the old landline phones, notorious for their unreliability. For the masses, email as a form of regular communication has been bypassed by the mobile phone, mainly because of the high cost of personal computers and the marginal literacy of new urban immigrants, although internet access is widespread and relatively inexpensive. Mobile phones are used by everyone from street vendors and taxi drivers to bureaucrats for basic communication. They have become invaluable for the increasingly efficient culture of the prompt appointment, once the subject of jokes that an hour or more should be added to any 'fixed' meeting time, and to the maintenance of social relations (*munasaba*) rendered problematic by traffic jams and busy schedules.

Mobile phone reception throughout the country is excellent for both domestic and international calls. I called the US from the far North in Dongola in 2004 and the far South in Juba in 2008, and the reception was better than my current experience in rural New Hampshire. While conducting research I also received calls from Juba in Khartoum and called Juba from Khartoum and received calls from Darfur, and this was likewise clear and affordable. Young people rely on text messaging in Sudan for the same reasons that they do in the West; it is instantaneous and extends the life of the phone cards.

Table 5.5   Students admitted to higher education in 2005 (p.293):

Student Type	Number of Students	Percentage (%)
Females	18,639	53
Males	16,415	47
Total	35,054	100

The larger proportion of females admitted to institutions of higher education reflects regional and global patterns that are nonetheless worthy of comment. The attraction of higher salaries in the Gulf both for unmarried as well as married men has been an established social pattern since the 1980s. Like other labor supplying nations their remittances from abroad represent a major part of the Sudanese economy. These males tend to be semi-skilled or unskilled workers with secondary school education. In the past they would work in the Gulf to earn enough money to marry, needing funds for the considerable dower (*mahr*), a house and furniture for their younger, relatively uneducated wives. However, the new part of this social equation is the dramatic increase in university women who are postponing marriage into their later twenties, apparently without the old fears that an unmarried 25 year old was an 'old maid.' These days university women are working during and after university study, and some complain about the lack of available 'good' men, while others are delaying marriage by choice without fear or regret.

On a trip I made to Shendi town, a few hours North of Khartoum and a center of the major ruling ethnic groups, the Shayqiya and Ja'alinin, to attend a conference in 2007 entitled 'Shari'a Debates,'[39] I learned that the University of Shendi is overwhelmingly female, 80 per cent in Medicine with women predominating in the law, as well as the more traditional *al-Adab wa al-'Ulum*, (Arts and Sciences). I asked, 'Where are the young men?' The response was that by the end of secondary school, or before, they leave for work in the Gulf or in the Kingdom of Saudi Arabia, and they do not intend to get a university education which they view as unnecessary since the degree will not earn them the money they need to succeed in the 'new Sudan.'

Table 5.6   Gender Differences in Marriage Ages, 1983–93 (p.62):

MARRIED (%)	Males Married (%)		Females Married (%)	
Age Group	1983	1993	1983	1993
15–19	3.3	1.7	28.2	19.7
25–29	51.2	41.7	63.3	52.1
30–34	78.0	65.7	84.5	75.6

In Table 5.6 the decreasing percentage of both males and females who have married by the ages of 20–24 and 25–29 from 1983–93 is evident. That number, too, has likely significantly increased in the fifteen years since this data was collected.

The differences between rural and urban men and women (Table 5.7) during this same time period shows a sharp decline of 7 per cent of the young women who are married at age 15–19 between 1983 and 1993; 13 per cent for women aged 20–24; and the most dramatic 20 per cent reduction for women aged 25–29. This is matched by a rising age for the percent of men to be married at comparable ages or above. Most significant is the 13 per cent decrease for men who are married by the age 30–34. The differences for rural men and women are also noteworthy, although they are not as great as for the urban areas, they do reflect a growing convergence of rural and urban life.

Official statistics can be misleading, as the number of Sudanese in Egypt in the Yearbook is stated as 783, an extremely low number for the known and well-studied huge refugee population of Sudanese

Table 5.7   Changes in Marital Age of Rural and Urban Men and Women (p.63):

1983 Marriage Age	Male/Urban (%)	Female/Urban (%)	Male/Rural (%)	Female/Rural (%)
15–19	2.2	21.4	3.6	31.3
20–24	14.0	57.6	24.6	73.6
25–29	41.7	83.5	60.7	92.5
30–34	70.8	92.9	85.0	96.9
35–39	86.2	96.5	93.6	98.5
1993 Marriage Age	Male/Urban (%)	Female/Urban (%)	Male/Rural (%)	Female/Rural (%)
15–19	0.9	14.5	2.3	23.8
20–24	8.8	44.7	18.5	61.7
25–29	32.0	72.4	52.2	84.5
30–34	57.6	85.3	76.1	92.1
35–39	80.5	93.8	90.6	97.1

(Status distributions from 1983 and 1993 Censuses)

Table 5.8   New Demographic – Sudanese in the Diaspora

Country	Number of Sudanese
Saudi Arabia	456,074
Libya	52,445
Iraq	51,843
UAE	45,901
Yemen	19,352

According to the Yearbook (p.393) for Sudanese living abroad, the overwhelming majority in 2005 were in Saudi Arabia. (Source: Sudanese in the Diaspora (p.393))

in the country estimated to be several million economic and political migrants seeking temporary or semi-permanent residence in this neighboring and accessible Nile Valley country (Fabos, 2001). This no doubt reflects sensitive politics of exile and out-migration, as Egypt does not recognize – by way of accepting refugees – the extreme conditions of harassment and hardship caused by Sudan's chronic wars that had made long term exile in Egypt a necessity. No western country is mentioned although we know at least that at least 3,000 'Lost Boys' from southern Sudan have received asylum in the US, and the number of Sudanese from other parts of the country is higher. The official number of Sudanese in Europe UK, and the USA is 822, and for all other African countries is 601 (p.392), again these are numbers that are seriously to be questioned in terms of realities on the ground. As a result of the CPA and the partial withdrawal of the Islamist program there has also been a noticeable return, or reconnection, of exiles from the Diaspora. In many cases these are people who have spent years or even decades in exile and have established roots in Europe and North America, and increasingly in Australia, thus their 'reconnection' is one of finding ways to be of use to the mother country through teaching or working with an NGO. Increasingly, these exiles take dual citizenship.

The following statistics may be useful for estimates of the percentages of African nationals who have fled to Sudan for refuge. At one point in the 1980s Sudan was a far greater recipient nation for refugees than it was a 'donor' nation, so to speak, for sending refugees.

Table 5.9   Refugees in Sudan, by number and percentage in 2005 (p.411):

Nationality	Number of Refugees	Percentage
Eritrean	405,529	60.7
Ugandan	157,000	23.5
Ethiopian	91,400	13.7
Chadian	6,400	1.0
Congolese	5,000	0.7

Table 5.10   Sudanese Refugees Abroad by country (p.412):

Country	Number of Refugees
Uganda	223,000
Chad	209,000
Ethiopia	88,000
DR Congo	75,009
Kenya	69,804
CAR	36,000
Egypt	30,000
Eritrea	645

Table 5.11   Major Diseases for 2005 (p.239):

	Diarrhea 2003	Diarrhea 2005	Malaria 2003	Malaria 2005
Out-patient	2,053,254	1,895,748	3,084,320	2,515,693
In-patient	19,792	28,890	152,686	132,617
Out-patient per 1,000	61	53	92	71
Deaths at admission (%)	2.0	3.3	1.3	1.6

The last table from the Central Bureau of Statistics reveals the continued presence of the major diseases of malaria and diarrhea that debilitate the poor, displaced, and especially children from all classes. Eradication and education programs to ameliorate and treat these diseases are relatively inexpensive, but have not been a government priority and have been left to the international aid agencies.

The 'State of Emergency' Still in Effect

The State of Emergency that al-Bashir instituted at the time of the NIF-backed coup in 1989 has never been lifted. This means that Sudanese in cities and towns have been living under a protracted period of martial law where any disturbance can be quelled with impunity of the state and its judicial authorities. Demonstrations of more than three persons, not organized by the regime, are illegal and are subject to immediate dispersal by the police assigned to this detail, *Shurtat al-Ihtiyat al-Markazi* (Central Reserve Police), with potential arrest of the participants. The Public Order Police and armed private militias are deployed in obvious positions in the major popular gathering places, such as in the former locations of central transport, Mahata Wusta, the *suq al-'Arabi*, and along the side streets that would potentially defend the main streets of the capital. This daily show of force reminds the populace that any spontaneous action would be dealt with swiftly and decisively. Curfews are still in effect, meaning that no gatherings may extend beyond 11.00pm. Although they are rarely or only selectively enforced since the easing of such restrictions, late wedding parties and travel on the streets after curfew can still be subject to police intervention.

During my research stays in 2005 and 2007, I lived in the city center in a flat with a good balcony for viewing street life on Shari'a Jama'a. On 7 April 2007, a Saturday evening about 6:00pm, there was an explosion near to the military barracks across the railroad tracks near to the University of Khartoum. I heard the explosion and the subsequent sirens that brought me out to the balcony where I saw a continuous flow of the small Toyota trucks that the militias in their clearly identifiable blue-purple camouflage uniforms use, each loaded with armed soldiers at the ready with visible arms and show of force. My first thought was instinctive from past experience, that a coup was underway, or that there were demonstrations at the University of Khartoum. The continuation of loud booms, as well as the spontaneous gathering and visible fear of people observed from my balcony, confirmed in my mind that something volatile was going on. When fire trucks began to speed down Sharia al-Gamhouriya and the smell of smoke was in the air more Toyotas full of soldiers sped by. I turned on the TV thinking there might be a report and then went to my internet café at the Hotel Sahara where I learned that the bridges to Bahari and Omdurman were closed and all public transport had been shut down. The three towns of the capital city were in lock down for 24 hours. Later on Sudan TV the report was that there was an accidental explosion of an ammunition truck due to poor road conditions just next the army barracks.

Immediately the rumor underground circulated alternative reports that the incident was a planned attack to bring the Darfur war to Khartoum, as there had been skirmishes in Omdurman with eight killed the previous week, and the Khartoum army barracks is highly strategic. Moreover, the rumors continued, 'ammunition does not blow up due to the road conditions,' many commented. From my ethnographic perspective the reality that the city was almost immediately in a 'lock down' mode was most instructive. The public understood the danger and that they needed to do to get home safely as soon as possible. Most walked home, as they did during the days of the disturbances following the death of John Garang.

A New Social Order – *al-Nizam al-Am*

The most visible face of the Islamist 'Civilization Project' (*al-Mashru' al-Hadari*) after 1989 were the changes instituted by the *Inqaz* regime in 'Public Order' (*al-Nizam al-Am*) and morality, primarily through the new Penal Code. From the institution of the new codified criminal law in 1991, a Saudi-like public morality was enforced through a series of Public Order laws with its own Public Order Police (*Shurtat al-Nizam al-Am*). Initial fear and intimidation among the populace eventually gave way both to acquiescence and subtle and overt forms of resistance to a 'public order' that was essentially foreign to old Sudanese ways. During the decade of the strictest application of these laws an entire generation grew up in the changing cities and towns of the country that has created lasting effects of the culture of the new public order.

Shari'a: The Ideological Underpinning of the 'Civilization Project'

Public Order Laws

In 1991 the government issued a new codified Penal Code (discussed in chapter 4) that sought to fill in the gaps not addressed in the September Laws. The Public Order section provided that 'a person who, in public, commits an act, or conducts himself in a manner, contrary to public morality or wears an "immodest" dress commits an offence punishable by flogging.' This provision was elaborated by a 1996 Public Order Decree for Khartoum State that penalized and provided for flogging for a wide range of hitherto common practices, such as ... a women being in the company of a male other than a *mahram* (a near relative with whom marriage amounts to incest).[40]

Section 5 (3) of the Penal Code of 1991 made the punishments of *hudud* and *qisas* not applicable in the southern States and exempted the region from the provisions of the law relating to apostasy, adultery, manufacture, use and possession of alcohol and wearing 'immodest' dress. Despite this exception, the public order laws were applied to many Southerners in the North, especially its harsh application for men and women in the IDP camps where beer brewing and sale are often the only means of self-support in the general absence of government assistance. The *al-Nizam al-Am* laws regarding alcohol brewing, sale, and consumption were still being applied in the IDP camps in the years after the CPA when I was conducting research, primarily still enforced by the Public Order police.

Alcohol consumption never disappeared, before or after 1989, according to multiple informants who gave me precise details of where *'aragi* and *merissa* were, and are still, sold and how much to pay. Of course, none is for public sale, except the known 'secret' places of alcohol sale, e.g. Amarat, along Cemetery road, or a certain Chinese restaurant in Khartoum Two where imbibers can purchase a 'special pot of tea' containing cold Heinekin beer. This was true for the northern consumers of brew even during the harshest days of the *Inqaz*, according to one acquaintance, a confessed alcoholic. 'Now it only appears to be enforced on the wrong people, the non-Muslims in the camps,' he commented.

In the criminal courts in Khartoum I observed in 2007, the story was different. Cases were regularly dismissed involving Southerners in possession of alcohol in their homes. Public consumption of alcohol in Khartoum would likely be another matter, although public drunkenness in sections of the city where large numbers of Southerners reside, such as the Hajj Youssef neighborhood in Khartoum North, generally has not been subject to prosecution. This may be due to class as well as political factors for the Southerners who live in the suburbs are often home owners or renters and are more respected than the people in the IDP camps.

The Public Order Courts are still selectively prosecuting the 'crimes' of improper dress (pants or indecent dress) and the production of *merissa* sorghum beer, which is now subject to fines. For bribes the police turn a blind eye to the distribution and sale of *merissa* in the IDP camps.[41]

According to attorney Sonia Abdel Malik, application of *hudud* on non-Muslims was mainly directed against the southern women beer brewers, *sitat al- merissa*, which was heavily prosecuted until the eve of the signing of the CPA, and many remained in jail until two years after the peace accords. She says that 'women were targeted because they are vulnerable.' These were prosecuted in the Nizam al-Am courts near to the IDP camps.

The same is true for harassment of women not wearing proper *hijab* until it eased in 2001–02, after the political isolation of Hasan al-Turabi and the beginning of the flow of oil. Interviewing leaders of the women's empowerment group SUWEP, Zaynab Elsawi and Fahima Hashim, they recalled their experiences during the years of the strictest imposition of public order. Fahima was in high school in the early 1990s and as she refused to wear the most conservative *hijab* she was instructed to sit in the back of the lecture hall where she could not hear the lectures. Refusing to cover her head, she carried with her a thin head scarf she dubbed 'just in case' – just in case she was stopped by the Public Morals Police. On one occasion in Khartoum's suq al-'Arabi she was accosted by the Nizam al-Am police and reluctantly donned 'just in case' while pointedly questioning the officer to quote the Qur'anic passages that mandate her wearing this veil. 'Where in the Qur'an, why, and how do I veil according to our Holy Book,' she asked, with the response from the officer that she move along. On another occasion she was stopped because her skirt was too open in the front, and in response to her retort 'So what?!', the police injected a form of sexual harassment implying that he could take her skirt off, reminding her of his legitimated power of the state

Sonia Abdel Malik argues that al-Turabi pushed the wearing of veils for obtaining political backing from the conservative Ansar al-Sunna. She noted that in Omdurman the essence of their message that women must veil is still overwhelmingly observed in the streets and universities. As such, she argued that there has been little to no advance for women during the Islamist period, and there have even been some retreats. Moreover, many pioneers of the vibrant Sudanese women's movement are either in exile or their voices have been suppressed, leaving a gap and sense of frustration among younger women activists. 'Our pioneering women judges have disappointed us' noted SUWEP leader Fahima Hashim, implying that they have failed to speak out on the repressive laws affecting women the most. However, Sudan's most prominent woman leader, Fatima Ahmed Ibrahim, did criticize the repressive laws during the early years of the *Inqaz* from exile in the UK. She returned to the country at the time of the CPA and allowed a public role, along with other leaders of Sudan's weakened communist movement.

Although various government bodies decreed modest dress for women, contemporary enforcement of such decrees is less common and opportunistic, usually for political purposes. The arrest and flogging of Muslim Northerner Lubna Hussein and twelve others, mostly non-Muslim, women in 2009 for wearing trousers was protested internationally and contested in Khartoum. The required head covering was extended to Christian women for official purposes, such as a photo ID. In the past Nizam al-Am police on occasion entered university campuses to enforce dress codes. But today women wearing trousers in residential areas, or with their heads uncovered, generally are not accosted by the police as they were in the past. At private weddings where unmarried youth freely mix, revealing dresses and glamorous night gowns for young women have replaced the former full body wrap, the *tobe*. In 2000, the Wali of Khartoum State issued a decree forbidding women from working in businesses that serve the public, such as hotels, restaurants, and gas stations. However, in 2001 the Constitutional Court overturned the decree and women now work in many of these same service industries. Once considered acts of 'public indecency,' the Nizam al-Am police have recently only issued warnings for improper dress. The uneven and sometimes unpredictable alternate enforcement and relaxation of the public order morals-dress codes make this arena a delicate one for young women to negotiate, but also a sensitive one for assessing the relative withdrawal of the public order codes.

The law restricting the independent travel of women has been in effect since the Sadiq al Mahdi years (late 1980s), an important reminder that Islamist restrictions are not confined to the NIF nor the *Inqaz* regime. In immigration law a Sudanese woman is not free to marry a foreigner (*ejnabi*), without the permission of a male guardian. Sonia Abdel Malik was acquainted with a woman who was married in Germany but could not obtain identity papers for her children because she married without this specific guardianship (*wilaya*). Moreover, a woman cannot obtain a passport without *wilaya*, first from the Father, then the husband, brother or son, or one of the *'asaba*, core males in her family. Sonia herself had a conference to attend in Nairobi, but because she has custody of her children she was unable to get permission from the children's father. As guardian (*hadina*) of the children, if she traveled the father could claim she is 'neglecting' them and file suit for their custody.

One of the few studies of the early effects of the new public order was of single female teachers outside of the central North of Sudan was in al-Fasher, Darfur in 1991 (Willemse, 2001). Under the Nizam al-Am, single women in public were described as the most 'dangerous' element in society, which caused young women not only to be cautious but to locate ways and means of undermining the program. Work hours appropriate for women were legally set at between 5.00am and 5.00pm (article 17). In more remote parts of the Muslim North, the push was to make people, in this case Darfuris, 'better Muslims.' The poor, the slum dwellers, and the lady public tea sellers were targeted.

Although young, single women teachers were not of this class and were living in boarding houses, they were still considered potentially troublesome. Willemse reports that they began to memorize *suras* from the Qur'an and *Hadith* from the Prophet Muhammad in order to be able to defend their rights if accosted by the Nizam al-Am police. However, these women resisted the government call to marry in one of their sponsored public group marriages, *zawaj jamiya* or *zawaj al-kora*, despite the financial incentives, preferring to delay the marriage that would have made their life and work in Darfur easier.

My research assistant Salma M. Abdalmunim who was born into emerging Islamism in 1984 and grew up during its extremist period represents the youth who have known nothing other than a social system associated with Islamism. She described being required to cover her head from primary school (a break with past tradition where young girls first put on the *tarha*, a simple veil that adolescents wore before donning the adult woman's *tobe*, about nine meters of cloth wrapped about the body. She also described her 'brainwashing' with a religious curriculum that made primary school almost like a *khalwa* (traditional Qur'anic school) where reading and memorizing passages from the Qur'an were part of government schools. There was study of Qur'an, Sunna, and Shari'a law throughout primary and second-ary school and two years of study of the Shari'a are mandated in the public universities.[42] Ironically, many of the elite have enrolled their children in private schools, such as the Christian Unity and Comboni High Schools for girls and boys where the language of instruction is English, or the British Victoria and American Schools, that still operate in the suburbs where students study a secular curriculum in English.

Salma grew into a youth who became highly concerned about the conditions of southern refugees and the displaced in the North, even-tually conducting her Master's degree research on Christian-Muslim relations since the CPA. She reflected that in her primary school class of 60 students only four were Southerners and they were often har-assed and ridiculed as *kufar* or heathens. This reminded me of my own high school years in the 1960s in the then segregated southern city of Atlanta before its social transformation, like that for Khartoum's future, depended upon transformation of racial relations. She is now studying for her doctoral degree in Beyrouth, Germany.

One indication of the extremism and essentially foreign Saudi Wahhabist influences of the *al-Mashru'* was the prosecution of 'excessive dying of the hands and feet with henna,' a deeply embedded aesthetic tradition for northern women strongly associated with rites of passage, circumcision, marriage, and the birth of children, as well as personal beautification. Interestingly, the government argued that henna poisons the body through the skin, contradicting the likely thousands of years of use of henna products in the Nile Valley, (interview with attorney Sonia Abdel Malik, 14 February 2005).

Entirely new institutions of policing the 'public order' came into being to enforce the new laws. They function primarily in urban public space, and are often seen driving around as a show of force, and permanently stationed in sensitive places such as the *Suq al-Arabi* in central Khartoum.[43] These include:

> *Shurtat al-Nidham al-Am* (colloquial, *al-Nizam al-Am*, public order, green uniforms)
> *Shurtat al-Mujtama' al-'Am* (social order)
> *Shurtat al-Najda wa al-'Amaliyat* (Rescue and Operations Police, blue uniforms)
> *Shurtat al-Ihtiyat al-Markazi* (Central Reserve Police, especially used for control of political demonstrations)
> *Shurtat al-Quwwat al-Khasa* (Army Special Forces, only Northerners)
> *Private militias*

The new public order was imposed with seemingly little formal protest after the introduction of the laws and the sacking of judges believed to be opposed to this brand of Shari'a. All of the women judges survived – despite allegations from international human rights groups to the contrary, and two women judges were promoted to the Supreme Court, the Honorable Moalanas Rabab Abu Gusaysa and Amal Mohamed Hasan, while Justice Sinia Rashid was appointed to the Constitutional Court. When I returned to resume research in 2004–05, I expected to find few of my old friends in the Judiciary, but I found them all

Image 6   The author with senior women judges at Sudan Judiciary, 2005 (author photo)

and they hosted a party for me for the occasion of the 'sacked women judges who are still employed! (*lisa mojudin*).'

The Arabic translation of my 1987 book did not pass muster on this point with the Censorship Board on this point before its release in Sudan in 2004, and Mahgoub al-Tigani and I made the necessary correction to state clearly that the women judges has not been sacked during the early years of the *Inqaz*.

Few new women judges were appointed in the 1990s decade of Islamism, but overall the number of women in the Sudan Judiciary is about 10 per cent of the total, a figure that compares favorably with the overall statistics in the American Judiciary. However, the sacking of male judges opposed to the new Shari'a order in the early 1990s was widely reported inside and outside of Sudan.

Defying the 'New Social Order' of the Islamist Program

Cultural Resistance

Three types of Muslims may be detected in present day Sudan, according to Haydar Ibrahim, Director of the Sudanese Studies Center in Khartoum, (2003): 1) the *real* believers, representing the traditional practice of Islam in Sudan, heavily influenced by Sufis; 2) those involved with *al-harakat al-islamiya* (the Islamic movements), many of whom are entwined with the regime and have learned how to manipulate the faith to achieve their goals; and 3) those who are resisting the Islamist project in their behavior, a popular trend evidencing a passive resistance to the Islamists.

Resuming research after nearly 15 years of absence from Sudan and Khartoum, I was constantly aware of the visible transformations as well as the dramatic social changes, both physically observable and intuited. As I spoke with Sudanese colleagues in the social sciences, I began to process these observations through an analysis not only of unintended consequences of the 'Civilization Project' but of the extent to which there was popular cultural and social resistance to the project. A major statistic that flew in the face of the project was the sharp rise in the number of women in universities and in the work force during the 1990s when public order laws restricted their movement, dress, freedom of association, and areas of acceptable employment. A comparable resistance was observed for the Islamic Revolution in Iran and this subject will be treated in chapter 7 on comparable cases with the Sudan.

The dramatic rise in university attendance is just one form of cultural resistance to the Islamist project during the decade of the 1990s. Other expressions of resistance that I observed included the following:

Resistance in dress

As young Muslim women entered the universities and the formal work force in unprecedented numbers, their modest dress evolved and modernized under the strictures of the 'Civilization Project.' Among northern Muslim youth, long skirts, fitted blouses, and tied headscarf revealing no hair, or the more casual veil (*tarha*, revealing the hair) have replaced the more modest traditional *tobe*. Older women who still wear the *tobe* adopted a more conservative mode of covering the hair during the *Inqaz* with a scarf or headband that hides all of a woman's hair added to the *tobe* that naturally covers the head but not the hair. Among youth in the affluent suburbs loose fitting shirts over jeans or pants – with or without headscarf – are observed. Make-up among unmarried women is common, and in recent years, skin-lightening foundation has become popular. This new ensemble of the urban young woman is alluring, long skirt, fitted blouse or shirt and loose or tightly pinned head covering, and is consistent with the wardrobe of secular youth in Cairo or the Gulf.

During this same period for most literate youth the world of the internet and global culture penetrated the Sudan. These youth saw a world outside of that enforced by the *Inqaz* dictates of public propriety. They shared this new culture with others at safe meeting places as social restrictions relaxed after 1999. Internet cafes provide such a meeting place, as do public parks and outdoor cafes. At these meeting places a new counter-culture – so to speak – emerged that was undermining the *Inqaz* Civilization Project. During my visit to Shendi University in February 2007 university women were wearing the 'uniform' of the *'al-Mashru*,' full *hijab*, no hair showing, long sleeves and long skirts. However, some of the bolder girls wore heavy make up and tight fitting clothes which they still claim was 'Shari'i,' lawful, since their shirt sleeves and skirts were long and modest.

Resistance in public behavior

With known places for public mixing of youth at night – often near to markets where every night after the *maghrib* sunset prayers – there is mixing of unmarried boys and girls without any intervention of the Nizam al-Am police, especially in the more affluent suburbs. Like youth around the globe, they share a music that binds them. A number of young singers openly critical of the government and its policies, such as Taha Ismail and Awad Dakan, are popular. These singers have also brought into Sudanese music elements of Ethiopian dancing that has now become an expected and much anticipated part of wedding celebrations among elite northern families.

Resistance in social organization

The most dramatic source of resistance to the traditional order is the dramatic increase in *zawaj 'urfi*, a controversial form of marriage, new to Sudan but now common in Cairo. It involves the contracting of marriage between the men and women themselves, generally without the usual parental and familial guidance and approval, and usually without the payment of *mahr*, the dower requisite in Muslim marriages. It is widely viewed as a form of temporary marriage – like that which Sunni Muslims accuse Shi'a of practicing – and together with a more recent form of seeming temporary marriage, *misyar*, they bear a dangerously close resemblance to informal sexual arrangements that are so criticized in the West.

Female Circumcision

Also known as female genital mutilation or cutting (FGM, FGC) has been one of the most widely reported and discussed of Sudanese customs. It has been condemned by feminist and human rights organizations and has been debated as a harmful tradition understandable as a cultural norm but violating universal standards of human rights (Fluehr-Lobban, 1996). During the decades of the demographic and social transformation under discussion in this chapter and in chapter 6, overall female circumcision has been reduced and the most severe forms of the practice have been ameliorated. A study in 2001 (Islam and Uddin) surveying the reproductive health of 1,000 ever-married woman in the urban areas of Khartoum, Shendi and Juba revealed a significant shift away from *Pharaonic* circumcision or infibulation to the simpler and less traumatic Sunna form of the operation. Knowing the sensitivity in the West to the continuation of this custom, several of my educated women friends offered without my prompting that female circumcision was 'finished' (*khalas*) in the cities nowadays.

Zawaj 'urfi

This is instantly a hot topic once it is introduced, and is treated separately in chapter 6. Haydar Ibrahim sees this not only as a result of the difficult economy, but also of globalization. 'They see Arabs acting like westerners on TV and conclude that to be modern is to act in this way with casual relations. The culture of the Egyptians as superficial, apolitical and fun seeking is also affecting Sudan. They are lacking a serious culture; they do not read or reflect, and there is really no significant student movement as in the past' (Interview, 8 February 2007).

Southern Harassment and Voices of Resistance to **al-Mashru'**

Southern presence in the public areas of Khartoum and environs must be careful not to offend anything that has to do with the faith of Islam or the Prophet Muhammad. Freedom of dress and of personal habit is often reported as liberating when Southerners travel outside the North, especially to the South. The resistance of Southerners is political as well as cultural. Presidential advisor Bona Malwal reported an example of southern youths arriving to Khartoum via Dubai. They were observed buying only alcohol in the Duty Free Shops and were intent upon openly carrying their purchases into the Khartoum airport. This resulted in a confrontation at the airport. Once a fierce opponent of the regime and now an advisor to President al-Bashir, Malwal remarked that this act was 'deliberately provocative' (interview 7 February 2007). Another view of this story is that of cultural resistance to *al-Mashru'* on the part of these southern youth.

The renaming of the IDP camps by their residents, substituting African for northern political names, is a clear form of resistance. The names 'Mandela' and 'Angola' were substituted for the oldest and largest camp 'Mayo,' this camp dating from the Numieri years.

A young Dinka lady, a Christian secondary school student described harassment in Khartoum when wearing a short sleeved blouse. The Public Order police accosted her with the question, 'Is this your home town? You should dress like that in Juba, not in Khartoum. Christian or not, you should respect the Muslims here,' said the policeman.

Voices from the IDP camps perhaps offer the most incisive commentary on resistance to the civilization program and are suggestive of the current state of Christian-Muslim relations.[44]

Paulino Jandolor asks, 'How could there be jihad against "the infidel" when I am a Christian and Christians are "People of the Book"? Why should I, as a law student, have to sit for a bar exam on Muslim personal status law of 1991? My father tried to work for al-Higra Construction Company (reputed to be founded by Osama Bin Laden during his six years in Sudan) but the condition of employment was to be a Muslim. I tried to get a job with SUNA (Sudan News Agency), but in the job interview I had to recite a verse from the Qur'an and I did not do very well.'

Bol Chan Bol, resident of Mandela camp comments, 'TV is a problem – all of the programs are for Muslims, there is nothing for Christians. Also in the curriculum, even the poetry is Islamic. They only show the formal [token] government participation of Christian officials, while the whole state is an Islamic state. In many southern families some members know the Qur'an by heart because they faced pressure to learn it. For me it is important to have a lot of information about Islam to succeed in this society.'

Romeo Bor Akec observes, 'If I have a girlfriend who is Muslim I wear appropriate clothes to her house, but with my family I just wear ordinary clothes. When their daughter comes to our parties she dresses like us. When we are together, we ignore religion and just are Sudanese.'

From a pious Muslim camp resident, Wad al-Bashir, Osama Abdel Fadeel, 'The Islamic Dawa is more active these days compared to before. There is a new mosque, *al Hamduilah* (praise God), but there are no *khalwas* (Qur'anic schools) at present.'

However, Maryam Eddini says, 'It is not so easy to differentiate between the true Islam and the political Islam. My suggestion to the politicians is not to mix religion with politics. My only problem now is with university studies I must attend lectures on Sunday and it is hard to go to church.'

From a Christian Mandela camp resident, Solomon Oduho, 'I go to the civil court. I have Muslim friends there. I attend hearings of cases from Mandela and Jebel Awlia (IDP camps). Not a single law suit was connected to religion. However, once I attended a case of a woman from Mayo who makes *'aragi* (liquor from dates). She was captured and fined although she denied possession of the liquor. A photograph by the police proved the case against her. She was convicted; the judgment was a fine of 50,000 SD (about $250) or three months prison. To me such deeds are prohibited in Shari'a law, yet living conditions compelled people to commit such acts.'

Perhaps the best summary comment describing the asymmetrical relations between Christians and Muslims is from Oliver Njoro, 'Christians know much more about Islam than the other way around.'

The Decline and Partial Withdrawal
of the 'Civilization Project'

My 2007–08 US Institute of Peace grant was titled 'Shari'a in Sudan: Post-Islamism or Renewal of Conflict' and was funded after a period of research in 2005 supported by the European Union. It seemed to me that Sudan was transitioning to a post-Islamist phase of the state and I began to suggest this to Sudanist colleagues in Sudan and in the US. The idea of post-Islamism had been discussed in Europe in connection with other Islamist movements, in North Africa and the Middle East (Roy, 1994), but Sudan was left out of this debate despite its obvious importance. Post-Islamism as a trend or transitional phase of the *Inqaz* state was formally discussed at a panel of the Sudan Studies Association in 2008 (Fluehr-Lobban, Salomon, 2008) and a blog discussion entitled 'Is Sudan a Post-Islamist State' was organized by Alex de Waal around an online discussion of Abdullahi Gallab's book, *The First Islamist Republic: Development and Disintegration of Islamism in Sudan* (2008). Gallab sees Sudan as unique, apart from the Islamist states erected in Iran and Afghanistan, and as 'the first Islamist Republic' largely because he sees the other cases as based upon religious rather than political movements. For Gallab the Islamist Republic dates from 1989 to 1999, and does not begin with the establishing of the September Laws in 1983 (blog discussion, 2008). In this book, I address the broader subject of Sudan's process of Islamization, for which I start this clock in 1983. These efforts followed upon earlier works by Sudanese who witnessed and began the analysis of the withdrawal of extremist Islamist politics. These include Haydar Ibrahim's *Suqut al-Mashru al-Hadari* (2003, The End of the Civilization Project), Khalid al-Mubarak's *Al-Turabi's Islamist Venture, Failures and Implications* (in English, Cairo, 2001), written while Mubarak was at the Woodrow Wilson Center in Washington, DC. A number of former regime supporters, or acknowledged apologists, are also important writers on the subject including Hassan Mekki's *al-Islamiya fi Sudan, 1969–1985,* Khartoum, 2008); and Abdelwahab Elaffendi's *Al-Turabi's Revolution: Islam and Power in Sudan* (1991). Indeed, Sudan's failed Islamism is acknowledged by its very founder, al-Turabi (Salomon, blog discussion,

2008) whose political twists and turns are legendary. These works and analyses are reviewed in depth in chapter 8 along with my own observations and theoretical contributions to this important question of the extent, breadth and depth of Sudan's 'post-Islamism.'

The subtle and obvious changes in the 'Public Moral Order' imposed, pursued, withdrawn or partially withdrawn that are introduced here are relevant to this later discussion. Some of the tantalizing suggestions by Sudanists commenting upon the reasons for the withdrawal or failure of the Islamist project include the following:

1) The loss of the civil war in the South, and the CPA mandated by international pressures;
2) The huge ambition behind the 1989 coup with the mantra that the ends justify the means, resulting in an extremism that now has run its course (Khalid Mubarak);
3) The effects of international sanctions and isolation;
4) Islamism as foreign to Sudanese Sufi Islam (al-Tigani Mahmoud SHRO Report);
5) The flow and export of substantial amounts of commercial oil after 1999;
6) 'Nizam al-am' was relaxed after 9/11, not after the flow of the oil but the regime's real fear was of retribution for their collaboration with Osama bin Laden, according to some local human rights activists; and
7) The Islamist project failed to deal with Sudan's central problem of racism (de Waal, blog introduction, 2008).

'The theater of the Islamist project is still visible,' says Haydar Ibahim. 'The gentlemen with the beards and prayer mark on their foreheads (ura al-salat) are a common sight on the streets of the three towns. They may be doing this out of genuine piety, or because they want to obtain or hold on to a job. The girls are wearing a different and more revealing hijab with a lot of cosmetics. There is a study in the "ethnography of hair"!' Ibrahim remarks. 'How to reveal the amount of hair you want to show is a subtle, but in the matter of the hairstyle there is clear indication of the acceptance or rejection of the Islamist program. The ultimate in mixed messages is you don't show your hair, but wear tight pants!' (Haydar Ibrahim interview, 8 February 2007).

Ali Suleiman Fadlalla, University of Khartoum Law School Professor, argues that what remains of the Islamic project is just the façade of Islamism. What is left is just the superficial, public face of Islamism through 'public order' displays for public consumption, however at the core is the fabric of a changing society with greed, corruption, and social disintegration occurring. He told me one of the best jokes that I heard about the Islamic project: 'You know how the girls are dressing these days, with blouses that expose their midriff, well, that is the space between *din wa dawla*, where lies the separation of religion and the state.'

IDP Camps: Sudanese nationals denied full citizenship

The south in the North, a new permanent underclass?

There are five official camps for IDPs ringing the greater Khartoum 'three towns' – Mayo/Mandela and Soba Eradi/Aradi (population of 344,000) 30 km south of Khartoum, Wad al-Bashir and El-Salaam (population of 400,000) outside of Omdurman, and Haj Yusuf outside of Khartoum North 'Bahari.' Jebel Aulia, Baraka, Hamas Koreib, and Navaisha settlement areas also constitute parts of the official UN statistics for IDPs in Khartoum state for a total of 2,072,320 (dated 8 July 2008). Some people have been in the camps since the mid-1980s, while others arrived in the 1990s, and still others are arriving from Darfur and Kordofan after the outbreak of hostilities in 2003. The Arabic word used for the camps is *mu'askarat*, the word for military encampment, literally 'full of soldiers.' The IDP camps are the result of wars, and are extensions of the coercive arm of the state, its army and police who run the camps. Humanitarian aid in the camps is largely left to international donors, except for the state run Muslim Humanitarian Assistance Commission that provides the overarching regulation of camp life.

Until the Iraq war the number of IDPs in the Sudan was the largest worldwide, with about 11.9 per cent of the population considered

Image 7   Darfur Internally displaced

displaced mainly as a result of war. It is estimated that more than one half of the population of the southern Sudan is now either living in northern Sudan or has fled to neighboring countries. Perhaps 25 per cent of Sudan's population lives in and around Khartoum. Of the IDPs, the greatest number is located in Greater Khartoum (over 44 per cent).

The CPA mandated census was conducted, but not trusted, because it was controlled by the GoS and linked to their desired outcomes in the elections. Official results released in March 2009 were immediately contested by the SPLM and a legal suit demanding its review was filed, with implications for constituencies and voters in the 2010 elections. The commonly cited population of Khartoum at 7–8 million may or may not include the approximate 2 million in the IDP camps. For this CPA mandated census, people in the camps were not counted as they are considered temporary residents in the capital and were required to travel home in order to be recorded. Thus, this latest official census will exclude millions of displaced persons whose citizenship status is fundamentally compromised. Not surprisingly, the outcome of the elections in April 2010 drew mixed reactions for their lack of inclusion of the historically disenfranchised.

Nevertheless, the people of the camps come and go to the capital city every day, especially women. Travel to and from the camps is controlled, but public transport reaches into the camps and tens of thousands of displaced person workers in the informal sector travel to and from the city every day. The situation is comparable to the African townships that surrounded the major cities under apartheid in South Africa, and like the apartheid comparison the camps reflect the politics of both fear and hope. Thus far, only a small percentage of targeted returnees have gone home from camps.

My research assistant Salma was conducting research in the IDP camps in the year the CPA was signed and she reported that after 'Black Monday,' the day after Garang's death was announced, everything changed. On that day she could not get home along with thousands of others, she had to walk from the University of Khartoum to Omdurman via the Blue Nile Bridge. Continuing her research after these events, she observed that the people divide time in the camps from before Garang's death and after. Certainly, trust by Southerners of their government was once again broken. In the aftermath of the violence, some of the Southerners arrested for their role in the riots were subjected to the *hadd* punishment of lashing for 'disturbing the public order.'

In Mayo camp, founded in 1991, 80 per cent of people report that they are displaced due to war. In this oldest camp there are eight schools, five mosques, twelve chapels, three health centers, two cultural clubs, three native music bands, and three water wells. Although there are many churches in the camps, I did not see clear evidence of a church building or cross, except for crosses worn by people, although the mosques are evident in the centers of the camps. There is no pubic supply of electricity or water in Mayo.

Police stations dot the camps' centers and peripheries. There is a tension between the traditional authority of the chiefs, the salatin, and the police. The authority should rest with the chiefs, but the government has taken this away. The police are made up of all of the ethnic groups present in the camps, but the running of the camps is basically carried out by the police who are mostly northerners. At Mayo (South of Khartoum), Wad al-Bashir (Omdurman) and Hajj Youssef

(Khartoum North) it was reported to my research assistant that *merissa* is taxed and sold for revenue to the state. There are Chief's Courts specialized by ethnic group and subject, such as special courts for water, electricity, other public services, but the problem is that the judges are hired by the corporations.

Few Khartoum residents have ever visited the camps or have a clear idea of where they are located. Our taxi driver had never visited any of the camps and was fascinated by each visit and genuinely enjoyed listening to the interviews. Popular interest has to do with the illegal alcohol production prevalent in the camps. There is an imagined reality in a society that has officially banned public use of alcohol, but all or most know that the 'brew' is still flowing and available (like the war on drugs in the US), yet it remains behind closed doors whether it is the expensive imported whiskey of the elites or the *merissa* and *aragi* locally made. The fascination is with public drunkenness, Sonia Abdel Malik observed. She noted in an independent study there was a random sampling of men in Mandela camp where researchers apparently saw many openly drunk individuals, about which there is great interest among northern Muslims.

The following is a relatively raw description from my research journal that I reproduce here for recording the details of these visits and research and for the vividness of the immediate reactions I had upon my return each day.

15 April 2007: together with Salma Abdelmunim, my research assistant from the University of Khartoum, we spent our first day in Mayo/Mandela camp just outside of Khartoum. I hired a taxi for the day negotiated at 80,000 SD for the taxi, about $40.

Before this first visit, I had to obtain permission to conduct research in the camps through the Muslim Humanitarian Assistance Commission (MHAC), a government agency responsible for the running of the camps.[45] Beyond Erkoweit is Mayo which is the older camp and displays signs of long term occupation by displaced people, mainly beginning in the early 1990s as the war was waged again in earnest in an effort to 'win' it militarily. As such Mayo, for me, resembled the lower class areas of the old Khartoum Diem section – mud houses, with limited water delivered by donkey cart. These ubiquitous donkeys that used to be a part of Khartoum life are now transporting goods in Mayo. There is a tarmac road to Mayo – *Shar'ia al-Mayo* – and a bustling *suq* for everything plus a transport hub. The camp area is vast with rickshaws serving as a means of local transport.

But nothing really prepares you for the vast areas of Mayo and the huge number of 'homes' made up of nothing more than sticks and burlap, with the desert winds easily blowing through them. This is beyond *'masakeen'* (pitiful) and if the south was often referred to as the fourth world, then this is the fifth world There are no proper streets, few visible services, except for the government police, about which more will be related.

We parked next to a mosque that surprised me since I saw no comparable churches, confirming reports about Islamist penetration of the camps viewing them as potential recruits to Islam. There we waited until Khalid (representative of the MHAC who accompanied us on every visit) had made arrangements for me to meet the *'salatin'* or chiefs from the Dinka who will respond to my questions. The appointed translator is Francis, a Latuka, who knows Dinka and will translate my questions from Arabic to English and then back to Arabic from Dinka. Salma wrote the transcriptions.Exterior photography in the camps is not permitted, but photographs of persons with their permission was allowed.

The 'salateen' with whom we met are eight in number and only one speaks some limited Arabic that suggests isolation from Khartoum,

Table 5.12   *House types in Wad al-Bashir and Mayo* (Abdalmunim, 2008)

House Type	Percentage
Mud	42.4
Carton	23.8
Straw Hut/Cloth	14.0
Others	8.4
Unidentified	11.3

media and meaningful contact with the capital city. The courts each have 12–13 chiefs who reach their decisions collectively by consensus (*qararat jamiya*). There are two functioning Salateen Courts organized along ethnic lines which are basically customary courts dealing with marriages, divorces, and quarrels between people. We tried on several occasions to observe court sessions in progress, but the courts meet so infrequently that we had to settle for interviews with the chiefs. There is a joint council of the salateen that meets as need arises for community matters and responses to government action or inaction.

According to the salateen the marriage and divorce cases are working well in Mandela. There are 64 different 'tribes' – Dinka, Nuer, Shilluk, Zaghawa, Birgu (Fur), Hausa, Messiriya, Rizegat, Masalit, Equatorians – Latuko, Moro, etc. The language of the courts is by the ethnicity of the litigants, by each '*gabila*.' In the camps people are looking for the *grush* (money) to marry. Questions such as how to determine the number cows sufficient for a marriage that is made in the North; how to write what in effect are promissory notes for the delivery of cows once they are home; who are the effective representatives of the two families? I saw one of these marriage documents neatly typed with the bride and groom, their paternal uncles standing for them with the promise of future cows as brideweath once normal life has been restored.

There is a Secretary who takes notes and keeps these records in his house and to underscore the marginal status of IDPs as incomplete citizens, these records are not kept in official government offices nor in the Sudan Judiciary. 'Sudan is *balad wahid*' (Sudan is one country), but there is a problem with this state; you see the state does not care about the '*mahakim salatin*,' Sultan John Deng[46] complained. When there is a problem between people of two different ethnic groups then they bring in the sultans from each to resolve, as before. The large cases that used to be heard in Salateen Courts now are now going to Mahkama Niaba.

'We have a system here. There is a big tent, adult people meet there. Those under 15 cannot go there. When a dispute arises, it is settled there. This morning there was a dispute, but instead of going to the formal authorities, we solved it in *judiya* (folk mediation) there under that tent. We solve our problems by ourselves. When somebody comes here for the first time, we invite him to attend meetings to know where he comes from, and to introduce him to the community, and we make a meal' (Kafino Satarnino, interviewed by Salma Abdalmunim).

The 'al-Nizam al-Am' courts are quite another matter; they are government operated and are still enforcing Shari'a, despite the mandates in the CPA about the non-application of Islamic law upon non-Muslims, a fact about which they complain bitterly. The fine (gharama) for alcohol possession and/or consumption is 150,000 SD or $75, and the physical punishment is 40 lashes for a non-Muslim and 100 for a Muslim. On another visit we interviewed Salateen in Wad al-Bashir camp who were from Aweil, Dinka. The party included Khalid from the MHAC, Salma and our driver Elias who by now has become interested in the conversations we have and in camp conditions in general. I greeted them in Dinka with 'jeebak' and used this as an occasion to relate a story about a murder case in the US for which I was consulted where the Dinka murder suspect refused to speak to his lawyer who was desperate for an opening to begin communication. I recommended that he greet him with 'jeebak' and this was key to commencing a successful relationship and reduction of a serious murder charge to manslaughter. They liked the story and began to recite a litany of complaints about their ability to manage affairs in the camp.

In Wad al-Bashir there are 12 sultans, one 'umda or 'mayor,' and a Court President, Rais al-Mahkama. As with Mandela camp, they also reported that after the CPA the government closed the Salatin Court,

If the police are there to preserve order (the nizam), now they are the nizam. Before the sultans were strong and people were afraid of them. They were able to levy fines for minor crimes and deal with problems for which people could be sentenced for up to 3 years imprisonment. But now we have lost the respect of people because we have no power. They want to go home where they can be real salateen in real customary courts. It was better before the CPA when we had some power. We are the Salateen bidun sulta – the Chiefs without power.

They laughed, we all laughed with a shared sense of irony and sarcasm. Actually there were many sardonic, bitingly critical comments made this day – without any fear of Khalid's presence – and with much cynical laughter about the absurdity of their situation.

Women in the Camps

At Muaskar Wad al-Bashir, we met Sudanese indigenous worker Um Abdu Al-Jabber who is responsible for assisting and providing information (*shubak mu'amalat*) to refugees returning to their home areas after the CPA. She is from Talodi in the Nuba Mountains, is divorced and has eight daughters: five are married and three are still in school. She came to Wad al-Bashir in 1994, and has worked for the UN International Organization for Migration (IMO), among the largest NGOs operating in the camps, for two years. The week we visited (22–24 April 2007) repatriation trips to Bahr al Ghazal and also South Kordofan were being organized. She works with UN colleagues in Haj Yusef and the Wali of Khartoum who delivers the lorries for transport.

She expressed frustration that after the CPA very little has changed. She is especially concerned about the heavy burdens that women in the camps carry.

They work in the house and are the major source of economic income for their families. 'The majority of women are working outside their homes, the children are without care and the men don't do anything but sit around – the only ones helping out are the foreigners,' she says.

Men in the camps have been almost entirely emasculated both in terms of culture as well as gender. Lacking the traditional base of a cattle economy and with a plentiful supply of cheap labor for construction projects in booming Khartoum, they remain isolated in the camps in almost every respect from linguistic skills in Arabic to basic literacy in any language. For some this is the case despite decades of living in the camps. The limited education available is primary school in Arabic with the standard Islamist curriculum focus on religious studies. Loss of dignity, hope, and a resulting despair create conditions for alcoholism, domestic abuse, and fights between men.

Women have moved in to fill this economic void. During our visits to the camps in the daytime hours, few women are visible or available for interviews as they are working in a variety of informal sector jobs in the three towns and peripheries. They are tea sellers in the outdoor markets in *Suq al-'Arabi* in Khartoum, or in Omdurman suq. They sell small bags of sunflower seeds, peanuts (*ful Sudani*) and peanut products such as ground peanuts (*dakwa*) used in Sudanese cooking. They also supply most of the nearly ubiquitous cheap domestic labor for urban and suburban middle class families. These are the legal economic activities for which camp women may nonetheless suffer some ethnic or racial discrimination in the homes where they work, but they also learn Arabic and are familiar with the intimate details of northern family life. Harassment and criminal prosecution has accompanied the illegal brewing of beer and other types of *khamra*.

Um Abdu reports, 'In the camps the woman has the two jobs – daytime outside the camps and night work at home – the men just sit *sakit* (doing nothing) in the camps while the women do all the work. If there is problem between the husband and wife they can go the sultan or sheikh; if she is Muslim they go to the Shari'a Court, if they are Christian, the case goes to the Salateen Courts. For major problems between husband and wife they can go to the police. Men are still able to marry five or six wives just with a present (referred to in the interview as *zawaj mut'a*, temporary marriage, as in *'urfi* marriage described above for Muslims). The children are the woman's responsibility and the family unit is really just the woman and her children; this was present in earlier time in the South but it has really changed with the life in the camps.'

Um Abdu described a Tira woman who makes *khamra* (alcohol) but her man takes the money. She makes a tray seeds and *ful Sudani* (peanuts), *waka*, salsa, dried meat, *dakwa* (peanut butter) and she sells tea in the *Suq al-'Arabi* alternating her trade with the Suq in Omdurman. She observes that the CPA has opened more space for trade by camp women. However, the police steal from them with impunity, while they take the local brews *khamra baladiya*, the one and only thing they are interested in, she reports. A woman she knows had 75 SD ($35) taken from her house by the police whom people view as thieves, operating in the open without fear with guaranteed immunity from any accountability for their actions (interview 22 April 2007). She repeats the widely held view that the police run the camps, and are given free reign to seize alcohol and property as an incentive to carry out this work which is neither attractive nor prestigious in the hierarchical structure of Sudan's professional police service: 'When police come and they take *merissa*, it is for themselves to drink'; (600 ml = 1500sd) (laughing again).

There were several reports of the police seizing property from peoples' houses on their searches for *khamra*. If the house if locked, they break in, and no search warrant (*tasreeh*) is needed. The police are local from different 'tribes' ('shorta *sha'biya*'), young men with little formal knowledge of the law. Flogging (*jald*) is still meted out as a Shari'a punishment for khamra violations – 80 lashes for a Muslim, 40 for a Christian.

The youth in the Suq al-Arabi may steal to buy a bottle of *merissa*, the going rate for a small water bottle 600 ml = 1500SD, or $3.00 (a kofta or fish sandwich in a central Khartoum restaurant can be had for about a quarter of that amount, even less in the popular suqs); a stolen mobile = 3 bottles of *merissa*. They can be sentenced to prison for four months, and/or receive a SD200,000 fine. 'They will send you to prison for possession of the ingredients to make *merissa*, the dates, the sugar, reports one women beer brewer. This is the only work for us women and this is how we are carrying on. Our children need to eat, milk, sugar.'

As many as 3,000 women were prosecuted for beer and alcohol brewing and served extended sentences in Omdurman Women's Prison. They were held for several years until 2007 after the signing of the CPA, despite their new amnesty from prosecution or further imprisonment under Shari'a law. They were fined $75, which they could not pay or were given three months' sentences that have been indefinitely extended, perhaps as a form of preventative detention to prevent them from resuming alcohol production after their release. They say directly to me 'You should go to the prison and see for yourself.'

With the inauguration of the work of the CPA mandated Commission on the Status of Non-Muslims in the National Capital in August of 2007, 858 non-Muslim female prisoner inmates accompanied by 147 children were released. The head of the Judiciary Muhamad Osman Jelal Eddin Osman made the announcement: 'It has been decided by virtue of our prerogatives in Art 185 of the Code of Criminal Procedure, to drop the remainder of the terms and release the 858 prison inmates and 147 children, without prejudicing fines or civil liabilities ensuing from the crimes committed, provided that none of them is waiting for sentence to be passed or wanted in another crime' (2 August 2007 from Sudan TV, Omdurman). Joshwa Gaido, the head of the Commission for non-Muslims revealed that a number of courts for non-Muslims have been formed (in the capital) and that training courses are being given to judges who will be assigned to them. He expressed happiness at the release, considering this another step and new beginning of co-existence between Muslims and non-Muslims within the CPA framework. At the same time a special committee was formed to promote awareness through the media between Muslims and non-Muslims, again part of the CPA agreement.

Christian-Muslim Relations

Many leaders and indigenous relief workers with whom I spoke wanted to point out that with so many of Sudan's ethnic groups represented in the camps that there is considerable mixing of Christians and Muslims, approximately 70 per cent Christian and 30 per cent Muslim. Recalling that Southerners comprise the largest number of IDPs, it is important to reiterate that a number of Southerners have become Muslim, either through a process of forcible conversion, indoctrination through Islamist education, opportunism while living in the North, or a sincere embracing of Islam – or a combination of the above. This 30 per cent Muslim population explains the visible presence of mosques in the camps, especially in the central market areas.

'There are no problems between Christians and Muslims in the camps,' I was told repeatedly, often without raising the question myself. 'It is all about politics (*siyasa*)'; the problems are over food and money – the most important thing is to have faith. The Saudis try to stir up problems bringing their extremist *da'wa* (religious propaganda).

Likewise, the Ministry of Awqaf (Religious Endowments) are involved with Muslim *da'wa* as they are the responsible for the permits and construction of new mosques.

However, besides the support for mosques over churches Muslims are favored with better houses in the realm of the limited good that is available in the camps. Jobs are granted to those with Muslim names, that is why there are so many Southerners with Muslim names. The worst houses, *beut showlat* (lean-tos for houses covered with cloth), are not occupied by Muslims. But in the end most agreed that the fundamental problems between people are not about religion, as the foreign press suggests, but are about food and money (*akil wa grush, bas!*).

Still the sentiment of solidarity as camp residents overrides religious difference. 'They [Christians and Muslims] are in the camps together and help one another out quite naturally – the government needs to act like we do here in Wad al-Bashir,' says Fatma Hamdan. Salma Abdalmunim agreed to share some of her interviews that reflect the essence of camp residents' views of Christian-Muslim relations, and the changes, or lack thereof, after the signing of the CPA.

Conditions after the CPA

The CPA stopped the war but it did not end our troubles. Conditions were supposed to improve but they did not, in fact some of the police harassment increased because some of the police were against the CPA, as they saws it as a loss of their power. After the CPA the police became rougher with us, and they do not need the same proof of our wrongdoing as before. Just the word of the police against any accused person is sufficient to convict that person of *merissa* or *khamra*, and this has opened wide the door to corruption of the police – the protection money is 400,000 SD per day.

After CPA the salateen were 'laid off' and no longer took any government salary. '*Iza ma fi shughul, ma fi akil*' – If there is no work, there is no food. 'We want to return to the south because that is where we can survive and live on our own with cows and agriculture.' Finally one frank sultan spoke up, 'We have not told you the worst – we are not speaking freely as we do not know if you will go and tell the government what we have said. We need your help to tell the truth about these things. We still do not feel free to speak without fear.'

They talked further about racial discrimination and the 'problem' of the color of their skin. I talked about the SSA and the work we try to do and our good relations with prominent southern leaders like Francis Deng and Bona Malwal. There are rarely problems between the people of the world themselves, but many problems and wars that governments and politicians make. A few human words between human beings. May I never forget this day or the sights I have seen, and be unafraid to bear witness. We took some pictures with my throwaway wind-the-film camera (digital cameras and all electronic equipment were forbidden to bring under US sanctions), but the light was insufficient and flash wouldn't work so they are useless and the salateen did not want to go outside to pose for a photograph.

After multiple visits to the IDP camps I left with a feeling not of pity for the victims, but the immense admiration for the triumph of the people to survive creatively under the worst of conditions. I only heard evidence of voluntary return, not forced, and of the enormous and unacknowledged contribution of women, who are holding this all together, while the men are disempowered and drinking, despairing and angry. However, I did not see a single drunken man nor smell alcohol on anyone's breath.

Other Voices from the Camps[47]

Maliki Abdalla Adam, Muslim merchant, Mima 'tribe' West Darfur, 'It would be enough if one receives a piece of land to settle in a house, nothing more.'

Jane Ayoro, 'All of the people rose up at the time of Garang's death, Christian and Muslim. All people are one tribe in the face of government.'

Osama Abdel Fadeel: 'We have become suspicious of the people who come and ask us questions and don't come back.'

Tabaan Hokuma (this name means 'tired of the government'),
'My father is treated as a 'martyr' but I don't agree with that.
He was wounded in the army and died on the way to hospital in
Khartoum. He was buried in Sahafa; sadly there is even discrimination in the cemetery – the deceased are divided into Christian
and Muslim. When I graduated military college I won top hon-
ors in marching and height climbing. The award ceremony was
attended by President Bashir. When I received the award I had
to shout 'Allahu Akbar.' In fact, the martyr foundation is religious and not military. Muslim martyrs receive a sheep on 'Eid
al-Fitr (holiday at the end of Ramadan), but we do not get a
sheep or anything at Christmas.'

Issues of Race, Unaddressed and Unresolved

Race (al-ansur), and racism, (al-ansuriya), are major issues in Sudan
that, like in the US, are central to understanding society and politics,
yet they remain largely unaddressed and unresolved. In the current
era race has entered political, academic and popular discourse as never
before. After the CPA, but with conflict continuing in Darfur, it is a
time rife with despair as well as hope that the society can begin the
process of healing its racial wounds that have proved so deadly. The
CPA admonition to 'make unity attractive' or prepare for separation
of the South was really coded language for the country to engage in
reckoning with its race problems, described after South Africa's positive experience as 'truth and reconciliation.'

Sudan's truth and reconciliation would acknowledge a complex and
lengthy legacy of slavery and enslaved in the Nile Valley that resulted
in a genetic co-evolution of peoples (Keita, 2008) tied by blood and a
bloody history. A number of scholarly works (Spaulding and Beswick,
2000; Sikainga, 1996; Ewald, 1990; and Jok, 2004) have tackled this
subject, and the novels of Francis Deng – 'Seed of Redemption' and
'Cry of the Owl' – dramatized the human story of shame and the
secrets of an intermingling of peoples engulfed in slavery and con-
cubinage. Now available in Arabic, these novels have the potential
for initiating conversations leading in the direction of healing and

reconciliation. The most potent legacy of this history is embodied in one word – ''Abd,' slave – that has the same power in Sudanese society as 'nigger' has in English or 'kafir' has in South Africa. When a Northerner calls to a Southerner, 'ya, 'abd' – 'Hey, you slave,' it is at least a word that wounds establishing the hierarchy of relations in an instant. But in today's climate it can be explosive for its potent message and racial politics in the interim period between unity and separation. Jimmy Wongo, a prominent southern SPLM leader, described in a public forum how in the immediate post CPA urban environment he can still be addressed as 'abd – recalling a recent incident where the boy who collects fares on public transport said to him, an older gentleman, 'Gom, ya 'abd' – 'get up on the bus, slave.' The use of the term 'abeed/slaves as a generic reference to Southerners has become politically incorrect in public discourse, but it can be heard, or overheard, in casual conversation, oftentimes heard by Southerners themselves who supply most of the domestic service in northern households.

A racial hierarchy in the Nile Valley was established by British colonialism in an effective system of divide and rule and sophisticated manipulation of race by phenotype and closeness or distanced from 'Arab identity' (Fluehr-Lobban, 2004). The complexity of social-racial formations in the two major Nile Valley countries is best explored by Eve Troutt Powell in her 2003 breakthrough work *A Different Shade of Colonialism, Egypt, Great Britain and the Mastery of the Sudan*. Racialized references separating 'Arab' from 'African,' and brown from black, are embedded in the colonial system erected by politicians and anthropologists to offer a scientific veneer. The colonial system ranked Delta Egyptians over Nubians of Upper Egypt; it offered Nubians, especially those who had become Arabized (that is, they speak Arabic as a first language), the Shayqiya and Ja'alin of northern Sudan, superiority over the peoples of the South and the Nuba Mountains. This system descends to the present in a homogenized, monolithic use of 'northern Sudanese.' In the 22-year civil war between North and south Sudan, it was alleged that Muslim 'Arab' was pitted against Christian 'Black African,' while this confusion or misrepresentation was mirrored in the western press that described the conflicting parties in Darfur as 'Arab' against 'Black African,' dropping the religious referent since Darfur is an overwhelmingly Muslim region. These terms are becoming highly contested in just about every facet of contemporary public discourse. 'African' is as much about geography as race, and 'Black' is a moving target in the social construction of race. 'Northerner' and 'Southerner' in Sudanese discourse have become akin to the 'Black-White binary' in the US where people with complex social, ethnic-racial histories are homogenized and categorized as one or the other. The conflict in Darfur devolved to race alone as the majority of Darfuris are Muslim.

For most of the post-colonial era matters of race were little addressed. But the persistent resistance of the South, resulting after decades of struggle in the achievement of the CPA has brought the issue more to the public consciousness than ever before.

The relevant factors shaping this new reality include the displacement of massive numbers of Southerners into the North where their interface was unavoidable despite apartheid-like relations, as well as the growing realization and fear in the North that a great historic injustice had been perpetrated against the south.

Nonetheless, many Northerners remain in a state of denial about the reality of race discrimination and emphasize differences of a 'tribal' or ethnic nature over that of race, best described as phenotype, or outward physical appearance (Fluehr-Lobban, 2006). Southern Sudanese are physically and culturally distinct with tall, lean bodies, darker skin color often described as the color of eggplant, and scarification marks on many male foreheads from ethnically-based rites of passage. To the trained eye, Darfuris and other westerners are racially distinctive, and can be also identified by name, origin, and their accent if they speak ·Arabic as a second language. Al-Baqir Mukhtar's provocative article 'The Crisis of Identity in Northern Sudan: the dilemma of a Black People with a White Culture,' (2004) was translated from *Race and Identity in the Nile Valley* to Arabic and prompted strong reaction with some grudging acknowledgement from elite Jaʿali and Shayqiya, such as 'our grandmothers were slaves and were as black as any Dinka.' In the same volume Jennings' observation that Egyptian Nubians (whom she studied in Aswan) more readily accept their color while their Arabized cousins in Sudan were trying to escape it. Meanwhile, Egyptian Nubians are coming to Sudan in increasing numbers particularly to visit the National Museum where ancient Nubian history of Kush and Meroe is celebrated, while in Egypt there is a gloss or indifference to this classical tradition that is an independent from Pharaonic history.

Debates over 'Arab' identity invigorate northern Sudanese intellectual life where linguistic-religious markers have been emphasized by the current regime and Khartoum proudly accepted the honor of being 'a capital of Arab culture' for the year 2005, in the same year that the CPA was signed to the consternation of many Southerners. Increasingly, intellectuals and politicians specifically deny possessing 'Arab' culture, including followers of the old NIF now divided into two competing parties. Northern elite academics may diffuse the overt politics of this attribution of Arab identity by adopting the language of western scholars as people who have been 'Arabized' (*must'arabiyin*). Until the matter of center-marginalized politics is resolved, the question of Arab or non-Arab identity will remain contested ground in the realm of ideas and society. In response to critics of their simple renderings of race and ethnicity in Sudan, the term 'non-Arab' has begun to be more used journalists writing about Sudan. Many reflective people today, no matter from which region, comment that 'race is the central issue we need to discuss.'

CHAPTER 6

SOCIAL TRANSFORMATION: THE INTENDED AND UNINTENDED CONSEQUENCES OF THE ISLAMIST 'CIVILIZATION PROJECT'

The 'Civilization Project,' (*al-Mashru' al-Hadari*), was intended to create a renewed Muslim man, woman and social order through the al-Bashir-al-Turabi *Inqaz* program in order to construct a proper Islamic civilization based on conservative interpretations of Qur'an, Sunna (words and deeds of Prophet Muhammad), and *fiqh* (Islamic jurisprudence). Measures, such as the banning of alcohol and the purification of popular visual culture and the media, were intended to build a more perfect Islamic 'civilization' to replace the imperfect and uncontrollable indigenous Sufi Islam of the Sudanese Muslim and corrupting influences of the West supplanting it with MB ideology and practice.

A façade of this new public order was created during the early years of the *Inqaz* government as young bearded men and closely veiled young women moved discretely in public while more jaded citizens still found ways to purchase bootleg *merissa* and *'aragi*. But by the time that the al-Bashir-al-Turabi alliance fell apart in 1999, the 'Civilization Project' had run its course, the dream of the perfect

Islamic society was described by various Sudanese intellectuals as a failure (al-Mubarak, 2001) and in a state of 'collapse' (Ibrahim, 2003). When I returned to conduct research on the status of the Shari'a in 2005, I observed a social transformation of a different sort, not all of which were the intended outcomes of the Islamist project. During the years of my research 2005–09, initial shock at what I was seeing and hearing about the reality of the 'new social order' gave way to examination of the new patterns of family life that are emerging at the core of society – in marriage, divorce, the welfare of children, and inheritance. Having studied family law intensively in the 'old' Sudan, I admit to a certain initial disbelief – for example the presence and dramatic growth of *'urfi* (in effect, temporary) marriage that I had formerly relegated to the extreme social conditions found in Cairo, or the acceptance in Shari'a of fosterage and adoption of illegitimate and abandoned children – each of which was previously unheard of in Khartoum. Disbelief yielded the findings described in this chapter as to what have, in fact, been some of the *real* social consequences of the 'Civilization Project.' I do not posit the 'Civilization Project' as mono-causal in regard to the social transformation documented here, but I do associate it strongly with the broader general context wherein other demographic and economic changes have occurred.

Gender and Shari'a in Sudan: Intended and Unintended Consequences of Islamism

Sudan, once a pioneer in legal reform for improving women's status, began its Islamization in 1983 and became an Islamic state in 1989 under the rule of al-Bashir and al-Turabi, respectively the armed and intellectual wings of Sudan's Islamist movement. Instituting a 'Civilization Project,' Islamic law was applied more strictly toward Sudan's vulnerable citizens – women, Southerners and other margin-alized citizens – who became the targets of a legal and social reform program intended to build a more perfect Muslim society. The new 'Public Order' laws imposed conservative dress and public behavior codes upon Muslim women of the North and made criminals of dis-placed southern non-Muslim women who were prosecuted, fined and imprisoned for brewing beer. The comprehensive codified Shariʻa law from 1991 brought a new legal order for which there has been both compliance and resistance.

In 2009, journalist and UN employee Lubna Hussain, rejected an amnesty from the al-Bashir Government seeking to put the matter to rest, and mounted a court challenge to article 152 of the Public Order law (for indecency) requesting a permanent freeze of the ban on the 'indecent' wearing of trousers. The autonomy and lack of legal oversight of the Nizam al-Am police were evident in this case, as the arrest of Lubna and 12 others took place in Khartoum and not in the poorer suburbs or IDP camps and was reportedly the result of overzealous police. As predicted the case was dropped in court.

Khartoum is a diverse, teeming city with its millions comprised of a rising new middle class of Northerners, voluntary and involuntary migrants from the margins, and war-related refugees sharing its public spaces. The demographic transformation of the primate city has major social implications for gender, class and race relations in the 'new Sudan' that is presently under construction. The state-controlled Shariʻa and their courts struggle to keep up with the emerging new social relations – new forms of marriage, and informal liaisons that are developing in a nation transformed by its unique history of chronic conflict and its newfound oil wealth. The dialectic of intended and unintended consequences of the use of Shariʻa as the main instrument of Sudan's Islamism is critically examined in this chapter.

Marriage and Family Transformed: *Zawaj Jamiya*, *Zawaj ʻUrfi*, (group and customary marriage) and the Adoption of Orphans

The fundamental changes in the 'new Khartoum' and the 'new Sudan' are most evident in the utterly new, flexible types of marriage that are commonplace in the urban areas. This product of demographic transformation is also a reflection of economic forces, rapid class formation and polarization, with super rich and hyper-poor, and the beginning of the triumph of class over ethnicity in the North. It also reflects the growing independence of the young Sudanese woman who is seeking agency apart from her family, is delaying marriage, and beginning to negotiate it on her own terms.

The opportunities for women to obtain a university education have greatly expanded with the proliferation of universities, not only in the capital city but in the major towns of the 26 states, now numbering 62 post-secondary institutions. This democratization of higher education is a generally unacknowledged achievement of the *Inqaz*, albeit as a vehicle for Islamist education but it has been criticized for the quality of objective instruction due to the hiring 'politically correct' professors. Women have come to the universities in their droves, in most instances they represent a majority in the universities, except in the South. One factor, given the travel restrictions placed on women through male guardianship, is that women have not become labor migrants to the Gulf countries as have men. Predictably, the extensive male labor out-migration has produced a crisis in the contemporary marriage market, such that old class requirements for traditional arranged marriages, 'equality of standard' (*kafa'a fi zawaj*) in marriage, and the tradition of intra-ethnic marriages are disappearing in the 'new Sudan' in Khartoum. With so many men absent, and so many women educated and in the work force, the postponement of marriage by women – sometimes into previously unheard of ages ranging of the late 20s or early 30s – has become both apparent and accepted.

The increased educational opportunities, however, have not translated into fundamental transformation of the economic situation of women or greater personal autonomy under Islamist strictures. The number of women in the labor force has increased to as much as a third of the overall formal urban workforce, yet most women still do not have the earning power to be independent, nor would all wish to be. Ironically, the number of working women rose dramatically during the years of the *Inqaz* when women were supposedly secluded by Islamic mores and withdrawn from public life. Instead, they packed the universities and flooded into the workforce, all the while delaying by choice or necessity the prospect of marriage. In the long term they are still dependent upon getting married for their economic security. In the short term, however, some are tempted to make more casual arrangements with an older, financially secure man in what Sonia Abdel Malik describes as 'disguised prostitution.' And, although this is officially denied, HIV/AIDS infection rates have risen, although the numbers can only be estimated in the Muslim North. I was questioned at the Khartoum airport upon my departure in 2005 for having in my luggage a book published by Ahfad University for Women on the international AIDS epidemic. I was asked, 'Do you think we have an AIDS epidemic in Sudan?' I responded that the book was about the global AIDS epidemic, and the book was returned to me.

University of Khartoum social anthropologist Osman Mohamed Osman observed the rise of temporary and 'brittle' marriages that began to look like Shiʿa temporary marriage, (*al-mutʿa* marriage), long condemned by Sunni Muslims in Sudan. *Mahr* (the dower) has been rendered a formality, or it has become meaningless. He notes reports – that are interesting even if they result from gossip – about a rise in clandestine prostitution where male kin prostitute female family members for the additional income she can bring. *Zawaj ʿurfi* (customary marriage), has increased dramatically, even to the point that it is recognized as a social problem by the *Inqaz*. Divorce is also increasing with the main cause *talaq al-ghayaba* (the missing or absent husband), amounting to cases of desertion, as the husband leaves to work in the Gulf and may return home only rarely, if at all, and ceases to support his wife and family. One obvious difference with respect to divorce between the present moment and my previous study of family law is that now women are seeking divorce, not just the *nafaqa* (support) they used to demand in court.

The degree and depth of the social changes in the basic institutions of marriage and divorce in the 'new Sudan' are sufficient so as to render the old Sudan virtually unrecognizable. Few of the norms and mores that I learned through research and life in Sudan a generation ago still hold. The dynamics of their change offer a prism through which to view an emergent new social order. Despite efforts to make Sudan look and act more like the Kingdom of Saudi Arabia, to my eyes Khartoum is looking and acting more like Cairo than Riyadh.

SOCIAL TRANSFORMATION   211

New Marriage Forms since the 'Civilization Project:'
Zawaj Jamiya *and* Zawaj 'Urfi

Zawaj jamiya ('group' marriage), became a vehicle for the official promotion of marriage by the *Inqaz* government shortly after it came
to power in 1989. Marriages in large groups were promoted by the
government as a way to gain support of the masses, many of whom
were forced to delay marriage by expensive dowers and the inability
to afford the other multiple costs of marriage in the city, such as housing and furnishing a home. In the early 1990s, President al-Bashir
set a personal example of marrying a second wife whose husband had
been killed in the civil war that was being fiercely waged at the time.
Presumably, many women in the North were being widowed as the
result of the surge of the war in the South, so the regime employed
the Qur'anic injunction (allowing polygamy) to 'marry the widows
whom you find suitable, two, three, four ...' (Surat al-Nisa', Aya 3),
offering government sanctioning of polygamy for the first time since
independence.

Group marriages are held in public, in football stadiums or other
large gathering places, perhaps several times a month. As many as
100–300 couples are married at one time with President al-Bashir, or
his designee, acting as the *al-Wali al-'Am*, Public Marriage Guardian.
The two required witnesses for a valid Muslim marriage might be
the president and vice-president Ali Osman Taha, another inner circle
Islamist, or a local banker who bankrolls the event. No *mahr* (dower)
is required or expected, and marriage presents of small kitchen appliances or furniture are offered by the government and/or sponsor. The
marriage engagement, the *'aqid*, and the marriage contract, *qassima*,
are signed on the same day, and all marriages are registered on the spot
with the Ma'azun, the Registrar of Marriages and Divorces. The event
usually does not involve the families of the bride and groom, and such
marriages are said to have little security or durability.

Zawaj Jamiya is marriage sponsored by the government for poorer
people, without negotiated *mahr* – or with the government paying
the *mahr* and a few necessities for the married couple. In this form of
marriage the woman's traditional rights may be lost, as she may not

be educated as to her rights and the couple might separate as easily as they married without seeking an official divorce and the rights and responsibilities that would normally accrue as a result. A popular joke reveals a great deal about changing attitudes: A marriage carried out by *zawaj jamiya* is breaking down and the husband's family says 'send her back to her parents,' but the woman's family says 'send her back to the stadium!'

During a visit to Shendi in February 2007, I met with local Judge Mohamed Dirar, lawyer Abu Talib Osman, and other legal professionals.[48] They noted that these days a woman with a university education will marry a young man (they used the term *walad*, 'boy') with only a high school education. They further observed that if he is coming from the Gulf with money, few questions are asked. Thus, the old requirement of 'equality of standard' in marriage references (*kafaʾa fi zawaj*) as a requirement for marriage in my 1987 book (1987: 125–129) has dramatically changed. Indeed, they laughed heartily when I brought the up subject. However, inter-marriage between the Shagiya and Jaʾalin, the core ethnic groups of the traditional northern political elite, has increased as never before, the result of their mushrooming economic growth since oil and their historic clout in national politics. They also reported that *zawaj ʿurfi* is not as prevalent in Shendi as it is in Khartoum, which also fits with this type of marriage being a reflection of the increasingly heterogeneous capital city of Khartoum, and not so prevalent in the smaller towns and rural areas.

These novel types of marriages would have been strongly disapproved of in the past, but their dramatic increase in the past 15 years has made them more accepted as a fact of contemporary life. They result from multiple, complex factors – economic, political, the easier mixing of young men and women, the reduction of family influence, and, not the least of which, are unintended consequences of the 'Civilization Project.' They are also a response to economic constraints, the high costs of marriage, and youthful rebellion against the strength of the traditional marriage guardianship system, (*wiyala fi zawaj*), moving society more in the direction of individual choice over extended family demands. Whether they are characterized in the public mind as 'a student thing,' or criticized as temporary marriage like the Shiʿa, or seen as a necessary accommodation to the changing demographics of the city with more 'stranger' marriages, they have become a fact of life.

'These easy marriages and divorces are destroying our society – it could be that the family does not know the couple are married until she becomes pregnant. Because the cost of marriage has gone down so much and there is little or no *mahr*, the immigrants from marginal areas and the poor have welcomed this ease of marriage and the *Inqaz* has benefited when public shows of support for the regime are needed.' A young graduate student from eastern Blue Nile, migrant to the city, says he had 'enough money to marry but not to purchase a house anywhere in the three towns. The situation is growing more and more like Cairo' (interview with Mohamed Mukhtar).[49]

Zawaj 'Urfi, 'customary' marriage: is this Zina (fornication), or an evolving New Marriage Form?

Zawaj 'urfi ('customary' marriage) is a contract of marriage that the man and woman draw up themselves that does not contain the usual features of a Muslim marriage, the negotiation and payment of *mahr* (the dower), the signing of the contract in the presence of a marriage guardian, two full witnesses (two men, or one man and two women), and by custom, a public celebration of the marriage. *'Urfi* marriage was unknown in Sudan before the 'Civilization Project,' rapid urbanization, and demographic shifts in the capital city. Once a source for gossip in Egypt, *'urfi* marriage was viewed by conservatives as a consequence of fast city life in Cairo and declining morals. In the past, the ease of these 'customary' marriages reflected, in the eyes of the many Sudanese who frequented Cairo, the decadence of Egyptian life that was so unlike their own. Now Cairo has come to Khartoum, and the social problem of *zawaj 'urfi* is being discussed by sociologists and theologians in both Nile Valley countries.

In 2007, I attended a forum (*nadwa*) on *'urfi* marriage, invited by my colleague Dr. Hatim Babiker Hillawi, Nilein University, who was presenting his views as a sociologist on the subject (6 February 2007 at the Zubeir Hall, Khartoum). *Zawaj 'urfi* has become prevalent among youth unwilling or unable to afford or arrange the traditional, more expensive Sudanese marriage. The day-long conference was organized by the Commission for the Defense of the Nation, and *al-Nazan al-sha'biya* Council with co-sponsorship of the Sudanese Women's and Youth Unions. The dialectic energizing this debate is that *zawaj 'urfi* is seen as a social problem by most Islamists who view it as an irregular or invalid form of 'marriage,' closer to fornication or prostitution than to a legitimate Muslim marriage, while social scientists, who themselves tend to be secular Muslims, view it as a valid, emerging form of marriage chosen by young couples for its economy and relative lack of traditional restrictions.

The conference's organizer introduced a prevalent religious view of *zawaj 'urfi* as an informal liaison, 'just making a paper between a so-called husband and a so-called wife, without witnesses and without *mahr.*' She continued, 'It emerges from dating so that they can ease their consciences that somehow they are married. Clearly this is not marriage but *zina,* fornication.' This is not *nikah al-Shari'a,* marriage according to the Shari'a, but this is a new form of 'stranger marriage.'

Another speaker from the Ministry of the Family and Child (*Wizarat al-Usra wa al-Tifl*) opined that 'in our religion there is *zawaj shari'i* (Shari'a marriage) with all of the requisite elements of Islamic marriage, and all the rest is *haram,* forbidden. Thus, '*urfi* marriage should be opposed because it is against the religion of Islam.' In addition, he argued, 'it is alien to Sudanese society and is really *zina*' [at this people in audience indicated their approval with the political-religious response *Allahu Akbar* – God is great].

The speaker turned from religion to sociology saying that the reason for the increase of customary marriage is that in the capital city all are strangers and traditional family ties no longer prevail in such important matters. 'This is one of our responsibilities to discuss and to solve this problem – *Allahu Akbar* again from the audience – and the law protecting the needy child (*tifl miskeen*) is also our responsibility. Marriage that does not secure the rights of the child is also non-Islamic and it violates the international agreements on the rights of the child' he concluded. In sum, *zawaj 'urfi* is a social, economic, and religious problem, and the Ministry of Higher Education needs to pay more attention to the issue because so many university students are engaging in the practice.

A speaker representing the National Defense (*al-Difa' al-Watani*) focused the problem on university students living in dormitories (*sanduq al-tulab*):

> This is a real problem for the youth, particularly those 88,000 students in the capital which is a great increase over prior years. What we are seeing is one of the major trends of secularism (*'ilmaniya*) and it needs research to see if this is a phenomenon of the students, the middle class, or the poor? The biggest problem is the dakhiliyat, dormitories, where the girls from outside the capital are living and studying, without their families, or the *'asaba*, on her own. They succumb to temptations and are producing illegitimate children (*ghayr shari'iyin*), or *bil haram*.

Dr. Fatima Osman, from the College of Shari'a and Fiqh, Omdurman Islamic University, Girls Branch, also took the position that this is not true marriage (*zawaj sahi*):

> This was present in the *Jahiliyya* (time of ignorance) before Islam and this is not the true marriage (*nikah*) that Islam intended. The young people make this 'contract,' they photocopy it and can present it as an official document of marriage. This is really 'secret marriage' (*zawaj bil sir*) and it is *zina*, and by all means it is against the Maliki school of jurisprudence (*al-madhhab al-Maliki*) lawful in Sudan. Abu Hanifa [one of the early Islamic jurists for whom a school of jurisprudence is named] spoke to the *zawaj al-sir*, but we do not follow this school after 1991, and in Maliki law the marriage must be public. [*Allahu Akbar*, from the audience]
>
> In the family there must be a guardian (*wali*), and without a *wali* there is no marriage, correct? *Yaktabu waraq wa hatgha zawaj* – We need to return to Islam, and this custom takes us away from Islam. Let us go back to the marriage of our grandmothers; this is not zawaj, and it is something that the universities and responsible government agencies need to attend to.

She alleged that 90 per cent of the AIDS cases are the result of this type of marriage, and continued, 'some of the male administrators at Omduman Islamic University do not want girls as students, but we argued for their enrollment. Whether they are from Darfur or from the east, we want them to have the right Islamic education. What we really have is a social problem. We are urgently in need of an official judgment from the scholars (*hokum fiqh*).' A *fatwa* on '*urfi* marriage was issued in 2008 and is discussed below.

Her talk was followed by a brief commentary from Dr. Haggar Bakheit, Dean of the College of Arts (*al-Adab*), Omdurman Islamic University (Girls). He noted that *zawaj 'urfi* is here, and whether it is *zina* or not, it is still here and is a problem in need of a solution, whatever reasons have caused it. 'The context is that after the evening prayer (*salat al-maghrib*) the dormitory girls (*talibiyat dakhlikyat*), and even girls living at home, go out looking for boys. This is a problem of religion and society, but also a family problem because it does not have the power that it used to have. These wars (civil and chronic regional conflicts) are killing our families – these marriages are taking place without the knowledge of the families. *Al-usra biqa ghayabu*, the family is disappearing.'

Dr. Hatim Babiker Hillawi, a secular sociologist, remarked that many types of marriage exist in Sudan's customs. 'Here we are debating the religious Shari'a order (*nizam Shari'i*) versus the culture of the boyfriend/girlfriend that is the West's '*urfi*, custom. Of course, in the past marriage was the family's decision with the negotiation and payment of *mahr*, the signing of the marriage contract (*gassima*), and through these fundamental rights for women were protected.' He continued,

> Now, socially the door is open to students to make relations with each other, especially those from outside the capital. For the Khartoum girl it is for the father or the '*asaba* (core males) in the family to negotiate if the father is not present. But, with *zawaj 'urfi* there is no need to register the marriage with the *ma'azuun*, so they would not be subject to adjudication in court proceedings. If they want to change they can break the relationship as

easily as they made it- and all of this is done quietly without public attention or celebration. Public guardianship (*al-wilaya al-'ama*) is being practiced more widely in this marriage form, without family involvement in vital contract negotiations that protect the rights of the woman. These are the most visible things missing in *zawaj 'urfi*.

After the *Intifah* al-Sudan ('opening,' economic liberalism), like in Egypt's Intifah, this irregular (or invalid) marriage became common leaving the woman without rights, and, for the man, he can just say 'good-bye' and leave the relationship without responsibilities or penalty.

The problem, he argued, is that if they have children their legitimacy is at issue. The 'Public Order' (*al-Nizam al-am*) is at risk with this new phenomenon, recalling that the conference is sponsored by the Committee for the Defense of the Nation. He concluded that there are many social and economic factors at work, but this stunning, unanticipated development during the years of the Civilization Project calls for objective study and analysis.

The only study I was able to locate of *zawaj 'urfi* is a 2005 doctoral thesis in Arabic at the University of Khartoum, (supervisor Farouq Osman) entitled *Zawaj 'Urfi: asbabu, atharu, hokumu fi al-Islam* ('Customary marriage: its causes, consequences, and rulings in Islam') by Mohamed Gibreel Fadl Haroun.

The study is both sociological and religious, dealing with such subjects as how to protect women from this 'illegal' form of marriage in the author's view, what is legitimate Muslim marriage, and what are the types of *zawaj 'urfi* and what are the social attitudes to this marriage form. The study located 100 individuals who had contracted *'urfi* marriage and they were interviewed and also responded to a questionnaire.

The study asserts that the underlying causes for *'urfi* marriage include: 1) the rising costs of marriage and dower (*mahr*) payments; 2) the dramatic decline of male responsibility for protecting women and looking after their interests – there is no '*kafeel al-mar'a*' looking out for women which is derived from Maliki law; 3) public mixing of the sexes in the universities and at work as a major cause; 4) the decline of religious life making sex relations more relaxed – 'the Islamic way is weakening;' 5) too much freedom for women (*hurriyat al-mar'a*) and lack of values (*inhilal*); 6) easy sexual values (*akhlaq jinsiya*) that used to be impossible before marriage are now common; 7) girls are dressing too freely; 8) rising materialism and interest in possessions over good values; 9) girls are more influenced by friends, not family as in the days of her mother; and 10) physiological aspect – girls are naturally weak and vulnerable to temptation and this sexual freedom is destroying the family, the basic unit of society.

Zawaj ʿUrfi *Questionnaire results*

The results of Haroun's questionnaire (2005: 155–163) are most telling about the breadth of the changes that have undermined traditional Sudanese marriage in the North. Nearly 60 per cent of women who contract *ʿurfi* marriage are between the ages of 20 and 30, but a surprising 29 per cent are under 20 years of age. Most live in university dormitories (*dakhliyat*) (46 per cent) giving credence to the popular view that this is a student innovation, but again a surprising 40 per cent are living at home with their families. A wholly new 13 per cent of women are renting their accommodations. Not unexpected, most of the female university students attend the largest public university Nilein (37 per cent) that currently enrolls about 60,000 students in Khartoum; after this the University of Khartoum (18 per cent), Ahliya and Sudan Universities each at 16.8 per cent, and perhaps most surprising is that the Islamic University had 9 per cent of such marriages. It may be that a large number of *ʿurfi* marriages are found among women in universities because they have the freedom, the opportunity, and the time for such meetings.

The age of men and women in *ʿurfi* marriages is significantly discrepant. 41 per cent of men are over 40 years of age, while 35 per cent are between the ages of 30 and 40 years. The 24 per cent remaining are under 30 years of age. By a slim majority men in *ʿurfi* marriages are not university students or graduates, but are high school graduates (51 per cent), while 29 per cent are university undergraduate students and 19 per cent are post-graduate students. In the main the couple met at work (55 per cent) with the university setting being the next most frequent place for initial meeting (38 per cent).

The process of contracting the *'urfi* marriage and its length are perhaps its most controversial aspects and the reasons for its being condemned by Muslim educators and theologians. Only about a third of *'urfi* marriages reported the presence of the requisite two full witnesses (29 per cent). A majority (54 per cent) had no witnesses and 15 per cent reported using only one witness. In my interviews on the subject, I was told that when two witnesses were present at the contract signing – if indeed a contract was drawn up between the man and woman, that often the witnesses were persons who themselves were involved in *'urfi* marriages. Likewise, the length of the 'marriage' was most often counted in months (61 per cent) or days (18 per cent), not years (19 per cent).

Strikingly, most of the women in *'urfi* marriages in response to Haroun's questionnaire said they neither experienced pregnancies nor were there children born of these relationships, indicating, of course, the necessity for the use of birth control. In the past it was nearly impossible for an unmarried woman to obtain birth control, meaning that young women in *'urfi* marriages present themselves to doctors and pharmacists as married women seeking birth control. One woman reported that she had undergone an abortion.

On the subject of changing morals (*akhlaq*) and what might be deduced as another unintended consequence of the Islamist experiment in Sudan, most women (44 per cent) viewed their participation in *zawaj 'urfi* as forbidden in Islam (*haram*) from their studies of Shari'a and jurisprudence (*fiqh*) in school. About a third were not sure if what they were doing was *haram* (forbidden) or *halal* (lawful), and 22 per cent thought that they had contracted a lawful form of marriage, perhaps those who reported using two witnesses. The female respondents were about evenly divided by thirds as to whether they 'often' (33 per cent), 'sometimes' (36 per cent), or are 'not sure' (30 per cent) that what they are doing is wrong. The men were not questioned on this point. A majority of women (63 per cent) reported that they 'sometimes' have problems with the *'urfi* marriage arrangement, while 14 per cent responded 'often' to the question of problems in the relationship and 23 per cent reported 'no problems.'

One question that both men and women currently involved in such marriages were asked was to evaluate the positive aspects of 'urfi marriage: 36 per cent responded that there are 'many positive features,' while 35 per cent said there are 'few positive features' and 26 per cent 'no positive features.' The last statistic begs the question as to whether women and men understand in advance the implications of this new marriage form to Sudan.

That most of the women are young, 20–30 years of age, and at Nilein University, where they may be working part-time to support themselves suggests that they may be from outside of the city, living on their own whereby family ties and restrictions are loosened. Older women over 30 would, perhaps, be more cautious or skeptical about these liaisons. While working in Khartoum women are part time students, yet they have needs for tuition money and books, as well as their transportation expenses, even if they are living at home. The older men can help these female students through *zawaj 'urfi*. Other factors are that the dorms are sometimes far from the universities and there is no *'isma* (male protection) for these university girls. They may use excuses to leave the dorms, such as I am 'visiting my relations.' Under the public order laws she has the permission for travel as a student, so this gives her a freedom that girls living at home may not have. The author of the study recommends that students live at home, and that the city services are expanded to keep women students off of the streets.

At Omdurman Islamic university sexual segregation on the campus is very strict, women must dress in *hijab*, and they must be in the dormitories by 7.00pm, thus *zawaj 'urfi* has been avoided in large numbers. One case that was described to me was that of a girl from Islamic University who had an *'ishhad 'arabiya*,' or right to use a private car for transport to and from the university. She and her driver entered into an *'urfi* marriage.

As for the men in *'urfi* marriages, most are assumed already to be married (although, interestingly, the study did not ask this question of male respondents). These men above 40 may be seeking a polygamous solution to an older wife who stays at home and is unaware of her husband's activities outside of the home. For the men under 40 who may not have sufficient money to marry, they would be tempted by the lack of *mahr* payments in *'urfi* marriage. But according to Haroun, the corrupting aspect now is that with the old 'equality of standard' in marriage no longer operative today 'money alone makes marriage' (*al-grush al-kafa'a fi zawaj*).

Some Muslim observers who are critical of *'urfi* marriage nonetheless see in it a positive aspect that it is less costly. The most frequently cited disadvantage made by both legal professionals and religious figures alike is that in customary marriage a woman loses her rights to the dower and to subsequent litigation over any of her rights or the responsibilities of a husband. The religious scholars, the *'ulama*, cite more objections that in *zawaj 'urfi* there is no obligatory support of the wife (*nafaqa*) required in a valid Muslim marriage. Moreover, without the public signing of the marriage contract (*al-aqid*) there is no legal access to support. They argue that *'urfi* marriage is a form of secret marriage (*zawaj al-sir*) and that they are one and the same; both are secret, with no witnesses or less than the fully legal requirements. They see the underlying reasons for *zawaj 'urfi* as economical, while the western-inspired method to solve the economic problem is inspired by the media (*afwadiyat*) and encourages the sexual impulses (Haroun, 191).

Haroun's study is neither religiously authoritative nor government-funded, yet it reflects an interpretation that is consistent with what the scholars in the quasi-official *Majma' al-Fiqh al-Islami* (Islamic Jurisprudence Council) might argue. The study concludes that because of all of the above factors, marriages should only be conducted in the mosques where their validity can be assured. If *zawaj 'urfi* is not *zina*, it leads to *zina*. 'The youth are following the European way, and it is the culture of the foreigner that is bringing these values that are against Islam. The result is the loss of the traditional values of patience, denial, and discipline values which is bad for the future of society. Equality for women has been lost and their lack of financial and moral support leads to temptation. All have weakened with *zawaj 'urfi*' (p.125).

I spoke with many judges and lawyers about *zawaj 'urfi*, including one focused conversation with a woman judge Sayeda Sanaa al-Fadil who was presiding at Omdurman Shari'a court (a court I had visited 25 years ago). She was clear that there is a valid marriage only if there are: 1) contract (*qassima*); 2) two witnesses; 3) dower (*mahr*); and 4) the marriage guardian (*wali*) (in Maliki law and not necessary in Hanafi). If any of these elements is missing, then it is not a valid marriage. Justice Sanaa reported that she has never seen a case involving *zawaj 'urfi* – no woman has raised a case for divorce or made a claim for *nafaqa* resulting from an *'urfi* marriage in her 17 years of experience, 7 of which were at the Omdurman court. She said that if there was proof of a valid marriage, she would hear the case on the same day. On the day that I visited she had an apprentice judge who also agreed adding that there had been a '*rai faqih*' (an opinion from an *'alim* or religious scholar) that *zawaj 'urfi* is invalid (*fasad*). Their main concern, as with others, is the legitimate genealogy of any children (*nasab*), which relates to the possibility that *'urfi* marriage couples are purposely not having children, or are abandoning them, as is also alleged. Justice Sanaa said that there was still a lot of Hanafi law in the new personal status law. Although the Maliki school is the main source, they did not abrogate the existing Hanafi law in the 1991 comprehensive codified Shari'a (interview 1 May 2007, Omdurman Shari'a Court). Justice Kawther Awad who presides at Diem Shari'a court in Khartoum is very clear about *zawaj 'urfi*, that it is *ghayr zawaj sahih*, not a valid Muslim marriage. Moreover, the woman has given up all of her rights. 'How can she come with this piece of paper and claim rights to *nafaqa*, or most importantly, what about the legitimacy, *nasab*, and support, *nafaqa*, of any children born to the "paper".' (Interview, 14 April 2007).

My research assistant asked her university friends about what they see as the reasons for the increase in *zawaj 'urfi*. They point to the following: 1) It is cheaper to rent a furnished apartment (*shogag mafrusha*) together, and the landlords do not ask for any proof of marriage; 2) After the CPA, youth noticed that the Government had relaxed about Shari'a implementation in Khartoum – 'Khartoum became like Addis Ababa'; 3) The law supervising control of student housing was not being implemented; 4) That *'urfi* marriage is common among diploma students (*banat al-diplomat*) and Ethiopian men who live and work around Khartoum; and 5) There are many stories about dead babies in the bathrooms and dustbins (*koshat*) in 'Al-baracks,' student hostels for girls near to the Khartoum Army barracks for the University of Khartoum students, and in Ali Abdel Fatah house, a dormitory in Omdurman. You can see how many cars come to pick up girls from outside these dorms (personal communication, Salma Abdalmunim, 11 March 2007).

In February 2007 the government channel – Sudan TV – broadcast a drama about *zawaj 'urfi* in which a University of Khartoum girl from one of the marginalized areas outside Khartoum contracted an *'urfi* marriage without any family involvement. When she went back home to her village for the holidays, her cousin requested to marry her. She refused, but her father nonetheless imposed this marriage forcing her to agree and ordered her to leave the university to get married immediately. Conflicted, she resolved her personal crisis by killing herself.

The sociological subject of *'urfi* marriage is a major index of social change and is worthy of more in-depth study for its relationship to popular views of Shari'a that challenge Islamist views of marriage. It is also a significant indicator of the demographic changes in the capital city where 'strangers' are meeting, forming relationships, and marrying in new ways.

Zawaj Misyar: *Public Controversy and Debates*

Zawaj or Nikah Misyar – translated variously as 'marriage of altruism' or 'selflessness,' or 'marriage in motion'[50] – was the subject of much public debate in the early months of 2009 after the *Majma' al-Fiqh al-Islami* issued a *fatwa* declaring that it is a valid form of marriage, despite the key feature of the woman giving up several key rights in traditional Muslim marriage, including the rights to accommodation and support by her husband and the right to inheritance from her husband. The Islamic Jurisprudence Council had already determined that *zawaj 'urfi* was a valid form of Muslim marriage in 2008 in a move that likely reflected the general rule of the *Inqaz* that marriage – even irregular ones – are preferable to *zina* or fornication.

Within a matter of days after the *fatwa* was issued, Justice Kawther Awad (sitting in the Diem section of Khartoum) issued a ruling to a couple requesting a *misyar* marriage claiming that a marriage in which

women give up their rights to maintenance, housing and also the custody of their young children is not acceptable. This interpretation of
Shari'a family law and a woman judge's rejection of it reflected deep
controversy in the capital city and sparked much public debate.

Nikah misyar may be viewed as a further extension of the existing
'urfi marriage, so popular among young women and university students. It appears to give women more freedom to control the conditions of marriage, which she can only enter into with her full consent,
in exchange for giving up her traditional rights. As mentioned earlier,
increasing numbers of Sudanese women are delaying marriage, refusing proposals, and, in some cases, choosing to remain single. Since
the NIF took power and instituted the 'Public Order' there has been
an emphasis on promoting marriage to prevent women from falling
prey to temptation that would lead to *zina* (fornication and promiscuity) and resulting social breakdown (*fitna*). Indeed, from 1977, divorce
due to the fear of fitna (*talaq khof al-fitna*) was legalized as a ground
to free women to remarry their husbands who had abandoned them
or did not support them adequately due to lengthy periods of working abroad (Judicial Circular 61, 1977).[51] In this case, *nikah misyar*
allows for marriage of a couple where the husband is not resident in
the country, may only visit the wife infrequently, and where the couple cohabits in *her* place of residence, making it a temporary conjugal
home. But, the Sudanese religious scholars have argued that this does
not constitute 'temporary marriage' – the *mut'a* marriage of the Shi'a –
but represents conditions of life that the wife understands and accepts
upon the contracting of marriage into which she enters freely. As such,
the marriage is described as 'altruism' on the part of the wife – for her
voluntary surrender of certain basic rights for the sake of being in a
state of marriage.

So, who would benefit from such a marriage? Is validation of *misyar*
marriage by the Majma' Fiqhi a stretch of the interpretation of the
legal Muslim marriage to its limits in order to promote marriage over
inevitable *zina*? Is *misyar* the latest chapter in the 'Civilization Project'
to propagate virtue and reduce vice? Have the scholars stretched the
Shari'a law of valid marriages to the breaking point? Is *misyar* marriage, marriage in name only, or minimal marriage? Or, is *misyar*

marriage an extension of the right of women to the fullest consent, including a woman's right to offer up her rights? These are all power-ful and provocative questions.

As *'urfi* marriage is appealing to students seeking liaisons without permanence, or to displaced women in the major urban centers where family ties ensuring economic and emotional security are lacking, *misyar* marriage could be of interest to older divorced, never married, or widowed women who are not in need of the economic security that traditional marriage offers. A post-menopausal woman with an inde-pendent income, a secure place of residence, who is beyond childbear-ing age and is indifferent to the traditional benefits of marriage may only be interested in the status of being married for a variety of social reasons, including respectability and greater freedom of movement. A man who is moving between Sudan and the Gulf for work may be interested in having a wife in Khartoum whenever he returns, or he may have wives in two countries. 'Altruistic' marriage could appeal to young couples who cannot afford the high costs of traditional mar-riage with the dower or the provision of lodging in a teeming city with limited housing. The young bride gives up her rights in order to make marriage a realistic and affordable prospect. The issue of the high cost of the dower (*mahr*), that is subject to inflation rates, rising costs and standards of living, has been raised for decades as a social problem inhibiting marriage. In the past men were forced to delay marriage into their thirties or forties and often selected brides who were much younger. Now, it is women who are willfully delaying marriage, who are seeking options that offer legitimate marriage with fewer strings attached that afford them greater freedom, such as living in an apart-ment of their own without the stigma of being unchaste.

Public critics quickly began to label this form of marriage as 'pass-port' or 'airline marriage' with jokes about couples living in airplanes and hotels. But such jokes on the surface masked deeper anger, cyni-cism, and uncertainty about the fundamental changes to the old social order that now, are not only evident in daily life, but are sanctioned by the highest religious authorities. Citizen commentary[52] in the national press was mainly negative and one referred to *misyar* mar-riage as 'an abortion to the values of religion, customs, and culture of the community,' or as another way to practice 'secret marriage' (*zawaj al-sir*) that is condemned. Others opined that while 'altruistic marriage' may solve the problem of spinsterhood, it opens the door to the frivolous second marriage option for the man which is not treated with full respect. 'The door is open to supply and demand' in the marriage market where the responsibilities, as well as the rights inherent in marriage are abandoned. Others compared *misyar* marriage to *'urfi* and to the legitimization of 'pleasure' marriage which is fundamentally corrupted and close to *zina*. Still others blamed this 'uprooting of the traditional society' on the universities 'that now educate more females than males' and they [the educated] should be the ones to uphold the core values, but can no longer do so.

'Urfi and *misyar* marriages may be correcting the age difference in marriage, with the man traditionally being 10–15 years older than the woman in the past. The mutual consent of the couple implies a weakening of the family role in marriage guardianship, especially for the woman, and can be viewed as emancipating from male guardianship and patriarchy in this respect. This is another unintended consequence of the Civilization Project. The trade-off of the woman relinquishing her rights in traditional Muslim marriage for greater freedom may well be the perceived benefit that outweighs the risks of loss of her key economic rights in marriage. It also may be an important indicator of the increasing economic independence of women who have flooded into the universities during the years of Islamism, while reflecting the realities of the young male labor migrant who must spend months of the year outside of the country. Female migrants to neighboring countries for work is still a rarity, and *al-Nizam al-Am* restrictions on female travel have prevented women from getting passports without the permission of fathers, husbands, or male guardians. It may be that families have become content, or do not interfere, with such marital arrangements that require sons to travel abroad for work but keep daughters close to home.

The Shari'a and its interpreters in the collective law-making body, the *Majma' al-Fiqh al-Islami*, are struggling to keep up with the speed and magnitude of the social changes the urban areas of northern Sudan are experiencing. Their flexible and socially sensitive interpretations are commendable. As one commentator in the online postings put it: 'the circle of tolerance in the Shari'a must widen, and thankfully our religion has the capacity to do this' (Abdel Latif Abuni, 6 February 2009). Together *'urfi* and *misyar* marriage have turned the old social order upside down. And, perhaps without intending to do so, the Islamic scholars have legitimized a new social order that may one day upturn the Islamist 'Civilization Project.'

Other changes in marriage in a diverse and changing Khartoum

The following cases were observed by me in Family law courts and are selected to shed light upon some of the broad patterns of contemporary social change that are reflected in the Sudanese courts.

18 April 2007: In Marriage and Divorce Registration office of Ma'azun Moalana Yusef Akasha, I observed these marriage cases:

1) Two Egyptian men came to the office asking for a permission to marry, *'Izn al-zawaj*,' in Sudan as foreigners. They are intending to marry two Ethiopian women.

2) In the Ma'azun's office this case was both interesting and emotional for me to observe as an American: An Iraqi woman came with three male witnesses and supporters (not from her Sudanese family, but friends who were willing to help out. She was living in Baghdad when Saddam was overthrown and saw the statue coming down. She is widowed and has a son 16 years old (4 months and 10 days passed after her husband's death so she was able to marry). She married a Sudanese and they want to live in the Kingdom of Saudi Arabia (KSA), so she needs an official contract of marriage, *qassima*, for permission from the Ministry of Foreign Affairs of the KSA to prove their marriage so they can live together. Two of the men act as her witnesses, and the ma'azun proceeds with an *'aqid* (terms of the marriage contract), he recites prayers from the Qur'an, while holding the hand of the first witness, the *tawkil*, while the Iraqi lady and I

observe. Once it was over I made a little uulation for the joyous
occasion that pleased them and brought tears to my eyes at this
accidental intersection of the lives of two women, an Iraqi and
American.[53] The Ma'azun and Justice Kawther comment that all
foreigners have to take permission from the relevant embassy of
their nationality before marrying in a Sudanese court, to prove
that they are free to marry.

3) The family of a young woman came to court on her behalf
seeking 'wilaya al-am' – public guardianship of marriage –
because the father of the girl refused to give his permission and
blessing to her choice of husband. The parents are divorced, and
the father's refusal may be because his daughter is marrying one
of his divorced wife's relatives. The father has been intransigent
so the maternal grandfather and the woman's brother testified
that they approve of the marriage and they request the permission and guardianship (wilaya) of the court. The mahr is 10 million SD, prompt (muajjil) and 500,000 SD deferred (muakhir)
which appears to be average for a 'middle class' family (this =
$5,000 or 50,000, probably the former as mahr is also debased
along with everything else.

Adoption and Fosterage: Accepted and De-stigmatized

In the past illegitimacy in Muslim Sudan was so stigmatized that
in my 1970–72 study of homicide the killing of children born out of
wedlock was the main context in which women committed murder
(Fluehr-Lobban, 1976), far more than killing husbands that is statistically more common globally. During my studies of Shari'a in the late
1970s and early 1980s, discussions about the legitimacy of children
focused on how the law can even create the legal fiction of a halal,
legitimate birth – such as the Maliki interpretation that a child born
even up to four years after the dissolution of a valid marriage could be
considered legitimate. In Islamic law the consequences of illicit sexual
relations are intended to be grave and adoption is forbidden. Nasab,
or legitimate parentage and genealogy, cannot easily be invented. A
child without a legitimate genealogy cannot take the foster family's

name or inherit the father's property, and a woman must cover in the
presence of non-kin members of opposite sex. Adoption by foreigners
is forbidden.

The shame of illegitimacy remains great and reports of the death of
28 parentless children in Maygoma as recently as September of 2007
reveal that the problem is still critical. The main cause of death is malnutrition resulting from neglect. Meanwhile the police report a continued rise in the number of abandoned infants, 546 in 2007, mainly in
the slums outside of Khartoum (al-Khartoum, 5 September 2007).

With a case of a single mother raising her child born out of wedlock in my own family, there was intense interest among my female
friends as to how she was managing this social and economic challenge. Children of forbidden sexual relations were considered born bil
haram – and could be hidden in extended families raised with ambiguous genealogy.

One neglected consequence of Sudan's chronic wars and conflict are
the large number of children born to refugees, non-marital relations,
and often abandoned. Refugees who have flooded into the capital city
and the burgeoning urban centers of the North often seek human refuge in one another. The children that result cannot be supported by
such desperate people and are known to be discarded in refuse bins
in outlying areas of the city. Clearly these were 'throw away' children
born as much of a society in crisis as the parents who produced them.

Care of orphans is strongly favored in Islam. As mentioned above,
the Qur'anic verse on polygamy begins with the admonition to 'for the
sake of the orphans, marry of the widows two, three, four ...' (Sura
IV: Aya 3). In order to get the help of the state, or at least for the state
not to interfere, an Islamic solution was needed to assist the growing
numbers of abandoned, orphaned, and out of wedlock children that
the chronic wars and conflict have wrought.

As a result the Shari'a norm that 'adoption' and 'fosterage' are
unrecognized has been modified in Sudan, adapting the law to the
urgent needs of contemporary life. It is to the credit of the Sudanese
'ulama that an Islamic solution was sought and found for this pressing
and poignant problem of orphans. Orphanages, once unknown, are
now an accepted part of the new picture, the most famous of which

is Maygoma Orphanage located in the North Khartoum district in what used to be the old city suburbs. At any given time there are 300 or more children from various ethnic backgrounds who have been orphaned by desperate mothers or relatives who are too poor to care for them. What is also new is that there are over 200 foster/adoptive families – mainly working class families who are taking in these children and raising them as their own, according to Wendy Wallace, a British journalist who has been writing about Maygoma and has written a book, *Daughter of Dust*, based on interviews with one of the former residents of the orphanage who has become an activist and adoptive parent herself (2009).

'It's really a social revolution,' says Mona Abdalla al-Feki, a social worker at Maygoma, 'It was very difficult to persuade people that adoption is not forbidden in Islam.' (Polgreen, *The New York Times*, 5 April 2008). Until just a few years ago 80 per cent of the abandoned children left at Maygoma died there, but now many are placed in foster homes and/or adopted. As an excellent case of successful cooperation with foreign aid groups, the Sudan government worked with UNICEF and local aid organizations. They consulted with hundreds of religious and social leaders, met with women's groups, and encouraged the news media to visit Maygoma and report on the terrible conditions there. The Maygoma children were truly Sudan's untouchables with reports that abandoned children were not held or touched, could not speak, and a majority died of neglect, a slow death sentence not unlike their murders by disgraced mothers in the past.

The most important change was among the Muslim religious scholars, the *'ulama*. In 2006 the Islamic Jurisprudence Council, (*Majma' al-Fiqh al-Islami*) that issues *fatwas*, followed upon a 2004 law recommending that, as much as possible, children should be raised by families, not institutions. In the past in Islamic law only children whose parents had died were considered orphans worthy of charity. But the innovative *fatwa* declared that abandoned children should be considered as orphans with the legal result that an Islamic society has a duty to care for them. The *fatwa* also said that pregnancy in and of itself is not sufficient to convict a woman of adultery, and that children born out of wedlock should not suffer because of the misdeeds of their parents. This line of argument also figured importantly in discussions among Nigerian *'ulama* ameliorating the stoning sentence leveled against Amina Lawal for having given birth to a child out of wedlock. This interpretation also means that barren women and couples can adopt, and single parents who leave their babies at Maygoma and do not abandon them are entitled to reunite with the child. Orientalist scholars who have long argued that Shari'a is fixed, incapable of development or flexibility to changing times and circumstances, might take a lesson from contemporary Sudan.

Journalist Wendy Wallace,[54] who has a lengthy experience in Sudan, writes about the subject of abandonment: the introduction of Shari'a law in Sudan coincided with a huge increase in the abandonment of babies. About sixteen hundred babies are left in public places in the capital every year. Some perish by roadsides or are eaten by the feral dogs that roam the city. One newborn, in October 2006, was dumped in a pit latrine and – more surprisingly – rescued by police. Up to half a dozen newborn babies arrive at the orphanage, some days.

It is shame that prompts their abandonment. Sex outside marriage is illegal under Shari'a law. The punishment for an unmarried woman is 100 lashes, to be administered by a female policewoman, with a stick, in the presence of an audience of believers. The woman is beaten on her back, between her neck and ankles. According to the Qur'an, men too should be punished for sex outside marriage, although no one I spoke to could recall this ever happening.

The birth of a baby to a single woman provides definitive proof of the crime of *zina*. Midwives are forced to report illegitimate births to the police – or risk losing their license to practice. Some of the unwanted babies are adopted informally; traditional midwives may for a small sum negotiate the transfer from one household to another. Not all are unwanted. But whatever women's feelings about their newborns, social pressures to get rid of them usually prevail.

Ayesha's boyfriend is a 40 year old suitor and a father of eight with two wives already. He invited the 16 year old to his house on her birthday, saying he was making a celebration for her, and then raped her. Although worried by the absence of her periods,

Ayesha was instructed by the man that she should keep her condition quiet, until he married her. She obeyed, and told no one. Her mother learned of the pregnancy when Ayesha was admitted to Khartoum hospital as an emergency. After three days in labor, Ayesha had a Caesarean section. Her mother was prostrated with shock and shame, unable to eat or drink. She roused herself, immediately after the delivery, to take the infant boy to the city's orphanage, the notorious Maygoma, where until recently eight out of ten babies died.

No one else in the family ever knew. The boyfriend stopped answering his mobile when Ayesha went into labor, and hasn't been in touch since. Ayesha is studying accountancy at college.

Aloom Mahjoub, age 35, took in Ayesha's son Mohamed when he was aged six months, after getting the idea from a program she heard on the radio about the problem of abandoned babies. She undertook three days training in how to be a foster parent – a whirlwind tour of nutrition, hygiene, stigma, religious obligation – and collected the baby immediately afterwards. That was a year ago. 'I treat him like my own child,' she says. 'No one here has a bad attitude towards him.'

Aloom makes little of her role as a social pioneer. But that is what she is. Many Sudanese believe that to bring in a child born outside marriage would jinx the entire household. 'Adopting a child is like building on another man's land,' is one commonly known expression.

But the Mahjoub family have chosen to interpret things differently. Aloom already has four children of her own, aged from 20 to 14 years. When she brought Mohamed home from the orphanage, they held the kind of party they would have held if a baby had been born into the family, burning sandalwood incense and inviting the neighbors in for dates, sweets and soft drinks. Foster parents are paid a nominal monthly allowance, but that is not Aloom's motivation. 'I never think about the money,' she says. 'I love babies and I believe God will reward me for doing this work.' Aloom did not immediately realize that she would be adopting Mohamed's mother, too.

As soon as she was able after giving birth, Ayesha got into a rickshaw and refused to get out until the driver located the orphanage. Under the guise of being at college, she began to visit him regularly and when he was fostered she came to Aloom's house, to see him there. She now seems like a daughter of the house herself, sitting with her adored infant in the yard, or in the room reserved for the best occasions. She is paler-skinned than Aloom's family; in Sudan's fiercely hierarchical color caste system, it is darker women who tend to look after the '*laqueet*,' or found infants. But she appears more at ease here than she can be in her own home, where the birth of her child still goes unmentioned by her mother.

When she graduates from college, she hopes to get a job, leave home and take her son, she says. 'I want to keep him by any means possible, even if it means estrangement from my family.' Ayesha tells her story shyly, her eyes cast down, her voice low. She is still only 18. She scoops up Mohamed and cuddles him one last time, wiping his drool off her shirt before she goes back to college.

Charitable organizations such as 'Hope and Homes for Children' report modest successes in the public campaign for adoption over abandonment or killing of illegitimate babies. In the two and a half years of its existence, two hundred and fifty foster parents have been recruited, their small cash incentive paid by the state. After a campaign on the risks of street abandonment, fewer babies are found on roadsides and more are left in hospitals. Adoption has risen twelve-fold. And some 200 babies have been re-united with their mothers.

Amal's grandson, as soon as he was born, went to Maygoma orphanage. Amal paid weekly visits. At the same time, she put herself forward as an emergency provider of foster care. As soon as she had completed the three-day training and paperwork, she took her first foster child. Only she and her closest family knew it was the family's own baby. They subsequently adopted him. 'Who is his mother now, Amal or her daughter?' 'Both of us,' she says, and the daughter smiles for the first time. She fosters two other children now, one with cerebral palsy. The cot is for him.

Amal sheds tears as she tells the story. She is still traumatized by the injustice that is the lot of her grandchild. She calls her grandson by terms of endearment. But she knows that society will call him *'wad haram.'* Bastard. Or, literally, 'son of shame.'

Amal's husband stands outside in the tidy yard, under a grass roofed shade, ironing a pair of trousers. The grandfather of the baby is an understanding man, who works as a driver for an oil company. Not all men are as enlightened as he. Often, it is the fathers and brothers of unmarried woman who report their pregnancies to the police. 'Girls usually tell their mothers their condition,' says Nawal. 'Then they help them escape from the hospital, the community, the fathers and brothers. Social stigma is lower among women.'

Seventy year old Sheikh Mohamed Ahmad Hassan is an influential Imam who has come out in support of children born outside marriage, saying that the prejudice against them comes from society, not from Islam.' They are innocent and they are normal,' he says. 'But people stigmatize their mothers and them. Children should be able to stay with their mothers for at least two years,' he says, as was the case of the woman called Amrya at the time of the Prophet, as described in the *Hadith*. The punishment of 100 lashes for an unmarried mother is just though, he says. 'It is a protective legal measure, to defend society against adultery and protect the social fabric.'[55] In 2007, the supervisor of statistics at Maygoma, Majda Naeem, reported that between August-September, 28 children had died in just 35 days. She said the major cause of death is malnutrition. Clearly, despite the advances, the orphanage is still massively under-resourced. Meanwhile, the child and family protection unit in the Khartoum police department reported that number of sexual offenses has risen and that more frequent reports of abandoned infants have been received, commenting that this is a function of 'large degree of ignorance and poverty' (*al-Khartoum*, Khartoum Press Summary, British Embassy, 5 September 2007).

Divorce Rising

As soon as I returned to Khartoum after 15 years absence, old friends and new remarked that divorce rates had skyrocketed since my last research on family law. In 1979–80, I had roughly calculated an urban divorce rate of about 28 per cent on the basis of statistics provided by the Sudan Judiciary. For this round of research I gathered statistics directly from the Ma'azun's Record book (*Daftar al-Ma'dhun*) that reveal a considerable increase in urban divorce, although it had not climbed to reported European, US, and Russian statistics of nearly 50 per cent of contracted marriages.

However, Justice Kawther Awad, (Family court, Khartoum Diem district) estimated that the divorce rate is perhaps 50 per cent of all marriages (interview 11 April 2007). One newspaper columnist reported a 33 per cent divorce rate. Probably both are estimates, but in either case the numbers are higher than the 28 per cent I calculated almost three decades ago. Justice Kawther opined that this is because women have more grounds to apply for divorce since the 1991 law was instituted. In the past women mostly did not seek divorce, but only the support payments (*nafaqa*) to which they were entitled in Shari'a. However, as a result of reforms in the 1970s responding to agitation from the women's movement, grounds for divorce were expanded from abuse or harm – beating and insulting (*darar*), imprisonment, and impotence (*'ayb*) in the husband that were instituted as early as 1916 (cf. Fluehr-Lobban, 1987). In a series of reforms during the 1970s, a woman could raise a case for divorce based on harm or abuse, *talaq al darar*, for which she was the only witness (reforming the usual requirement of two witnesses), or on the ground of 'fear of temptation' to commit adultery or zina, *talaq khof al fitna*, due to the prolonged absence of the husband. And in a novel innovation, a woman could in effect ransom herself out of a marriage, *talaq ala fidya*, whereby she offers the return of part of her dower in exchange for the husband's release of her from the marriage by his right of divorce pronouncement. *Khula*, or negotiated divorce, was also available, but little used, although preferred by the richer classes. Justice Kawther indicated that *darar* as a ground for divorce has decreased because other grounds have been extended, including *huruj al zawaj* (absent husband in the marriage), or extreme neglect and lack of support that results from prolonged absence, both of which are considered *darar* or harm. *Talaq ala mal* is also new, which is derived from *khula* and has expanded with the class that historically preferred it, and is still done in front of the Ma'azun. There is now a formal recognition in the law for the woman who claims she is abused but does not have the requisite witnesses in *talaq al-shuqaq*. In such cases the wife can be divorced if she claims her husband beats her and that the beating has continued for at least three months. This strengthens the woman's ability to end her own suffering in the marriage because she is the only one who can testify to her own abuse. In this way, these matters can be kept private, as in Sudanese culture domestic violence has yet to be publicly addressed, although feminists have been agitating for its recognition in the Shari'a family law for decades. Naziq Mahgoub, a researcher from Ahfad University for Women, in her study of divorce after the 1991 law reports the increase of *shuqaq* due to rising domestic violence (in Badri, 2006). There are major gaps in the protection of the rights of women after the 1991 law, she says, and there are at least two kinds of harm to the wife, the physical harm, *darar* or *'onf*, and the missing husband, resulting in economic neglect.

Bayt al-ta'a, (obedience to the house), the forced obedience of wives who flee the conjugal home usually as a result of abuse, was abolished in 1969 during the early relatively progressive years of the Numeiri regime. It has apparently been partially restored during the years of the *Inqaz*. Justice Kawther reports that a *hokum al-ta'a* (an order for obedience), can be issued if she has fled the home so that she can claim the support to which she is not entitled due to her being in a state of 'disobedience,' (*nashiz*). As described in chapter 4, *bayt al-ta'a* in the old sense of a husband getting an order from the Shari'a court for the police to return – with force if necessary – a defiant or recalcitrant wife – does not exist, but obtaining a *hokum al-ta'a* is still possible for other situations when a woman is *nashiz*, such as going out regularly at night, or working at night without her husband's permission. Thus, *bayt al-ta'a* was reformed by removing the element of the use of police force to execute judicial orders for obedience (defined as the wife co-habiting with the husband), but the essential principle of a wife owing obedience to her husband was not fundamentally altered. Recalling the deep connections among the Abrahamic faiths, I am reminded of the recent ruling of the southern Baptist Convention that a wife owes 'gracious obedience' to her husband. Judge Kawther mused that because this court is near to Diem which is a working class area, sometimes the husband and wife who have been fighting in the night come before the court in the morning – or 'he hauls here to the court by the front of her *tobe.*'

Both Judge Kawther and Moalana Yusef, the Ma'azun (Registrar of Marriage and Divorce), offered related opinions about the causes of the increasingly high divorce rate. Justice Kawther answered 'the economy' to my question about rising divorce, and Moalana Yusef said the missing or absent husband, '*al-ghayaba,*' who is either working abroad or neglecting his responsibilities. They both agree that nowadays women are asking for divorce, whereas in the past they just wanted financial support. Or, they want to get out of a second marriage that the husband has contracted. Polygamy has also increased, encouraged by the *Inqaz*, and has been made more attainable for the men employed by or associated with the regime (Interview, 18 April 2008).

Indeed, while divorce due to harm or abuse was the most common type of divorce in my previous research, the most common ground for judicial divorce reported by the judges is *al-ghayaba* (the absent husband). If he cannot be located to respond to demands for support payments for two to three weeks, the wife can initiate divorce and be divorced easily in court, in contrast with the past where women sought support for husbands working for long periods in the Gulf. Apparently Sudanese men working abroad cannot emigrate to the Kingdom of Saudi Arabia because the Saudis demand a certain income level for residence and Sudanese usually cannot meet this class standard. Some allege that issues of race are also involved in such emigration denials. So, this means that the largest number of migrants from Sudan cannot obtain residency and must remain in KSA on long term work contracts so the husband is unable to meet his family demands. He does not come home, so the wife seeks divorce.

Both the types and frequency of divorce represent breaks with the past. Marriage and the family has been under increased pressure to perform their traditional tasks. The past closeness and solidarity of the family, physically and socially, is breaking down, as reflected in the looser forms of marriage already described and in the figures below from one of Khartoum's major courts.

However, most divorces do not take place in court, contrary to western practice. Divorce in Shari'a law is lawful if pronounced by the husband on three separate occasions, each separated by three months during which time reconciliation of the couple should be pursued. During the period when pronunciations of divorce are occurring, the couple should not have conjugal relations and their agents – usually relatives – should make efforts to reconcile them. The first two divorce pronouncements are revocable, but the third is final and irrevocable rendering the couple unable to remarry until the wife has been married and divorced by another man. It should be clear that divorce pronouncement is intended to be given careful consideration with an emphasis on the passage of time to allow opportunities for reconciliation, if possible.

Most divorce pronouncements are of the first revocable kind, the so-called warning divorce sending an alarm to the couple and their families that the marriage is in trouble. It affords an opportunity to get to the bottom of their mutual difficulties. That was true during my earlier study in the late 1970s and early 1980s, and it is still true today. However, what is evident is that judicial divorce by women, the only kind which they initiate, is increasing, according to anecdotal evidence from family court judges. Also, the following statistics I gathered also indicate a steady increase in the number of third and final divorces pronounced by men over a twenty year period from 1985 to 2005. This period was selected because the past two decades have been the years of rapid urbanization and of the various Islamist projects that manipulated family law, from Numieri's September Laws in 1983 to the law's codification and reform of 1991.

It is difficult to determine statistically the total number of Muslim and non-Muslim marriages in the capital city or in the country at large. Muslim Marriages are registered in mosques, with Ma'azuns' in their record books, *'urfi* marriages are self-contracted and almost by definition are not registered, and southern marriage is negotiated with cattle and only mediated in the courts if there are subsequent questions or problems. There is no mandatory civil registration of marriage making the following sample of divorce statistics an indirect method of determining the rising divorce rates that are so widely alleged.

The following divorce statistics were collected from the record books in Khartoum Diem Court for the years 1985, 1995–96, and 2005. These divorces are uncontested by wives insofar as they are the unilateral right of men in the three stages prescribed by Shari'a. Ideally the couple should not cohabit nor engage in conjugal relations as the pronouncements are made, but no studies of which I am aware exist to confirm that the ideal is matched by reality.

The statistics reveal that in absolute terms, the first form of revocable divorce – *talaq awal rajia*, the co-called 'warning' divorce – is increasing, perhaps consonant with overall population increase between 1985 and 2005. It remains, as it was in my 1979–80 study the most common form of divorce that may not in the end lead to the final irrevocable divorce. However, the second and more serious revocable divorce, *talaq thani rajia*, and the third final and irrevocable divorce are increasing dramatically. For the 'second revocable divorce' it increased from 1 per cent of the total number of pronounced divorces in 1985 to 7 per cent in 1995 and 13 per cent in 2005. The third and final divorce *talaq thani rajia* increased from 7 per cent 1985 to 16 per cent in 1995 and 18 per cent in 2005. Thus, declaration of final divorce, *talaq thalatha*, nearly tripled from 7 per cent to 18 per cent between 1985 and 2005. These figures are for one court in one of central Khartoum's neighborhoods. In my previous study of Shari'a divorce in Khartoum (the three towns), statistics in 1998 from the National Judiciary had the third, final divorce at 6 per cent of the total (n. 840) and the first 'warning' divorce at 80 per cent of the total; that number had dropped 12 percentage points to 68 per cent in 2005 for the Khartoum Diem court.

Table 6.1   Divorce in Khartoum, Khartoum Court Registry 1978, cited in Fluehr-Lobban, 1987: 147

Ma'azun Divorces	1978 Number (and percentage)
Talaq awal rajia, first revocable	677 (80)
Talaq thani rajia, second revocable	107 (12.7)
Talaq thalatha/baina, final	56 (6.6)
TOTAL	840

Table 6.2   Divorce in Khartoum Diem, 1985, 1995, 2005

Ma'azun Divorces	1985 Number (and percentage)	1985 Number (and percentage)	1995–96 Number (and percentage)	2005 Number (and percentage)	TOTAL Number (and percentage)
Talaq al-awal (revocable)	262 (92)	262 (92)	329 (74)	401 (68)	992 (75)
Talaq thani (revocable)	2 (1)	2 (1)	36 (7)	80 (13)	118 (9)
Talaq Thalatha (baina)	20 (7)	20 (7)	74 (16)	106 (18)	200 (15)
TOTAL	284	284	439	587	1310

Divorce (*talaq*) Statistics collected from the Diem Court, Khartoum Ma'azun Daftars/Record Books Registering Marriages and Divorces, 1985; 1995; 2005.[56]

Over a period of several months in 2007, I observed family law court sessions and sat with the Ma'azun Yusef Akasha in his official capacity. The following is a sample of cases from these sessions.

1) 18 April 2007

'Talaq awal rajia' – first revocable divorce – was recorded simply as a matter of fact after the pronouncement. The husband and his two witnesses chatted casually, but the reasons for the divorce were not revealed. Despite the seeming air of indifference about the 'warning divorce' Moalana Yusef explains to me that he often counsels people against divorce, especially if there are children.

Al-Ghayaba – the missing or absent husband

By all accounts, most cases of the absent husband stem from the husband who is a labor migrant to the Gulf, or elsewhere. However,

I observed an interesting case of *Al-Ghayaba* that involved an 'absent' husband who is currently serving a prison sentence. A very pregnant woman and a man wearing a *jellabiya* and *tagia*, skullcap, accompanied by two policemen who brought him from prison entered the court. A lawyer for the woman was present, but there was no representation for the man who spoke on his own behalf, as litigants have the right to represent themselves, and in my previous research, most litigants did.

1) On 16 September 2006 they were divorced – that is, the husband divorced the wife while he was in prison, with witnesses and with registration by a ma'azun. Between them there is a two year old boy, and it is the present pregnancy that is apparently in question. The imprisoned husband is furious as he describes what he believes happened – he is speaking passionately and with a fury. The judge advises him to calm down but does not berate him, and the wife does not say anything to protest what he is alleging. She is 7–8 months pregnant, and the only time that they had a conjugal visit (permissible once a month, over the weekend, Thursday night-Friday) was in January of 2007, so it is impossible, he contends, that this child is his. 'How can I pay her anything when I don't know who is the father?'

He has been in prison a year with another year to go. The judge did not ask him what he is in prison for – nor did the policemen who brought him to court asked anything to say about his crime. The case is clearly one of divorce and legitimacy, and prisoners' right to adjudicate personal matters is not affected by their incarceration. The case was continued to two weeks hence.

The case was continued so that the woman could bring her witnesses. Also, the head of the prison will appear to testify about the date(s) of the conjugal visit(s). For now, the question rests on how she can be legitimately seven months pregnant from a conjugal visit only three months ago? In a subsequent discussion with Justice Kawther, I asked about DNA testing, which is not currently available, but she regards as very important to introduce. She also offered an unsolicited, but interesting comment about the witnesses in the case, where there was a missing male or two female witnesses. She does not accept that a woman represents half a witness, 'I am a judge; I can hand down decisions and my word is the application of the law, but if I appear in front of this court, I am half a witness! This is wrong!' This is a view I have heard expressed over the years from women judges, but for me the importance lay in the fact that this younger judge brought up the subject. This indicates to me in the spoken language of Sudanese sensibilities where subtlety is the norm that this was a point of view she saw as important to project.

> 2) A Sudanese couple were married and then became estranged after they moved to the US. He came back to Sudan and she remained in the US from where she filed a case for support and for divorce to be conducted remotely from America. All present found this highly amusing, including me. She also claimed *talaq al-darar* by telephone because she alleged that he threatened her by phone. The judge queried, 'how can she substantiate this claim without witnesses?' The woman's lawyer then recommended that the woman take the case to courts in Abu Dhabi court since it has relations with the Sudanese courts and from there she make her case and appeal.

This was the only time that I was called upon to comment in court about any possibility of litigating a Muslim divorce case in the US. I noted not only are there no diplomatic relations between the US and Sudan but that relations between the courts in the US and Sudan are doubly difficult as there is also ignorance of Islam and Shari'a and that I am often called to be a *mustashara* (consultant) on cases involving Islamic law.

Nafaqa (marital support) Cases
8 April 2007, Family Law Court

1) A husband and wife (she does not look Sudanese – maybe North African Maghribi) appear together, they are cohabiting, but there is a clear deep chill between them. She previously appealed for and obtained the support he was not providing for her and the children. He has the money in his hand, shows

it to the judge, counts it out – 380 SD – then the wife asks
'This makes up for the past, what about what is due soon?' It is
agreed that 230 SD is the correct amount (I am not sure what
period it covers), but the wife asks for it by Saturday; the husband responds that this is not possible. They agree that it is due
in ten days time, on 18 April. Satisfied, the woman leaves the
court alone and the husband is left standing alone in front of the
judge. What makes the case interesting is that a wife pursued
her husband for *nafaqa*, and he is not an absent husband, out of
the country working. This is yet another index of the extent of
the economic strains on urban working class couples, but for
now, the wife is not seeking divorce and this reflects the older
social patterns.

Court of Justice Sanaa al-Fadil, Shari'a Court, Omdurman

2) The case was originally divorce for harm, *talaq al-darar*,
and the couple was divorced, but she neglected to collect her
nafaqat al-'idda, the support to which she is entitled for the
three months and ten days during which she passed 'three
monthly courses' to prove that she was not pregnant from
the former husband. So the question before the court was
whether she was still entitled to the uncollected payments
of *nafaqa*. Judge Sanaa said that the *nafaqat al-'idda* begins
from the date of the divorce and she still had fifteen days to
file her claim.

14 April 2007, M. Kawther's court

3) After identification cards were presented to assure that the parties before the court are who they claim to be, a lady represented
by a woman lawyer initiated a case of *nafaqa*. She brought one
witness. The husband is not represented by an attorney. The witness is asked about whether the husband has been working. He
has a rough idea that he has not been working. (He says '*fi rayi*'
(in my opinion), and the judge interrupts, 'we want facts, not

opinions.' 'How much do you want per month?' she asks of the
woman. She replies that 200S£ (about $100 at the time), and that
she wants that amount established for the coming six months.

Female headed households are now at 13 per cent in Sudan according to one scholar (Badri, 2005), but are probably much higher if
the IDP camps are taken into consideration, as well as the large
number of women who are effective heads of households for husbands who are working for long periods of time in the Gulf. The
soaring number of 'missing or absent husband cases needs recognition in law' (Mahgoub, 2005).

Dramatic Increase of Cases Disposing
of Family Estates (*Terikat*)

In my previous research in the Shari'a Courts in 1970s and 1980s,
the smallest number of cases were those dealing with the disposition
of family estates after the death of a family member. Since inheritance is strictly regulated by Qur'anic shares that apportion shares
to prescribed relations – the majority of whom are female – and can
only be slightly modified by religious testamentary bequests, *waqf/
awqaf*, estates were straightforward and uncontested. In the past,
I mostly witnessed estate cases in courts located in upper middle
class areas, and were among the few cases that I recall having legal
representation to ensure that the large estates would be portioned
accurately. In the past, most litigants represented themselves in
court.

Now estate cases have come to dominate daily court proceedings according to my own observations and from judges and lawyers whom I interviewed. And, like most other cases I observed in
2007, they all had lawyers representing the various family members
utilizing the court as a third party to ensure that there was clarity
and no quarrels between family members. Justice Kawther was of
the opinion that when families were living one extended household
there was little to divide since most of their wealth was shared in
common. Now that extended families are breaking down and are

living in different locales, each of the heirs wants to be sure he/she has their share.

Obviously, the expansion of the urban upper class, particularly that enriched by the *Inqaz* and its business and financial ventures, has made the transfer of wealth within these newly rich families more crucial to the maintenance of their new class position. Moreover, rivalries between Muslim family members of both old and new wealth can only be legally determined in a Shari'a Family Law Court, not in a secular, civil court of law. This places great power in the hands of the judges who are professionals generally not from this class. Likewise it places judges under great pressure from these powerful families. One judge who was relating adjudicating a family estate dispute from within a powerful corporation seemed to delight in the recollection of the power of their decision over the distribution of such wealth.

The following is a representative sampling of estate cases that I observed:

Family Law Court, Diem, 11 April 2007 M. Kawther Awad

An estate case is the first of the day. There are eight heirs present, each there to claim their share. From the deep *shillukh* (facial scarification) on the older woman's face I deduce they are Mahas, probably from Tuti Island or Burri al-Mahas. The presiding judge first confirms that they are the lawful heirs of the deceased (*al-mutwaf*). Each of the heirs took his or her turn to show identity papers proving their relationship to the deceased. They are represented by lawyer(s), and are spread out between Abu Dhabi and Khartoum, and the extended family no longer live in one house. Some are showing Government ID cards, others their passports, and one older woman without official identification has her fingerprint taken. The case was continued to 21 April 2007.

In the past proof of identity was established in court with witnesses and bearing personal witness on the Qur'an. Nowadays, litigants must have papers in hand to prove identity – otherwise they are asked to leave and return with the requisite proof on another day.

Sample of estate (*terika*) cases from one morning in court, 7 April 2007, Khartoum Diem Court.

1) A case of a Moroccan woman married in Morocco to a Sudanese and all of their children were born in Morocco – they are ages 14, 10, 5 and 3. Her 14 year old daughter came with her. The husband died, and she wants to claim his inheritance for his children. She proved her nationality with her passport.
2) Another terika case where there were no sons and only daughters, so the calculations have to be carefully drawn up since there are no living core males (*'asaba*). The male *wakil* and his lawyer used his mobile to do the calculations and the judge stopped them reminding them that she will do the calculations and continued the case for several days.

14 April 2007:

1) A lawyer representing a *terika* case did not bring an official death certificate (*ishhad al mutwafa*), moreover the names on the petition and the name of the deceased are different. 'The papers you brought are wrong, they won't work here. We're done, *khalas*, leave!'
2) An older woman inquired of the court about making religious bequests (*al-awqaf al-Islamiya*) and the judge respectfully informed her that this is the wrong court for the family *waqf* and that she should go to the '*Tamimi*' court in Khartoum.

Islamic Banks and an Interest-Free Economy

Islamic banks and finance companies are a monopoly in the Sudanese economy in the North, and they had a near monopoly in the southern cities during the decades of Islamization and Islamism. Islamic banks remained in Juba after the CPA, but as reminders of a bitter past there was a call to close them. However, southern economists and politicians advised a pragmatic approach whereby, irrespective of separation or unity, the South will need to conduct business with the North.

The Islamic banking movement was introduced in the early years of Islamization in the late 1970s as an alternative to interest-based banks that dominated in colonial times, such as Barclay's and later Citibank. The national Bank of Sudan was modeled on these western banks. Originally the Faisal Islamic and al-Baraka banks developed from oil capital in the Gulf created this new sector. With Islamization followed by state Islamism the Islamic banking sector came to monopolize all economic transactions finalizing the shift to an interest-free public economy.

Novel forms of Islamic investment involving benevolent loans (*qard hasan*) and forms of shared risk and profit sharing known as *Mudaraba* and *Musharaka*, and *Murabaha*, cost-plus financing, were developed and debated over the decades of progressive Islamization. One study (Ahmed al-Hassab, 2007) found that a majority of financial transactions in Islamic banks are *Murabaha*. These include options offered by the bank whereby the client borrows from the bank for an investment and negotiates in advance a portion of the profit which is settled at the time of the loan. Variations of this model involve the bank purchasing goods on behalf of the client which are then sold to the client at an agreed mark-up. *Murabaha* is actually a concept in Islamic Fiqh which is lawful when based upon the seller disclosing the cost incurred in acquiring the commodity and then adds to the actual cost some profit (*ribh*). What is forbidden in Islam is *riba*, which is the charging of interest, the act of loaning money for money at an agreed upon percentage of the loan.

The high demand for *Murabaha* loans probably came from commercial loans that would not be covered by Islamic profit-loss sharing models, particularly the market in durable goods, such as cars or household appliances, real estate, or machinery and equipment for large scale businesses. With the rapid expansion of the Sudanese oil economy a new capitalist class required accommodation by the Islamic establishment, entrenched since the early days of the NIF. The close ties between them and Islamic banking sector has been well-documented (El-Affendi, 1991: 1116–17; Gallab, 2008: 91). What was added to the original Muslim concept is that the loan occurs in two stages: first the bank purchases the commodity and the second stage in which the

bank sells it to the client. These should be separate transactions conducted between parties who have different capacities at different stages;
they are transactions of sale and not financing. Al-Hassab argues that
standard practice has become the latter and that Murabaya is masquer-
ading as being in conformity with Shari'a averring *riba* (usury) when
it is in fact a transaction with built-in interest taking. Some Shari'a
scholars think that by permitting a higher price for deferred payment
is making the same mistake as the Jews when they opened the door to
interest, as well as the yielding to interest that the western Christian
world took after the Reformation. Both Jews and Christians had bans
on usury that fell to pragmatic capitalist development. The critical
attitude toward this tendency in Murabaha loans is as much a concern
to Muslim scholars as is the fear that it is hiding usury in a legitimized
Islamic institution. The deepening economic crisis in the US and the
West, due in no small part to interest-based economies, is a powerful
lesson in point that this debate in the Muslim world and in Sudan is
more than simply religious or academic.

Al-Hassab writes that the although Sudanese government abolished interest, all it really managed to do was to effectively raise what
amounts to an interest rate from 4–16 per cent but giving it the name
of 'profit' (*ribh*). By using a devious method of 'deferred payment' (*bay
al-muajjal*) it has introduced interest in effect, if not in name. Other
critics see this as the 'ghost of interest' haunting Islamic banks to convince them to charge fixed rates of payment per annum in their investment financing and loans transactions. This, he notes, is a world-wide
tendency, and is a special problem for various Islamist programs that
seek both capitalist economic growth and religiously approved practices and institutions.

The Unintended Consequences of the 'Civilization Project'

The darker side of the 'Civilization Project' was first suggested to
a western audience by American Muslim T. Malique Simone in his
In Whose Image? published in 1994. Simone had been employed by
the '*Inqaz*' regime to study and transmit to the broader world the
achievements and benefits of al-Mashru' al-Hadari. Instead he found

opportunism and social corruption among the legions of the regime tasked with erecting and implementing the Islamist program, and he hinted at the unraveling of the Sudanese social order.

But the dialectic of a deeper social evolution is also at work here – as the old order was assaulted and has yielded, a new synthesis is under construction. This is the real 'new Sudan' where the base of a new, vastly more heterogeneous and hierarchical society is replacing the old homogeneous, egalitarian ways. This new social fabric is a richer, more complex set of realities, and has the potential of yielding a more tolerant, heterogeneous society. Residential apartheid by class, race, and ethnicity is still the norm and will remain so, but the multiple opportunities for intersection, interaction, and knowledge of the other in everyday life – with inevitable social discord as well as harmony – is the more accurate version of the long terms effects of the 'Civilization Project' in contemporary Sudan.

Adopting a dialectical approach to the emerging social patterns discussed in this chapter yields a fresh analysis of social construction as well as social breakdown. The breakdown of old marriage patterns and of the family that is acknowledged by most Sudanese observers, right and left alike, is often referenced with disapproving shaking heads and clicking tongues. Despite the Islamist regime's emphasis of 'family values,' much like the George W. Bush evangelical vision of an ideal American society, the conservative political program is reacting to rapid social mobility and change. The dramatic yet uneven economic development of the nation has pitted the periphery against the core and forced a majority of young men from the North to migrate abroad for a sustainable income. Untold others have sought refuge abroad from political repression and war, yet their ties to home and country remain strong, and this Diaspora of Sudanese may yet have a significant role to play in the construction of the 'New Sudan.' The facts of emigration and displacement have been undermining the stability of marriage for some time. In the early 1980s, I witnessed numerous cases of wives suing their labor migrant husbands for non-support, the same women who as young brides sang of their joy and anticipation of the rich bridegroom coming from the Gulf with a large dower for their marriage. Today, that married woman, with an independent income, fearlessly and with family support, sues her husband for divorce. The displacement of millions of Sudanese from decades of war and chronic conflict has dislodged deep social patterns of intra-ethnic marriage resulting in many inter-ethnic liaisons among Southerners and many international marriages of Sudanese and non-Sudanese living in the metropolitan Khartoum region.

The irregular forms of marriage and sexual liaison that have emerged in the capital city, such as *'urfi* and *misyar*, that once were condemned by Islamists are now interpreted as consistent with Shari'a. Social scientists and intellectuals are more intrigued by these developments and tend to see these changes as stemming from urbanization and globalization. Others link the change to a passive, or even active, resistance to the 'Civilization Project.'

Study of the emergent and divergent social patterns evolving in the periphery and center is urgent. At present I can only hint at this. Northern towns like Shendi and Atbara and major urban areas such as Wad Medani are now within easy driving distance of Khartoum making commerce and social intercourse easy, so that the social changes evident in Khartoum are present in these urban areas as well. Shendi, where the core of the present elite is based, is yielding to more class-based marriages rather than the intra-familial, intra-ethnic marriages of the past where up to half of the marriages were of first cousins, preferring the tradition of marrying the father's brother's daughter, *bint 'amm*.

The periphery may be idealizing and attempting to preserve the old order, even as it is physically and militarily challenged. A study of the social pressures exerted on female teachers from the center employed in al-Fasher before the conflict erupted in Darfur is illustrative (Wilemse, 2001). Meanwhile in the capital city, instead of marrying young to preserve a girl's virginity and family reputation, men and women are delaying marriage well into their late twenties and thirties from economic necessity, but increasingly as a matter of personal choice.

The rising number of illegitimate and abandoned children was perhaps the most shocking change for me. Although Maygoma Orphanage was established in the 1980s, its existence was generally unmentioned and unrecognized. Such children were living proof of the old order gone wrong. The most extreme forms of social stigma were attached to illegitimate birth and the one remaining *hadd* punishment from the *'al-Mashru'*,' that of lashing, is still applied to unwed mothers giving birth in public hospitals. However, an attitude of compassion and care for the innocents created by disorder, conflict and economic privation has overwhelmed the 'remedy' of punishment by lashing to the credit of the Sudanese *'ulama* interpreting the Shari'a. Abandonment of infants and children born into conditions of conflict, displacement, and poverty has been recognized as a social problem, with a commendable legal accommodation of fosterage and adoption by the Shari'a as applied in Sudan.

Zainab Osman al-Hussain, former Director (1985–91) of the Social Welfare Department at the Ministry of Social Affairs and Zakah (welfare) said that when she was director the Dutch and Japanese NGOs approached her about available funds earmarked especially for orphans and other special needs groups, such as illegitimate children, orphans, juveniles, and the handicapped. Mrs. Zaynab reports that the Ministry refused to accept these funds indicating that their need was not demonstrated in the society at the time. Indeed, the Ministry was working to improve its services for the handicapped, but the increased demand for services for illegitimate children and orphans could have been anticipated as outcomes of chronic war and social dislocation.

The rising divorce in Sudan may seem modest by comparison with its mentor state, Saudi Arabia, where the divorce rate is reported as having skyrocketed from 25–60 per cent in the last 20 years, according to Noura al-Shamlan, head of research department at the Center for University Study for Girls (Abu-Nasr, 2008). There is no single cause explaining Khartoum's rising divorce rate, but certainly rapid urbanization, class formation, and the social stresses of external labor migration and chronic internal conflict – especially in the families of the military and their targets – have exerted their inevitable influences. The impact of the 'Civilization Project' is also significant for its state promotion of marriage to avoid *zina* that made marriage easy and accessible for many who in the past would have been restrained by the high cost of marriage. Such arrangements substituted the guardianship of the state for the family and became brittle, and thus served to weaken both marriage and the family that they intended to strengthen. The effect of globalization accessible by the internet and satellite TV is often cited by Sudanese as 'corrupting' the morals of youth by normalizing easy and promiscuous sexual relations. However, for decades, regional television with a steady diet of Egyptian soap operas, now produced locally with Sudanese themes, have served as a social sounding board and barometer for many social issues.

Finally, the rapidity of class formation as the economy boomed in urban Sudan is evident indirectly in the significant rise in estate (*terika*) cases in the courts. What formerly had been the province of private family affairs for people living in extended family compounds in lineage-based neighborhoods is now the province of a service provided by the state courts for scattered families differentiated by class and social position. Those families with members close to the apparatus of the regime may find themselves in a family court determining how best to divide the enriched estate of the deceased. The cadre of Islamist supporters, rewarded by the *Inqaz* with economic opportunities and special advantages, have differentiated from other family members and have weakened old family ties, even as they have become more enriched. These cases in the courts, inevitably having family members represented by lawyers all around, tell a much larger tale of growing social differentiation, breakdown of the old order and vivid construction of the new.

CHAPTER 7

COMPARATIVE CASES: IRAN, NORTHERN NIGERIA[57]

As a global phenomenon, Islamism has many faces and multiple cases. Among those having the greatest parallels and relevance for Sudan, Iran and northern Nigeria stand out. Although the Iranian Revolution was populist, while Sudan's persistent moves toward Islamism occurred over successive military regimes, Iran's Islamic Republic and Sudan under Numeiri, al-Turabi, and al-Bashir and the *Inqaz* bear many similarities. Indeed, the two Islamist nations have been close allies and have hosted each other's leaders on many occasions. The three decades of a mature Islamist government in Iran mirrors the aging Islamism of Sudan after two decades and both are increasingly vulnerable from within and without. In northern Nigeria, the dramatic events between 1999 and 2002, when all thirteen Provinces of the North declared Shari'a as provincial law was reminiscent of the top down Islamization in Sudan moves nearly two decades earlier. Sudan and Nigeria are linked by culture and politics from the early days of Islam through the colonial and post-independence periods and their African-influenced Islam is both deeply spiritual and Sufist, historically marked by Islamist reformers and jihadists. Nigeria's federal system is being tested even as Sudan is trying once again to achieve a federal solution after decades of civil war that would stave off the looming division of the country. The comparison of these two African giants, one geographic and the other demographic, is apt, illuminating, and filled with lessons for the rest of the continent and for nations having experience with Islamism.

Iran and Sudan

Iran and Sudan are parallel cases in most respects, except for their respective political routes to Islamism. Both dealt with major wars, resulting in huge losses of life (nearly a million lost in the Iran-Iraq war and untold numbers lost in the 22 years of civil war between the North and south). Iran supported Sudan at the United Nations throughout its struggle and embarrassment with resolutions condemning its actions in Darfur and South Sudan. Iran's historic close ties to the *Inqaz* was evident as it was the first country to oppose the ICC arrest warrant for crimes against humanity levied against al-Bashir in March 2009. Both have histories of successful popular resistance that have overturned military and/or dictatorial regimes, the Iranian revolution overturning the monarchy of the Shah Reza Pahlavi and two Sudanese popular revolutions against military rule, in 1964 against General Abboud and 1985 against General Ja'afar Numeiri.

A great deal is often a made of the fundamental differences between Sunni and Shi'a Islam, while their historical breach dealt with succession to the caliphate, not theological or doctrinal disputes, as with historical Christianity. The convergence between the two is evident in the idea of an 'expected' deliverer and cleanser of Muslim society envisioned as the 'hidden Imam' or a gifted and timely Ayatollah in Shi'a Islam and a Mahdi in Sunni Islam. Sudan and Iran share this powerful tradition. And in their contemporary societies they share many parallels in response to devastating wars with a flexible approach that has made marriage easier for the widows, the soldiers, the poor, and the dilemma of the educated woman. Each country has used the state apparatus to support marriage over *zina*.

In the first year of the Iranian Islamic Revolution, by December 1979, an Islamic constitution was drafted making the Ayatollah Khomeini the Supreme Religious Authority, thus the highest ranking Shi'a jurist with control over all branches of government. By the end of its first year, 1989, the al-Bashir-al-Turabi regime had eliminated all opposition but those supporting the Islamist agenda, however neither declared themselves as religious head of state. By 1981, Ayatollah Khomeini's Islamic Republican Party dismissed the presiding Prime Minister Bani-Sadr making Iran a full theocracy. His *fatwas* became the basis of legal interpretation giving the state full control of Shari'a, and then with the establishment of the Council of Guardians comprised of religious scholars Ayatollah Khomeini was made supreme religious authority and highest ranking Shari'a jurist. When the *Inqaz* seized power, Islamization was already advanced since 1983, and al-Turabi appeared to assume the role of 'Imam,' even speaking about himself in Shi'a-like terms as 'expected,' at the Roundtable with American scholars in 1992 which I attended. In Sudan, the *Inqaz* institutionalized its rule through codification of Shari'a, thus ensuring its permanent role in state governance. Al-Turabi's public self-aggrandizement as 'expected' Imam, although disingenuous was nonetheless revelatory of his international ambitions. His surprising dismissal in an internal power struggle in 2000 signaled the withdrawal of the Islamic 'experiment.'

Extreme political repression, terror, and executions were used in the early years of both regimes. The Iranian revolution from 1980–83, executed 6,027 opponents of the regime while the 1983 September Laws heralded the coming of Shari'a as national law with the over 200 amputations in its first two years. In the first years of the *Inqaz*, thousands of regime opponents were detained, tortured in 'ghost houses,' and effectively neutralized or forced into exile. The effects of extreme repression can be long lasting as a general fear is spread throughout the citizenry. However, the Iranian popular resistance to the elections outcome in May-June of 2009, revealed deep fissures in the fabric of governance with general protests against the degree of religious centralism and lack of democracy in the Iranian polity. Sudanese, who have twice successfully risen up, overthrown military regimes, and initiated the country's two periods of democracy are capable and overdue for their coming *intifada*.

In September 1980, the Iran-Iraq war began and lasted until 1988 with estimates of one million dead on each side. In 1983 Sudan resumed its civil war with the South with estimates of 2 million Southerners dead and untold northern troop casualties in 22 years of war. Each war was justified in terms of either defense of the Islamic revolution or as jihad against the 'unbelievers.' In the years of the most intense jihad against the South as military victory was pursued, the number of soldier-martyrs increased. President al-Bashir personally encouraged polygamy to marry the increasing numbers of war widows allegedly by marrying the widow of a close aide who died in a military aircraft accident in the South. Aid to 'unprotected women,' war widows, was enacted in 1987 after popular pressure was exerted on the state to improve the pension allowance of widows whose husbands were state employees and were killed in the war, in an amount equal to the husband's last paid salary. In 1983 seminars in the Islamic Republic were held to ensure a unified, national interpretation of Shari'a tensions between the Judiciary and the NIF activists, while feminists, historically active on the issue of Shari'a, insisted on multiple, flexible interpretations.

1989 was the focus on the public appearance and behavior of women, and restrictions on their employment and contact with the public. 'Public order' tied to an Islamic morality, with state enforcement backed by Islamist militias, are common to the two experiences. Marriage in groups (*Zawaj jamiya* discussed in chapter 6), was officially promoted with state supported marriage gifts for the lower class couples unable to afford traditional expensive dowers and increasingly expensive urban housing.

One of the first acts of the Islamic Revolution was the repeal of the Shah's 1967 Family Protection Law, abrogated on 26 February 1979. On 3 March 1979, Ayatollah Khomeini declared that 'women cannot be judges'; on 6 March the declaration that women must wear *hijab* in the work place – scarf and long dress covering whole body to 'fight western culture.' Beaches and sporting events were legally segregated by gender on 29 March. Nearly twenty years later in November 1997 in a move of pure patriotism women broke down the gates and forcibly entered the Azadi soccer stadium in capital to encourage Iranian team against Australia as Iran qualified for the World Cup.

On International Women's Day, 8 March 1979, thousands of women protested these formal restrictions in Tehran but they were attacked by

Hezbollah. After these initial restrictions on women and an election in April 1979 in which voters were given the option of 'yes' or 'no' to the Islamic Republic (and voted 98 per cent yes), the governance of the Islamic Republic was basically secure.[58]

Still unsure about student resistance, in June 1980 Iranian universities were shut down in advance of the announcement of the 'Islamic Cultural Revolution,' a program of social and economic transformation to which to 'al-Mashru' al-Hadari,' the Islamic Civilization Project, bears close resemblance in Sudan. Revealing no absolute ban on women's participation in Islamism – as is the case with Saudi Wahhabism – four women were elected to the first Majlis (1980–84) in Iran for their proficiency in Qur'an and religious matters, while in Sudan no female jurist was sacked, and those who sided with the *Inqaz* were elevated to high positions in the Judiciary and in government ministries.

Cracks in the Façade

In Iran the political benefit of capture and release of the American hostages, from 1979 to their release at the hour of the swearing in of the new American president Ronald Reagan intended to humiliate Jimmy Carter, demonstrated to the Iranians the strength of their revolution. Nonetheless, within a few years, 1982–83, contradictions in the Islamic Republic began to appear.

As the social fabric was torn apart by war and radical social change, dissension over women as custodians of young children came to the fore as the number of dead soldiers and fathers mounted in the war with Iraq. By February 1985 it was determined that women can have full custody of her children if father is incapable of assuming custody. The Iranian state passed legislation to loan funds to poor couples to enable them to marry, organized by *Bonyad-e Shahid* (Martyr's Foundation) to aid war veterans. 'Siqeh' (temporary marriage) was legalized by a *fatwa* issued by Ayatollah Khomeini and remains in effect in Iranian law today. 'Marriage can be either permanent or temporary,' according to article 1075 of the civil code. *Siqeh* marriage lasts for a specified period of time, and the wife leaves the husband's home as soon as the period has expired, or if the husband waives the remaining time, the wife is not entitled to support or inheritance from the husband.

By the summer of 1984 the Morals police (*Gasht-e Ershad*) were mobilized to enforce *hijab* rules (showing of hair, lipstick) and the Majlis passed a law enforcing 74 lashes for non-compliant women. Meanwhile efforts to strengthen the religious base in the rural areas were made, and Qom University (in one of Iran's most conservative regions) in an unprecedented move admitted over 400 women directly from high school. Likewise under the *Inqaz* in Sudan, the number of women in Islamic and in all universities soared to its present majority of students, 65 per cent of the total.

A Women's Religious Studies Center was initiated at Qom University even as certain professions were considered inappropriate to women and were disallowed, such as management (no woman could be in charge over a man) and mining-engineering, considered too physically demanding. In 1986 the Revolutionary Guards announced military training of women (in an apparent contradictory move for professions inappropriate to women) and admitted 500 recruits. The restrictions placed upon women resulted in inevitable resistance; in March 2000 600 female medical students from Qom University protested the lack of women faculty to teach them while at the same time the Popular Assembly debated whether the increasing number of women in the Majlis were required to wear the long chador or just a head scarf and long dress.

In 1994 women were admitted to the courts as legal consultants but were still barred from being appointed as judges in marked contrast to Sudan where having women judges was both a reflection of women's historic activism and a sign that the new Islamism was non-discriminatory toward women. To its credit, the Sudanese *'ulama* have not interpreted the most important Aya in the Qur'an (4:34) – *Men are in charge of women because God has made one of them to excel the pother and because they spend of their wealth* – to exclude women as judges.

Sudan, Iran, and other Islamist nations formed something of an Islamist feminist bloc at the fourth World Congress of Women in Beijing in advocating women's rights from an Islamic perspective. They argued that Muslim women do not need global feminism for women's rights are fully represented in Islam and the Shari'a. These include full rights in marriage, divorce, inheritance and other aspects of family and civil law. Secular activists from Arab and Muslim nations disagreed and advocated equality in inheritance. However, both Iran and Sudan are signatories to the United Nations Convention on the Elimination of all forms of Discrimination Against Women (CEDAW) while the US is not.

Progressive women from both Iran and Sudan have received international recognition for their human rights work for women and girls. In 1997 Human Rights Watch recognized lawyer Shireen Ebadi for her work with non-profit Children's Rights organizations and she later received the Nobel Peace Prize in 2003. Veteran Sudanese communist and feminist pioneer Fatma Ibrahim, the first woman elected to Parliament in 1965 and Sudan's 'Passionaria' for women's rights was given the United Nations' Human Rights Award accepting on behalf of the Sudanese Women's Union, of which she was a founder. Ebadi has maintained that the problem for women is not Islam but interpretations of Islam; change never will come from without, but within.

Unintended Consequences and Social Transformation

As the years passed the fervor of the Iranian Islamic Republic faded. Efforts to maintain male-female segregated hospitals and clinics failed due to the expense and difficulty of enforcement of gender separation. Since the birth of the Revolution in 1979, 60 per cent of university students are women; they were in the forefront of the demonstrations after the election results of 2009 with the iconic martyr of the uprising the female student Neda Ali. During the years of the Islamic Republic female literacy increased to 97 per cent nationally for women aged 15–24; in 1975 female *illiteracy* was 90 per cent in the rural areas and 45 per cent in the urban areas. Representation of women in the professions likewise dramatically increased with one-third of all doctors, 60 per cent of civil servants and 80 per cent of teachers being women. The birth rate in Iran (once among the world's highest) has plummeted thanks to the enhanced education of women. Condoms and birth control pills are free and state supported despite president Ahmedinejad's encouraging larger families and state support for women who stay at home to raise them.

This outcome of female advancement under Islamism, although counterintuitive from the West's viewpoint, is nonetheless observed in both Iran and Sudan. It demonstrates that there is not a fundamental contradiction between emancipation of women and Islamism. The overriding contradictions lie elsewhere. Before 1979 in Iran and 1989 in Sudan a majority of women chose to wear some sort of *hijab*, whether the traditional Sudanese *tobe* or a scarf to cover their heads. Patriarchal traditions preceded both Islam and Islamism in the Middle East and Islamic world and are not mainly about dress styles.

What is more interesting than dress in these two cases is the promotion, or sanctioning, by both states of temporary marriage. Iran first started promoting temporary marriage in the early 1990s as an alternative to 'living in sin.' Then President Hashemi-Rafsanjani said it was a way for men and women to satisfy their sexual needs. He declared there was no need for a cleric to validate the marriage, but the couple could recite their oaths in private. As recently as 2007 Iran's Interior Minister Imam Mostafa Pour-Mohamed that 'marriage should not be just used for sex but to solve social problems' (BBC News, 2 June 2007). Couples should marry at an earlier age and a man can have unlimited temporary marriages, or *siqeh*, although conservative Iranian society might still disapprove of this as a cover for prostitution. A religiously conservative newspaper in Iran complained of a travel agent advertising for Caspian Sea holidays for couples seeking a temporary marriage for a holiday, offering both hotel accommodation and a cleric to register the marriage. A positive outcome is that couples who are 'marrying' in this way do not want to have children and they are, thus, encouraged to seek sex education and family planning to which they are accustomed at the time of the permanent marriage.

Comparable developments in Sunni Sudan legitimized various forms of temporary marriage such as *zawaj 'urfi* and *misyar*, documented and discussed in chapter 6. Social workers and social commentators in both societies ask about the effects of the temporarily marriage(s) on the real permanent marriage. Likewise, in Iran there are allegedly tens of thousands of children from these temporary marriages whose fathers will not acknowledge them, they are considered illegitimate and are therefore not entitled to a proper *nasab*, a legitimate genealogy giving them rights in a father's patrimony with his name passed to his children and rights to inheritance, as well as other family matters. In both cases this amounts to a tearing down of the old social order, both patrilineal and patriarchal, which some welcome, especially as it appears to have religious legitimacy.

Two-thirds of Iran's and Sudan's population are under 30 years of age. Youth have grown up and only known only Islamism; its culture is normative. Youth are likewise tired of having their nations constantly vilified as international pariahs. They may view such relationships, made possible through forms of temporary 'marriage,' as a way to behave more like youth in the West.

While new forms of temporary marriage are legitimated, the old order regarding bans, intimidation and potential execution of homosexuals continues unabated. In this respect Sudan and Iran are different, with Iran taking a more public and aggressive posture regarding homosexuals, while Sudanese jurists have not addressed homosexuality to my knowledge. Since few studies exist of the practice of homosexuality, its relative acceptance in Muslim or non-Muslim contexts in Africa or the Middle East, it is risky to venture an explanation for the difference. Sudan's pronounced Sufi traditions of egalitarianism, tolerance, and mutual respect have promoted a 'live and let live' attitude to all manner of lawbreaking, including use and abuse of alcohol, as well as irregular social-sexual relations, including heterosexual cohabitation without marriage and acceptance of their offspring. If one's public life is apparently upright, what happens in private remains there.

Iran's assault on homosexuals may be a part of what has been argued in this book, that Islamism targets vulnerable populations, women, the poor, and marginalized as an early and repeated signal that they are in charge. Since 1979, an estimated 4000 gay males and lesbian females have been executed in Iran. Same-sex sexuality between consenting partners is a crime in Iran, as it is in Sudan, but Iran chose to enforce its law with special vigor. Iranian law condemns men involved in sexual penetrative acts with the death penalty, and non-penetrative acts with flogging, until the fourth offence, which warrants the death penalty. Women accused of engaging in same-sex acts are flogged, until the fourth time when they too are punished with death. Examples are many. As recently as 2005, two homosexual male teenagers (aged 18 and 17) were hung in Edalat [Justice] Square in Mashbad, (19 July 2005). Reports of widespread repression of homosexuals in Iran have been verified by Human Rights Watch (Blumenfeld, 2009). Sudan's first raid receiving international attention on an allegedly homosexual party occurred in 2010.

There is likewise imperfect comparability when it comes to the application of the *hadd* penalties. The use of flogging (*jald*), is most common in both countries, but amputations for theft appear to have been more numerous at particular times in Sudan's Islamism than in Iran, while stoning for adultery have been both sentenced and executed in Iran, but not in Sudan. Anti-stoning activists in Iran, such as Shahla Herkat, argue that Shari'a law is not the problem, but patriarchy is. Both Iranian and Sudanese state security apparatuses reign supreme and neither hesitates to use brutality when needed. They can block a demonstration or a movement and work well at the local level. However, the overheated era of 'Death to America' in Iranian political culture is ending and Sudan's relationships with the West are improving, especially since the CPA. In neither case have USA sanctions been effective and in some cases they have blocked desired economic relationships.

Iran's religious scholars are as diverse as Sudan's but a significant change was made in both the Iranian and Sudanese Islamic Republics when they went from the venerable oral traditions in Shari'a to the written law. The traditional legal culture of negotiation and compromise with a pragmatic style shifted decisively to the anonymous bureaucracy of the state and laws applied to the letter, rather than through a more informal human process. Shari'a lost to the Islamist projects its locality, its flexibility, and its adaptability.

Nigeria and Sudan

Between 1999 and 2001, Nigeria's 13 northern states adopted Shari'a as the sole law in force exercising their right to local rule and judicial autonomy under the national federal system. Parallel patterns of Islamization are evident for Sudan in the 1970s and 1980s and Nigeria in the 1990s. Bans on alcohol production, sale, and consumption began the process in both nations. *Hadd* penalties were legalized and applied with the imposition of lashing or flogging sentences for immorality, amputation of limbs for theft, and of stoning for adultery.

After independence in Nigeria, a uniform code of law applicable to all Muslims and non-Muslims throughout the North was brokered in the run-up to independence in 1960 under the influence of the departing British colonialists and consultation with other former colonies in the Muslim world, including the Sudan (Ostien, 2004). After Islamization in Nigeria, the sentiment of 'no going back on Shari'a' was proclaimed throughout its northern states. Although not erupting into civil war, inter-communal violence between Nigeria's Muslims and Christians resulted in tens of thousands of deaths, often in and around religious sites. In Katsina state, the case of Amina Lawal attracted world attention for the Shari'a court's sentence of the *hadd* penalty of stoning for her conviction of adultery. This precipitated a governmental crisis, with the federal government opposing the sentence but refusing to interfere directly for fear of a confrontation between the Muslim North over the case.

Parallel Islamization: Sudan in 1983; Nigeria from 1999–2001

Progressive Islamization in Sudan, from 1977 to 1983, and in Nigeria, from 1999 to 2001, proceeded in comparable fashion from initial bans on alcohol production, sale, and consumption to the suppression of public prostitution, to an enforced public morality and dress codes, including gender segregation in public transport. Courts of 'prompt' or 'emergency' justice where appeals are limited were instituted as was the institution of *zakat* (religious alms), and, finally, the application of public punishments of *hudud*. The outcomes, leading to civil war and chronic instability in Sudan, and a constitutional crisis in Nigeria, are parallel in several respects, but also differ in their social magnitude, especially in regard to loss of life, with an estimated two million persons either killed or displaced in Sudan and tens of thousands of persons killed or injured in northern Nigeria's religious violence.

In Nigeria moves towards Islamization in northern Nigeria were increasing for years before the formal declaration of Islamic law throughout the northern region. The Muslim Brothers under the leadership of Ibrahim el-Zak Zaky became more active in the late 1980s raising the familiar Islamist slogan – 'there is no government except that of Islam' (Quinn, 2003). In 1999, Zamfara state was the first to declare Shari'a as the sole law in force in the state, and it was also the first state to execute a sentence of amputation in 2001. Yobe, Kebbi, Katsina, and Niger states followed suit by January 2000, with Kano state following shortly thereafter. By November 2001 the entire northern bloc of twelve Muslim states had adopted Shari'a, including the states of Niger and Kaduna close to the national capital, Abuja. Sokoto state, the historic center of Islam and headquarters of the Nigerian Supreme Council for Islamic Affairs, adopted Shari'a where the powerful Sultan of the Sokoto Caliphate, Alhaji Muhammad Maccido presided until his death in an airline crash in 2006. Anti-Shari'a demonstrations occurred in many state capitals south of the predominantly Muslim North – some threatening to declare Christian states if the federal government did not intervene to stop the spread of Shari'a. A previous challenge to the federal constitution failed in 1979 when Muslims unsuccessfully argued for a separate Federal Shari'a Court of Appeals between the northern states and the National Supreme Court. Nigerian Muslim revival has focused on a return to the purity of worship ('Ibada) and the uncompromising application of Shari'a Law.

In one exception in Kaduna state, non-Muslims threatened secession if the government implemented the law, and the state government decided not to apply Shari'a on non-Muslims who instead would be subject to customary courts. Shari'a courts would apply family law and local governments would only be allowed to restrict the sale of alcohol in Muslim areas. A clear motivation for the Islamization move was its unifying effect for the northern bloc of Muslim states against misuse of power by the Nigerian central government. Nonetheless, many southern and northern Muslims oppose the Shari'a as a comprehensive law because of its potential divisiveness.

For decades before Islamization, Kano, the North's largest Muslim city, became the center of a radical brand of Islamist preaching. This inflamed Muslim-Christian relations and precipitated rioting in Jos and in Kaduna state in the aftermath of the events of 9/11. It is noteworthy that Evangelical Christian groups have targeted this 'fault line' in the Sahel in the post 9/11 world, where fears of growing Islamism in the region have spawned an aggressive Christianist response.

While Shari'a was a major political device for ensuring northern Muslim dominance in Sudan, in Nigeria Shari'a became the driving force for a greater political role for the Muslim North. Some observers allege that Islamist forces seized their opportunity after the end of 16 years military rule and the return of 'the South' to power with the ascendance of General Obasanjo in 1999. The Christian Association of Nigeria (CAN) warned that a more general religious conflict would ensue if Shari'a is accepted. In an open letter addressed to the president during the constitutional drafting meeting, they mentioned that 'Sudanese experience was enough for Nigeria to profit from and eschew anything which has to do with the Shari'a in our constitution. If not, the consequences will be too grave and obvious' (Bunza, 2006).

In both Nigeria and Sudan popular Muslim sentiment holds that political systems have failed the public since independence devolving to chronic militarism. For many Muslims Shari'a law represents traditional governance, not the foreign law of colonizers. Those seeking to limit the influence of Shari'a are often accused of being blind imitators of the West by Islamist agitators. Whereas Sudan since the CPA non-Muslims are theoretically immune from prosecution using the Shari'a, Nigeria is actively in the throes of early Islamization with an outcome regarding Muslim-Christian relations that is yet to be determined.

Parallel Islamic History

Both Sudan and Nigeria had significant pre-colonial Islamic Sultanates across the Sahel, connected through pilgrimage routes and Muslim jihadist expansion in *bilad al-Sudan* (Arabic 'land of the blacks') especially after the sixteenth century CE. In the cases of Kano, Kanem-Bornu in Nigeria, and Darfur in Sudan, feudal sultanates continued into the twentieth century. Better protected by indirect rule in Nigeria, the sultanates not only survived but thrived, while the last remaining Sudanese sultanate of Darfur was overthrown and the sultan assassinated in 1916, one of the last acts of *Pax Britannica* in the Anglo-Egyptian Condominium. Christian Nubia effectively blocked the introduction of Islam into northern Sudan through a unique *baqt* non-aggression treaty with Muslim Egypt until the sixteenth century (Lobban, 2006). Continuous Hajj routes west to east across the Sahel brought a steady influx of Nigerian and other West African Muslims for centuries to and through Sudan as they made their way to pilgrimage in the Holy lands of the Hijaz. The Maliki African school of Islamic jurisprudence (*madhhab*) both introduced and reinforced legal and customary practice through this West-East exchange. Intellectual and theological exchange among religious scholars, *'ulama*, impacts both the pre-colonial and post-independence history of Islam in the Sahel. Informal exchange by peripatetic scholars in the centuries of the great and small Muslim states of West Africa was formally adopted as policy by British colonial authorities and post-independence rulers who sent and received scholar-experts in Islamic law between the great universities and Islamic institutions of Sudan and Nigeria. A continuous tradition of Sunni *'ulama* educated at al-Azhar University in Cairo developed Islamic jurisprudence, *fiqh*, in Sudanic Africa. Likewise, folk traditions and Sufi brotherhoods across the Sahara – the Qadiriyya, Sanusiyya, or Tijaniyya – remain influential and have generally peacefully co-existed with the tradition of respected scholars. A detailed history of this centuries-long Sahelian exchange is a relevant and significant area for continuing future research.

Parallel jihadist expansionist movements

A comparable history of Muslim expansionist movements is evident in the two countries, especially in reaction to European colonial expansion in the nineteenth century. The jihadist movements of Uthman Dan Fodio (1804–17) and Muhammadu Bello (1853–64), in future Nigeria, and Muhammad Ahmed al-Mahdi and his successor the Khalifa Abdullahi (1884–98) in a future Sudan, have far reaching political ramifications continuing to the present time. Dynastic tendencies are evident in both.

The political careers of the son and grandsons of Muhammad Ahmed al-Mahdi and their Umma party exerted a dominant force in Sudanese pre and post-colonial politics, from the Mahdi's son, Abdel Rahman al-Mahdi during colonialism to the enduring career of great grandson and twice Prime Minister in Sudan, Sadiq al-Mahdi. These living traditions embody the religious and political legitimacy across the Muslim Sahel afforded by virtue of lineage.

The history of the Caliphate and its administration remain as an inspiring source for Islamists and their demands. Dan Fodio's jihad founded an Islamic state with Shari'a as its sole law in 1809 and Sokoto as its capital. The jihadist movement of Dan Fodio did not have the same impact in England that the Mahdist uprising in Sudan had, due to the murder of the popular imperialist figure General Charles Gordon in 1884 during the Mahdi's 'siege of Khartoum.' However, both the Sudanese Mahdists and the Nigerian jihadist movements had the effect of shaping colonial and post-colonial relations in each between North and south, between Muslim and non-Muslim, and between center and periphery.

In Sudan, slave raids, known as *ghazwa*, were waged against Southerners, while the rank and file of the Mahdist army, although under the control of northern officers, was drawn heavily from the western ethnic groups in Darfur and Kordofan. This pattern continued from the Mahdiya to the post-independence Sudan army. While early European scholars saw the Mahdiya as an anti-modernist movement fighting against the forces of progress, post-independence Sudanese and other scholars have viewed it as anti-imperialist and an early 'fundamentalist' Islamic movement part of contemporary Islamic reform and renewal (Lobban, Kramer and Fluehr-Lobban, 2002). While slavery was significant in the growth of all Sahelian sultanates, the moral and human rights dimension of slavery has not been part of the otherwise heated political debates over Islamization in Nigeria. The Hausa-Fulani jihadists of the eighteenth- and early-nineteenth-century leaders were revivalists more intent upon purifying the lands of 'paganism' and polytheism, introducing Shari'a as a systematic law for the first time, replacing the informal mix of customary and Islamic law that had prevailed (Hiskett, 1976).

In both Sudan and Nigeria the nineteenth-century jihads empowered a new governing elite as they as they spread Muslim literacy
through Qur'anic schools known as *kuttab* or *khalwa* in Sahelian
Africa. The creation of a socio-religious solidarity through politics
and Muslim education that these movements engendered in the eighteenth and nineteenth centuries resonates today. 'Neo-jihadist' movements have destabilized both countries at the end of the twentieth
century and into the millennium. In Nigeria, the Maitatsine (lead
by Yan Tatsine) movement was blamed for the religious riots of the
1980s. The chronic Sudanese civil war waged against the south has
been described as jihadist, especially by Southerners in their legitimate
claim that Arabization or Arab colonialism, as well as Islamization,
were the goals of the central government's protracted war.

Contrasting Societies

Sudan's approximately 70 per cent Muslim population is concentrated
in then northern two-thirds of Africa's largest geographical nation.
For nearly five centuries Islam has been close to state power, from the
sixteenth century Funj sultanate in central Sudan, through the nineteenth century Turkiya and Mahdiya states, to the present rule of the
National Islamic Front/National Congress Party since 1989. During
the 58 years of British rule Islam was marginalized from centralized
power in the predominantly Muslim northern tier of the Sudanese
colonial state. Meanwhile peoples of the South practiced indigenous
African faiths and were introduced to Christian missionary activity during colonialism. This created a Christian base from which
Southerners could respond and expand Christianity when campaigns
to Arabize and Islamize the South were waged by various post-
independence governments in Khartoum.

In the decades of civil war since 1983, several millions of Southerners
fled to and have settled in the northern cities, especially Khartoum,
making these cities more animist and Christian, although officially
governed by Shari'a law until the CPA in 2005. In Nigeria, numerically
Africa's largest Muslim nation with a population estimated at 130 million, 80 per cent of the North and 30 per cent of the South is Muslim.

In the North, Muslim personalities and institutions dominate regional politics, and after independence northern leaders often became heads of state. In the southern capital city Lagos a Christian-animist majority predominates, although a significant Muslim population has a history of peaceful co-existence with the dominant non-Muslim majority. The 'border' states and cities between North and South – Bauchi, Kaduna, Katsina, Kano, Maiduguri, and Jos – have all experienced Christian-Muslim inter-communal violence and serious loss of life in reaction to Islamization and other factors.

Both countries have serious Muslim-Christian fault lines with the issue of the status of Shari'a acting as a theater for multiple symbolic and real conflicts. Failure to resolve the civil war in Sudan centered on the issue of Shari'a as the symbol mobilizing southern resistance and Sudan government intransigence. Although civil war was never threatened, inter-communal violence between Nigeria's Muslims, often in and around religious sites, has been extensive. Like Sudan, the sentiment of 'no going back on Shari'a' is widespread in the northern states of Nigeria.

Parallel British Colonial Policies Toward Islamic Institutions

After the Berlin Congress the British moved quickly from 1886 to colonize Nigeria, first the South and then the North, despite massive local resistance. The emirs of the North pledged to die defending Islam against the 'infidel,' but their armies succumbed in northern Nigeria as they did elsewhere to the superiority of British firepower (Adu Bouahen, 1990). When the British took control of the North after 1900 they banned the *hudud* punishments of amputation, stoning and crucifixion as 'repugnant to natural justice, equity, and good conscience' (Anderson, 1976), the English colonial standard to which all indigenous legal application was held. But otherwise, the introduction of British governmental and legal institutions was tempered by attention both to 'Mohammedan' traditions and 'native custom.'

In 1900 Lord Frederick Lugard declared the Caliphate a protectorate of the British crown. He recognized the sensitivity of preserving Muslim institutions, and committed not to interfere with them, including the power of the 'Native Courts' to administer Muslim law and custom. The center of the Caliphate and the capitol of Sokoto were subjugated by British forces in February and March of 1903. The conquest was followed by political and religious structural changes. Shari'a was restricted to civil matters only. Criminal cases were handled by the British High Commissioner or their designate. The preserved judicial institutions of Shari'a became symbolic of Muslim identity and stood as a barrier to English cultural hegemony. The scholars and judges, *Alkalai*, were respected and their courts were preferred by locals. Aware of the power of the Shari'a the British kept it in control and ultimately subject to English law. However, an open confrontation with the learned *'ulama* was not advised, and a policy of subordination and secularization was pursued (Tabiu, 2001).

In Sudan the story was dramatically different with its successful anti-colonial resistance mounted by Muhammad Ahmed, the Mahdi that staved off British colonization from 1884 to 1898 while an Islamist state was erected under the rule of the Khalifa Abdullahi al-Taisha. The 're-conquest' was a bloody affair with over 10,000 Mahdist resisters falling to English Gatling machine guns in a single morning in 1898. The successful Sudanese resistance both tempered the British approach to Islam and Muslim institutions and, inspired later nationalist activism seeking an Islamic constitution or state after independence.

British colonial policies erected by Lord Lugard were similar in both countries, with indirect rule for Islamic institutions. Shari'a (referenced under the Orientalist designation of 'Mohammedan' law) was relegated in both colonies to a personal status law only, leaving important civil and criminal matters to English-derived law. The *mallams* (religious scholars and judges) in Nigeria perhaps derived more influence from their extant feudal traditions than did the Sudanese scholars and judges, the *'ulama*. In order to stabilize their indirect rule in northern Nigeria, the British ensured that the students of the law school were children of existing British-backed judges and Imams they controlled throughout the North. In this way the old legal order was perpetuated and there was little significant resistance to the continuous erosion of the Shari'a by the British.

The religious intelligentsia in both Sudan and Nigeria were carefully observed by the colonial authorities. The history of early colonial Sudan with respect to Islamic activism reveals a careful management of Islamic institutions once the British colonized the country. A policy at once asserting dominance after military pacification of the Mahdists also moved to placate, yet control, the *'ulama* who the colonialists understood had their own credibility to protect. After the early period of constraining and colonizing Muslim law and legal personnel, colonial fear of a Pan-Islamism (dating back to the Mahdist period) was renewed in the First World War. With a growing pan-Arabic Islamic movement the English demanded loyalty from the indigenous Muslim leaders against the Ottoman Empire, responsible for the guardianship of the Holy Places at Mecca and Medina.

According to Bunza (2006), the Islamists' fight in modern times originated in the opposition to the British imperial occupation of the Caliphate of Sokoto. The history of the resistance of the *'ulama* and the *mallams* in Sudan and Nigeria during colonial times is relevant as they preserved or attempted to conserve essential principles of Islam despite the demands of the colonial masters.

The colonial government in Sudan left a legacy both of entitlement to full political-religious status and respect for Islamic institutions, but also the unfinished business of the restoration of Muslim institutions. This was especially strong among the *'ulama* and the 'second class' Shari'a judges who administered the Shari'a as a separate and distinctly inferior system of law and courts. In Sudan Shari'a courts in 1979 were still separate with inferior facilities and lower salaries for judges and employees of the courts.

Contrasting Post-Independence Histories

At independence in 1960, Nigeria instituted a federal system that permitted autonomy of governance for northern regions, where Shari'a remained the law in force for family and personal status matters. Sir Ahmadu Bello, co-founder of the Northern People's Congress (NPC) was the leading spokesman for the northern view of federal government, and from 1954 he was the first Premier of northern Nigeria.

Despite his influential voice, Shari'a lost status in the national system
of law that in effect abrogated Islamic criminal law (Ostien, 2004).
This loss was ameliorated by the creation of a new Shari'a Court of
Appeal for the northern region that was placed on a par with the
Regional High Court. This meant that judgments in areas of Islamic
family law were rendered final and not subject to appeal. It is noteworthy that the first Grand Kadi of the newly created Shari'a Court
of Appeal was the Sudanese Sheikh Awad Muhammad Ahmed who
had spent several years teaching at Kano School of Arabic Studies. The
powerful voice of Ahmadu Bello was silenced by his assassination in
the 1966 coup toppling Nigeria's first independence government.

In 1967 Nigeria sub-divided its four regions and in the North
each new state had its own Shari'a Court of Appeal. With federalism extended to individual states and no overriding national Appeals
Court to harmonize the work of all courts, the question of the preservation of the uniform legal system of 1960 arose as early as 1976. A
new Federal or 'Final' Shari'a Court of Appeal (limited to family law
jurisdiction) was proposed to resolve any conflicts, but the objections
of influential Christian federalists was intense and they succeeded in
eliminating it from the new constitution of 1979. This reduced the
effective implementation of Shari'a and its jurisdiction to its weakest
position since British colonial times. Moreover, the Shari'a seat on the
National High Court was lost with a resulting loss of national status
and prestige for this key Islamic position (Ostein, 2004). After these
events, claims of Muslim victimization by Christian politicians per-
meated political discourse and set the stage for the Muslim-Christian
inter-communal violence that began in the 1980s and continued into
the next decades before and after the institution of Shari'a as state law
throughout the North (Sanusi, 2003).

The federal system may have staved off the chronic civil war that
afflicted Sudan for most of its post-independence history (1955–72;
1983–2004). Nigeria's brief Biafran war (1967–70) was certainly costly
both in loss of life and in confidence that the federal system would
prevail. Sanusi (2003) argues that one effect of the Biafran war was
the construction of a monolithic identity of 'northern Nigerian' without much nuance, although differences about the place of religion and

the state among the northern cadre of the Nigerian Armed Forces was reflected in the military ranks competing for state power from the 1970s through the 1990s. Thus, competing ideas about greater Islamization or strengthening of the federal system were evident among northern elites for decades preceding the institution of Shari'a as state law throughout the North.

In 1979, nearly two decades after Nigerian independence and federalism, a constitutional challenge was precipitated when northern Muslims argued again for a separate federal Shari'a Court of Appeals, adding a layer of judicial review between the states and the Nigerian Supreme Court. The idea was defeated. Instead the issue of federated autonomy for the North and some national status for Shari'a simmered and came to a boil in 1999 when Obasanjo returned to power and the first northern state declared Shari'a as its sole law in force. Years of inattention of the deeply held views of many Nigerian Muslims left the politics and emotions to harden and polarize.

Sudan's independence in 1956 established a parliamentary system of government, not a federal system. In both countries politics devolved to persistent militarism. However, Nigeria's military rulers executed more of a balance of power between the major regions of south, North, and east than have the Sudanese. The status of Shari'a was a persistent unresolved issue after independence, with various northern forces seeking greater implementation of Shari'a and a state governed more by Muslim institutions. It is noteworthy that the nineteenth century Mahdi is referred to by northern Muslim Sudanese as 'Abu al-Istiqlal,' the father of independence, for having united through Islam various ethnic groups of the North and driving out foreign rule. The Mahdist state was the only truly anti-imperialist Islamic state of its time in Africa, thus, the twentieth century movement for restoration of Islam to a central role in the state is viewed by Islamists as grounded in real Sudanese history, and not messianic hope.

Review of this history shows consistent support for a greater role for Shari'a after independence. The MB was founded in 1953, on the eve of independence. Its lobbying group, the Islamic Front for the Constitution, promoted a program for an Islamic state based upon an Islamic constitution with constitution and law based solely upon

Qur'an and Sunna. After 1964, it was led by al-Turabi. In 1957, the Umma party (whose leaders descend from the Mahdist lineage) and the Khatmiya Sufi order (with followers loyal to the noble Mirghani family) both advocated a parliamentary Islamic republic with Shari'a as the sole source of legislation.

Southern non-Muslim regions were ignored politically as resistance to elite, northern Muslim rule became entrenched and chronic civil war pursued. The western, eastern and Blue Nile regions were politically marginalized. The first military coup of General Ibrahim Abboud began the ultimately failed policy of forced Islamization and spread of the Arabic language in the south, the other major factors – besides Shari'a – that have inflamed relations between the North and South.

Oil and Post-independence Civil Wars

The Nigerian Biafran civil war of 1966–68 erupted with assertion of ethnic and regional autonomy after the vast oil reserves were discovered in Biafra. The war was quelled and a lasting peace was negotiated. By contrast, the Sudanese civil war began on the eve of independence in 1955 prompted by the political isolation of the South. Resolution of the war occurred in the wake of the discovery of vast oil reserves in southern Sudan and the beginning of production in 1999. The pipeline for Sudan's oil was located in the North for export from Port Sudan after the NIF came to power and various western oil interests were driven out by the civil war in the south (Chevron Oil), or shamed out (Talisman of Canada) after international outcry from human rights groups. Currently, approximately 10 per cent of China's oil imports come from Sudan. The factor of oil is believed to have been a major stimulus to advance in peace negotiations.

As described in this book, the symbolic and real issue was Shari'a, which SPLM leader John Garang demanded be withdrawn, and the GoS contended was non-negotiable. Until pressure from the international community mounted and the Bush administration placed Sudan near the top of its first administration agenda – under influence from the Christian right to protect southern Christians and vigorously oppose an Islamist regime that once gave haven to Osama bin Laden

– the peace process was stymied. In the end, compromise over Shari'a paved the way to the CPA, with the withdrawal of Shari'a from the South and its retention in the North, theoretically excepting the considerable non-Muslim population residing there. However, as events revealed uneven enforcement of the CPA, in July 2009, a dozen, primarily Christian and animist women wearing trousers, were arrested at a prominent Khartoum restaurant and sentenced to 40 lashes for 'indecent' dress (BBC, 13 July 2009).

Politics of Shari'a in Sudan and Nigeria

Until the riveting events in Sudan in the 1980s and 1990s, and in Nigeria at the turn of the new millennium, Islam and its relationship to the state in Africa was viewed as peripheral by western policy makers. Generally overlooked until the Islamist regime in Sudan afforded safe haven to Osama bin Laden from 1990–96, since the bombings of American embassies in East Africa in 1998 Islam and Islamism in Africa are no longer at the margins of western foreign policy. Today Islamic Africa has achieved a high profile status in western geopolitical strategy due to the politics of Islamism (McCormick, 2005) under review here, the vast stretches of Sahara and savanna lands that are sparsely populated and little regulated by any state – Islamist or otherwise – and finally, by the precarious situation of the states in the Sahel, especially the Sudan which holds the dubious distinction of one of the world's failed states.

In Nigeria, Shari'a quickly became the symbol of a revived northern power as old ethnic-based power rivalries between northern Muslim Hausa and southern Yoruba and Igbo Christians reheated. Sanusi (2005) argues that the attempt to construct a new Muslim identity in Nigeria is partly the result of the loss of control of the state machinery and the armed forces by the northern Muslim elite. Moreover, he argues that the debate over Shari'a was just one stage in a long historical process between opposing religious identities *within* northern Nigeria, especially among the important national players of the Nigerian Army.

Shari'a law in Sudan became state law by presidential fiat, not mass mobilization, under military rule of Ja'afar Numeiri (1969–85); it was neither popularly supported nor protested by masses of northern Muslims. Southern public trust was destroyed, and in the words and title of the classic work by former southern vice-president Abel Alier (1990) 'too many agreements [were] dishonored.' Shari'a became the major symbol of northern dominance and a critical stumbling block to peace. Peace negotiations advanced with significant oil wealth; chronic war fatigue of northern and southern leaders set in; and international pressure – primarily from the US – mounted for a settlement. With the signing of the CPA in 2005 the issue of Shari'a retreated substantially, reconfirming its symbolic role in politics. Yet, it is still able to inflame passions.

Debating the Politics of Shari'a in Nigeria

Although Islamization has advanced dramatically, there is no Islamic party *per se* in Nigeria, no national Islamist movement comparable to Sudan's National Islamic Front. Ironically, some argue that it is secular democracy that is the most effective device of the Islamists. Madeleine Albright, on a visit to Kano was taken aback when she was thanked for introducing Shari'a – 'it was due to democracy,' she was told (Bunza, 2002: 15). Islamist ideology was sharply critical of the series of corrupt military regimes, economic mismanagement, and years of political repression and was an established presence once democracy was restored in 1999 (McCormack, 2005: 9).

The rapid move toward Islamization of northern Nigeria precipitated vigorous internal debate regarding threats to national unity as well as constitutional federalism. Events in Sudan did not escape notice. As the case for Shari'a was being pressed, the Christian Association of Nigeria (CAN) warned of open religious conflict if Shari'a is accepted. In an open letter to the president they argued that the 'Sudanese experience was enough for Nigeria to profit from and eschew anything that has to do with the Shari'a in our constitution. If not, the consequences will be too grave and obvious' (Yadudu, 1993).

In an effort to dissuade Nigeria's further Islamization, the Assembly of Muslims in Nigeria (AMIN) invited Umma party head and former Sudanese prime minister Sadiq al-Mahdi to Nigeria in an attempt to convince Nigerian Muslims that the Shari'a is not feasible as state law in its northern region. Although sponsored by the federal government of Nigeria, al-Mahdi failed. Al-Mahdi's legitimacy in opposition to the application of Shari'a as an Arabic speaking African Muslim, the great grandson of the Sudanese Mahdi, was clearly being sought. Ironically, he had not opposed Shari'a as state law in 1989 at a critical moment in Sudan's fragile democracy and in negotiations over the status of Islamic law to end the civil war in the South.

Political pressure exerted by the Nigerian federal government to prevent the implementation of Shari'a was intense. The Kaduna State House of Assembly attempted to consider debating the case for and against installation of the Shari'a, and federal officials in Abuja issued an order to halt the adoption of the Shari'a and return to the Nigerian Penal Code (Yadudu, 2001). This proved widely unpopular and resulted in a federal government retreat on the issue in the early years of the adoption of Shari'a in the North. The opposition of Nigerian President Obasanjo proved equally ineffective. Initially he predicted the move would be temporary, but he later revised his view by asserting that the 'real' Shari'a would prevail, while the 'political' Shari'a would fade (Ibid).

Intense debate among Muslim intellectuals has ensued since 1999, along the lines of traditionalists – those who adhere strictly to Maliki legal interpretations and those who might be described as modernists. Sanusi Lamido Sanusi is regarded as one of the boldest of the modernists. He is a banker and a writer with an excellent knowledge of Arabic gained at Omdurman Islamic University in Sudan. Although not trained as an '*alim*, Sanusi's knowledge of Arabic gives him standing in the debate among the '*ulama* in Nigeria. In Nigeria's growing polarization over Islamization and Shari'a, he has his detractors. Labeled a secularist reformer comparable to Mohamed Abduh and Kemal Ataturk, he has also been likened to Sudanese Republican writer Abdullahi an-Na'im in the current era (Mohamed, 2002). Sanusi uses the methodology of other contemporary Muslim reformers, such as Sudan's Mahmoud Taha and Egypt's Sa'id al-'Ashmawy (1998), to demonstrate that what is thought of as a fixed and unchanging Shari'a actually reflects its interpretation by the religious scholars at different points in time in a manner consistent with the dominant world-view of the leaders in that society. As such, Islamic jurisprudence (*fiqh*) is not an unchanging law revealed by God, but a man-made law whose interpretation is relative to time and space.

National debate on Shari'a generally has occurred in times of crises. The dialogue regarding the retention of a federal state and constitution, but with fuller legal recognition of Islamic law and norms is yet to be decisive. Nigeria is perhaps in its intense period of Islamization, closer to Sudan in the mid-1980s. Yadudu (2001) summarized the debate – North versus South generally – as non-Muslims conceding that the constitution already recognizes Shari'a, but that its status cannot be permitted to intrude on the secular purity of the state. Muslims contend that there is sufficient constitutional support for them to have full legal rights in the state which is empowered to expand the jurisdiction of the Shari'a and its courts.

Shari'a, Federalism, Self-Determinism

Shari'a political and theoretical debates go to the heart of the political futures of other states in Africa and the Muslim world. Pointedly, the movement attempting to resurrect the failed Somali state has called itself 'The Islamic Courts.' They also go to the heart of contemporary debates about the nature of the state itself – federal and secular, or theocratic. Theocratic models of the state, normally characterized as undemocratic, are evolving new forms, such as the experience of Islamic rule in Iran has shown.

The federal 'solution' to Sudan's chronic civil wars was adopted in 1991, after its third military government fulfilled the Islamist direction begun in 1983 during its second period of military rule. That federalism triumphed at the moment that Islamism was officially installed is a telling point in the pragmatic politics of the Islamist movement. Also, in 1991 Shari'a was codified in Sudan, for the first time in its five centuries of history in the country since the Funj state. In 1998 Sudan's new 'permanent' constitution enshrined the principle of 'Islamic federalism.' The Machakos Protocol of 2003–04, leading to the CPA, instituted the right of self-determination for the South, federalism, and the Islamic character of Sudan outside of the South.

Nigerian Muslims never accepted the colonial policy that undermined Shari'a and subordinated its judicial system. The Emirs and *Alkalai* (judges) resisted the substitution of Islamic criminal law with an English-based Penal Code and Criminal Procedure Codes. The decision at independence to remove a substantial part of Islamic law, the criminal law, was accomplished through pressure from the British Government on the newly installed ruling NPC party. The colonial policy was reinforced in 1977 when the Emirs courts were abolished and the Alkali courts were changed into Area Courts (Tabiu, 2001). The 1999 Constitution reaffirmed the federal principle, and it was this principle that was cited as accommodating the first act to implement Shari'a as provincial law in Zamfara state.

The principle of the right of self-determination has been enunciated over the decades as key to the future of the Sudanese state, whether ultimately unified or divided. It has been recently developed as basis for the desirable outcome of retaining Sudanese unity (An-Na'im and Deng, 2009) using a localized political framework that respects the rights of a people freely determining their political and social future. However, unity – whether based in law, language, culture or politics – cannot be used to eclipse the more fundamental right of self-determination. With this perspective a federal 'solution' can never be imposed.

Global Human Rights activism over Shari'a
in Nigeria and Sudan

International and indigenous human rights have taken an interest in Shari'a in Sudan and Nigeria by condemning their application of *hadd* punishments. However, their efforts at the level of local politics were challenged. In the first case of amputation in Zamfara state the amputee resisted pressure to sue the government for amputating his right wrist, saying he was satisfied with his conviction and that he had no right to challenge the Shari'a (Mohamed 2002). Issues of cultural relativism and universal rights sharpened in both Sudan and Nigeria after the *hadd* punishments were applied by Shari'a criminal law. When *hadd* penalties were imposed on non-Muslims – as in Sudan from 1983 to the eve of the peace agreement – they were condemned for their glaring religious and political contradictions. During research in 2005, I questioned the frequency of application of *hadd* punishments and found it to be sensitive among a broad spectrum of persons – from attorneys, to judges, social scientists and journalists – similar to their reaction during the western campaign against female circumcision, as though Islamic law was itself being challenged. Although statistics are difficult to obtain in Sudan, it is likely that the 'lesser' punishment of flogging was more frequently applied than the debilitating punishment of amputation, most used in the earlier, intesnse period of their Islamism in 1983–85 (Layish and Warburg, 2002). The international human rights outcry in response to the stoning sentence of Amina Lawal and its confirmation was unprecedented, both for African Islam and an individual case of Islamic law. In Katsina state – the home of Amina Lawal, who attracted the attention of international human rights activists for her sentence of stoning for adultery – the government at first refused to intervene to overturn her sentence, and then upheld the sentence in the context of the national presidential elections, fearing a northern backlash if the sentence was overturned. In the end the Katsina State Shari'a Court of Appeals did overturn her conviction due to procedural irregularities – her confession was uttered once instead of the required four times, and the first trial was presided over by one judge instead of three (Sengupta, 2003). This legal solution, nonetheless, does not resolve the issue of the status of Shari'a within the Federal Republic of Nigeria, and will undoubtedly resurface especially as new elections replacing president Obasanjo are scheduled for 2007. Adultery is not an offense against the state, and it was predictable that the state would not risk its own stability to save a woman convicted by a Shari'a court. The female attorney for Amina Lawal made the interesting argument that pregnancy as evidence of a crime inherently discriminates against women, and that this is a violation of the Islamic principle that men and women are equal before God and the law. What is most instructive in the Lawal case is that Islamic procedures and principles were consistently invoked without any interference from presumably 'superior' western legal ideas still operative in national Nigerian law. This stands as a political victory for the integrity of Shari'a.

Like Sudan, the issue of Shari'a became incendiary when its jurisdiction was expanded beyond a personal status law alone. Once mostly uncontested by Christians after independence while it remained a Muslim family law, its status in Sudan became a symbol of the preservation or loss of national unity. Presently in Nigeria the issue of Shari'a is poised to become more of a central issue in the coming years and, perhaps, a fundamental test to its federal system.

The examples of Sudan and Nigeria, respectively Africa's largest countries geographically and having the largest Muslim population, underscore the significance of the issue of Shari'a and Islamization in nation building and in the maintenance of national stability. Beyond their specifics of region and history, they are likely to recur between North-south, Muslim-Christian fault lines across the Sahel in the continent. Shari'a and related issues are demonstrably capable of mobilizing masses.

The issue of Islamization of law across Africa and among nations in the formerly colonized Muslim world is not simple and outcomes are likely affected by the following: 1) the historical experience of colonialism and its policies toward Shari'a and Islamic institutions; 2) the multiple forms of Muslim identity embedded in the indigenous processing of this history, including the symbolic issues of Shari'a; 3) diverse political experiences in nation-building in post-independence Muslim Africa; and 4) politicization of religious institutions, such as Shari'a, and the growing appeal and strength of Islamism.

Beyond these, personal status and criminal applications of the Shari'a, especially the *hadd* criminal punishments, have proven problematical in international human rights discourse, and in African Muslim societies that are more complex politically and sociologically than is often held. While the political dimension of the issue of Islamization and Shari'a appear paramount, their underlying symbolism for religious mobilization cannot be ignored.

Whether Sudan's dubious distinction as one of the world's failed and most repressive states is the direct result of its failed Islamist policy from 1983 to the present is a matter of debate. What is clear is that

Sudan began its withdrawal from its own brand of Islamism, albeit under intense international pressure and as a matter of pragmatic politics. There are obvious potential insights to be gained, for Nigeria – now in its own advanced stage of Islamism, and for Sudan as it enters early post-Islamism.

The persistence and tenacity of holding on to the Shari'a in Sudan after its installation as state law in 1983, despite decades of civil war, international outcry, and pressure to withdraw Shari'a is notable. The steadfast commitment not to compromise on Shari'a in the post-colonial, post-9/11 politics of Muslim Africa has relevance beyond these cases. Significant and still largely unresolved questions in Sudan and Nigeria include: 1) implementation of the peace accords remains ambiguous and problematical in Sudan, while Nigeria is possibly heading for a constitutional crisis over Shari'a; 2) social polarization over Shari'a in both nations makes objective dialogue/debate difficult, if not impossible; 3) damage to Muslim/ non-Muslim relations in both countries over decades of increasing mistrust is probably irreparable. Both nations have reacted more to political crises over Shari'a rather than by developing a strategy of respectful, sustained dialogue over the relevant issues; and 4) Constitutional issues remain central.

Both Nigerian and Sudanese constitutions guarantee freedom of religion. A constitutional convention, long been advocated by Sudanese democrats, has repeatedly stalled by a lack of political will. Implementation of Shari'a in Nigeria through legislation will likely lead to its challenge as constitutional or unconstitutional (Yadudu, 2001). The southern non-Muslim legal establishment has already dismissed any implementation of Shari'a as unconstitutional in violation of Section 10 of the 1999 Constitution defining Nigeria as a secular state. How far can the *hadd* penalties stand the test of constitutional validity?

It is clear from a review of history that the issue of Shari'a is sensitive to the interests of Islam and Muslims in both Sudan and Nigeria. The colonial policy of indirect rule at the local level, but restriction of Shari'a on the national level, left a strong desire after independence to restore or install Islamic institutions, chief among them the Shari'a. Oil in both nations exerts both internal and external pressures favoring stable governments. Nigeria is the sixth largest world oil producer at 2.5 million barrels per day (mbd), while Sudan's oil reserves are extensive, potentially as large, but with current production of 500,000 mbd, expected to double or treble soon.

In the realm of international Islamist politics Sudan is advantaged by Arabic language, and Nigerian Muslim intellectuals are often judged by their ability in classical or modern standard Arabic. But the influence of the Iranian experience and Saudi monetary support has been substantial in both countries that have advanced the issue of Shari'a in national politics.

Finally, the future of the state – secular, federalist, or Islamist – remains an open question for both countries. Nigeria's rapid and dramatic Islamization in the North (1999–2001) is comparable in content but not in form to the historically prior experience of Sudan (1977–83). The early, dramatic application of the stricter *hadd* penalties is similar, but the political paths of a Nigerian federal, state-by-state adoption of Shari'a versus the Sudanese military-presidential decree in 1983 is noteworthy. Nigerian federalism, with autonomous Islamic states under a national, secular constitution remains a potentially destabilizing force, while the two decades of civil war and the lack of an unambiguous status of Shari'a in North and south Sudan remains a source of potential instability. Democracy and the ballot box is a tool increasingly used by the Islamists providing a legitimacy the West finds difficult to contest. For the present any 'final' status of Shari'a in Nigeria and in the Sudan remains unclear and contested.

Concluding Remarks

Contrary to the parallels I have invoked with Iran and northern Nigeria, both Abdullahi Gallab (2008) and Abdelwahab Elaffendi argue that the Sudanese case is unique. Gallab sees in Sudan a first historical and unique international case, while Elaffendi[59] sees a special case where a historical movement – the Sudanese MB/NIF – seized power and held to it. Unlike the cases of electoral success by Islamist movements, Hamas in Palestine or Rifaa in Turkey, Sudan's history of Islamism has been entirely in the context of militarism,[60] sees a special case where a historical movement – the Sudanese MB/NIF – seized power and held to it. Unlike the cases of electoral success by Islamist movements, Hamas in Palestine or Rifaa in Turkey, Sudan's history of Islamism has been entirely in the context of militarism, more like Pakistan than either Iran or northern Nigeria.

Also, the resistance of the South to Islamization and the issue of the status of non-Muslims and self-determination also make Sudan a unique case. As a result Elaffendi observes that from the outset 'there was a lot of novel "experimentation".'

CHAPTER 8

SHARI'A AND THE FUTURE OF THE SUDANESE STATE

In much of social science literature the role of religion has been down-played as secondary to economics or politics in the analysis of chronic conflict. However, the Sudanese case reveals religion to be the fulcrum on which the levers of Islamization and resistance have turned for over a half century. There are majority-minority issues, of course, where the religion of the majority was imposed upon the beliefs of minority groups impacting basic economic and political outcomes. But for sheer consistency Sudan's core elites have deployed a politicized Islam, tied to Arab language and identity, against its non-Muslim minorities to seize and maintain power since independence. This politicized Islam was used to mobilize a bought-off, or coerced, Muslim base in the North, effectively neutralizing them from a sustained or effective resistance to decades of military and undemocratic rule. Democracy in Sudan does not mean eliminating Shari'a, but it does mean depoliticizing it.

Sudan, one of the world's most recognized 'deeply divided societies,'[61] makes it an important case for analysis of the role of religion as a major issue in the post-independence history of national conflict. It is often remarked that Sudanese are lovely, hospitable people who have become expert at killing one another. Among the root causes of war and conflict religious factors – if not primary, such as unequal wealth and power sharing – they are certainly close collaborators to these root causes. While any analysis focusing on a single cause of conflict must be avoided, religion – its beliefs, practitioners, leaders and its power to mobilize for both good and ill – cannot be ignored (Appleby 1999).

The centrality of religion in Sudan's North-south wars is reflected in part by the fact that the question of a national religious identity appears in each of Sudan's multiple constitutions. Yet, reference to a national religious identity is significantly missing from the CPA 2005 section 'Nature of the State' where neither Islam nor Christianity are mentioned, no doubt due to this incendiary history. Likewise, the divisive history of Shariʿa is glossed in the CPA, both as a tactic and diversion from the bloody history so embedded in religious mobilization. However, in the struggling post-peace Sudan the specific language of the CPA for the withdrawal of Shariʿa is: 'The judicial discretion of courts to impose penalties on non-Muslims shall observe the long-established legal [Shariʿa] principle that non-Muslims are not subject to prescribed penalties, and therefore remitted penalties shall apply' (CPA, 2005) is reinstated. Of course oil, northern ethnic chauvinism and monopoly of power, boundaries, issues and actors at the center and in the margins all are part of any comprehensive analysis, but religion deserves its place at this table where conflicts are generated, managed, and eventually reconciled.

The dominant northern political parties have been religiously based, while the major southern movements have been secular, largely in reaction to this fact. Both of the two major northern parties – the Umma and the Democratic Unionist Parties – descend through hereditary lines where the mantle of religious legitimacy meshes with political entitlement, the line of the nineteenth-century Mahdi to the present day Sadiq al-Mahdi and the Khatmiyya religious brotherhood led by the Mirghani family. Both power and allegiances are hereditary. Two important religious leaders have stood outside of this pattern – Mahmoud Mohamed Taha, leader of the Republican Brothers and Islamic reformer who was hung for apostasy in 1985, and al-Turabi who likely backed his execution order as Attorney General at the time. The strength of religion in the Muslim North is such that once powerful Sudanese Communist Party did not oppose Shariʿa as state law in 1983, nor did the northern dominated, secular National Democratic Alliance (NDA) call for its immediate withdrawal after the 1989 Islamist coup. They all did, however, oppose the 'incorrect' application of the Shariʿa after the September Laws of 1983, although to no avail. The NDA Charter called for Sudan to be ruled by constitutional law reflecting international human rights norms according to the Nairobi Declaration.

Historically the bedrock of Sudanese Islam has been a Sufi folk system, decentralized, tolerant, and for some a transcendental mysticism expressed through various religious brotherhoods (*turuq*), Qadiriyya, Khatmiyya, Tijaniyya, and others. This was altered by top-down Islamism, imposed and institutionalized under two military regimes (Generals Numeiri and al-Bashir, respectively), both under the influence of the Muslim Brothers, later evolved to the NIF created by al-Turabi and its successor the National Congress Party (NCP) of the al-Bashir regime. For a significant period (1992–96) the tactical alliance of Hasan al-Turabi and Osama bin Laden, then resident in Sudan, shaped not only Sudan's Islamism but had global ramifications. This politicized Islam required implementation of a strategic cultural agenda that would transform the historical Sufi popular social order into a new Islamic 'moral order' embodied in a 'Civilization Project' imposed top to bottom, penetrating every institution, and eventually displacing the old order through terror and fear.

Shari'a was the main instrument of Sudanese Islamism, as it was in Iran, Pakistan, Afghanistan and northern Nigeria. It is critical to emphasize the point again that criticism of the use (some argue the abuse) of Shari'a in a political Islamist agenda is not a fundamental criticism of the body of Shari'a writings and interpretations over 14 centuries of jurisprudence. Islamic law stands as one of the world's great juristic traditions on a par with any law associated with state and empire. However, its recent entry into the 'clash of civilizations' between the West and East after 9/11 and attacks in Europe and in the East have demonized the law using the extreme cases as proof of its 'backwardness' and inappropriateness to the 'modern era.' The early entry of Shari'a into Islamist activism in every case is both symbolic and real signaling that an Islamic alternative program is ascendant and that the goal of an Islamic state is now achievable. Sudan's Islamism is described as both an 'experiment' (Warburg and Layish, 2002), but more often as 'extremist' after the *Inqaz*'s brutal repression of all dissent in the North in 1989 and its intensified jihad against the South, believing military victory was within its reach.

After several decades of the *Inqaz* regime and more than a quarter-century since the September Laws, Sudan Islamism is experienced, mature, pliable, and durable. The political isolation of al-Turabi from the *Inqaz* in 2000 signaled a pragmatic turn that relaxed the Islamist program and paved the way for major compromise on the issue of Shari'a with the 'one state/two systems' agreement at Machakos in 2004. This led directly to the historic CPA.

Throughout the decades of Sudan's Islamism, it is clear that Shari'a has succeeded. Its laws are now codified and hold an unchallenged monopoly as a comprehensive law in the North; its history and principles now are a mandatory part of basic secondary and university education irrespective of the religion of the student; and its institutions and practice are now embedded in Sudanese society in a myriad unprecedented ways. Shari'a may be the one lasting legacy of Sudan's Islamism after the anticipated separation of the country. There is little question that Shari'a will remain, but what of Sudan's Islamist actors and programs as the two decades-old *Inqaz* faced mandated elections in 2010 and the referendum on southern separation? No matter what scenario – whether costly secession, return of civil war, or muddling through as the US Institute of Peace Report suggested[62] – the years leading up to 2011 and its aftermath are a turning point for Sudan. The question is at what stage is the Islamist program and how will it weather the changes that are on the horizon?

One question is whether Sudan entered a post-Islamist phase with the isolation of al-Turabi and the flow of oil in 2000, or with the mandates of the CPA in 2005. The post CPA period shows that Sudan has not decisively withdrawn from Islamism, despite the concessions the regime made in the CPA under intense international pressure. I originally posed this question between 2005 and 2007 as the optimism created by the CPA was high and the promise of full withdrawal of Shari'a from non-Muslims in the North meant a retreat of Islamism. But, as the CPA implementation has been slow and utterly lacking in good will, and as Shari'a continued to be used to harass both non-Muslim and vulnerable Muslims, the skeptics were proven correct.

And while the GoS engaged in foot dragging on the CPA the internal politics of the South became divisive along traditional ethnic lines, the potency of Islamism has stirred once again. The security and public order police have not lost their grip over the citizenry, nor has the regime reined them in. From time to time the symbols of Islamism are exercised for domestic and international consumption such as the teddy bear named 'Mohamed' incident. Such international dramas demonstrate that Sudan can still play the role of 'bad Muslim' (Mamdani, 2005). However, unlike Iran and northern Nigeria, Sudan's Islamist surge was met with resistance from a southern non-Muslim minority at every turn, and by anti-*Inqaz* Muslims in the North. That resistance continues to the present post-CPA period where unity has been rendered unattractive to the overwhelming majority of Southerners whose bitter grievances are nurtured in memories of a host of injustices, not least of which is the abuse of Shari'a against them. John Garang understood this, but he also knew that respect for Islam and the retention of Shari'a were key to northern sensibilities and that without compromise there would be no peace agreement.

Just as Shari'a was the main instrument in the erection of Islamism and in the waging of civil war, it was likewise the main vehicle for peace. The Machakos protocols of one state, two systems were built around withdrawal of Shari'a from the South and from non-Muslims in the North as a cornerstone of the CPA. But the peace that was fragile at the beginning is more vulnerable now with the final status of non-Muslims in the North still a major issue. And in the IDP camps the Shari'a of the *Inqaz* continues to play an oppressive role where the Nizam al-Am police are the tip of the lash, literally and figuratively, and are still mobilized with impunity against the vulnerable, the restive, the marginalized, and both Muslim and non-Muslim women.

Although strongly driven by ideology, Sudan's Islamism adopted a pragmatic approach to the Shari'a whose judicial rule evolved to accommodate the needs of a changed and changing society. For Islamic interest-free banking, the practical principle of 'necessity,' *darura*, for economic exchange with interest-bearing banks was applied to lubricate the international financial system in order to do business with Sudan's oil revenues. In family law, adoption and

fosterage, considered unlawful or irregular in traditional jurisprudence (*fiqh*), Sudan's religious scholars permitted the Shari'a to address
the increasing numbers of orphaned and abandoned children who are
the tragic face of the country's chronic wars, displacement of its citizens, and their impoverishment. Beyond these, the types of marriage
legitimated under the *Inqaz* (*'urfi* and *misyar*), although irregular or
forbidden in terms of strict Sunni Shari'a, was also adapted to the
needs of large number of immigrant women seeking attachment in
the city – so-called 'stranger marriage.' This is also a response to
the large male labor out-migration that has made traditional intra-
familial marriage more difficult to sustain. Government promotion
of marriage over sexual misconduct (*zina*) has aided the poor through
government support of public mass weddings (*zawaj jamiya*), while
the reduction in monetary amounts of marriage dowers have lessened
some economic demands on marriage. However in the end, it is the
lack of sufficient economic opportunity inside the country added to
the decades of political repression that has resulted in a huge male
out-migration that skews the economy toward dependence upon foreign remittances and has, thus, had a drag effect on marriage and
family life. Likewise, the increase in educated women in the cities during the decades of Islamism has created a dilemma of either
delaying or postponing marriage indefinitely, or marrying a man
who is less well-educated but is 'Gulf rich.'

This transformation has occurred in the context of a modernizing
capital city where gleaming buildings, suburbs, slum and IDP camp
dwellers coexist and class formation has intensified. Rising aspirations
of youth have mounted with expanding university education, while
large numbers of the marginalized are excluded from the prospect
of prosperity and advancement. With every day these contradictions
increase. Only years of government suppression and threatened or real
application of strict Shari'a criminal laws have kept the lid on this
cauldron of contradictions. The volatility of this mix in the capital
city was made apparent in the days after the death of John Garang in
2005, when the city was in lock-down for a week as northern citizens
faced a southern urban insurrection. Any government mishandling
of the 2010 elections or denial of the hard won right of the South to

self-determination could light the fires of uprising in the capital once again.

Apart from the story of its political use and abuse, on balance Shari'a is now more unified and better organized as a system of law, judges, and courts. It is decolonized, and established as a permanent part of Sudan's governance irrespective of the outcomes of the elections and referendum. It is also less compassionate than when I first studied it and recorded its laws and practice before Islamization. The secure future of Shari'a lies in its return to its core of compassion and community as part of the restoration of a more democratic society.

Abdullahi Ibrahim (2009) documented well the 'Manichean dilemma' of the Sudan Judiciary under colonialism and its tumultuous decolonization almost two decades after independence under Numeiri and al-Bashir. The prior inferior status of Shari'a law and its judges and courts lasted long after colonialism as a legacy, evident in lesser pay for judges and inferior court facilities, a fact I personally observed in my studies of Shari'a in 1979–80. Shari'a judges with their turbans and jellabiyas were ridiculed as 'women's judges' because of their restriction to Islamic family laws alone and their attachment to a presumed old and dying order. This state and legacy from colonialism no longer exists, the Shari'a establishment is fundamentally altered, unlikely to ever return to its former low status.

Shari'a law is now more unified as a comprehensive law that is easier for judges to apply as a uniform code. Codifying Shari'a law gave structure and uniformity to a system that lacked full legitimate status and predictable order. The Shari'a judges, no longer second class legal professionals, proudly wear turbans and jellabiyas or suits and ties or other forms of western-derived dress as a matter of personal preference, not status markers. The court facilities are modern and are housed in new buildings, or in renovated older structures. They are air conditioned and orderly without the presence of court police that were usual in my previous study. They are no longer places where women predominate as litigants, as family law is only one part of the unified law. Criminal, civil, labor courts share space with what were once only personal status courts. Justice is meted out in a timely and affordable way for the average Sudanese.

Historically the Islamist political instrumentation of Shari'a was not protested on a mass basis by Muslims either in 1983 or 1989 as both were instituted under military regimes that forbade public demonstrations under protracted periods of martial law. However, the democratic impulse of the Sudanese defied Numeiri's harsh application of the *hadd* penalties and was a part of the mass mobilization and *intifada* that overthrew Numeiri in the spring of 1985. Besides military suppression of political dissent, the lack of protest also is indicative of Shari'a's potent symbolism for Muslims. The few intellectuals who disagreed with Islamization of Shari'a were punished with charges of apostasy and execution in the case of Mahmud Mohamed Taha, or were forced into exile, such as democracy advocates Abdullahi An-Na'im, Mohamed Mahmoud, and Mahgoub al-Tigani Mahmoud.

An-Na'im and Francis Deng maintain that historic application of Shari'a in South Sudan was a violation of the principle of self-determination, and they extend this logic to the application of Shari'a in the North where millions of Southerners reside also as a denial of full citizenship rights if they are bound by Islamic law. They further argue that an Islamic state applying Shari'a categorically repudiates any possibility of self-determination for most Sudanese because it denies equal citizenship to non-Muslims and women as well as to those Muslims who do not believe in the desirability of an Islamic state (1996: 199–223).

It is notable that protest against the laws has come from individual cases involving women where *hadd* criminal law penalties of stoning or lashing for alleged violations of Shari'a garnered international attention. These are the acts of everyday rebellion that are closely observed, celebrated in private and on the internet, and may prove even more transformative as processes already underway proceed. It is more likely that any future mass protest for reform or amelioration of the application of Shari'a will be a part of larger movements, involving the critical participation of women, for restoration of democracy where a just and non-discriminatory rule of law is demanded.

Islamization, while enhancing the status of Shari'a, also disfigured it through its abuse as a political tool under Numeiri and al-Bashir. The *hadd* penalties that had not been applied since the nineteenth century

Mahdiya were wrongly enforced on the poor, the vulnerable, and on non-Muslims. This became the harsh new face of Shari'a, essentializing it from Iran to Sudan to Afghanistan and northern Nigeria. Successful cases of a non-controversial applied Shari'a in limited democracies, such as Lebanon or Israel, or in the monarchies of Morocco and Jordon, or in military regimes of Tunisia, Egypt, or Turkey, are overlooked in favor of 'bad Muslim' stories like those generated for the Sudan case. Unfortunately, the best known cases in the West about Shari'a are, in practice, the worst examples. The truth is that all examples, including Sudan's experience with Islamism, are more complex than journalists or propagandists suppose or convey.

Balancing the damage done to Shari'a from decades of a politicized Islam with its benefits will be the task of future generations of citizens, lawyers, judges, and law interpreters (the *'ulama*) in future Sudan. The compassionate Shari'a that I learned and studied before 1983 would return – its history well-documented in the Judicial Circulars, in the cases part of public record, and in my own research and that of others. Stripped of the foreign Iranian and Wahhabist-like harsh application, it would return to its Sufi roots of toleration and compassion. Shari'a is a Sudanese law whose application will be for Muslims who are a majority in Sudan, but in a diverse, more democratic future it will not retain its monopoly on the law but will incorporate the diverse legal traditions of the citizenry. Even after the separation of the South millions of non-Muslims will remain in the North and a national law appropriate to their needs is required.

Post-Islamism? Is Sudan Transitioning to a post-Islamist State?[63]

Islamism, understood as 'political Islam' or a 'politicized Islam,' emerged as the major western diagnostic reference for 'extremism' in Muslim nations after terms such as Islamic 'revival,' 'resurgence,' or 'militant' were generally abandoned. Olivier Roy (1992) argued that Islamism – 'defined as the populist and often revolutionary ideology with the goal of the establishment of an Islamic state and govern-ance according to Islamic principles' – peaked in the late 1970s with the Iranian Revolution, and thereafter declined. Post-Islamist theory emerged in the early 1990s as the differing outcomes of various Islamist experiments were examined in Europe. Sudan was not one of the cases reviewed, perhaps due to its historic liminal status. Gallab dates the 'first Islamic Republic' from the 1983 mandate noting it is the only African state to apply Shari'a comprehensively as a national law.

Post-Islamism has been analyzed as (Lauzière 2005: 241):

1) Post-Islamists who evolve more modest agendas;
2) Post-Islamists who create a secular space by re-routing religious activism away from the state, such as the revival of Sufi orders; and
3) Post-Islamists who employ reformist theology.

If the case is to be made for post-Islamism in Sudan, it would be a relatively weak one based upon a more modest agenda mandated by the CPA. As the CPA goes, so would a course of post-Islamism. The disengagement of Islamism has not been clear or decisive as implementation of the CPA has slow and lacking in political will. Withdrawal of Shari'a from non-Muslims in the North has been partial, and the CPA-mandated Commission on their status in the capital city was delayed for two years.

Al-Turabi's reformist ideology came after he was isolated from the ruling center. Nonetheless, Gallab argues that the MB movement – later the NIF and NCP, in other words Sudan's Islamist movement – has undergone remarkable evolution. Gallab argues that al-Turabi, who led the movement for 40 years, signaled a shift from idealistic MB Islamism to rank opportunism after his downfall in 1999. Rank opportunism is not mentioned by Lauzière as criteria for post-Islamism.

Gallab continues that the fall of the Islamist regime was marked by the split in the movement after al-Turabi's fall in 1999. Some scholars I interviewed in Sudan refer to the present era as 'post-extremist.' Sudanese and Sudanist scholars in the West may be reluctant to accept the post-CPA period as 'post-Islamist' as so much anti-regime rhetoric is invested in the abuses associated with its pursuit of an Islamist agenda. Moreover, international press coverage of incidents such as the Teddy bear named Muhammad and Lubna Hussein, the 'pants

protester,' with the arrest and detention of a British teacher, as well as
al-Bashir's references to the 'Crusaders and Zionists' behind the troubles in Darfur, leave western observers and Sudanese in the Diaspora
cool to the idea of 'post-Islamism.' The few active western researchers
and the Sudanese who have returned, in some cases after decades of
exile, are seeing a different and transformed reality on the ground.
Beyond the present work, this new reality needs further documentation and analysis.

Gallab concludes that the Sudanese Islamist model is actively being
contested, an observation with which I agree based on my own research
between 2005–09. However, in my view, this space has been opened
more by the historic CPA than by the internal politics of the 'fall' of
Islamism. As with the collapse of other colonialist and authoritarian
regimes in Africa – such as the end of Portuguese rule and apartheid
in South Africa – the potential for liberation among the communities
of the oppressor state is a fortunate by-product of the successful struggles by the oppressed. The democratic space opened by the CPA in the
demographically transformed North is just one important factor in
the evolving Sudanese polity as are the squabbles and rivalries of the
core elites.

Islamism has been critiqued by both Muslim and non-Muslim
scholars for its apparent focus on the faith of Islam as the source of
the alleged extremism and resulting abuses in Islamist states. These
critics observe that a comparable use of 'Christianism' for extremist
advocates of Christian values or rule in a state has not been applied,
thus Islam has been singled out as having a particular penchant for
religious extremism.

One important indicator of post-Islamism is the shift away from
state-imposed Islamist rule by militarist or autocratic regimes.
Although Sudan is a military state, the CPA changed the fundamental
governance model for a time with shared rule by the GoS and SPLM
and its mandated withdrawal of Shari'a.

However, the disengagement of Islamism has not been clear or decisive with the plodding implementation of the CPA. US Special Envoy
General Scott Gration and other diplomats now openly acknowledge that years of focus on the Darfur conflict diverted international

attention from the centrality of the CPA and critical time was lost. Efforts by the US Envoy to speed up the process in the lead up to elections and the referendum were delayed and insufficient. For the case to be made that Sudan is transitioning to post-Islamism in Sudan, evolution of the Islamist movement should be evident. Gallab (2008) argues that Sudan's Islamist movement has undergone remarkable evolution from the MB movement to the NIF and NCP. The jettisoning of al-Turabi, who led the movement for 40 years until his downfall in 1999, signaled a shift from ideological Islamism to a pragmatic opportunism whose sole focus is to remain in power.

But Islamism has been embedded for too long in too many institutions to be affected by the departure of a single individual. Opportunistically, Sudan began to move away from Shari'a after 9/11 and the association of the regime with Osama bin Laden and al-Qaeda that had been nurtured in Sudan in the early 1990s was subjected to closer scrutiny. Sudan's cooperation with American intelligence was crucial to a new, pragmatic relationship with the US. Add to this the commercial flow of oil that dismantled key elements of the Islamist project, such as acceptance of dealing with western interest-based banks.

Assessing post-Islamism is a vital part of the analysis of the future of Sudan – as a less or more peaceful unified state with a more restrained Shari'a, or as or as belligerent, conflict-ridden, and divided into two nations.

Al-Turabi's Last Stand?

The question today is how far from the levers of power and for how long has been al-Turabi's fall from power? His ability to reinvent himself is legend, and his role as an instigator and backer of JEM and of internally divisive Darfur national politics is clear. A further question is whether this is a new stage in Sudan's Islamism, shifting the political base from the center to the West, or simply a new game in the old rivalry among the unchanging national elite power base?

Psychological profiles of al-Turabi trace his Islamism to his father, an allegedly humiliated clerk in the colonial judiciary where Shari'a was not respected. Al-Turabi may be said to personally vindicate his father in this analysis. Gallab sees his involvement in fomenting the Darfur crisis as resulting from his political isolation in 2000. The influential *Black Book* detailing the history of rule by central Sudan core elites, excluding Muslims from Darfur, laid the political base for the Darfur movements for autonomy or a greater role in the central government. Released as a secret document, al-Turabi is widely believed to be behind this provocative book. Although his disciples are still in power and still fear his charisma and intellect, his isolation from the Islamist agenda was rendered complete when the Islamic Jurisprudence Council declared him an apostate after remarks made in public and in print in 2006 about women and men praying together and women being able to be Imams and to marry Christian men. The Council admonished that 'al-Turabi should declare his repentance or face the Shari'a *hadd* for heresy.'

With the CPA mandates of the withdrawal of Shari'a from the South and from non-Muslims in the North, the CPA appeared to be a clear break with *the* symbol of Islamism, the Shari'a. Once on the ground in 2007 with grant in hand, I began to ask the question of colleagues, 'has Sudan entered a post-Islamist period?' There is an Arabic equivalent of Islamism carrying the same meaning, so I was confident in using the term *al-Islamiya* for the question. Sociologist Hatim Babiker Hillawi, an old friend and collaborator on the translation of the Judicial Circulars in 1979–80, immediately responded – 'post-extremist, but not post-Islamist.' Extremism, he argued in agreement with other colleagues, ended with the ousting of al-Turabi from the al-Bashir inner circle. Some argue that extremism never sat well with Sudanese Muslims and even Numeiri was said to have declared there would be 'no Khomeninism in Sudan.'

Haydar Ibrahim, Director of the Sudan Studies Center, whose book in Arabic *Suqut al-Mashru' al-Hadari* (2003, *Collapse of the Civilization Project*) was one by several indigenous scholars that analyzes the decline of Sudan's Islamism. We discussed post-Islamism. He responded, 'not post-Islamism, disintegration, of the Islamist movement. The defenders of the *al-Mashru' al-Hadari*, such as Abdelwahab El-Affendi, are confused if you read their columns in the newspapers. How can they be critical of their obvious failures without condemning "the project" or their mentors?' (7 February 2007).

Shortly after meeting Dr. Ibrahim, I interviewed El-Affendi in London in 2007, now a professor of Islamic studies at Westminster University, on the status and standing of Shari'a among Sudanese and world Muslims after the Sudanese experience is weighed and evaluated. He opined that 'Shari'a needs a little rethinking – the spirit of Shari'a is the issue, and not the letter of the law. It is better to think about the Shari'a in light of the Sudanese experience through vision of justice and equity, but instead there was victimization of the poor in the name of Shari'a' (25 February 2007).

Haydar Ibrahim argued that 'al-Turabi was never really isolated; he is still the symbol of the movement and he is still influential.' His political isolation in 1999 was only theatrical; he is his usual clever self never leaving an obvious trace of his work, but just by looking at the composition of JEM, it has al-Turabi written all over it. He continued, 'the real pressure to get al-Turabi out of the inner circle was from the Egyptians, and the American government was keen to have access to Sudanese intelligence after 9/11, so there was a convergence of interests. The key to this all was Salah Ghosh, Head of Security and alleged former torturer in the infamous ghost houses of the early 1990s. He has been flown in to Washington, DC several times for high level and highly secretive consultations.'

Another staunch critic of the Islamist project is Mohamed Mahmoud who referred to the current period as 'post-al-Turabism,' in apparent variance with Ibrahim, but arguing that al-Turabi and 'al-Turabism' can be seen as two different things. The al-Turabi of today appears not to agree with 'al-Turabism.' The apparent withdrawal from Islamism is only symbolic and the essentials of the Islamist program are still in effect (interview in Birmingham 26 February 2007).

Lawyer and feminist Sonia Abdel Malik noted that the 1972 Permanent Constitution was the first to name Shari'a as the main source of legislation. She was critical of the composition of the draft constitution commission since there was no female representation and women's rights were not a consideration. The debate over Shari'a as *the* main source of legislation, or *a* source will remain for some time, she argued. Several Sudanists argue that Islamism in Sudan today at an impasse (de Waal blog, Gallab, 2008). I would add that the movement is internally divided with unclear direction ahead as the country faces its greatest crises determining its future. The turning point for Sudan is also the turning point for its long experience with Islamism.

Ultimately, whether the 'collapse' or 'failure' of the Islamist agenda is post-al-Turabism or post-Islamism, Sudan Sudan has undergone a period of transition in 2011, and as external pressure mounts, internal social transformation may lead the way toward reshaping what was once Africa's largest nation.

The CPA, Shari'a, and Future of the Sudanese state

The national status of Shari'a so profoundly affected by the CPA none-theless has proven its resilience. Its ultimate effect on non-Muslims living in the majority Muslim North is inconclusive. The only certainty is that intensified or unreconstructed Islamism will be met with resistance, as it has since 1983 and the Abboud era. Before Islamization of the Shari'a customary law and a variety of religiously based personal status laws, such as for the once strong Greek Orthodox community, were formally recognized in national law. While the language of the CPA and the new permanent constitution speaks to a 'multiracial, multicultural, and multi-confessional' state – from which a multi-legal model could logically be derived – the core problem remains religious chauvinism linked to claims of a majority Muslim population being served by *their* religious law.

Shari'a may remain the sole law in force in the North, but the unity of the state has been sacrificed. We have seen how important a politicized Islamic law was as a grievance initiating and sustaining the civil war, and was the ostensible cause for years of delay in the peace negotiations. The central role of Shari'a in the lead up to CPA is clear. Its withdrawal from the South has been accomplished and a remarkable lack of rancor displayed by the southern government has permitted mosques to continue to operate and Shari'a to be an option for southern Muslims who choose to have their affairs resolved in an Islamic court. However, its status in regard to non-Muslims in the North remains problematical and is a key factor making unity unattractive to Southerners in general. It has not been an incentive for Southerners to remain in the North. The harassment that Southerners experience is an accepted part of life in their trade-off for the economic opportunities of the North contrasted with the underdevelopment of the south.

However, many Southerners commented to me that Shari'a was never the real problem, only its incorrect imposition on southern non-Muslims and its direct role in their poor treatment by a succession of national governments. For peace building and civil society, Shari'a must never be imposed upon non-Muslims again. If alcohol consumption by Southerners creates disturbances of the social order by public drunkenness, the problem is the alcohol abuse and its control, not the religion of the drinker. Likewise, the growing multiculturalism of Sudan's cities demands a respect for diversity of dress, public association, and affiliation without threatening the state or its laws.

Eventually the Public Order laws, erected using the instrument of Shari'a, will be fully relaxed as a necessary response to an evolved cosmopolitan city of 8–10 million, that will likely resemble Cairo more than Riyadh. Piety has never been lacking in Sudanese Islam, but imposed religion and a social order in its name have spoiled the genuineness of old Sufi Muslim traditions. After decades of Islamism, there is the question as to whether a man is bearded out of piety or opportunism to keep his government job; or if the lady whose head is covered so as not to show a wisp of hair, is doing so out of genuine religiosity, or because she will be criticized as immoral if she reveals her hair. And what of the youth – a quarter of more of the population who have grown up only with Islamist versions of education, morality, and ways of speaking. For example, the old greetings '*Izzay al-hal?*' ('How are you, how're things going?') have all but disappeared replaced by '*Salam wa Rahma*,' a shortened version of the universal Muslim greeting '*Salam 'alaykum wa Rahmat Allah*' ('Peace be on you and God's mercy'). Political rallies and university lectures may be punctuated with approving cries of '*Allahu Akbar!*' – including in my own experience as I described in Arabic to an anthropology class at the University of Khartoum that I frequently take my non-Muslim students to visit local mosques so that they learn about Islam and American Muslims experientially.

Public lectures in secular universities are opened with Muslim prayer, as would not have been the case in the past, while rarely is a Christian or other prayer included. Domestic airlines, even those traveling to the South, play lengthy recordings of Qur'anic chanting before take-off. TV programs are universally in Arabic with a heavy emphasis on Muslim religious programming. Modesty is a deep seated cultural characteristic of male-female interactions all over the country, and especially among Muslims, so imposing 'modest' dress and behavior – described as 'Shari'i,' i.e. derived from Shari'a law – was never a necessity. Used as a tool for its political program and taken to multiple extremes, today many men who would have greeted me and shaken my hand in the past, or slapped it as a friendly, familiar gesture, will not do so. Those who do shake my hand do so briefly and may avoid all eye contact as a clear sign of Islamic 'modesty.' Nonetheless, the old core values of hospitality, generosity, honest and direct communication, and a wry sense of humor remain in place.

Despite the decades of Islamism, the Sudanese are still the Sudanese. Youth, of course, have access to the outside world as never before and they are consuming global culture, though they may not be entirely digesting it as they lack the experience of other cultures and ways of life. Few Sudanese have visited parts of their own country to which they do not have a direct ancestral connection, and fewer still have traveled abroad, except for the male labor migrants to the Gulf and the more educated elites who travel to the US and Europe. None of the Khartoumites I met had ever seen or visited the IDP camps that ring their city. Nonetheless, the taxi driver who took us to the camps for research was fascinated. Ethnically, racially, and in terms of class, Khartoum is an apartheid-like world – not significantly different from the suburbanite who has never visited the south of Chicago or North Philadelphia. It may be that democracy and the liberation of the northern Sudanese society will be delivered by the long history of southern resistance ending in separation or a federalized unity. Separation forces all of the North-south contradictions finally to be confronted, as did the African wars of liberation liberate the Portuguese from fascism in 1974.

A small, but significant (estimated population of 23,500 in 1976) of southern Muslims (Wani, 2006) has likely swelled to double or triple that size under the influence of forced or opportunistic conversions during the decades of imposed Islamization and Arabization in government schools, IDP camps, and locations of war resettlement of Southerners in the North. The estimated (and decimated) post-war population of the South is 2.7 million. In a democratic, secular Sudan, Shariʿa would be a law of choice for Muslims and for non-Muslims who prefer it as an option for a desired legal outcome, for example a Christian women seeking equitable lodging or maintenance from a Muslim husband required by Islamic law in a polygamous marriage. It would share a pluralistic legal stage with the myriad different customary laws of the nation, and reflect an historical legacy that is Anglo-Islamic, as well as indigenous.

Elections in 2010 and the 2011 Referendum on the South

How did the 2010 elections and 2011 referendum on separation of the South reflect the history of the issue of Shariʿa? Or how will Shariʿa be raised as a part of future politics? First, the fact that the elections took place was a success in spite of some international complaints of irregularities. Al-Bashir received 67 per cent of the votes for president instead of the 99 per cent tallies from the Numeiri era. Elections outside of the capital were pronounced a success in general and those in the South were viewed as a prologue to the major event of the referendum in 2011.

For decades Shariʿa was referenced by Southerners in a litany of grievances against a succession of northern governments, and Shariʿa remains a live issue for those living in the North where little has been done to 'make unity attractive.' Active harassment using Shariʿa as a bludgeon continues for alcohol-related offenses in the IDP camps. Meeting CPA terms and mandates by the GoS and GoSS has differed on the issues related to Shariʿa. It took two years before the CPA mandated Commission on the Status of Non-Muslims in the Capital City was formulated, and its majority were Muslim. The first special courts for non-Muslims were not reportedly established until 2008. By contrast, in the South removal of official presence of Shariʿa courts in the major town was swift and Shariʿa only has standing for personal affairs between Muslims. Islamic banks in the South were either closed after the CPA or phased-out due to lack of customers.

Candidates for the 2010 elections did not develop any new platform regarding Shari'a, but in potential future elections liberals from the northern opposition Umma, DUP and Communist parties will likely advocate relaxation of the Nizam al-Am laws that have already been challenged, while the conservatives will likely argue that any weakening of the Shari'a rule of law would undermine the entire Islamist project. While a real, new political base for Islamism has been built over the past several decades, mass sentiment – were free and fair elections held – would favor a more liberal approach, primarily because of the generalized unpopularity of the *Inqaz* and its close association with harsh application of Shari'a. The remaining hard core supporters are those of the new middle class ethnic northerners – Ja'alin, Mahas, and Shayqiya – who have personally benefited most from the years of the *Inqaz*. Their homes are no longer the mud houses of the past, but are concrete, large, and well-appointed. For them, the *Inqaz* has meant opportunity for class advancement. Overall, Shari'a is still more of an issue for Southerners than for Muslims in the North who still fear an open confrontation that might question the religious legitimacy that the law represents.

The historic referendum vote overwhelmingly (98 per cent) favored separation with a voter turnout of 97.5 per cent with a new independent Republic of South Sudan joining the world of nations in July 2011. While the outcome may seem straightforward, disentangling Shari'a South Sudan is not an easy matter. The idea of one country and two systems hammered out in Machakos is untenable for the long term. The matter of Shari'a cannot be determined by simple geography – North and South – there are far too many Christians in the North and a surprising number of Muslims in the south for this to be the case. Likewise, the resident immigrant population of Christian Ethiopians whose religious status has not been challenged or directly threatened by Islamism represents a potential alliance with the resident Christian southern populations once the Islamist program has lost its teeth in the wake of the 2011 referendum that will demonstrate overwhelming southern support for separation. It is likely this new state will receive international support in the region and in the West. Such an outcome would strengthen the hard liners in Khartoum who would accentuate the differences between Muslim and non-Muslim Sudanese, and again Shari'a would be used to underscore the differences.

Muslim-Christian Relations in a Divided Sudan

The subject of Muslim-Christian relations, also a theme of this book, has received much attention in the US, fueled for years by the Christian Evangelical movement so closely tied to the years of the Bush administrations. As described in chapter two, the South has a half-century of resisting Islamization which it correctly identified in the 1963 Petition to the United Nations signed by many of the South's leading political figures across regional and ethnic divides. It is a notable feature of the decades of conflict in Sudan that no religiously-based mass peace movement has emerged either from the Muslim or Christian constituencies, although there have been a number of noble small collective or individual efforts. The movements by western-based Christians have been far more influential. Now with the fate of the country hanging in the balance, a measure of what developments might shape the future of Muslim-Christian relations in a divided or unified Sudan.

Of the myriad issues this subject raises, there are a number relating to the law and society require mention. Islamist government and Islamization as the main objectives of the *Inqaz* meant that Muslim proselytizers were free to spread Islam in government controlled areas of the South and the Nuba Mountains. A report by the Christian group World Vision states clearly the effects of historic Islamization from Ottoman times upon southern customary law as well as the fears of its potential for continuation to be troublesome in the post-conflict period.

Of all the factors affecting southern Sudanese customary law, Shari'a law has traditionally been the greatest threat to its continued existence. Islamisation that began in the Ottoman Empire was only temporarily halted during British colonialism. Shari'a law does not easily accommodate other forms of law. The potential for conflict is twofold: a resumption of Islamisation through the government and courts of the northern regions; secondly, conflict between the authorities of southern Sudan and the not insignificant Muslim communities indigenous to the southern regions. At this state in the post-conflict era it would be ill-advised to develop arguments regarding the future accommodation between Islam and the customs, practices, and beliefs of the southern peoples. It is sufficient to recognize the potential for conflict between them and the need to find an enduring and mutually acceptable solution.

(Aleu Akechak Jok, Robert A Leitch, and
Carrie Vanderbilt, 2004: 30–31).

The present codification of southern Customary Law as a unified system is an ambitious project that should strengthen the status of traditional law in the South making it more of a bulwark against the more powerful systems of law that have challenged it.

In the northern towns preferential hiring of Muslims was reported throughout *Inqaz* rule. Christian missionaries are still active in the South, and are also visibly working the North where they are part of an international evangelical drive across the Sahel from Kano to Khartoum. Interestingly, the GoS has not halted their activities, even in the early days of the regime, in including a Billy Graham style rally that was held in Omdurman Stadium in 1991, led by the German evangelical preacher Reinhard Bonnke. It is assumed that government-backed Islamic proselytizing in the South will cease, although there are still remnants of the years of Islamization evident in the Khartoum-Juba axis, such as government air line routes between the two capital cities. On the other hand, southern leaders need to exercise caution against the ambitious agendas of overzealous foreign missions keen to expand their historical bases in the south.

The law that permits non-Muslims to convert to Islam while conversion to another faith by a Muslim is punishable by death is still on the books in the national law, although there are no reports of prosecution and capital punishment for this offense. Some non-Muslims converted to Islam to obtain or keep a job, for promotions and job advancement, or for other social services or benefits, there has been no evidence of forced conversions in recent years (2007 US State Department Human Rights Report). So, this aggressive face of the Islamist program has also ceased, but the question of the status of the South's Muslim population is still yet to be determined. There is mixed evidence of both discrimination and non-discrimination. It is likely that southern Muslims who practice their faith discretely will not suffer harm and that an unwritten policy of absolute non-proselytizing be observed. As to the genuine depth of their commitment to Islam, there is no reason to doubt it, although in the 'New South' a fluidity between Christianity, indigenous beliefs, and Islam is likely to become the new normal.

In the North, all Christians, including Southerners, are still required to seek legal permits to build new churches, while mosque building requires no such government review. Christian cemeteries are also curtailed, the government arguing that space is limited in the capital. Friday is recognized as the official day of worship, while Sunday as a working day forces Christians to worship on Fridays, or to take time off from work, if possible. Christian holidays often become political displays of strength with public parades on Christmas days in Khartoum, for example. In the short term it is unlikely that this present pattern of discrimination will cease altogether, but it should continue to ameliorate in the urban areas as part of the CPA legacy, while the overt discriminatory practices in the IDP camps will likely continue unless they are addressed by the international community. The indigenous Sudanese possess little knowledge, thus little concern, about the plight of their fellow citizens in these camps. Their status in the 2010–11 elections/referendum is compromised with the GoS arguing that displaced persons need to vote from their home districts, thus the fundamental citizenship status of the camp residents is second class, rather than one of full citizenship. One interviewee argued that he would rather be a first class citizen in the poorer South than a second class citizen in the North.

Reaction to decades of indoctrination of non-Muslims in the Islamic faith are complex and varied in the South. Beyond active proselytizing in schools, incentives were used to induce conversions in any government institution, even in prisons and juvenile detention facilities where early release was offered in exchange for conversion. In government controlled IDP camps children categorized as 'abandoned' or 'vagrant minors' were required to study the Qur'an, and were pressured to convert to Islam. Given this history, the 'call to prayer' can be seen as indoctrination. While most ultimately see neither Islam nor Muslims, per se, as the source of their problematic relations with 'Khartoum,' nonetheless bitter tastes of the past still remain. Thus, it is not surprising that after the CPA the government of Upper Nile State banned the use of public loudspeakers at mosques in the towns of Malakal and Nasir, claiming that the call to prayer disturbed the public.

As a general rule in the South, Christians, Muslims, and followers of traditional indigenous beliefs worship freely. Many of the region's Muslim residents have departed voluntarily over the years. And, although the GoSS officially declares secular government, Christians dominate the bureaucracies, perhaps a correlation with the more educated sectors of the southern workforce. Local government authorities often had a very close relationship with local Christian religious authorities. Greater consciousness of this phenomenon will foster continuation of the secular nature of the GoSS.

In the impatient countdown to independence by Southerners, any concerted act on the part of the Islamist government perceived to be against Christians, or their places of worship, could spark violent resistance. And it cannot be ruled out that an increased militancy of Southerners in the North could involve attacks on mosques, as has occurred in Nigeria. Only belief in miracles sustains the hope that the two Sudans will collaborate effectively after 2011. Until political transformation in the North, the two states will evolve to separate and unequal states, religiously identified as Muslim and Christian.

Race and Language in Future Sudan

An underrepresented factor in Sudan's conflicts is the role of race. Sudan's manifold complexities of race, ethnicity, region, as well as religion (that has often mistakenly been conflated with race) demand critical analysis. The ways in which 'race' has been deployed encouraging violence are better documented than are the unifying aspects of shared genetics and culture of Sudan's antiquity in the Nile Valley and environs (Keita, 2008). The racial hierarchy constructed by the English from the first days of colonialism, including the designation of a generic 'Arab' North and 'Black' South, has barely begun to be reconstructed (Fluehr-Lobban, 2004).

However, 'race talk' and the existence of racism (*al-ʿabudiya*) pervades political discourse as never before. As elsewhere race is a separate construct from ethnicity and religion, although they are often confused in Sudan's conflicts – 'Arab against Black African' in Darfur and 'Arab Muslim against Christian African' in the South. Light skin preference is openly addressed in the aesthetics of marriage and skin lighteners have found their way into popular markets. Dark-skinned Sudanis may object to their description as 'black,' and the ebony toned Southerners are the only ones to extol the beauty of a blue-black, 'eggplant' color of the skin. As in America, black has been associated with slavery and this status in one's background continues to be a bar to marriage and social advancement in the North. The politics of race can no longer be submerged in the 'we are all Sudanese' rhetoric of the past, and a genuine confrontation of race as a powerful marker and determiner of social status is long overdue. In a transformed, post-conflict culture some version of 'truth and reconciliation' would be appropriate, especially as a foundation for needed trust building between and among Sudan's diverse racial and ethnic groups, broadly cast as among the formerly enslaved and the darker skin-toned marginalized peoples.

The interpenetration of race, religion, and ethnicity as identity markers in Sudan, and elsewhere, begs for more sophisticated analysis as to how each of these, separately or in interplay, can trigger, ameliorate, reduce or prevent violent conflict. It is tempting to assert that religion consistently trumps the others in Sudan, but in truth, after the CPA it is interethnic violence in the South that has risen as the region prepares for its independence and various ethnic groups jockey for position in the new government. Nonetheless, while overt religious conflict has been reduced, nearly all of the forces that produced it and sustained it over the decades are still basically in place.

As for the future of the languages, Arabic and English, that were so closely associated with Islamization and Christianization, their future is tied to the resumption of conflict or normalization of relations between the regions and the religions. In the North for years the government forbade use of the English language in public instruction in conjunction with its policies of Arabization and Islamization. While this policy has relaxed considerably, it has left a generation of Sudanese youth lacking practical facility in English, even after some years of study. This was dramatized for me when young journalists working for English language newspapers preferred to interview me in Arabic to ensure mutual comprehension. Many Southerners raised in the North are most fluent in Arabic from schooling and daily life. They may only know their indigenous language for minimal conversational use and prefer the colloquial Arabic with which they are more familiar. However, English as the global language of communication is valued by all and is no longer is stigmatized through extremist Islamist propaganda. English will enjoy a revival in the 'new Sudan' while Arabic is already evolving to a neutral position with some practical utility for dealing with 'Arabs,' but of secondary value. In the unlikely event that another round of Islamism stresses Arab identity and Arabic language, the divide between North and South will widen and unity of the nation may be a dead issue.

Within the Muslim community the *Inqaz* has a history of monitoring Islamic groups not close to its own politics, however only one Islamic group, *Takfir wa Hijra*, is officially restricted. Extremist Islamist groups to the right of *Inqaz* (those, for example, such as Ansar al-Sunna, who opposed the CPA) focus most of their activities on the regime and have not targeted Christians or other non-Muslims. Periodic clamp downs take place on such groups, such as the radical Muslim group who attacked a mosque during Ramadan in Khartoum in 2002 killing many worshipers and those who murdered the US/AID worker John Granville and his driver in the early morning hours of New Year's Day in 2008. In the former case, all but those directly involved in the bombing were released after 'lengthy dialogue with Islamic scholars' (US State Department International Religious Freedom Report 2004, Sudan). In the latter case the family of the driver victim exercised their Shari'a right to be a part of the sentence and asked for a compassionate sentence of imprisonment instead of the death penalty. Insurgent groups from Darfur, such as the anti-regime but Islamist Justice and Equality Movement, attacked the outskirts of Omdurman in May 2008 bringing that 'other war' home and underscoring the fundamental nature of the struggles of the marginalized over any inherent Muslim-Christian divisions.

It is a telling point that IDP residents interviewed by Salma Abdalmunim[64] in the years after the CPA wanted to declare that in the camps religion is never an issue among people and that the government made it a source of social tension. Even Sudan's most vulnerable and least fortunate understand the abuse of religion and religious affiliation by politicians. It is a complex equation to sort out the measure of the use and abuse of religion as cause and effect in Sudan's chronic conflicts. Among the ordinary people, religion is not a source of daily tension. Its power lies in its symbolism, like the Shari'a itself, a church or mosque, a seat in Parliament or a Ministerial appointment, the public impression of exclusion or inclusion along religious lines is what makes the difference between peace and tranquility, or conflict and war.

Persistent importance of Gender in the Islamist and anti-Islamist camps

The 'emancipation' of Muslim women has often been cited as a rationale for US and western military interventions, whether in Afghanistan or Iraq. The low status of Muslim women is a presumption, not a question. Facts contradicting this presumption are ignored or re-interpreted. For example, the woman's considerable dower (*mahr*) at the time of marriage is often believed to be owned or controlled by a man, the wife's husband, father, or brother when it is in fact legally the bride's. However, unprecedented even for Sudan that has had women judges since the 1960s, more women Shari'a judges are sitting publicly in court *after* Islamization. This is another of the unexpected outcomes of the Islamist project. Some of these lady judges have differed publicly with the Islamic Jurisprudence Council that issues *fatwas*, indicating that they are empowered by their public role as custodians as well as appliers of the law. The presence of women judges – at about 10 per cent of the Judiciary, comparable to the US percentage – is worthy of further comment. The Islamist agenda under al-Turabi's tutelage was not hostile to women as a class, indeed it saw itself as both liberal and modern, and these attitudes are reflected in his recent advocacy of reforms for women in religion and marriage. The majority of Islamic states do not permit women to be judges, and some, such as Egypt, have only recently authorized women judges. Sudan's first women judges date from 1964, after the first democratic revolution. Although the numbers never reached parity, and there are many qualified women lawyers who might be elevated, Sudan never retreated from its acceptance of women as judges whether under secular, or military-Islamist governments. During the *Inqaz*, female judges advanced to the High Court and the Constitutional Court, as well as to the influential Majma' al-Fiqh al-Islami. Qualified women, who also did not disagree with the Islamist agenda, advanced. Now, some of these younger women judges are challenging the rulings of the male religious scholars.

The status of women is a sensitive barometer in any changing polity, but it is predictive in Islamist states. The resistance of women to Islamism has been generally overlooked in favor of viewing them primarily as victims of men, Islam, and Islamic states. The case for feminine resistance can be made in parallel ways for Iran and Sudan, but not as much for Nigeria. A key difference is the extension of education to women in Islamizing societies and Islamist states. In the case of Iran and Sudan women predominate in the universities and in some professions. However, in Nigeria a conservative culture and theology have meshed well in the North as female confinement and low levels of literacy and higher education have constrained their movement and activism. Nonetheless important cases of specific resistance to harsh application of Shari'a on women in northern Nigeria have attracted world attention. And reform movements in 2009, in both Iran and Sudan, have had courageous women as symbols of resistance – Neda Ali whose death was recorded on a cell phone as she participating in anti-regime demonstration after the alleged corrupted elections became the symbol of the reform movement, while Lubna Hussain

Ahmed defied her arrest and challenged the Public Order law mandating the *hadd* penalty of lashing for 'indecent dress,' because she and other were wearing trousers.

Intended and unintended consequences of Islamism

As Islamist regimes promote and enforce their programs, the old adage to 'be careful what you ask' may be invoked as multiple unintended outcomes of Islamism have been witnessed. The 'Marriage over *zina*' clarion call of the *Inqaz* with its official promotion of marriage has weakened the traditional role of the family through state-run 'group' marriages (*zawaj jam'iya*) even as it has strengthened the hand of the male marriage guardian to approve of the marriage of a ten year old girl, reducing the official age of marriage from 18 to 10 years of age. In an unprecedented response to chronic wars and conflict, polygamy was officially promoted, especially in regard to the high toll of casualties resulting from the civil war. The acceptance of *'urfi* and *misyar* as valid forms of Muslim marriage violate long held standards of Muslim marriage and Sudanese practice where women's rights to property and maintenance are indispensable to a lawful marriage.

It can also be suggested that the recognition of these new forms of marriage are in fact intended and reflect the flexibility and wisdom of the religious establishment and their scholars to make acceptable entirely new forms of male-female relations in a rapidly changing society. Such novel interpretations may be intended as a way to keep the youth from protesting their lack of opportunities in a climate of rising expectations with Sudan's oil economy and new skyscrapers. Their low wages and inadequate employment levels have either compelled them to migrate abroad for employment or to postpone marriage until they could afford to pay the expensive dowers. By accommodating their need to spend less on marriage, eliminating in the case of *misyar* the requirement to provide housing and other specified forms of maintenance to the wife, the state solves a major impediment to marriage. The legitimacy the state has given to these irregular marriages reveals the practical politics of Islamism. Meanwhile the zealots and hard core theological Islamists have themselves protested saying, in effect, that Sudanese society is going to hell.

Objective Assessment of Shari'a

Al-Turabi (and others before him) has said that the West has the wrong idea about Islam and that he had discussed this with Pope John Paul II in 1993. It is my view that if the West is to engage at all with Islamist regimes, it must do so within a framework of a respectful and culturally appropriate dialogue. President Barack Obama has declared the same in his Cairo speech that engagement based on mutual respect is the appropriate way forward to improve relations with the Muslim world. The Obama administration has the Sudan at the top of its list of priorities for its African foreign policy. However, most policy makers, and regrettably even human rights and NGO consultants, are woefully ignorant of Islam and its basic institutions, such as Shari'a law. Some harbor views of Islamic law as a backward or primitive law 'in need of reform,' as I have been told. Few bother to learn the basics of the law or can appreciate its thirteen centuries of legal-religious interpretations.

The West must devise ways to engage in informed dialogue with Islamist regimes, particularly those where post-Islamism is taking some tentative steps, such as in present day Sudan. Khartoum-based UNDP human rights attorney, Heba al-Kholy, expressed the view that now it is especially important for the Muslims who oppose extremist Shari'a to speak out (27 February 2005 interview). For the policy makers it helps to understand that the harsh *hadd* punishments have been imposed under extremist regimes, such as Afghanistan under the Taliban, in the Islamic Republic of Iran, and in Wahhabist Saudi Arabia, as well as during Sudan's period of extremism from 1983–85 and after 1989. Many in the West argue that *hadd* penalties violate international standards of human rights, but this is often asserted as part of a monologue the West is having with itself. It is important to include not only dissimilar views of Muslim scholars, but also to acknowledge the similar view expressed by Sudan's Chief Justice, for example, who described the punishments of lashing and stoning as 'excessive and cruel.' It is important for the West to accept the equal standing of Shari'a as a fully legitimate system of law, even when there are disagreements, and for the Shari'a to demonstrate to the international community its ability to evolve and adapt to contemporary conditions within its structures and methods of jurisprudence. Attorney al-Kholy argued that the West can be most helpful in facilitating internal debates, drawing on the local expertise of jurists. But productive dialogue between the West and emerging post-Islamist regimes, such as Sudan, requires an informed knowledge of history and a respect for the complex history and politics of its legal traditions, embodied here in the case of Shari'a in Sudan.

Final Thoughts

This book is both a documentation and an analysis of one of the most important cases of Islamism in Africa and the Arab-Muslim world. Its focus has been on a country that few study under the best of circumstances and most western scholars eschewed during the past two decades. Thanks to the peace initiatives brought about by years of struggle inside and outside of the country – by the SPLM/SPLA and democratic forces in Sudan and international forces – the Peace Agreements and especially the CPA opened the door for domestic civic discourse and the re-engagement of international scholars with their Sudanese colleagues. The case study of a quarter-century of Islamism in Sudan is significant both for the West as well as for Sudan. The media and concerned pubic in the West benefits from a better understanding of the development and complexity of what it often tends to simplify as 'Islamic militancy' or 'Islamic extremism.' western scholars benefit from an enhanced understanding of the case of Sudan from its initial Islamization of law through the present crisis as the nation faces division and separation. The study traces Islamism from the September Laws of 1983, effectively making Shari'a state law during the Numeiri regime, to the two decades of the al-Bashir-al-Turabi regime when Shari'a was institutionalized and became a major issue in waging war and negotiating peace under the *Inqaz*. In the end the issue that was once central to war also legitimized resistance to Islamization by non-Muslims and was ultimately rendered as a neutral factor in the peace process once the one state-two systems principle was agreed to at Machakos. In the most general terms, the peace has held and the future of Shari'a is secure.

The distinction between Islamic Shari'a of the ages, its careful interpreters and noble literature, on the one hand, and its potential for abuse under military and undemocratic regimes on the other hand is a vital one to be made and to be understood. This is true not only for Islamist Sudan but for the cases of Iran and Nigeria examined in this book, and also for other notable cases in Afghanistan, Pakistan, and Somalia. Scholars often observe that African Islam is rooted in Sufi thought and practice, and this is very true, but the case of Sudan reveals that Sufism is neither a guarantor from Islamism nor a protection from its potential harm to sincere and pious African Muslims. Islamism in Sudan, to a large extent, did transform the social order, allowing that other factors such as massive urbanization and a new oil-rich economy intensified class formation. An entire generation of Sudanese – Muslim and non-Muslim – were born and socialized in this 'new Muslim society' that Islamist ideologues dreamed of. Decades of intensive socialization in Arabic through a new religiously-based standard educational curriculum, control of all mass media, electronic and printed, and fear and intimidation, when needed, have all had profound effects on the population irrespective of religion. For those preferring to see the bases for social change in the factors of urbanization and class formation, the very least that can be said is that the social transformation occurred within an Islamist context. These changes, documented and analyzed in chapters 5 and 6, provide a base and, hopefully, an inspiration for future research as Africa's largest country faces its most critical years since independence.

The case of Sudan underscores the potential for abuse of the core values and teachings of a religion when it is politicized in any society. Shari'a as the religious law of Islam has been interpreted for fourteen centuries and certain strict conditions need to be met when, for example, the *hudud* penalties of amputation or stoning are applied and executed. For example, non-Muslims should not be subjected to these punishments, such as non-Muslims being prosecuted for alcohol production and consumption. Moreover, in the application of Shari'a conditions that weigh Islamic core values of compassion and mercy with retribution and compensation are to be observed. Amputation of limbs for theft should be restrained, performed publicly for the purposes of deterrence, and should not be for minor offenses, as was the case during the more instense Numeiri years. The sudden imposition of *hudud* penalties after the September Laws – having not being a part of Sudanese criminal law since the nineteenth century Mahdiya – was the dramatic announcement that Shari'a was a new instrument in the arsenal of the military and that it was to be a formidable force. None of this was part of the Shari'a that I had studied in the years just prior to September 1983 when it was limited to family law alone. However, neither had Shari'a been decolonized, which is an historical trend to be both acknowledged and respected.

Nonetheless, the implications for the Sudan polity of decades of Islamization, accompanying Arabization, war, resistance, and a tenuous peace are devastating as the nation is about to separate or attempt to go forward based on little promise of a sustainable unity. The South has pursued its case for separation in spite of John Garang's sincere desire that the country remain united. But Garang himself instructed that the North must work to 'make unity attractive' and there is widespread agreement that this has not been accomplished in the years since the CPA signing. For those in the North who oppose separation, the old saw of 'too little, too late' applies and, quite simply, there is little genuine familiarity and no trust between the peoples of the South and the North. The respective historic clarion calls of 'No going back on Shari'a' and 'Shari'a must go!' are just the symbolic tip of the human iceberg of deeply chilled relations.

It can be readily argued that the conflict in Darfur, emerging in 2003 as a fresh centrifugal force away from the Khartoum center at the same time as the southern conflict was beginning to end, is emblematic of similar forces of alienation of other marginalized peoples. In this case, Shari'a was deployed differently as a strategic assault on 'lawlessness' and brigandage among Muslims in a remote, insurgent region as the *hudud* were applied again to instill fear and suppress rebellion. Crucifixion and cross-amputations were reported and allegedly executed by government Shari'a courts during the early years of the Darfur conflict. Apart from human rights organizations there is no independent documentation of these reports, and most Khartoumites seemed genuinely ill-informed about events in this remote part of their vast country.

There is room for optimism that a new relationship can be forged between an independent South Sudan and the government in Khartoum. After over 50 years of poor decisions, poor governance and missed opportunities, the new realities of oil wealth potentially to be shared and the hope of an enduring peace forged by international pressures and facilitated by developing mutual respect as co-dependent nations could form the basis of a more promising future.

This book is a cautionary tale about the legal, social, and cultural effects of Islamism for a state and its people. This works grows from a deep respect for the faith of Islam and an adult lifelong collaboration and friendship with Muslims, Sudanese and others. However, Islamism as a political movement is a distant cry from the religion of Islam and has been responsible for harm both to Islam and Muslims as well as to numerous non-Muslim victims of the ideology and practice of Islamism in Sudan.

The US, the West and their policy makers need to better understand the complex and intriguing lessons of significant cases of Islamism, like that of Sudan. The first of these lessons is that Islamism is neither monolithic nor static. The cases of Nigeria and Iran, while comparable to Sudan, are nonetheless separate and unique in their historical and cultural contexts. Secondly, Sudan demonstrates clearly that Islamism in its early heated, dramatic announcement phase is not sustainable. It evolved, then matured as Islamic institutions and practice developed, first by imposition and later without the need of coercion. In its latter decade, after the al-Bashir regime had suppressed all opposition and instituted a security state, it revealed surprising flexibility, including the ousting of its own mentor al-Turabi. And it was capable of compromise on fundamental issues, such as the Shari'a, to move the country toward a negotiated peace after decades of civil war. That peace is fragile while Shari'a appears secure. The Government of South Sudan, as well as its people, have shown remarkable tolerance toward the faith of Islam and the Arabic language, given the bitter history, and this reveals a confidence in their hard-won right to self-determination. The GoSS has been less tolerant of the institutions of Islamism and have fundamentally changed the law, the school curriculum, and the Islamic Banks are being replaced.

Perhaps the greatest lesson to be gained from the analysis of cases of Islamism such as Sudan's is the fact of the unintended consequences of programs like the 'Civilization Project' of the *Inqaz*. The familiar piece of folk wisdom 'to be careful what you ask for' applies in the Sudanese case. The Sudanese Islamists envisioned a model Islamic society that they imposed from the top down using the Shari'a as its main instrument for the new order and for its legitimacy. The legal banning of all things deemed forbidden was improperly extended to non-Muslims and to Muslims whose tolerant brand of Sufi Islam had relied on compassion and forgiveness rather than the lash. The curtailing of female public space and restrictions placed upon their employment resulted in young women flooding into the new universities (much expanded under Islamism to its credit) and into the workforce. Thus freed by education and by increasing urbanization as the economy also expanded under Islamist rule, young women and men left the strictures of older social patterns of sexual segregation and arranged marriage for freer forms of association that resulted in entirely new forms of marriage and the family. Rising divorce rates, now virtually without stigma as in the past, are accepted as part of modern times as is the growing number of polygamous unions, notable among the new rich of the *Inqaz* and the war windows left by decades of chronic conflict.

Acknowledgement of new social problems, such as official recognition of rising numbers of illegitimate children and of orphans from years of war and displacement, has created a new, less judgmental attitude toward these taboo subjects. Female circumcision, long a topic of interest in the West, has been reduced both in numbers and severity of the operation on girls during the quarter-century of Islamism, not as a direct policy initiative but as part of the natural social evolution with which it did not seriously interfere.

Most important for the future of the nation as a whole, or a part of its former self depending on the outcome of the 2011 referendum, is the molding of the 'new Sudan' of which John Garang spoke under the circumstances and conditions outlined in this book. The 'new Sudan' *is* actively under construction and it is young, dynamic, and eager to leave the past behind and to build a nation, or nations, that are worthy of respect and are viable and vital parts of the anticipated growth and development on the African continent in the twenty-first century. The 'new Sudan' must also profit from the lessons of Islamism and its quarter-century legacy, for better and for worse, in order to move toward a post-Islamist social order and, perhaps, a new secular order, or a novel hybrid of sacred and secular, in which Shari'a retains its respected role in Sudanese society but never again is used as a rationale for war, or other harms to non-Muslims or Muslims.

APPENDICES

Zawaj 'Urfi

Questionnaire results from *Zawaj Urfi: Asbabu, Atharu, Hokumu fi al-Islam* ('Customary Marriage: Its Causes and Rulings in Islam') Doctoral Thesis by Mohamed Gibreel Dadl Haroun, University of Khartoum, 2005 (pp.155–163) (translated by C. Fluehr-Lobban with assistance from Salma Abdalmunim).

Age of Women	Number	Percentage
Under 20 years	30	29%
20–30 years	59	58%
30+ years	11	10%
Total	100	100%

Type of Accommodation (Female)		
Dormitory (dakhliya)	47	46.5%
Living with family	40	39.6%
Renting (ijar)	13	12.9%

University Women Attend		
University of Khartoum	19	18%
Nilein University	38	37.6%
Jam'at Sudan	17	16.8%
Jama't Islamiya	9	8.9%
Ahliya	17	16.8%

Age of Men at zu Marriage

Under 30 years	23	22.1%
30–40 years	35	34.7%
40+ years	42	41.6%

Education of Men in zu Marriages

Secondary school	52	51.5%
University	29	28.7%
Post-graduate	19	18.8%

Meeting Place of Couple

University	35	34.7%
Outside of university/workplace	56	55.4%
Other	9	8.9%

Witnesses to the Marriage (2 Required for Legal Muslim Marriage)

One witness	15	14.9%
Two witnesses	30	29.7%
None	55	54.5%

Length of the Marriage

Days	19	18%
Months	62	61.4%
Years	16	18.8%

Pregnancy-Living Children (banat)

Existing pregnancy, yes	11	10.9%
Not existing	89	88.1%
Living children	5	
Abortion	1	

Knowledge of fiqh and zu (banat)

Zu is hilal (lawful)	22	21.8%
Zu is haram (forbidden)	45	44.6%
Not sure	33	32.7%

Positive Aspects of zu (from Men and
Women in Existing zu Unions; n = 20)

Few positive features	35	34.7%
Many positive features	39	38.6%
No positive features	26	25.7%

Problems with zu (banat)

Often	14	13.9%
sometimes	62	61.4%
No problems	24	23.4%

Sense of Right and Wrong (banat)

Often think it is wrong	33	32.7%
Sometimes think it's wrong	37	36.6%
Not sure	30	29.7%

NOTES

* A joint effort, to translate from Arabic to English and introduce the Judicial Circulars of the Shari'a Courts from 1902 to 1979, prior to the 1983 Islamization of law, was published in the *Journal of African Law*, 1983; vol. 27 (2):77–140).

1. Derived in part from *The Bookseller of Kabul*, Asne Seierstad, Little, Brown and Co., NY, 2003, pp.80–83.

2. I express most sincere gratitude to Dr. Osman Mohamed Osman and Wendy Wallace for their occasional, generous loan of their personal laptop computers.

3. *Islamic Law and Society in the Sudan* (London, 1987), translated by Mahgoub al-Tigani Mahmoud as *al-Shari'a al-Islamiya wa al-Mujtama' fi al-Sudan* (Cairo, 2004).

4. Thanks to the assistance of University of Khartoum graduate student Salma Mohamed Abdel-Moneim who was conducting Master's degree research in Political Science in the camps.

5. The first, Moalana Nagua Kemal Mohamed Farid was appointed to Shari'a division in 1970, Moalana Rabab Abu Gusaysa in 1974 to Shari'a, and appointed to the High Court in 1990; Moalana Amal Mohamed Hasan 1974, appointed to High Court 2002; M. Amira Yusef Ali Bilal 1974, appointed to High Court 1996; Farida 'Abd al-Moneim Hasouna 1974, Civil Court, appointed to High Court 1996; M. Farida Ibrahim Ahmed, 1982 Civil division, appointed to High Court 1990, currently serves as presidential legal adviser; M. Sinia Rashid, 1972, civil court (Mohamed Ibrahim, 2005: 270).

6. (*Manshurat al-Mahakim al-Shari'a*, 1902–1979; Judicial Circulars of the were translated and introduced by Hatim Babiker Hillawi and Carolyn Fluehr-Lobban, 1983).

7. Interview with lawyer Sonia Aziz Malik, 14 February 2005.

8. A series of interviews with Mahgoub al-Tigani Mahmoud was conducted on this period during July and August 2007.

9. Mohamed Mahmoud was documenting this period while still in Sudan through public record of the 'Popular Committee for the Defense of democracy,' one of many such groups during the 1985–89 period of democracy of which he was a part. Research assistants mined selected newspapers – al-Sahafa, al-Sudani, al-Ayyam and documentation was stored at the Lawyers' Club (Nadi al-Muhami-yin). Phase I, the collection period was completed, and Phase II, publication of the documents was beginning, but after 1989 all of the documents were seized and their radio station closed. This is only one example of the loss of historical documentation that Sudanese democrats have experienced.

10. (2007, http://www.photius.com/cuntries/sudan/national_security/sudan).

11. I interviewed Mohamed Mahmoud in his home in Birmingham, UK in February 2007.

12. Extracted from The Bookseller of Kabul, Asne Seierstad, Little, Brown and Co., NY, 2003, pp.80–83.

13. Muhammad Ibrahim Muhammad cites the six pioneering women judges; those appointed to the High Court: Sania Rasheed Mirghani (appointed 1972, High Court, 1995); Fareeda Ibrahim Ahmed (appointed 1972, High Court 1995); Rabab Abu Gusaysa (appointed 1974, High Court, 1995); Badria Abd al-Moneim Hassouna (appointed 1974, High Court, 1996); Amira Yousef Ali Bilal (appointed 1973, High Court, 1996); Amal M. al-Hassan (appointed 1974, High Court 2002); in his History of the Sudan Judiciary, 1899–2005 (Arabic), 2005.

14. Two Forums, in Arabic, that I attended were held on 2 and 9 February 2005 at the Sharjah Hall, University of Khartoum. Several hundred persons attended the first, while the second was held in seminar format. The 2 February Forum was co-sponsored with the University of Juba. The seminar discussed a paper by University of Khartoum political scientist Sir Adlan al-Hardul entitled 'Peace Protocols and the Rule of Law in the North during the Interim Period.' The paper argued that in the Machakos Accords the present solution of 'Islam in the North and secular society in the south' was hammered out. Now the CPA is about the construction of democratic, civil society. Democracy and transparency are essential, but he asked how can democracy and human rights be cultivated while militarism is still the system of governance? He argued that Sudan after the CPA needs an alliance of parties, not the continuance of single party rule.

15. However, it should be noted that the report of the summary dismissal of women judges after 1989 was not confirmed by my numerous visits and

meetings with them at the Judiciary. There is, however, a limited number of women on the High Court and none on being the total number of women judges of a total number of 800 judges, or about 8 per cent. The Constitutional Court, but two women sit on the influential Council on Islamic Interpretation (*Majma' al-Fiqhi*), and three new women judges were appointed in 2007. One of whom is a southern woman.

16. Special Courts established in Darfur in May 2001 – eight in the North and in South Darfur were changed to 'Specialized Criminal Courts' introduced in April 2003 as a result of international pressure and that of the NGOs. The Minister of Justice claimed these courts were needed to deal with the conflict in the region, and they are headed by a single civilian judge, with appeals within one week, rather than normal two. For these courts there is a lack of judicial review and supervision.

17. The editorial uses both 'the' source and 'a' source so it is not clear if he used the more moderate 'a' and I was unable to determine this from the Arabic texts as well.

18. The editorial continued: 'I do not hate a single Northern fellow. I only hate the policies. I was disgusted that at the way the Republican Palace church was turned into a colonial museum housing some of the belongings of former colonial masters of Sudan.' Brothers, let us go forward for separation. ('Undiplomatic chat, Which way?' by Michael Koma, *Khartoum Monitor*, 16 February 2005, p.12.)

19. English translation, courtesy of the Ministry of Foreign Affairs, will be available in 2012.

20. They included: Sir Edgar Bonham Carter (1899–1917); Sir Nigel Davidson (1926–30); Sir B.H. Bell (1930–36); Sir J.B. Gorham (1936–41); Sir Thomas Creed (1941–46); and Sir C.C.C. Cummings (1948–53) (p.82). The Muftis from 1900–56 were: 1) al-Tayeb Ahmed Hashim; 2) Ismail al-Azhari; 3) Ahmed al-Sayed Alfeel; 4) Ahmed al-Tahir; 5) Abu-Shama Abdel Mahmoud; 6) Hashim Abulgasim; and 7) Mohamed Hashim Abulgasim.

21. Post-Merger of the Unitary Judicial System were the following Chief Justices: Dafalla alHaj Yusef (1983–84); Fuad alAmin Abdul Rahman (1984–85; lasted only 6 months due to the 1985 *intifada*); Mohamed Mirghani Mabrouk (1985–89); Jalal Ali Lutfi (1989–94); Obeid Haj Ali (1994–98); Hafiz al-Sheikh El Zaki (1998–2001); and Jelal Eddin Mohamed Osman (2001-present).

22. Translated from the Arabic Jamhouriya al-Sudan, Wizarat al-'Adil, Al-Qanun al-Jana'y sana 1991. *Arab Law Quarterly*, Vol 9, Part 1, 1994.

23. Interview with Honorable Sinia Rashid, member Constitutional Court, 17 January 2008.

24. Natural features include: *Ithtilam* 'masturbation' for males, growth of hair on the face, menstruation or pregnancy for females, age for both males and females.

25. Mostly these High Court cases dealt with the question of whether the *hadd* penalty was properly applied in the specific case, that is, whether the requisite conditions were met.

26. See www.shro-cairo.org.

27. http://members.internettrash.com/rofbmiler/engl-akt2.html.

28. http://hrw.org/english/docs/2002/02/01/sudan3791_txt.htm.

29. Personal interview, 15 March 2007.

30. CEDAW is available in Arabic published by the Sudan Human Rights Organization-Cairo. Translation of the text regarding family law with the assistance of Salam Abdel-Moneim Mohamed.

31. For this I thank Moalana Boreii of Khartoum and Moalana Mirghani Hamad of Omdurman (*Mujemma Mahakim Kerreri*).

32. Justice Kawther Awad in Diem, Khartoum and Justice Sana'a in Omdurman Central Court.

33. Interview: Umm Asha al-Jabbu Eddoma, Muaskar Wad al-Bashir, 22 April 2007. She is responsible for providing relocation information for the returning refugees, United Nations, International Organization Migration. She is from Talodi in the Nuba Mountains, and came to Khartoum in 1994 and has worked in the IOM for two years. She is divorced and has eight daughters, five married and three still in school.

34. The men telling the story to the AP journalist were drinking an orange fermented drink called 'internet.' Ghazi Suleiman reports that such incidents have decreased considerably since the CPA. (Tanalee Smith, AP, 11 October 2005).

35. Available at www.gurtong.com.

36. See www.gurtong.com.

37. Presidential decree no. 72/207 relieved Justice Ambrose Riny Thiik as President of the Supreme Court of Southern Sudan effective 2 July 2007, replaced by Justice John Wol Makec and Justice Chan Reec Madut as Deputy, appointed by decree 73/2007. In January 2008 I visited the GoSS Judiciary we met with the Acting President of the Supreme Court, Justice Ayak der Kom Awan and Justice John Wol Makec and Justice Chan Reec Madut as Deputy, appointed by decree 73/2007. In January 2008 I visited the GoSS Judiciary we met with the Acting President of the Supreme Court, Justice Ayak der Kom Awan and Justice John Makec was still President of the Supreme Court.

38. I wish to express my thanks to sociologist Mrs. Magda Saeed of the Department of Statistics for the loan of the English copy of the Yearbook.

39. I extend my thanks to Dr. Osman Mohamed Osman of the Department of Anthropology at the University of Khartoum for this kind invitation and his hospitality.

40. Mohamed Ibrahim Khalil, 'Human Rights and Islamization of the Sudan Legal system,' in *Religion and Conflict in Sudan*, Pauline's publications Africa, Kenya, 1999, p.61; cited in Salma Albalmunim paper on Shari'a Debates, 2008.

41. Interview with Dr. Mohamed Mukhtar, Department of Political Science, Juba University, 1 February 2007 (at Political Science Department, University of Khartoum).

42. This perhaps explains the curious reaction of students at the University of Khartoum to me and my research on the Shari'a when I spoke to a class of anthropology students in January 2007. They were reading the translation of my study of the Shari'a before Islamization in 1983 brought to their attention by anthropology professor Osman Mohamed Osman, and the idea of an American non-Muslim carrying out this research perhaps seemed not only strange, but somehow inappropriate.

43. This central transportation hub has been removed to a more remote location, ostensibly as part of downtown development and improvement.

44. I gratefully acknowledge Salma M. Abdalmunim sharing some of the interviews she collected during her Master's research in the IDP camps on the subject of Christian-Muslim relations after the CPA.

45. My research assistant Salma took one week to obtain permission for her Master's research in the camps; she and I stayed a day at this office in Erkoweit, and after I gave them copies of my passport, visa, research proposal and questionnaire, and verbal assurance from Moalana Boreii head of the Organization of the Khartoum state courts, I was granted this permission. There were no restrictions placed upon my questions.

46. Interview 22 April 2007. The names of persons interviewed in the camps are either kept anonymous in the text, or are fictitious.

47. These interviews were made by Salma M. Abdalmunim and are reproduced here with her kind permission. As before, the names associated with these voices are fictitious.

48. I express my gratitude to Dr. Osman M. Osman for setting up this meeting for me.

49. Professor of Political Science, University of Juba, Khartoum.

50. *Misyar* is derived from the Arabic root *sara* meaning 'to be in motion,' or 'to get going,' or alternatively 'Ethar' marriage is derived from the *Hadith* of Prophet Muhammad, meaning 'sacrifice,' 'unselfishness' or 'altruism.'

51. 'Circulars of the Shari'a Courts in Sudan, 1902–1979,' Carolyn Fluehr-Lobban and Hatim Babiker Hillawi, Journal of African Law, vol. 27, no.2, 1983: 79–140.

52. Commentaries from the Sudanese Arabic press were posted at http://www.sudaneseonline.com on 6 February 2009.

53. When she was talking about the statue of Saddam coming down, the Sudanese witnesses asked me if the Americans could come and do that here as well! The bride said diplomatically that, 'foreigners don't comment about politics,' but we all had a good laugh.

54. Wendy and I shared an apartment in Khartoum in the spring of 2007 and she had kindly shared the text of her radio broadcast with me.

55. From 'Missing Angel: abandoned babies' Wendy Wallace, (BBC Radio 4 Broadcast, Women's Hour Programme, 27 February 2007).

56. I express my deep gratitude to the Khartoum Diem Court Ma'azun Moalana Yusef Akasha who graciously supported my research interests in the Court Records Office, and welcomed me to observe his work at the court during April-May 2007.

57. A version of this paper was originally presented at Institute for the Study of Islamic Thought in Africa Conference, May 2003, Northwestern University Program of African Studies. In 2005 I was funded by a grant jointly administered by the African Studies Centre of the University of Leiden and the Centre des Etudes Africaines Noir of the University of Bordeaux to conduct research on the status of Shari'a in Sudan after the CPA was signed in January. I express my gratitude to these institutions for their support.

58. 'Chronology of events Regarding Women in Iran since the Revolution of 1979' by Elham Gheytanchi.

59. Personal interview February 2007, London, Westminster University.

60. Personal interview February 2007, London, Westminster University.

61. The phrase is taken from the University of Denver project 'Religious Leaders and Conflict Management in Deeply Divided Societies,' directed by Timothy Sisk, Graduate School of International Studies to which I was privileged to contribute.

62. United States Institute of Peace Special Report, 'Scenarios for Sudan, Avoiding Political Violence through 2011,' Special Report 228, August 2009. www.esip.org.

63. Blogposting discussion of Abdullahi Gallab's book, *The First Islamic Republic*, and 'Is Sudan Transitioning to a Post-Islamist State?' 3 June 2008, Alex deWaal Darfur blogsite.

64. Salma Mohamed Abdalmunim, MA thesis.

REFERENCES

Abu-Nasr, Donna. 2008. 'Saudis distressed by child weddings.' *The Philadelphia Inquirer.* 7 August. p.A13.

Adu Boahen, A. (ed.). 1990. *General History of Africa, Vol. VII: Africa under Colonial Domination.* Abridged Edition. Aris: UNESCO Publications.

El-Affendi, Abdelwahab. 1991. *Turabi's Revolution: Islam and Power in Sudan.* London: Grey Seal.

El-Affendi, Abdelwahab. 2001. *Rethinking Islam and Modernity: Essays in Honour of Fathi Osman.* Leicester, UK: The Islamic Foundation.

El-Affendi, Abdelwahab. 2008. *Who Needs an Islamic State?* 2nd edition. London: Malaysia Think Tank London.

Alier, Abel. 1990. *Southern Sudan: Too Many Agreements Dishonored.* Exeter: Ithaca Press.

Amnesty International. 2005. *Sudan Memorandum to the National Constitutional Review Commission.* May 2005. AI Index: AFR 54/049/2005.

Anderson, J.N.D. 1976. *Law Reform in the Muslim World.* London: Frank Cass.

Appleby, Scott. 2000. *The Ambivalence of the Sacred: Religion, Violence and Reconciliation.* Lanham, MD: Rowan and Littlefield.

Al-'Ashmawy, Muhammad Sa'id. 1998. *Against Islamic Extremism: The Writings of Muhammad Sa'id al-'Ashmawy.* Edited and introduced by Carolyn Fluehr-Lobban. Gainesville: University Press of Florida.

Associated Press. 2009. 'Sudanese who killed American spared death sentence. 13 August 2009. http://www.google.com/hostednews/ap/article/ALeqM5gk9OSZF.

Badri, Balghis. (ed.). 2004. *Mashru' Muqtarah li Ta'dil ba'd Mu'ad Qanun al-Ahwal al-Shakhsiya* (Contesting Proposals some time after the [new] Personal Status Law). Center for Development Studies, Ahdaf University for Women.

Bayet, Asef. 1996. 'The Coming of a Post-Islamist Society.' *Critique: Critical Middle East Studies,* 5 (9), pp.43–52.

BBC News. 2007. 'Iran talks up temporary marriages.' 2 June 2007.

BBC News. 2009. 'Sudan women "lashed for trousers".' 13 July 2009. http://news.bbc.co.uk/2/hi/africa/8147329.stm.

Bechtold, Peter. 1993. 'May Revolution of Numeiri.' In Idris El-Hassan, *Religion in Society: Nemeiri and the Turuq, 1972–1980.* Khartoum: Khartoum University Press.

Beeman, William O. 2001. 'Iranian Women situation has improved under the Islamic Republic.' *Brown University News Service.* January 2001.

Bielefelt, Heiner. 1995. 'Muslim Voices in the Human Rights Debate.' *Human Rights Quarterly,* 17 (4), pp.587–617.

Blumenfeld, Warren J. 1907. 'Homosexuals: A Long Oppressed Group in Iran.' *Letter to Wingate from Cromer Commenting on Grand Kadi's Report.* 11 February 1907 (SA 280/2/82). Sudan Archives, Durham University, Durham, UK.

British Embassy. 2007a. 'Emptying Downtown Khartoum'. *(Sudan Vision), Khartoum Press Summary,* 17 July 2007.

British Embassy. 2007b. 'Release of 1,000 southern women and children detained for brewing alcohol.' *Khartoum Press Summary,* al-Sahafa. 6 August 2007.

Bunza, Mukhtar Umar. 2002. 'Islamism versus Secularism: a religious-political struggle in Nigeria.' *Journal for the Study of Religions and Ideologies,* 1 (2), pp.49–65.

Chan, Hoth, G. 2008. 'South Sudan and the Issues of Customary Laws.' *Sudan Studies Association Bulletin,* 26 (1), pp.18–21.

CNN. 2009. 'Sudanese lawyer calls woman's flogging punishment "degrading".' http://edition.cnn.com/2009/WORLD/africa/07/30/sudan.journalist.lashings/

Comprehensive Peace Agreement between The Government of the Republic of the Sudan and the Sudan People's Liberation Movement/Sudan People's Liberation Army, The. 2005. Nairobi, Kenya. 9 January 2005. Section 2.4.5.4.

Deng, Francis. 1986. *Seed of Redemption.* New York: Lilian Barber.

Deng, Francis. 1991. *Cry of the Owl.* Cairo: Midlight Books.

Draft Constitution. 2005. Distributed electronically. 16 March 2005.

Ewald, Janet J. 1990. *Soldiers, Traders, and Slaves: State Formation and Economic Transformation in the Greater Nile Valley, 1700–1885.* Madison: University of Wisconsin Press.

Fabos, Anita. 2001. 'Marriage Sudanese-style: Transnational patterns of citizen-ship and gender-making for Sudanese nationals in Egypt.' *Northeast African Studies,* 8 (3), pp.47–68.

Fluehr-Lobban, Carolyn. 1976. 'An Analysis of Homicide in the Afro-Arab Sudan.' *Journal of African Law,* 20 (1), pp.20–38.

Fluehr-Lobban, Carolyn. 1987. *Islamic Law and Society in the Sudan.* London: Frank Cass. Arabic translation, 2004. *al-Shariʿa al-Islamiya wa al-Mujtamaʿ fi al-Sudan.* Translated by Mahgoub al-Tigani Mahmoud. Cairo: Maktaba Madbouli.

Fluehr-Lobban, Carolyn. 1991. 'Islamization in Sudan: a Critical Assessment.' *Middle East Journal,* 44 (3), pp.620–633.

Fluehr-Lobban, Carolyn. 1995. 'Cultural Relativism and Universal Rights.' *The Chronicle of Higher Education,* 9 June 1995, pp.B1–2.

Fluehr-Lobban, Carolyn. 2006. *Race and Racism: An Introduction.* Lanham, MD: Alta Mira Press.

Fluehr-Lobban, Carolyn and Hatim Babiker Hillawi. 1983. 'Circulars of the Shari'a Courts in the Sudan (*Manshurat Mahakim al-Shari'a fi Sudan*), 1902–1979.' *Journal of African Law*, 27 (2), pp.79–141.

Fluehr-Lobban, Carolyn and Kharyssa Rhodes. (eds.). 2004. *Race and Identity in the Nile Valley: Ancient and Modern Perspectives.* Metuchen, NJ: Red Sea Press.

Gallab, Abdullahi A. 2008. *The First Islamist Republic, Development and Disintegration of Islamism in the Sudan.* London: Ashgate.

Garang, John. 2005. Speech at the Signing Ceremony. *Khartoum Monitor*, 11 January 2005, p.9.

Gettleman, Jeffrey. 2007. 'Sudan's President Pardons British Teacher.' *The New York Times International.* 4 December 2007, p.A8.

Haroun, Mohamed Gibreel Fadl. 2005. *Zawaj 'Urfi: Asbabu, Atharu, Hokumu fi al-Islam.* (Customary marriage, its causes, consequences, and rulings in Islam). Doctoral thesis in the Department of Islamic Studies, Faculty of Arts, University of Khartoum. Supervised by Dr. Farouq Osman.

Hasan, Yusuf Fadl. 2003. *Studies in Sudanese History.* Khartoum: SUDATEK Ltd.

Al-Hassab, Ahmed. 2007. 'Murabaha: A controversial model of Islamic financing.' Paper presented at 'Shari'a Debates' Conference, University of Shendi, 14 February 2007.

Hiskett, M. 1976. 'The nineteenth century jihads in West Africa.' In John E. Flint (ed.), *The Cambridge History of Africa: Volume 5, from c.1790 to c.1870.* Cambridge: Cambridge University Press.

Human Rights Watch. 2007. 'Sudan Justice: Stonings, Amputations.' 16 July 2007. http://frw.org/english/docs/2002/02/01/sudan3719_text.htm

Ibrahim, Abdullahi Ali. 2008. *Manichean Delirium: Decolonizing the Judiciary and Islamic Renewal in Sudan, 1898–1985.* Leiden: E.J.Brill.

Ibrahim, Haydar. 1991. 'The Crisis of Political Islam: the example of the NIF in Sudan.' Cairo, Unpublished paper.

Ibrahim, Haydar. 2003. *Suqut al-Mashru al-Hadari.* Summarized and Reviewed by Hashim al-Tinay. *Sudan Studies Association Newsletter*, 24 (1), Oct. 2005, pp. 18–22.

Islam, M. Mazharul and Misieh Uddin. 2001. 'Female Circumcision in Sudan: Future Prospects and Strategies for Eradication.' *Reproductive and Family Planning Perspectives*, 27 (2).

Johnson, Douglas H. 2003. *The Root Causes of Sudan's Civil Wars.* Bloomington: Indiana University Press.

Jok, Aleu Akechak, Robert A Leitch, and Carrie Vanderbilt. 2004. *Study of Customary Law in Contemporary Southern Sudan.* A study for World Vision International and the South Sudan Secretariat of Legal and Constitutional Affairs, August 2004.

Jok, Jok Madut. 2004. *Slavery and Race in the Sudan.* Philadelphia: University of Pennsylvania Press.

Juba Post, The. 2007. 'Bentiu Prisoners: 75% never convicted.' 20–27 April 2007. Dateline 20 April: p.7.

Al-Kabbashi, Taha al-Mukashfi. 1986. *Tatbiq al-Shari'a al-Islamiya fi al-Sudan bayn al-Haqiqa wa al-Thara* (Implementation of the Islamic Shari'a in the Sudan: between reality and political campaigning). Cairo: al-Zahra li al-I'lam al-'Arabi.

Keita, S.O.Y. 2008. 'Review Essay for Race and Identity in the Nile Valley: Ancient and Modern Perspectives.' *Bulletin of the Sudan Studies Association,* 26 (1), pp.23–32.

Khalifa, Babiker. 1989. 'Sudan: recent developments.' *Africa Today,* 36 (3&4), pp.5–10.

Al-Khartoum Daily. 2007. '28 Parentless children die in Maygoma child home.' British Embassy Khartoum Press Summary, 5 September 2007.

Khartoum Monitor. 2005. 'Welcome to the new Sudan.' Text of interview with Ali Osman Mohamed Taha. 13 January 2005, p.2.

Lauzière, Henri. 2005. 'Post-Islamism and the Religious Discourse of 'Abs al-Salam Yasin.' *International Journal of Middle East Studies,* 37 (2), pp.241–261.

Layish, Aharon and Gabriel R. Warburg. 2002. *The Reinstatement of Islamic Law in Sudan under Numayri: An Evaluation of a Legal Experiment in Light of its Historical Context, Methodology and Repercussions.* Leiden: E.J.Brill.

Lobban, Richard A. 2006. 'Relations between Islamic and Christian Nubia: The Case of the Baqt.' In Eleonora Kormysheva, (ed.) *Culture Heritage of Egypt and {the} Christian Orient, Volume 3.* Moscow: Institute of Oriental Studies, Golenishev Russian State University for the Humanities, pp.141–162.

Lobban, Richard A., Robert Kramer, and Carolyn Fluehr-Lobban. 2002. *Historical Dictionary of the Sudan.* 3rd edition. Lanham, MD and London: The Scarecrow Press.

Mahgoub, Nazik al Malik. 2004. 'Al-Nisa' wa al-Qanun' (Women and the Law), in *Mashru' Muqtarah li Ta'dil ba'd Mu'ad Qanun al-Ahwal al-Shakhsiya* (Contesting Proposals some time after the [new] Personal Status Law). Center for Development Studies, Ahfad University for Women.

Mahmoud, Mohamed. 1985. 'Sharia Victims Unite.' *Africa Now.* August 1985, p.31.

Mahmoud, Mohamed A. 2008. *Quest for Divinity: A Critical Examination of the thought of Mahmud Muhammad Taha.* Syracuse, NY: Syracuse University Press.

Majma' al-Fiqh al-Islami. 2006. *Risalat al-Qawl al-Fasl fi al-Radd 'ala man Kharaj 'an al-Asl* (The Last Word in Response to He Who Deviates from the Original). Khartoum: Majma' al-Fiqh al-Islami.

Mamdani, Mahmood. 2005. *Good Muslim, Bad Muslim: America, the Cold War and the Roots Of Terror.* New York: Pantheon Books.

Mekki, Hassan. *Al-Islamiya fi Sudan, 1969–1985.* Khartoum: Bait al-Ma'arifa.

Mohammed, Danladi Adamu. 2002. 'Muslim Intellectuals and the Sharia Debate in Nigeria.' Centre for Journalism Studies, Wales, March 2002.

Muhammad, Muhammad Ibrahim. 2005. *Tarikh al-Qadaiya al-Sudaniya bayn 'Ahdayn 1899–2005* (History of the Sudanese Judiciary between the period 1899–2005). Khartoum: Maktaba Watania al-Sudan.

al-Mubarak, Khalid. 2001. *Turabi's Islamist Venture, Failures and Implications*. Forward by Peter Woodward. Cairo: Dar al-Thaqafiya.

Mukhtar, Al-Baqir. 2004. 'The Crisis of Identity in Northern Sudan: The Dilemma of a Black People with a White Culture.' In Carolyn Fluehr-Lobban and Kharyssa Rhodes, *Race and Identity in the Nile Valley: Ancient and Modern Perspectives*. Metuchen, NJ: Red Sea Press.

an-Na'im, Abdullahi. 1989. 'Constitutionalism and Islamization in the Sudan.' *Africa Today*, 36 (3&4), pp.11–28.

an-Na'im, Abdullahi. 1990. *Toward an Islamic Reformation: Civil Liberties, Human Rights and International Law*. Syracuse, NY: Syracuse University Press.

an-Na'im, Abdullahi and Francis Deng. 1996. Self-Determination and Unity: The Case of the Sudan.' *Law and Politics*, 18, pp.199–223.

Osman Mohamed Osman Ali. 2004. *The Dynamics of Interpretation of Textual Islam in Northern Sudan: A Case Study among the Rural and Urban Population of Shendi Province*. Doctoral dissertation, Department of Sociology and Social Anthropology, University of Khartoum.

Ostein, Philip. 2004. 'The Shari'a Question in Nigeria: A Plea for Deeper Study of its History.' Paper presented at a conference on Shari'a Debates and their Perception by Muslims and Christians in Selected African Countries, held at Limuru, Kenya, 16–19 July 2004.

Quinn, Charlotte A. and Frederick Quinn. 2003. *Pride, Faith, and Fear: Islam in Sub-Saharan Africa*. Oxford: Oxford University Press.

Pickthall, Mohammad Marmaduke (translator), *The Meaning of the Glorious Quran*, Hyderabad Government Press, orig. 1930, reprinted by The Muslim World.

Polgreen, Lydia. 2006. 'Overcoming Customs and Stigma, Sudan gives Orphans a Lifeline.' *The New York Times*, 5 April 2006.

Powell, Eve Troutt. 2003. *A Different Shade of Colonialism: Egypt, Great Britain and the Mastery of Sudan*. California: University of California Press.

Protocol Between the GoS and The Sudan People's Liberation Movement (SPLM) on Power Sharing, 2004. Naivasha, Kenya, 26 May 2004.

Robert, Kanta. 2007. 'Sudan's CPA, another born-dead peace.' *Khartoum Monitor*. 1 February 2007: p.6.

Roy, Oliver. 1994. *The Failure of Political Islam*. London: I.B.Tauris.

Al-Saeed, Ann, 2007. 'Islamic Corporation shall be responsible for affairs of southern Muslims.' *Khartoum Monitor*, 24 April 2007, p.2.

Sanusi, Sanusi Lamido. 2003. 'The Shari'a Debate and the Construction of a "Muslim" Identity in Northern Nigeria: A Critical Perspective.' Seminar paper on 'The Shari'a Debate and the Construction of Muslim and Christian

Identities in Northern Nigeria,' University of Bayreuth, Bayreuth, Germany. 11–12 July 2003.

Scroggins, Deborah. 2004. *Emma's War*. New York: Vintage Books.

Sikainga, Ahmed A. 1996. *Slaves into Workers: Emancipation and Labor in Colonial Sudan*. Austin: University of Texas Press.

Simone, T. Abdou Magliqim. 1994. *In Whose Image: Political Islam and Urban Practice*. Chicago: University of Chicago Press.

Smith, Tanalee. 2005. 'Islamic Law still applies in Sudan.' Associated Press, 11 October 2005. www.washingtontimes.com

Spaulding, Jay. 2007. *The Heroic Age in Sinnar*. Trenton, NJ: The Red Sea Press.

Spaulding, Jay and Stephanie Beswick (eds.). 2000. *White Nile Black Blood: War, Leadership, and Ethnicity from Khartoum to Kampala*. Lawrenceville, NJ: The Red Sea Press.

Statement of the Mufti, Sheikh of the Ulamas of Sudan, Sherif Yusef al Hindi and 13 others representing the Ulamas Committee, dated 8 November 1914 (SA193/4/100). Sudan Archives, University of Durham, Durham, UK.

Sudan Human Rights Organization, Cairo Office. 2003. *Annual Report*. 'The Situation of Human Rights in Sudan.'

The Sudanese Judgments and Precedent Encyclopedia, 1956–1999, the Sudan Judiciary, CD Rom, www.sjprecedents.org.

Swangin, Isaac. 2007. 'Two Judicial systems leaves the Judiciary "confused".' *The Juba Post*, 6–13 April 2007, p.9.

Tabiu, Muhammad. 2001. 'Shari'a, Federalism and Nigerian Constitution.' Paper presented at an international conference on shari'a, The Nigerian Muslim Forum, London. 14 April 2001.

Al-Turabi. 1994. 'The Islamic State,' an interview with Dr. Hasan al-Turabi. *Islamic Conversations Series*. Princeton, NJ: Films for the Humanities and the Sciences.

Wallace, Wendy. 2009. *Daughter of Dust*. London: Simon and Schuster.

Willemse, Karin. 2001. 'A room of one's own: single female teachers negotiating the Islamist discourse in Sudan.' *Northeast African Studies*, 8 (3), pp.99–127.

Woodward, Peter (ed.). 1991. *Sudan After Nimeiri*. London: Routledge.

Yadudu, Auwalu Hamisu. 1993. 'The Prospect of Shari'a in Nigeria.' In N. Alkali, et al. (eds.), *Islam in Africa: A Proceeding of the Islam in Africa Conference*. Ibadan: Spectrum Books.

Yadudu, Auwalu Hamisu. 2001. 'Benefits of Shariah and Challenges of Reclaiming a Heritage.' Paper presented at an international conference on shari'a, The Nigerian Muslim Forum, London. 14 April 2001.

INDEX